Recasting Women

RECASTING WOMEN

Essays in Indian Colonial History

Edited by

KUMKUM SANGARI

SUDESH VAID

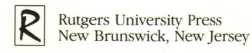

Rutgers University Press
New Brunswick, New Jersey

Third paperback printing, 1999

First published in cloth and paperback in the United States
by Rutgers University Press, 1990

First published in cloth in India by Kali for Women, 1989

Library of Congress Cataloging-in-Publication Data

Recasting women in India : essays in colonial history / edited by
Kumkum Sangari ; Sudesh Vaid.
p. cm.
ISBN 0-8135-1579-3. (cloth) ISBN 0-8135-1580-7 (pbk.)
1. Women—India—Social conditions. 2. India—History—British
occupation, 1765–1947. I. Sangari, Kumkum. II. Vaid, Sudesh,
1940–
HQ1743.R43 1990
305.4′0954—dc20 90-30892
CIP

Manufactured in the United States of America

CONTENTS

to our mothers

She must be refined, reorganised, recast, regenerated ...

KOYLASCHANDER BOSE,
"On the Education of Hindu Females," 1846

Recasting Women

Recasting Women: An Introduction

KUMKUM SANGARI and SUDESH VAID

THIS ANTHOLOGY has grown out of our need as academics and activists to understand the historical processes which reconstitute patriarchy in colonial India. We wish to focus primarily on the regulation and reproduction of patriarchy in the different class-caste formations within civil society. This is not in order to underplay the role of the state in maintaining, modifying or aggravating patriarchal practices. Rather, our political understanding and experience as observers and participants in women's protest movements of the seventies has left us, like many others, bedevilled with a host of questions about the nature of the social and cultural processes within civil society which determine the working of patriarchies in the daily lives of women. We feel that the implications of the reconstitution of patriarchies in the colonial period bear significantly upon the present, and this, in fact, is the justification for this venture.

There are two reasons for the consciously exploratory character of this book. Firstly given the regional, class and caste variation of patriarchal practices and their diverse histories, it is necessary to have specific studies, in order to build an adequate theoretical basis. Overarching theoretical formulations are helpful and necessary to undertake any work but they need constant testing and overhauling by historically and materially specific studies of patriarchal practice, social regulation and cultural production. If patriarchies are not, as we believe, systems either predating or superadded to class and caste but intrinsic to the very formation of, and changes within, these categories, then to rush into theoretical generalization at this stage would be to risk both simplification and rigidity. We are not however making a plea for theoretical eclecticism or "pluralism," but for flexibility within a field which is still being defined. Most of the essays have taken shape through discussing our idea of the book with the contributors. In turn, the richness and diversity of their essays has altered our own understanding as it is reflected in this introduction.

Secondly, the social and political developments of the past two decades have shattered the post-colonial complacency about the improving status of women and with it has gone the legitimacy of nationalist models of reform and 'development'. It is now apparent that far from enjoying the benefits of so-called development, the majority of women have in fact been pushed to the margins of the production process. Alongside this 'invisible' economic process, there is a visible escalation of communal conflicts and an increasing politicization of 'religious' identities. These latter developments have given a new lease of life to patriarchal practices unde 'religious' sanction. There has for example been a resurgence of widow-immolation in parts of northern India. The role of the state and its apparatus has also been far from negligible. In fact the urban women's protest movements in the 1970s were in part propelled by the frequency of dowry murders — usually treated by the police as a private 'family' matter — and custodial rape — a symptom of the acquisition of greater repressive powers by the state. All of these matters have given a pressing urgency to questions about the inter-relation of patriarchal practices with political economy, religion, law and culture — in sum, questions about the politics of social change. This situation has introduced into feminist research the need for a different object of enquiry.

I

Feminist historiography now implies in some sense a move towards the integrated domain of cultural history. It may be appropriate to describe what we mean by feminist historiography. Historiography may be feminist without being, exclusively, women's history. Such a historiography acknowledges that each aspect of reality is gendered, and is thus involved in questioning all that we think we know, in a sustained examination of analytical and epistemological apparatus, and in a dismantling of the ideological presuppositions of so called gender-neutral methodologies. A feminist historiography rethinks historiography as a whole and discards the idea of women as something to be *framed* by a context, in order to be able to think of gender difference as both structuring and structured by the wide set of social relations. In this sense, feminist historiography is a choice open to all historians. Not as a choice among competing perspectives, or even as one among personal predilections of the sort which dictate interest in a particular region or a particular historical period. Nor is the issue here the tokenist inclusion of women or the numerical or even qualitative evaluation of their participation in this or that movement. Rather as a choice which cannot but undergird *any* attempt at a historical reconstruction which undertakes to demonstrate our sociality in the *full* sense, and is ready to engage with its own presuppositions of an objective gender-neutral method of enquiry, as well as with the presuppositions of the social moments and movements it sets out to represent. The fact that this is a choice seldom excercised may perhaps even be partly ascribed to the emergence of women's studies in India which appears to be a convenience for mainstream historians who can now consign the onus on specialists in a 'separate' discipline, and so recreate yet another gender-based division of labour within the rarefied world of academia.

Cultural history seems to be the richest, most integrated, and yet most difficult form available for feminist historiograpy. Both its difficulty and its energy are, in one sense, generated by the obtuseness of the present situation. In order to understand the construction of gender difference — through ideologies, concepts and behaviour — and their relation to class and colonial economy, it is necessary to press against the boundaries of established disciplines. This not only involves knowledge of and working at the interface of various disciplines, but also a simultaneous questioning of the histories and assumptions of these disciplines. The act of understanding our construction as agents and subjects of social processes is itself a kind of intervention in the creation of exclusive knowledge systems. Perhaps the greatest difficulty lies in relating the ideological to the experiential; that is, of relating various symbolic constructs to the lives and actions of women, and in relating the often hegemonic ideologies produced about women (converging across region, caste and class) to existing divisions of labour and systems of production. Though there is no neat fit between symbolic constructs and the ordering of social relations or between consciousness and causality (as some sanitized versions of sociology and anthroplogy would have us believe) yet ideas, invented traditions, symbolic constructs do intrude upon the labour process in a number of ways ranging from the causative to the legitimizing.

The essays in this collection either attempt to construe the lived culture or social relations of a particular time and place through available records, or to show the making of a selective tradition through discursive and political processes. The essays are confined to the dominant Hindu community, largely in the north of India, and deal mainly with the middle classes. We feel that the exclusion of all other religious communities and of marginalized groups (dalit and tribal, agricultural and bonded labour) and the slender representation of women belonging to peasant and working class groups is a serious limitation because it is not possible to understand a dominant class or religious community without locating its relationship to other strata and religious groups. The geographical scope of the book is another kind of limitation considering the regionally differential intervention of colonialism. Finally, all except one essay are confined to areas under direct British rule. However, no anthology or even generalization about Indian women could hope to be representative. The book, though limited in terms of such representativeness is, however, held together by a common concern with the changing position of women both in its material specificity, and in its often inverse representations in the discourses which legitimize their social status. These may be useful for further work concerning the reconstitution of patriarchies.

Uma Chakravarty's paper traces the colonial and indigenous construction of a Hindu-Aryan identity. Lata Mani analyses the premises and parameters of the colonial discourse on *sati* (1805-1830). Sumanta Banerjee describes the making of a respectable Bengali middle class culture through the marginalization of the cultural forms of lower classes in Calcutta and the emergence of the *bhadramahila's* (educated wives and daughters of the bhadralok) literary voice. Vir Bharat Talwar gives an account of women's magazines and issues of reform taken up by the middle class within Uttar Pradesh during the same period. Partha Chatterjee addresses the "nationalist resolution" of the women's question, and shows how the new woman is the product of a new patriarchy formed along class lines. Susie Tharu traces the representation of the devoted wife, Savitri, within Indo-Anglian writing, in both its nationalist and post-independence incarnations. Nirmala Banerjee analyses the effects of industrialization on working class women in Bengal. Prem Chowdhry discusses the conjoining of colonial economic interests with the patriarchal practices of a local dominant peasant group, the Jats in Haryana. Kapil Kumar demonstrates the inter-relation of gender and class oppression among agricultural working women in Oudh (U.P.) and the nature of their participation in the movement led by Baba Ram Chandra. Vasantha Kannabiran and K. Lalitha discuss the perceptions of women who participated in the Telangana people's struggle (1946-50) showing both the liberating role of the movement and its limitations. Taken together, the papers elicit different kinds of relationships of patriarchal practices with class, nationalist reform, social movements and colonization. What emerges implicitly is the dialectical relation of 'feminisms' and patriarchies, both in the inventions of the colonial state and in the politics of the anti-colonial movements.

II

The relation between classes and patriarchies is complex and variable. Not only are patriarchal systems class differentiated, open to constant and consistent reformulation, but defining gender seems to be crucial to the formation of classes and dominant ideologies. Again, the relation between changing modes of production, patriarchal structures and class positions is both aligned and disjunct. For example, men and women in the same class often have a differential access to forms of social privilege, to wages, and to the means of production. Further, though patriarchies are entangled with modes of social ordering, for example, and with existing hierarchies and modes of subjection, they also appear to have no single one to one relation with a given mode of production but seem to change through overlap and reformulation. In this sense they have a relative 'autonomy' and a different duration. The lives of women exist at the interface of caste and class inequality, especially since the description and management of gender and female sexuality is involved in the maintenance and reproduction of social inequality.

The compulsion of colonial rule to extract surplus, create classes conducive to its rule, and to produce legitimizing ideologies, led in part to an aggravation of existing unequal relations within many sections of Indian society. Though there are many histories of social legislation and educational 'reforms' in relation to women there is as yet relatively less work on the relation between colonial intervention in the form of land revenue settlements and local patriarchal practices. Such ostensibly gender-neutral land settlements, whether guided by notions of preserving the 'village republic' or of creating a landed gentry, in fact, began a process of social restructuring which was simultaneously and necessarily a process of re-constituting patriarchies in every social strata. As most of this is either unrecorded or hidden history we can only briefly indicate some aspects of the changes in the agrarian economy which involved women.

Land settlements produced the following inter-related transformations. First, former landholding groups were re-empowered to a great extent within the new context of individual ownership of land and of market relations. This further impoverished both tenants and agricultural labour and exacerbated existing forms of extra-economic social coercion. It impinged thus on both the individual and social lives of women of these classes, and was perhaps one of the factors which later led to their wide participation in peasant struggles. Second, individual property rights were vested primarily in the hands of men, and women generally had only ancillary rights accruing from their subordinate relationships with men. In this there was both a continuation and a reinforcement of the exclusion of women from ownership or control of the means of production prevalent in the pre-colonial agrarian structure; where matrilineal systems did exist they were slowly transformed to patrilineal patterns of succession. Third, even when women of the subordinate classes did control some land (as tenants, for example), they had little access to the colonial legal and administrative machinery developed to manage the changed agrarian structure. The workings of an impersonal bureaucratic 'rule of law' administered from mofussil towns and district headquarters (as distinct from the working of the village panchayat) further marginalized the women from the 'public' sphere, even while it subjected them to its control. Such marginalization intensified their dependence on men. Fourth, along with land settlements, the colonial regime codified the customs of the dominant land owning and other rural groups. This froze custom into law and gave a juridical sanction to certain patriarchal practices regarding marriage, succession and adoption. Further, high caste Hindu norms in these matters, codified piece-meal as statutory Hindu law, were often privileged over customary law to the disadvantage of *all* Hindu women whether rural or urban.

A complex inter-relationship of contest and collusion between indigenous patriarchal norms, and those held by British administrators is visible in the colonial regulation of agrarian relations. For example, in Haryana (then the south-east part of the Punjab province), as Prem Chowdhry points out, the British while granting certain rights to widows in the interests of revenue extraction, were anxious to discourage them from availing of those very rights. Significantly, the attitudes of the British officials were determined by a conservative response to the feminist agitation in England which finally won the reforms in the Married Women's Property Law after a long struggle (1856-82). Many of these officials perceived the acquisition or control over property and money by women as both unfair to men and as socially dangerous, a perception which was shared locally. If the colonial regime, out of political and financial interests, sought to reinforce the local customary form of widow remarriage (*karewa*) in order to ensure male control over inheritance and property, reform organizations like the Arya Samaj found common ground with them and legitimized the custom as Vedic practice, and so enfolded the Jat landholding peasantry into the confines of high-caste Hinduism. It also gave a material grounding to the myth of the woman of the Vedic golden age, but at the expense of peasant women. Here the older form of the control of widows of ritually lower caste groups merges with the reformed Hinduism of the upper castes to make new instruments for ideological control of the widow through an acceptance of karewa — a process which is matched by the workings of the colonial law. The stability of both the home and of the agrarian economy was thus sought to be maintained.

In the princely state of Hyderabad, where the Telangana peasant struggle was later to take place, agrarian relations were a crucial determinant of the patriarchies experienced by both the women of ruling groups and by those from the exploited castes and classes. The system of subsidiary alliance with native rulers, one of the bulwarks of colonial rule, in one sense replicated, at a larger level, the effects of the land tenurial arrangements within regions in directly ruled territories. We are not in a position to indicate the nature of the change in patriarchies in states like Hyderabad where there was no direct colonial intervention in the agrarian economy but where a partial change in land tenurial arrangements was effected by the ruler. Perhaps future research in this area will facilitate comparison between the transformation of patriarchies within territories under direct British administration and those under indirect control.

In many parts of direct British administered regions, however, there are clear indications that colonial intervention in the agrarian economy generally intensified the oppression of the majority of rural women. For instance, in Oudh, the post-mutiny Taluqdari Settlement (1858) transformed the former ruling group of rajas, chiefs, and tax-collectors into landlords legally empowered to grant tenancies on the basis of a 'free market' economy.[1] This re-empowering of the *taluqdars* (landholders) along new juridical and economic principles at one level integrated an existing system of feudal agrarian relations within the framework of the colonial economy. Not only did this exacerbate patriarchal practices among the exploited classes (such as distress sales of daughters and harassment of women tenants), but it increased the regulatory power of landlords and upper castes (for example, through village and caste panchayats) in maintaining caste and class based marriage norms and sexual morality.

It may be noted that, contrary to popular notions, sections of the landed aristocracy created and supported by the British attempted to be as 'liberal' as the urban classes. Some Oudh taluqdars, for instance, took up matters of education and social reform for women.[2] The rural-urban divide was as such more spatial than social in the colonial context. Not only the urban landed aristocracy but the trading communities which later emerged as capitalists were also crucially linked to the agrarian economy and to rural society. This involved a certain degree of continuity in patriarchies practised in town and village.

On the other side, the working class both within and outside the industrial sector was also a product of a changed agrarian economy. Recurrent famines, the decline of artisan production, and the gradual emergence of the modern organized industrial sector all led to changes in occupational structure. These changes had special significance for women. Many were edged out of traditional village occupations and found only limited opportunities in the new sector, for instance in the textile and jute mills. Whether they were single (mostly widowed women) or with families, working women were, however, soon forced out of the new industries. Thus many women of the productive classes were pushed into the 'domestic' sphere, replicating to some extent the division between the 'private' and. 'public' domain as defined by middle class ideologies.

The middle class, to some extent, also derived from rural society. In addition to the urban professional and trading classes, the small landholders and village literati who sought jobs in the colonial administration and related professions, also became a part of the middle class. It was this middle class which was to develop ideologies of 'Hindu' and 'Indian' womanhood in contradistinction to the actual patriarchal norms prevalent among the other classes and in opposition to the 'western' woman. These notions were constructed and popularized through social reform and nationalist movements. As we shall see later, peasant movements were also to become carriers of such constructs.

III

Middle class reforms undertaken on behalf of women are tied up with the self-definition of the class, with a new division of the public from the private sphere and of course with a cultural nationalism. To some extent this book begins a sketch of cultural nationalism wherein the underbelly of every attempt towards identity has been a redescription of women of different classes. The imperatives have been both local and national, the ideologies have ranged from the conservative to the radical, and the class alignments have differed. This is a hidden history swept under the liberal carpet of 'reforms'; though these reforms have been stringently interrogated in terms of their class and caste character, their role in redefining gender and patriarchies has been largely ignored.

Through the nineteenth century different versions of female emancipation came to be slowly tied to the idea of national liberation and regeneration. The early colonial constellation of the Arya woman is a sternly elitist concept in class and caste terms, and finds its nationalist shape in social and political thought, in literature and in a dominant historiographic model of India wherein the Muslim interregnum is made to be responsible for all manner of deterioration in the status of women. The Vedic (and later, the Puranic) model becomes both a part of popular consciousness as well as of organized reform such as that of the Arya Samaj and is fed into the companionate models of the middle class family. The recovery of tradition throughout the proto-nationalist and nationalist period was always the recovery of the 'traditional' woman — her various shapes continuously readapt the 'eternal' past to the needs of the contingent present. Religion is the medium first for middle class and then for nationalist reform in the deepest sense. Selection from scriptural texts, and the construction of canons are not only serviceable in building an identity opposed to the colonial but are also related to the inegalitarian social structure. These reconstructions become ideological when highly selective and exclusive versions are sought to be universalized. The formation of desired notions of spirituality and of womanhood is thus a part of the formation of the middle class itself, wherein hierarchies and patriarchies are sought to be maintained on both material and spiritual grounds. The Vedic woman, both in her own time, and after her appropriation by upper castes and classes in the nineteenth century, is built upon the labour of lower social groups and is also a mark of distinction from them. Nowhere is the class character of middle class and nationalist reform of women more apparent than in the differential construction of the private and public sphere in the colonial period.

IV

The formation of the public and private spheres is a differential process which takes place on several levels, the discursive, the linguistic, the political and the economic, and usually in relation to other classes. The process of the formation of the private sphere as an indigenist alternative to western materialism is, in a sense, instituted at the beginning of the nineteenth century and comes into its own in nationalist discourse which sets out to establish, as Partha Chatterjee points out, a series of oppositions between male vs female, inner vs outer, public vs private, material vs spiritual. Since most middle class cultural production is tied, either explicitly or implicitly, both to its own formation within wider economic and political processes as well as to the anxieties of nationalism, the discursive production of public and private spheres occupies literature, popular writing as well as the writing on reform.

Sumanta Banerjee's essay gives an indication of how women are tied into the process of the cultural homogenization of the urban Bengali *bhadralok*. The need for a common middle class culture may have been produced as part of new economic market relations and the erosion of discrete caste cultures in the face of urbanization. Some degree of class polarization must also be taking place which requires a sharper differentiation at the cultural level. A new kind of segregation is imposed on women, whose identity is now to be defined in opposition to women from lower economic strata. This process is not dissimilar to the one which pushed the middle class woman into the seclusion of the private sphere as a mark of class status and superiority (among other things) in Victorian England. The channels for continuity between middle and lower class culture are domestic service, village and *kul* connections, as well as the transformation of rural landowners into middle-upper class urban groups. For women especially, organized social activities do not develop till the second half of the nineteenth century; till then they are restricted to *pujas, utsavs,* religious festivals, and ritual social functions like marriage. Upper caste women were barred from other public places. In the case of urban Calcutta it is popular culture, a space shared jointly by women of different social strata, which is pressed out by a hybrid middle class squaring colonial attitudes (to popular and vernacular performance and literature) with its own compulsion to 'modernize' patriarchy. For the Bengali bhadralok popular performative genres become opposed to a literary-ethical instruction which will eventually refine the 'soul' of their women. Popular cultural forms are virtually construed as sexual threats which will literally lure women into adultery. What is at issue here is both women themselves and the language in which they will speak, think, read and write.

The women who are sought to be excluded from the private space of the bhadralok home and from what is now seen to qualify as cultural activity are either relatively independent and literate such as the Vaisnavite women, or women from the lower strata, courtesans and prostitutes, i.e. women who have hitherto had greater access to a 'public' sphere of street, marketplace, fair and festival.

Significantly the principle of exclusion is at work here, and not as in the case of the bhadramahila, the procedures of reform. The women who are now sought to be excluded are in a sense outside rigid formations and part of a hitherto acceptable liminality, which perhaps because it is not so clearly contained by caste, class, gender or a demarcated space, is more threatening. The middle class public sphere which has come into existence, seeks not only to be somewhat different to this one but also to reposition it in relation to itself. The repositioning of cultural forms, then is implicated in the formation of a predominantly middle class public sphere, in a desired version of Indian culture and in desired versions of ideal women. It is also at the same time implicated in a new formation of the home as the insulated private sphere which is to be free from even temporary challenges to male authority. And indeed it is this guarantee which will ease the access of women to the middle class public sphere as both reformed women and as women reformers.

The relation between gender, speech and status, and the making of a 'literary' as opposed to a popular language is also of interest here. At one level it is orality which is under attack from the 'literacy' of written forms. For example *Vidya Sundar*, a courtly eighteenth century text, should have passed muster with the bhadralok, but for the fact that it had been appropriated by oral popular traditions. At another level, language itself is a site for contest in defining class, gender and the private sphere. This has been quite a protracted process. Thus Mritunjay Vidyalankar, himself a teacher of Bengali, disparaged the vernacular as a "naked and prostituted female" compared to Sanskrit — "a beautiful and virtuous woman".[3] The 'enrichment' of vernacular Bengali throughout the first half of the nineteenth century was a twin process of sanskritization and anglicization.[4] The purification of female vernacular may in fact be connected with both. William Carey, the Baptist missionary, deeply immersed in the Orientalist restorative project, produced in 1801 with the help of 'natives' a reader for the students of Fort William College called *Kathopakathan* or *Dialogues*. A compendium of sketches of various castes and classes, it depicts the idiomatic language, manners and customs of women, merchants, fishermen, beggars, labourers, and attempts to reproduce their speech patterns. Linguistic sophistication is proportionate to social status. Bengali women are identified as low caste through the 'vulgarity' of their speech while the vocabulary of higher caste women is represented as a mixture of refinement and vulgarity.[5] Even at the end of the nineteenth and beginning of the twentieth century the difference between vernacular and genteel Bengali obtains not merely between different classes but also between men and women in the same household. For the bhadralok it is the man who represents the mind and the woman the heart, and it is the heart of the woman which requires improvement. And so it is to the morally ennobling texts of English culture that middle class women are to turn. It is in this historical intersection that women begin to constitute themselves in journals, autobiographies, poems, narratives and diaries, and to which we owe the formation of an Anglo-Indian literature and the specific versions of a female sensibility that are present, for example, in Toru Dutt or Sarojini Naidu. Indeed the easy absorption of Victorian structures of feeling into the structures of Indian myth, as Susie Tharu describes, may well be related not only to the nature of the reforming venture, and to the specific acculturation of a section of the middle class on the 'English literary' model, but also to changes in the nature of the middle class and its definition of public and private spheres in opposition to the language, behaviour and culture of the lower strata.

The differential construction of the public sphere is also at issue. For middle class women it signals their partial emergence into a different kind of economic sphere (into which they will carry the constraints of conduct inculcated by the private sphere) — the service sector, professions etc. For poor women it signals a partial shift from the traditional 'public' sphere of agricultural labour into the modern industrialized sector, and also, as Nirmala Banerjee shows, a steady marginalization from both traditional activity and the modern industrial sector and hence from the productive process itself. And quite often the women who join the industrial sector have no supportive private sphere at all though they are sought to be regulated by its norms.[6] Thus most Bengali women workers in Calcutta's mills in the 1890s are widows or deserted women with no children to support them, often forced to live under male 'protection', and are consequently stigmatized and become virtual outcastes. So it is in fairly direct opposition to working class women that the private sphere of the bhadralok is built. The conditions of industrialization (wages, migration, housing), as well as attendant patriarchal practices constitute the social reasons for the exploitation of working women, but the bhadralok put the onus on the immorality and 'independence' of women in the public sphere. Among other kinds of labour, the intensified work of resident wives of migrant labourers, which invisibly subsidizes the industrial sector and the supply of labour to the city,[7] creates some of the material preconditions for a middle class private sphere.

For middle class women entry into the political movements of nationalist struggle did not naturally mean an entry into the economic sphere. For poor women, their subsistence labour or cottage industry may be carried out in the private space of the home but in that case the home should not qualify as a private sphere. And the definition of their labour as household work, i.e. unproductive labour, may work towards a derecognition of the 'public' nature of their labour. In fact, the redefinition of such public labour as an extension of private housework can and does open women to new and severe economic and patriarchal oppression. So not only do the familial ideologies of the middle class mediate in different ways the entry of women into the labour market and the economic sphere, they also become a constricting force which has often ensured that political or economic participation of women will not mean or be equal to a wider emancipation.

V

The social reform movements then are tied into the wide processes of defining class differentiated public and private spheres as well as into nationalism. Women internalize the offered models and constitute themselves with varying degrees of conformity — indeed the formation of the bhadramahila is paradigmatic in this respect. Towards the end of the century as women begin to organize and speak for themselves we find that many of the ambiguities in their own thought and practice have to do with this history of class based and male initiated reforms. For example in the Hindi speaking belt, women take up the issue of widowers remarrying with far more emotional involvement than that of widow remarriage. This is not surprising considering that at about the same time, Gandhi was quite wholeheartedly advocating the remarriage of virgin child widows but had many reservations about the remarriage of adult widows who, unlike the child, have understood the sacredness of marriage. So he too shifts some of the weight of the problem onto widowers and criticizes the social system which allowed men to remarry with ease. He advises young men to marry child widows.[8] Speaking of widowhood he said in 1920:

> Impatient reformers will merely say that remarriage is the only straight and simple remedy for this. I cannot say so. I too have a family of my own. There are so many widows in my family but I can never bring myself to advise them to remarry and they will not think of doing so either. The real remedy is for men to take a pledge that they will not remarry.[9]

Though reforms do seem to perform a service in a relative homogenizing of the middle class (perhaps nationalism itself also homogenizes the middle class culturally), the question of how many groups were actually touched by 'reform' issues such as sati, widow marriage, child marriage, female education, eradication of kulin polgygamy, remains. The cultural forms of the lower strata in urban Calcutta, for instance, scarcely reflect any involvement in these issues. Perhaps negotiating these areas itself becomes a way of being inscribed culturally into the middle class, and that is why they seem to preoccupy upwardly mobile groups as well as the innumerable caste associations which were formed in the latter part of the century.

Social legislation which set out to improve the situation of women, was at times counter-productive. The most notorious example is that of the Regulations (1812) introduced in Bengal Presidency to curb widow immolation. Based on a selective use of shastric interpretations made by pundits, the Regulations introduce the invidious category of 'illegal' and 'legal' sati and of opposed categories of 'voluntary' and coerced sati. Not only were the Regulations totally ineffective in their stated purpose (between 1812-16, out of 400 reported cases, only 10 illegal satis were prevented), but they also led to an actual increase in the number of incidents, for they were widely interpreted as being a sign of government approval of widow immolation.[10] What is not generally known is that though the Bentinck Abolition of Sati Act treated widow immolation as homicide, the category of "voluntary" sati (that is, suicide), was reintroduced a decade after, through an amendment of the Indian Penal Code (IPC). This amendment of "voluntary culpable homicide by consent," later incorporated in the IPC 1860, with some modifications, was an accommodation both to 'liberal' British opinion of so-called non-interference in the customs and religion of the 'natives' as well as to the opposition made to the abolition by the Dharma Sabha.[11] The notion of 'voluntary' sati foregrounded during the colonial period by both the British and the Indians, became a persistent component of the continuing ideology of sati. Its consquences for our own times are self-evident.

A product of the 'good' intentions of British administrators and the middle class, social legislation was often counter-productive because it did not distinguish between the forms of patriarchy which were cross caste or class and those which were specific to particular groups. Further, such legislation had its own conservative biases and later came to be dominated by the familial ideology of the middle class. Take, for instance, the Widow Remarriage Act (1856). Virtually a paper legislation in terms of the negligible number of marriages performed, it was of course important in raising, both before and after its enactment, social awareness about the condition of child widows in particular and high caste widows in general. However, there were certain important clauses in the Act, which in fact not only constituted a barrier to the marriage of high-caste widows but also affected women belonging to those castes which did not have a customary bar on widow remarriage or practised levirate marriage. These clauses debarred the widow, on remarriage, from any right to maintenance or inheritance from her husband's property, "as if she had died," and also vested the guardianship of her children with the relatives of her deceased husband.[12] In other words, the economic stake which the high castes had in not allowing widows to remarry, was firmly protected by the Act. Even if a widow were willing to forgo customary right to maintenance or to property, she would be faced with the painful dilemma of having to give up her children. And on top of that incur a social stigma. It is not surprising that apart from the obvious interests of the natal and in-law families, few widows would themselves have been willing to avail of the legal right to remarry. For most women of other castes, and they formed the majority, remarriage was customary. But where property interests were at stake, such as in the karewa form of marriage among the peasantry in Haryana, it meant that the widow lost it all if she violated custom and married outside her husband's family. Thus the Act served to reinforce karewa and allied practices among various social groups. In a sense, the Act homogenized at the legal level, the disabilities of upper caste Hindu widows attendant on remarriage.

Labour legislation was no exception. As Nirmala Banerjee points out, the industry employed the relatively cheap labour of women in the mines when the industry was expanding, and pushed them out when there was a recession. This was ostensibly in the interests of women's health. It should be noted that the ban on women working underground was lifted with the onset of World War II and reimposed at its end. Not only women but the entire family lost out since the women normally worked in family teams. There was hardly any alternative means of livelihood made available to the retrenched women. With a drop in what were in any case subsistence earnings, families migrated from the collieries in search of petty employment elsewhere.[13] What is noteworthy is that work in mines was extremely harmful for both men and women. Instead of granting them the right to safe conditions of work, a welfare ideology of protection of 'the weaker sex' was both invoked and perpetuated to deny what little opportunities the modernized sector of the economy afforded to working women.

VI

Both tradition and modernity have been, in India, carriers of patriarchal ideologies. As such neither is available to us in a value free or unproblematic sense, nor is either, as they are usually conceptualized, necessarily the solution. How then do we fight surviving and reconstructed feudal ideologies? Both tradition and modernity are eminently colonial constructs. We think it is time to dismantle this opposition altogether and to look at cultural processes in their actual complexity. Change has continued to occur (though it may not have been in the desired direction); we need to see how women and womanhood are inserted into, and affected by social change, and how change is made to appear as continuity. That is, the ideologies of women as carriers of tradition often disguise, mitigate, compensate, contest, actual changes taking place. Womanhood is often part of an asserted or desired, not an actual cultural continuity. Many kinds of distinctions need to be made, on the basis of future work, between actual continuity and desired continuity. And yet actual continuity is never either pure or uncontaminated. For it appears in different combinations at different historical junctures, has different social and ideological locations, and responds to different crises (colonial presence being one such). Further, the long duration and resilience of patriarchal practices makes the matter more complex.

Women's studies and feminist movements feel impelled to construct a positive and inspirational history. The danger here is both of literalizing and simplifying the 'model' women as well as of legitimizing the way in which reform and nationalist movements took up the woman question. Instead perhaps we need to admit that certain doors are opened, even that the consciousness of women exceeds quite often the ideologies which create it or enable it, but that class and caste have a formative role. Women may sometimes exceed or violate the prescriptions of a particular set of ideologies, precisely because they are members of a dominant group. The national movement too constructs an inspirational model of the past, and if feminism is to be different, it must acknowledge the ideological and problematic significance of its own past. Instead of creating yet another grand tradition or a cumulative history of emancipation, neither of which can deal with our present problems, we need to be attentive to how the past enters differently into the consciousness of other historical periods and is further subdivided by a host of factors including gender, caste, and class. Indeed the full ideological power of reconstructed Hinduisms and certain tendencies in nationalism can perhaps only be understood through the analysis of posited gender relations, and such analysis in turn will change the object of our enquiry.

Perhaps the most positive thing about the reforms is that though they shape women's entry into the public sphere, the labour market, and their self-constitution, they cannot entirely determine it. Through the very contradictions, pressures and inconsistencies of various ideologies in relation to their material circumstance, women began to articulate their position afresh, and to organize.

The history of reform — whether colonial or indigenous or nationalist — undertaken by men and by women does not seem very inspiring, freighted as it is with many kinds of patriarchal assumptions, and involved as it is in recasting women. This is not a matter of despair, nor is it merely or only a question of historical 'limits'. By this argument one is pushed to a position of sympathetic criticism which is to say that at that time, at that place, they tried to do their best but inevitably could not exceed the limits of their age; and if contemporary feminists wish they had done so, they are not only being unrealistic but are also reading history solely by hindsight. We think this is a more a question of being able to see how the history of feminism in India (and probably elsewhere) is inseparable from an history of anti-feminism. The questions which arise are: first, how in the face of conservative anti-feminism, projected reform and change can proceed no further since they are constantly being contested (thus despite the strategic/internalized use of scriptural sanction for prohibiting sati, or for allowing widows to remarry, the projected reforms were bitterly opposed); and second, that nowhere can or have reforms been directed at patriarchies alone, but they have also been involved in re-aligning patriarchy with social stratification (both existing and emerging) and with changing political formations. To be rid of patriarchies altogether then would consist in imagining and effecting a thoroughgoing social change.

VII

With regard to social movements we can perhaps make a broad distinction between the 'modernizing' of patriarchal modes of regulating women and the 'democratizing' of gender relations both in the home and the work place. Social movements which try to change, to whatever degree, both the base (the sexual division of labour in production and property relations) and the ideologies of a specific patriarchal formation may be termed 'democratizing' movements. Movements by working class and peasant women have a greater potential for democratizing patriarchal power relations than the 'modernizing' movements. Among the latter sort may be placed the social reform, the 'nativist' and nationalist movements, as discussed earlier, which provide a more 'liberal space' for middle class women. Whereas democratizing movements seek to alter class relations at the same time as undertaking some levelling of gender relations, the modernizing movements in colonial India seek to partially level gender relations either without attacking class inequality or by positively affirming it. In practice, however, there was an area of commonality between the two. The historical role of the modernizing movements was that of 'recasting' women for companionate marital relationships and attendant familial duties as well as of enabling middle-class women to enter the professions and participate in political movements, in a limited way. On the other hand, the democratizing movements which attacked both colonial and feudal structures were often themselves either infused with middle class familial ideologies and agendas for reform or unable to break entirely with feudal partriarchal forms.

Democratizing movements were potentially more revolutionary not only because they brought women of the most oppressed strata, who constitute the majority, into a struggle for their rights, but also because in fighting for their class rights women did attain an enhanced sense of self-respect as workers and producers rather than being confined simply to familial or caste-related 'identities.' Like the political movements for national freedom, these movements also surface some of the latent contradictions between the experiences of women and 'containing' patriarchal ideologies. Whether such contradictions are even acknowledged and in what manner they are handled by the organization leading the struggle is of course a crucial issue for feminist historiography. The broader question is what kind of abilities did peasant and nationalist movements need, and what kind of women — with what aspirations — did they make? How were the ensuing contradictions handled? The women active in these movements are usually a part of male-dominated societies and/or the middle class. The conditions of their formation would largely determine the possibilities for social action, the kind of 'self' formed and the modes of self expression. The relation between the experiential and ideological dimensions of female participation remains a complex and rich field for further investigation. Within the present materials available it is difficult to ascertain the full political significance of the demands of peasant women in the course of peasant struggles.

In this context, two aspects of the Oudh peasant movement are striking. The first is the repressive attitude of the Congress towards the movement. When Gandhi visited U.P in February 1921 where the peasants, both men and women, were facing large-scale police repression, he issued a set of 19 instructions asking them to treat the landlords as friends and not to resort to social boycott and other forms of protest to redress their grievances.[14] These instructions, as is well known, amounted to a call to abandon their struggle. What is seldom noticed is that the oppression women faced due to the agrarian class structure thereby remained intact. Thus we find that the resolutions of the Kisanin Panchayat reflect a set of oppressions in the thirties and forties similar to those which the women were subjected to in the 1920s. Ironically the Congress which curbed the movement and with it prolonged the class based forms of the patriarchal oppression of women, at the same time had a 'reform package' for women on its agenda.

Second, the middle class ideology of 'pure' womanhood enters the very working of the movement, which in the thirties and forties combined peasant issues with the nationalist programme. The Gandhian ideology on women as well as Baba Ram Chandra's own notions about gender relations combine into a visible attempt to regulate the mobility of women, and to restructure marriage norms and family life in conformity with upper caste patriarchal norms. In this respect, the reference to a "Kurmi-Kshatriya Sabha" in Baba Ram Chandra's papers is of interest.[15] Upper caste mobility for the Kurmis, who were the principal cultivating caste in the region, is being sought, in part, by reorganizing the patriarchal practices of the caste. If there is indeed a link between caste or group mobility and political movements, then here it finds its clearest expression in the attempt to reorder gender relations. There also appears to be some sort of relation here between 'Hinduisation' and the political movement. This connection is expressed both in terms of organizational needs — i.e. upper caste Hinduism appears to offer a model of regulated gender relations — and in an ideological sense — i.e. in the nature of the link forged with dominant nationalist tendencies.

In this sense a preoccupation which is common to both modernizing and democratizing movements is the preoccupation with the regulation of sexuality and different modes of control in the face of the emergence of women into a new public sphere, political participation, new labour processes and the consequent changes in the family structure. When Baba Ram Chandra seeks to introduce the companionate model of marriage upheld by middle class reformers, this involves both an erasure of certain freedoms as well as an access to respectability for the peasant women. Baba Ram Chandra's reorganization of marriage and morals bears a notable resemblance to Gandhi. The moral and austere new woman he tries to create, not only has a long genealogy in various kinds of middle class interdictions but is also related to the imperatives of active political participation by women and to a sanskritizing upward cultural mobility. Baba Ram Chandra does not advocate monogamy in the middle class sense but a quasi-legal regulation of male-female relationships, as well as certain associated middle class values. Firstly, upholding such norms equals a form of moral surveillance of female sexuality which does not square with the plural practices and different patriarchal modes prevailing in the lower strata. Widow remarriage in this area among the Kurmis was a form of cohabitation called *dharaua,* where certain features of the Hindu marriage were left out. (This may explain why it does not find a place in the Census). Secondly, since women are also bringing up their own issues it is not possible to determine how much of the initiative here was their own, reflecting a desire for one-to-one relationships, and how much was Baba Ram Chandra's. But Baba Ram Chandra's own equation of respectability, and eligibility for female political participation with a relatively more formal marriage is not very distant from Gandhi's attitude to marriage as one of the guarantors of a higher morality. Indeed Gandhi's extreme resentment at the inclusion of the prostitutes of Barisaal in the cause of the Congress party was on the ground of their immorality. Again like Gandhi, Baba Ram Chandra's relation to religion is both a matter of metaphor and mobilization. He too uses, though to different effect, symbolic constructs, to mobilize women and to change the social relations of rural women.

Perhaps the most ironic consequence of the attempt to introduce a middle class sexual morality into peasant movements is the fact that this morality is a product of the emergence of a middle class private sphere, and is sought to be superimposed on women who are already involved in the production process. Thus peasant women in Telangana, who must never have had an exclusively domestic role, are being given a role in the political movement which is perceived in part as an extension of their domestic role. In Telangana, there is a pressing contradiction between, on the one hand, an insertion of such domestic ideologies into the movement and, on the other, the representation of the movement as a higher cause for which women must, if called upon, give up even their children. Here we would like to make a few observations about the principal issues that arise from a study of that "magic time." Feminist writing in the past two decades has sought to analyse the problematic relation between class and gender oppression in the wake of ample empirical evidence of the continuance of patriarchy within post-revolutionary societies such as the Soviet Union and China — particularly the vexed relation between Marxist theory, the actual history of class struggles, the programmes of organized left parties, and the location of women in revolutionary movements.

Theoretical positions which locate patriarchy as the primary contradiction in society pose the following problem. To put it crudely, patriarchy becomes an ahistorical category within an originating myth of male coercion. The strength of this position, however, lies in the fact that it foregrounds patriarchal oppression as existing within all historically known modes of production and as a sociocultural system cutting across class divisions. Its weakness lies in treating women as a 'class' by themselves, leading to a disregard of the fact that women of the exploited classes may indeed have closer group interests with men of their own classes than with women belonging to the dominant classes. The problem with those Marxist positions which locate women's oppression solely within the system of production relations is that they tend to relegate patriarchy to the 'superstructure.' This ignores the fact that through the gender based division of labour within the production and procreation processes, patriarchy rests quite securely within the base itself. That is how it is reproduced both within social relations of production and within the family of the propertied as well as of the non-propertied classes. The resultant ideological formations invade all realms of state and civil society, reconstituting and strengthening patriarchies at the level of the base in different historical conjunctures.

In other words, class struggle will enable a fight only against those features of patriarchy which are directly related to the public productive sphere and to exploitation by the oppressor class — unequal wages, bonded labour, coerced sexual service, rape etc. It will not enable a struggle against those formations and ideologies which are carried within the movement itself both by middle class activists and by the people engaged in struggle. Recent Marxist and non-Marxist studies of the communist-led movements of the forties — Telangana, Tebhaga, Warli — have in different ways pointed to this crucial fact.[16] As these studies show, contradictions arising out of patriarchal power relations within the movement did surface, but they were either dealt with tangentially or suppressed. At that historical juncture, the Marxist theoretical position had honed itself on the practice of the Soviet Marxism. The Maoist position which takes patriarchy, both material and cultural, as a specific oppression which the Communist Party must include in its revolutionary struggles, did not become a model (see for instance, Hunan Report, 1927). The stringent yet constructive critique of the theory and practice of the left by socialist feminists also lay decades ahead. However, these contradictions cannot be treated as peripheral to the left. There are small signs, thanks principally to the feminists within the organized parties, that patriarchal relations within organizations are now beginning to receive some attention. Nevertheless, gender in an encompassing sense has yet to become central to the understanding of social inequality for the organized left and to replace 'women's issues' in the narrow sense; a revolutionary redefinition of public and private has yet to enter the agenda alongside class struggle.

VIII

The value of this collection may lie not necessarily in its provisional answers but in the fact that it sets out to interrogate the very nature of feminist questioning. In its seclusion or segregation of women's issues, much feminist research and practice has been contained within the colonial and nationalist historical paradigms of reform and reawakening. These paradigms by their very nature have designated the production processes, land and revenue settlements as in themselves gender neutral even when they acknowledge gender discrimination in practice. Gender difference is seldom seen as a structuring principle in economic processes. Again, in concentrating, like the reformers, on issues of family, education, and economic participation, feminist research often implicitly accepts and locates itself within the division of public and private spheres constructed in the colonial period and neglects the materiality of the wider economic and legal processes by which these spheres came into being. In one sense, peasant movements and urban 'feminist' reform have been opposite sides of the same coin. If peasant movements attempt to overthrow class oppression then questions of land, revenue, taxation are perceived as gender neutral, and questions relating to women as secondary.

The urban reforms which set out to demand greater egalitarianism for women in the home and in the work place do not challenge the binary construction of these spaces, and show little concern with class inequality.

If we take seriously the implications of the reconstitution of patriarchies in colonial India, there may be other ways of conceptualizing the feminist problematic. First arises the question of how much of its legacy remains in the structures of institutions, (both of the state and others), in the agrarian and industrial sectors, in the contemporary parodic and rhetorical nationalisms, in the emerging forms of religious fundamentalism, and in contemporary ideologies about women. Second, there is a perceptible relation between colonial reforms, especially in so far as they took juridical shape, and the homogenization (operating with a regional specificity) of different classes, both rural and urban. What is at issue here is both the relation of gender description to economic processes within a changing mode of production, and the mediatory power of superstructural discourses upon the base. Given the uneven development of capital and the changed location of India today in the wider global economy, these questions now have an even greater urgency. Patriarchies after all are *still* being reconstituted, and not all the modalities of this process have altered. In such a context existing anti-women practices are not feudal remnants alone which will vanish in time but are products of a sustained reformulation of patriarchies.

NOTES

1. See Jagdish Raj, *Economic Conflict in North India: A Study of Landlord-Tenant Relations in Oudh, 1870-90* (Delhi, Allied, 1978).
2. Thomas R. Metcalf, "Social Effects of British Land Policy in Oudh," in *Land Control and the Social Structure in Indian History*, ed. Robert Frykenberg (Delhi: Manohar, 1979), p. 149.
3. "Bedanta Chandrika," *Mritunjay Granthabali*, p. 28, quoted in David Kopf, *British Orientalism and the Bengal Renaissance* (Calcutta: Firma K.L. Mukhopadyay, 1969), p. 207.
4. See Hiranamay Banerjee, *Iswarchandra Vidyasagar* (1968; 2nd ed. Delhi: Sahitya Akademi, 1987), pp. 58-61.

5. See Kopf, *British Orientalism*, pp. 90-94.
6. See Radha Kumar, "Family and Factory : Women in the Bombay cotton textile industry 1919-1939," *Indian Economic and Social History Review*, 20 no. 1 (Jan-March, 1983), p.88,
7. Kalpana Bardhan, "Women's Work, Welfare and Status," *Economic and Political Weekly*, 20, no. 5 (Dec. 1985), p. 2208.
8. *Collected Works of Mahatma Gandhi*, vol. 30 (1926), p. 340.
9. Ibid, vol. 18 (1920), pp. 319-21.
10. V.N. Datta, *Sati: Widow Burning in India* (Delhi: Manohar, 1988). pp. 19-70.
11. Vasudha Dhagamvar, "Saint, Victim or Criminal," *Seminar*, 342 (Feb. 1988), pp. 34-39.
12. Kamaladevi Chattopadhyaya, *Indian Women's Battle for Freedom* (Delhi: Abhinav, 1983), p. 54.
13. Ibid, p. 89; and *Towards Equality: Report of the Committee on the Status of Women* (Delhi: Govt. of India, 1974), p. 191.
14. Gyan Pandey, "Peasant Revolt and Indian Nationalism, 1919-1922," in *Subaltern Studies*, ed. Ranajit Guha (1982; rpt. Delhi: Oxford University Press, 1986), pp. 143-45.
15. Sumit Sarkar, *Modern India* (Delhi: Macmillan, 1983), p. 203.
16. Indra Munshi Saldhana, "Tribal Women in the Warli Revolt, 1945-47; Class and Gender in the Left Perspective," Review of Women Studies, *Economic and Political Weekly*, 21, no 17(April 1986), pp. 41-52; Peter Custers, *Women in the Tebhaga Movement* (Calcutta: Noya Prokash, 1987); Stree Shakti Sanghatna, *We were making history: Life stories of women in the Telangana people's struggle* (Delhi: Kali for Women, 1989).

Whatever Happened to the Vedic *Dasi*?

Orientalism, Nationalism, and a Script for the Past

UMA CHAKRAVARTI

MEN AND WOMEN in India, whether or not they have formally learnt history, carry with them a sense of the past which they have internalized through the transmission of popular beliefs, mythology, tales of heroism and folklore. Formal history also percolates down, often in a transmuted form, to a wider range of people through articles in popular journals, discussions, and through what may be termed as the 'dispersal effect', so that elements of oral history may be overlaid by more serious historical conclusions forming a sort of medley of ideas. It is just such a medley of ideas that forms the basis of our understanding of the status of women in ancient times; and is also part of our deeply embedded perceptions of the past in a more general sense.

Particular elements that constitute a given community or group's sense of history are not, however, timeless and unchanging. Perceptions of the past are constantly being constituted and reconstituted anew. At specific junctures the sense of history may be heightened and the past may be dramatically reconstituted, bringing into sharp focus the need of a people for a different self-image from the one that they hold of themselves. One such juncture for India, when historical consciousness was being reshaped, came in the nineteenth century. In the new script for the past the women's question held a key place, but it is important to bear in mind that it was only one element in a set of related elements, all of which were being constituted at the same time and through the same process, ultimately ending in the creation of a Hindu-Aryan identity. The new self-image fulfilled a growing need of the emerging middle classes since it enabled them to contend with the 'burden' of the present, especially with the loss of self esteem following the British conquest of India.

What was gradually and carefully constituted, brick by brick, in the interaction between colonialism and nationalism is now so deeply embedded in the consciousness of the middle classes that ideas about the past have assumed the status of revealed truths. Any suggestion that we might fruitfully analyse the manner and the different stages by which this body of knowledge was built up, or how and when we came by our immediate intellectual and cultural heritage (which is often only a hundred and fifty years old) would therefore be considered quite unnecessary or even futile. But for women in particular this heritage, this perception of the past, of the 'lost glory', is almost a burden. It has led to a narrow and limiting circle in which the image of Indian womanhood has become both a shackle and a rhetorical device that nevertheless functions as a historical truth.

This paper attempts to demonstrate the factors and the stages spanning roughly the last century and a half, but focussing particularly on the second half of the nineteenth century, in the formation of the present historical consciousness; I will also outline here the different elements within a complex structure of ideas wherein knowledge about the past ultimately ended in the creation of a persuasive rhetoric, shared by Hindu liberals and conservatives alike, especially in relation to the myth of the golden age of Indian womanhood as located in the Vedic period. This image foregrounded the Aryan woman (the progenitor of the upper-caste woman) as the *only* object of historical concern. It is no wonder then that the Vedic *dasi* (woman in servitude), captured, subjugated, and enslaved by the conquering Aryans, but who also represents one aspect of Indian womanhood,[1] disappeared without leaving any trace of herself in nineteenth century history. Since no one had noticed her existence, it is natural that there was no one to mourn her disappearance.

My intention in this essay is not to rescue the Vedic dasi, which of course needs to be done and requires a separate study, but to situate the nineteenth century historiography of the women's question within the cultural and ideological encounter between England and India. This is the story of how the Aryan woman came to occupy the centre of the stage in the recounting of 'the wonder that was India' representing an amalgamation of brahminical and Kshatriya values. In this essay the process of the reconstruction of the past has been divided into three phases and is dealt with in three sections. Each phase was marked by certain trends although neither the phases nor the trends were watertight or exclusive. The first section provides a brief summary of the major ideas and themes in the work of the Orientalists, Anglicists and Evangelists, and the proto-nationalists, covering the period upto 1850; the next section deals with the succeeding group of Orientalists, namely Max Muller and two European women writers who extended his romantic reconstruction of the Aryan past to women, as well as the emergence of cultural nationalism in the period between 1850 and 1880. This was expressed in the writings of R.C. Dutt, Bankim Chandra Chatterji and Dayananda among others, and highlighted Kshatriya/Aryan values in the reconstruction of a new identity for Indian womanhood. The third section examines the relationship between such images of womanhood and the actual experiences of women in the closing decades of the nineteenth century.

I

> In the nineteenth century we recovered our long lost ancient literatures, Vedic and Buddhistic, as well as the buried architectural monuments of Hindu days. The Vedas and their commentaries had almost totally disappeared from the plains of Aryavarta where none could interpret them; none had even a complete manuscript of the texts. The English printed these ancient scriptures of the Indo-Aryans and brought them to our doors.
>
> JADUNATH SARKAR, 1928 [2]

The contribution of Europeans to the rediscovery of India's past was widely accepted by scholars and popular writers in the nineteenth and twentieth centuries. The perception of the past was influenced by European, more specifically British, perceptions in two separate and contradictory ways. One strand was represented by the Orientalists whose reconstruction of the glory of Indian civilization in the ancient past was taken over lock, stock, and barrel, by nineteenth century Indian writers to build a picture of Indian civilization not just for a particular region like Bengal (which contributed substantially to the building of this picture, especially in the early years of writing), but for the whole of India. The other strand was the Utilitarian and Evangelical attack on contemporary Indian society, especially on the visibly low status of women. Orientalism and Utilitarianism coalesced in the works of the early nationalist writers whose most enduring and successful construction was the image of womanhood in the lost past as a counter to the real existence of women in the humiliating present.

Among the Orientalists who contributed most substantially to the notion of a 'golden age' which had existed in a remote and unchartered period of Indian history were William Jones (1746-94) and H.T. Colebrooke. Closely associated with the Asiatic Society, their researches covered a wide range of themes in Sanskrit literature, history, and philosophy which were refined and elaborated in later years. It is significant, however, that glossing over certain aspects of the past was a characteristic feature of the work of the Orientalists who did not particularly react to the specific forms of inequality of caste, class, and gender prevailing in India. In part this may be due to the fact that status distinctions were deeply ingrained in British society, but partly the lack of concern may be explained as a natural consequence of their heavy reliance on the conservative indigenous literati, the Brahmin *pandits.*

The women's question, notably, was not one of the themes that were foregrounded in the earliest work of the Asiatic Society. Jones, for example, did not pay any attention to *sati* (widow immolation) and made only a passing reference to Gargi, whom he described as "eminent for her piety and learning."[3] More important than Jones in influencing the actual reconstruction of the past was the work of Colebrooke whose original researches earned for him the admiration of Max Muller. With Colebrooke the Orientalists came to focus their attention directly upon the women's question by compiling evidence bearing on women from the ancient texts; predictably, the focal starting point was the ritual of sati. One of Colebrooke's first pieces of research was "On the Duties of the Faithful Hindu Widow"[4] wherein he presented the textual position on sati. The essay reflects all the characteristic features of the historiography of the women's question: the reference to a variety of ancient texts, the special authority given to texts over custom, the search for the 'authentic' position as contained in the older and more authoritative texts, and the confusion in reconciling contradictory evidence. However, it is significant that there is nothing in Colebrooke's essay to suggest that the Vedas were recognized as either the oldest or the most authentic texts; the past was as yet unstratified and was perceived as one homogenous whole.

The focussing on the 'duties' of the 'faithful' Hindu widow, would most likely have had a great impact on Europeans who were the main readers of the *Asiatic Researches.* For many decades thereafter a reference to Hindus appears to have evoked the image of a burning woman as recorded by Max Muller almost eighty years later.[5] Whatever other research Colebrooke engaged himself with in reconstructing the 'glories' of the ancient Hindus, an unintended consequence of his essay on the 'faithful widow' was to add the weight of scholarship to the accounts of travellers and other lay writers whose descriptions of burning women came to represent an integral part of the perception of Indian reality. Colebrooke's account of sati highlighted an 'awesome' aspect of Indian womanhood, carrying both the associations of a barbaric society ***and*** of the mystique of the Hindu woman who 'voluntarily' and 'cheerfully' mounted the pyre of her husband.

Colebrooke's essay on the Vedas [6] was the first piece of work drawing attention to the texts as a major achievement of the ancient Aryans. Of interest to us are the references to Gargi and Maitreyi,[7] two of the oft-quoted examples of the glory of ancient Indian womanhood. It is significant that Colebrooke attributes no particular importance to the account of the conversation between Maitreyi and Yajnavalkya. Gargi too appears merely as one of the contenders, neither more nor less important than the other participants in the debate with Yajnavalkya.

Jones, Colebrooke and a whole range of students at the Fort William College who formed the earliest group of the Orientalists, saw themselves as engaged in reintroducing the Hindu elite to the 'impenetrable mystery' of its ancient lore. The Sanskritic tradition, 'locked up' till then in the hands of a closed priesthood, was being thrown open and its treasures made available to the people in its 'pristine' form;[8] the truths of indigenous traditions were being recuperated.[9] In sum, the Europeans who had successfully constituted their own 'true' history were now engaged in giving to Indians the greatest gift of all — a history.[10] But the first stage of the

Orientalist enterprise in reconstructing the past was hardly a case of "giving back to the natives the truths of their own little read and less understood Shaster (sic),"[11] as portrayed by the Orientalists. The indigenous intelligentsia were not functioning within a political and social vacuum. The natives were no passive recipients of the perception of the past, then in the process of being reconstituted. In fact the indigenous literati were *active agents* in constructing the past and were consciously engaged in choosing particular elements from the embryonic body of knowledge flowing from their own current social and political concerns.

The implications of the British position on social and cultural questions and the possibilities of generating certain changes through legislation became fairly clear in the early nineteenth century. The reconstruction of the past thereafter assumed a practical and utilitarian function. The question was no longer one of discovering fragments of texts, or translating them, but as the movement for abolition gained momentum, stratifying the texts to establish authenticity became crucial. All this meant that apart from a general increase in historical consciousness, the past was beginning to be classified and analysed more rigorously to argue the debates of the present. What was of lasting significance from the point of view of historical consciousness was the fact that the reconstruction of the past was no longer confined to the pages of the *Asiatic Researches,* read by a few select people. The reconstructed past was increasingly appearing in pamphlets and vernacular journals, made possible with the introduction of printing, and the participants in this were the newly emerging intelligentsia composed of both traditional and modern elements who perceived themselves as interpreters of tradition in a changing situation. This intelligentsia could regard itself as a product of an 'exhausted' culture but, through the work of the Orientalists, could simultaneously feel optimistic that despite the present circumstances they were representatives of a culture which had been "organically disrupted by historical circumstance but was capable of revitalisation."[12] Rammohun Roy epitomizes this dominant trend among the indigenous intelligentsia in the first quarter of the nineteenth century and is best known for his crusade against sati although his writing and thinking spanned a whole gamut of issues relating to Hinduism.

The case against sati had been argued forcefully even before Rammohun Roy by Mritunjay Vidyalankar. Together Rammohun and Mritunjay introduced into sati a highly intellectual argument, one that evoked the highest goal of religion which had never been evoked before in the case of women, except in the dissident tradition as exemplified by Buddhism. The goal for women, as spelt out by the ancient Hindu legislators was *pativrata dharma* (devotion to the husband). But Mritunjay, and then Rammohun, argued that the ultimate goal of *all* Hindus was selfless absorption in a divine essence, a union which could not flow from an action like sati. It was in this context, in response to the exigencies of social needs, that Roy imaginatively used the Maitreyi-Yajnavalkya episode[13] to argue against the subjection of women. He imbued the account with two features (neither of which could be seen in the Jones-Colebrooke accounts) both of which have survived into the twentieth century upper caste Hindu perception: one was the spiritual potential of women, and the second was that in the area of spirituality women were not inferior to men. From this followed the implicit assumption that the 'status' of women in the ancient past had been quite high unlike that of contemporary women. Rammohun used the Maitreyi episode to state that Yajnavalkya had imparted divine knowledge of the most difficult nature to Maitreyi and that she had not only been able to comprehend the high philosophy but had also actually attained divine knowledge. Roy thus provided a concrete example from the earliest antiquity to reinforce Mritunjay's position that women *had* pursued the highest goal of Hindu religion and in his view, it was the 'wicked' pandits who distorted the Shastras in subsequent times.

It is significant that the Maitreyi account should have been imbued with a normative value for Hindu womanhood during the course of the sati debate by a reformer arguing for change. While the Orientalists tried to write without taking a position, for the Indian writer that was virtually impossible. The entire series of arguments used by Mritunjay and Roy indicate their refusal to accept, albeit at an intellectual level, that the final goal of Hindu women was different from that of Hindu men. It was at the same time an implicit devaluation of the pativrata ideal, where salvation lay in unqualified devotion to the husband, until then the only legitimate aspiration conceded to women by the legislators.

Roy's search for an alternative to superstitious and ritualized Hinduism in its present degenerate form also led him to search for these strands in the glorious past which could be highlighted as providing an indigenous alternative to degenerate Hinduism in the form of the Vedanta. In scrapping everything except the Vedas and Upanishads, which were identified as the core of Hindu tradition, he thus created a precedent for the crucial nineteenth century foregrounding of the Vedas. Further, once the Upanishads were identified as the 'true' religion, the golden age was perceived as lasting upto the time the Upanishads were composed. Ultimately the golden age of Hindu womanhood would also have to be located within this era.

The emerging Indian intelligentsia in the first half of the nineteenth century were involved in a dual encounter with colonial ideology. Awareness of the past through Orientalist scholarship was countered by an equally strong negative perception of the present which missionaries, administrators, travellers, and others were engaged in writing about. Historical consciousness and especially the women's question were crucial components in this stream of writing too. In seeking a psychological advantage over their subjects colonial ideology felt compelled to assert the moral superiority of the rulers in many subtle and not so subtle ways. One of the not so subtle ways was in the area of gender relations. The 'higher' morality of the imperial masters could be effectively established by highlighting the low status of women among the subject population as it was an issue by which the moral 'inferiority' of the subject population could simultaneously be demonstrated. The women's question thus became a crucial tool in the colonial ideology. History in turn came to occupy a key position in the cultural conflict between the ruling power and the colonized subjects. This was the context for the obsessive concern with cultural questions in the reconstruction of the past.

The bulk of colonial writing in India focussed on demonstrating the peculiarities of Hindu civilization, and the barbaric practices pertaining to women. The circulation of this negative perception was much wider than that of Orientalist scholarship and probably preceded and outlasted the work of the Orientalists in revealing India's 'lost glory'. While they were writing and publishing mainly in learned journals the Anglican writers, especially Christian missionaries, were methodically building up an indictment, also in print, about the hideous state of Indian society.[14] Together their best representatives, Mill, Grant, and Duff drew up what has been termed as a 'national' account-sheet of moral lapses and strong points of Indian and western civilization.[15]

The best known work of this genre of writing is Mill's monumental account of India and her past; its reach and impact were tremendous because it was the first comprehensive history of India. In sharp contrast to the Orientalists who had suggested that the Hindus were a people of high culture now in a state of decline, Mill deemed Hindu civilization as crude from its very beginnings, and plunged in the lowest depths of immorality and crime.

Central to the criterion by which Mill judged the level of civilization was the position it accorded to its women. According to him Hindu women were in

> a state of dependence more strict and humiliating than that which is ordained for the weaker sex . . . . Nothing can exceed the habitual contempt which Hindus entertain for their women . . . . They are held in extreme degradation, excluded from the sacred books, deprived of education and (of a share) in the paternal property . . . . That remarkable barbarity, the wife held unworthy to eat with her husband, is prevalent in Hindustan.[16]

A major conclusion of Mill's was that the practice of segregating women did not come with the Mohammedans (p. 318); rather it was a consequence of the whole spirit of Hindu society where women must be constantly guarded at all times for fear of their innate tendency towards infidelity. Quoting from an ancient text he stated that the Hindus compared women with "a heifer on the plain that longeth for fresh grass", with reference to their uncontrollable sexuality (p. 314). Thus the conquest of Hindustan by Muslim invaders had nothing to do with the general degradation of women which, Mill argued, did not alter "the texture of society" (p. 318). Further Mill was not concerned with taking up specific social practices in demonstrating the degradation of women. He merely makes a passing mention of sati in the notes while discussing the indissolubility of the marriage tie that bound wives to their husbands even in death (p. 315).

The degeneration of Hindu civilization and the abject position of Hindu women, requiring the 'protection' and 'intervention' of the colonial state, were two aspects of colonial politics. The third aspect was the 'effeminacy' of the Hindu men who were unfit to rule themselves.[17] On all three counts British rule in India could be justified on grounds of moral superiority.

Throughout the first half of the nineteenth century, and even before, writers like Mill, Orme, Dubois, Macaulay and Bentinck were labouring to certify the 'natives' as a frail, cowardly, and soft bodied little people.[18] Reaction to the representation of Hindus as effete, and their womenfolk requiring protection from the barbarity of their customs was bound to come and it began to crystallize immediately after the banning of sati. There were three major elements that coalesced and triggered off the beginnings of cultural nationalism in the 1830s: one was the attack of the Utilitarians and Anglicists on Hindu civilization; the second was the perceived threat of the Christian missionaries as exemplified in the person of Duff whose ambition was to convert the whole of Calcutta, and the third was the abolition of sati, which was perceived as an intrusion into the Hindu family, the most sacred sphere of Hindu society. Compounding the sense of an attack was the threat from 'within' in the form of Derozio and the group called Young Bengal whose 'outrageous' behaviour included scoffing at the Gods.[19]

The explicit reaction to the attacks on Hindu civilization by the proto-nationalists in the 1840s was preceded by a growing historical consciousness of the past. As an important aspect of the ideological encounter between the west and Hinduism was contained in the writing of history, it is necessary to briefly review the early indigenous historical works and trace the subsequent shift as the century progresses.

For instance, the very first textbook published at Serampore press in 1801 was *Raja Pratapaditya Charita,* a historical sketch of the Raja of Jessore by Ramram Basu.[20] This was followed by*Rajaboli,* a story of kings, by Mritunjay Vidyalankar. Essentially anecdotal, it however included tales of heroes, Hindu, Muslim, and British, from the battles of Kurukshetra down to Plassey. It is significant that at this early stage heroism was not an attribute of nationalism in particular, that the Marathas are cast as "alien plunderers," and that valour was not associated with particular communities in India. Further, it should be noted that historical knowledge about ancient India was still not available. Vidyalankar says nothing of Ashoka, the Guptas or Buddhist India; the rediscoveries by nineteenth century scholarship which would establish the contours of the political history of ancient India were still to come.[21] *Rajaboli* was thus a reflection of the eighteenth century consciousness (often transmitted through the oral tradition) of the

Bengali pandits *before* the birth of cultural nationalism.

It was at this embryonic stage in the writing of history that Mill published his *History of British India* which influenced the direction historical consciousness would take. The Indian intelligentsia reacted violently to his grim picture of Hindu civilization and marshalled arguments against each of his major criticisms. In a sense therefore Mill defined the parameters of the nineteenth century discourse on history.

A small beginning, was made by Gobind Chandra Sen between October 1840 and May 1841 to rebut Mill and resuscitate the image of Hindu civilization. His account reflected in a rudimentary form some of the stereotypes now associated with Rajputs as "freedom lovers" and Muslims as "marauders."[22] Gobind Chandra Sen wrote mainly on medieval India but the proto-nationalist Peary Chand Mitra focussed squarely on pre-Muslim India which he characterized as the "state of Hindustan under the Hindus" and as the "scene of glorious exploits and actions."[23] Throughout Peary Chand's account it is clear that he is addressing, and contesting, the unseen presence of Mill. There had been, he asserted, no despotism under Hindu rulers. Further while the Hindus were as valiant as anybody else, they "did not encroach upon the dominions of any foreign power." This covert snipe against the British was accompanied by a reminder to his fellow countrymen that their ancestors had resisted the invasions of those who "allured by the wealth and grandeur of the country came to bring it to subjection." He argued that though the ignorant were branding the Indians as "barbarians" and men who were "*naturally inferior* to the Europeans" the former achievements of the Hindus in the field of intellectual glory and moral eminence remained as "splendid beacons."[24]

Apart from the general structure of Hindu civilization, the condition of women in the past was a key aspect of historical writing in the 1840s. It was not uncommon for Mill to be echoed by other writers particularly by those who have been termed the 'nativist-evangelists'. One such example was the account of women in the past provided by M.C. Deb, a Christian convert and a member of the Young Bengal group. Deb combined elements of Mill with what was then a widely circulating perception about the Muslim interregnum as the dark ages especially in its effects upon women. According to Deb men in India looked upon women as household slaves and treated them with a superciliousness which even the "Sultan of Turkestan does not show towards his meanest serf."[25] The primary responsibility for the "sad and deplorable" conditions was attributed to the ravages of Muslim rule.

In contrast to M.C. Deb, Peary Chand Mitra, also a member of the Young Bengal group, provided in 1842, a well argued response to the Mill approach on the position of women in Hindu civilization. Using the Orientalists and anticipating later nationalist historians, Mitra takes up different aspects of women's status, focussing on education and female seclusion as key contemporary issues. Admitting that the status of women in contemporary Bengal was bad, he sought to provide evidence for his argument that in the past women had access to Sanskrit learning and had produced many notable philosophers and debators. He quotes from the *MahanirbanTantra* which states that the daughter should be "nursed and educated with care" and married to a learned man, and uses Kalidasa's plays, Tamil literature, and accounts of well known philosophical debates to provide a series of examples of women like Leelavati and Avaiyar who were learned.[27] The example of Avaiyar, a Tamil Bhakti poetess, is particularly striking as it indicates a familiarity with a 'great Sanskritic tradition' to which the Orientalists had contributed substantially and which was an important dimension in the ultimate crystallization of a 'national' feminine identity based on 'high' culture.

The reaction to Mill, Grant, Duff and their kind of writing on Hindu women had been firmly set in motion by Peary Chand Mitra and it was to be developed and refined in the subsequent decades alongside the development of a nationalist ideology. The fact that this reaction to the women's question was launched by someone like Peary Chand is particularly notable as the Young Bengal group, to which he had belonged, had begun in the late 1820s and early 1830s with a severe onslaught on Hinduism. Now in the 1840s the women's question in particular seems to have touched a raw nerve and the Hindu intelligentsia was less willing to stand by and passively watch the attacks on its culture and the devaluation of its womanhood.

II

If the indigenous writing of the 1840s, broadly in the area of culture, represents elements of proto-nationalism, the writing of the period after the 1860s is directly imbued with nationalist fervour. The nationalist consciousness which permeated the writing of historical and semi-historical literature was greatly facilitated by an extension of British Orientalism through the work of Friedrich Max Muller (1823-1900) who more than any other of the Orientalists focussed upon the achievements of the 'Aryans' as contained in their ancient text of the Vedas. Under Max Muller the word 'Aryan' acquired such a range of normative connotations that it has left a permanent impress upon the collective consciousness of the upper strata of Indian society.

A product of the German Romantic movement (which departed from the eighteenth century Enlightenment and rationalism) and a sympathetic witness to the 1848 Paris revolt in his student days, Max Muller was initially part of the liberal tendency within Germany. However like other liberals in Germany he grew politically conservative about German nationalism and became a staunch admirer of Bismarck.[28] His initial interest in Sanskrit came as much from a romantic childhood interest in India[29] as from a pragmatic decision that he would have better career prospects in this area than in the already heavily saturated field of classical European studies.

The core of Max Muller's work which he himself valued most was his collation and publication of the full text of the Vedas.[30] According to him it was the only "natural basis of Indian history," which could throw light over the whole historical development of the Indian mind and therefore the task of fixing its age was of paramount significance.[31] Like the earlier Orientalists, Max Muller saw the recovery of the Vedas as bringing to Hindus the truths of their ancient tradition. He believed that the Veda is "the root of their religion, and to show what that root is, I feel sure, the only way of uprooting all that has sprung from it during the last 3,000 years."[32] Since the Veda was also the root of all religion, law, and philosophy, it was to trace the origin of these that one needed to reconstruct the Veda.

> So great an influence has the Vedic age . . . exercised upon all succeeding periods of Indian history, so deeply have the religious and moral ideas of that primitive era taken root in the mind of the Indian nation, so minutely has almost every private and public act of Indian life been regulated by old traditionary precepts that it is impossible to find the

> right point of view for judging of Indian religion, morals, and literature without a knowledge of the literary remains of the Vedic age.[33]

Regarding the Veda as the 'Bible' of the Aryans resulted in a great deal of importance being attributed to the term Aryan; although it was already well-known and often used, it gained tremendous currency following Max Muller's work. Starting from the researches on comparative philology Max Muller extended the meaning of the term Aryan to apply it to the unknown people who "spoke the assumed Indo-European original language common to all members of this language group." Sanskrit was the closest language to this unknown language group.[34] Later, the emphasis shifted from language to race and the 'unknown' Aryans were then described as the "true ancestors of our race."[35] For his European audience Max Muller attempted to establish the relationship between the Aryans in India who had, in their primitive glory, composed the Veda and the Aryans who now inhabited Europe; making a distinction between two major 'races': the Aryan (or the Indo-European) and the Semitic, he went on to imply that the Aryans were racially superior to the Turanian and Semitic races:

> The [Aryans] have been the prominent actors in the great drama of history, and have carried to their fullest growth all the elements of active life with which our nature is endowed. They have perfected society and morals .... In continual struggle with each other and with Semitic and Turanian races these Aryan nations have become the rulers of history and it seems to be their mission to link all parts of the world together by the chains of civilization and religion.[36]

The task of convincing the rulers of a nation that they were of the same race as their subjects was by no means easy, so Max Muller had to reiterate the theme of common origins in his writings: "Though the historian may shake his head, *though the physiologist may doubt* all must yield before the facts furnished by language"[37] (emphasis added). To bolster his argument that Europeans and Indians were of the same stock it was necessary to highlight the great achievements of ancient Aryans in India; knowledge of "universal history" according to Max Muller required that:

> . . . we should not leave out of sight our nearest intellectual relatives, the Aryas of India, the framers of the most wonderful language, the fellow workers in the constitution of the most wonderful concepts, the fathers of the most natural religions, the makers of the most transparent

> mythologies, the inventors of the most subtle philosophy and the givers of the most elaborate laws.[38]

Much of Max Muller's writing was directed at young I.C.S. trainees in England with the prospect of a career in post-Mutiny India, who were to be enthused with a sense of mission and injected with a feeling of excitement and adventure. Even if the conquests of soldiers were no longer possible there were other literary and historical conquests that were available for the asking such as retrieving the flagging Orientalist movement.

Though there are some references to women it is significant that at no point in his writings does Muller dwell at any length upon them. In fact there appears to be an implicit assumption that the Aryan patriarchal system did not itself pay too much attention to women and certainly did not regard them as equal. Like all writers on the Vedas he too narrated the Maitreyi-Yajnavalkya episode but he concluded the passage with the remark that although women participated in the ritual they were not initiated, and still less were they admitted to the highest knowledge of the *atman or brahman.* Cases like Maitreyi, according to him, were the exception not the rule.[39] He used Strabo's quotations on women in India in support of his views:

> Indians did not communicate their metaphysical doctrines to women thinking that if their wives understood these doctrines and learned to be indifferent to pleasure and pain, and to consider life and death as the same they would no longer continue to be the slaves of others; or if they failed to understand them they would be talkative and communicate their knowledge to those who had no right to do it.[40]

Max Muller goes on to say that this statement by the Greek writer was fully borne out by the later Sanskrit literature; he quotes from the *Srauta* and *Grihya Sutras* where it is stated that women were not allowed to learn the sacred songs of the Vedas. There is nothing in Max Muller's writing to suggest that he considered women to be spiritual, or learned, in the Vedic period. He himself attached little significance to the inferior position held by women.[41] Muller's contribution to nineteenth century historiography was thus clearly not in relation to the women's question; however, everything else that he wrote about was taken up with enthusiasm as I shall show presently. The different aspects of his work on the Vedas, Sanskrit literature more generally, and especially philosophy, had one connecting thread: all these were the achievements of the glorious Aryans. Max Muller vastly popularized a racist Aryan version of the Orientalist Hindu golden age and it was this newly formulated golden age that became so influential in later Indian thought.

Other British/European writers used the newly emerging body of knowledge on the Aryans in distinctive and less simplistic ways and these also had a bearing on the construction of the Aryan myth. One such example is W.W. Hunter's *The Annals of Rural Bengal* which argues that with the Aryan conquest of India there was a rigid division between the conquering Aryans and the aboriginal people which later resulted in the emergence of mixed castes.[42] Here we see a new element which was missing in the work of Max Muller who not only had concentrated exclusively on the Aryans but had treated Hindus, Brahmins, Aryans and Indians as synonymous, almost giving the impression that no other category had ever existed. Hunter's use of Aryan to show internal division, stratification and hierarchy is thus significant. So too is his notion of the 'vigorous' Aryan conquerors as getting degenerate through mixed breeding and ending up as effete Bengali Brahmins.

The use of the term Aryan by European scholars was varied but in all cases Aryan is clearly associated with vigour, with race and with a conquering group who came to India from elsewhere, and in their pure form possessed nothing but positive attributes. Directly or indirectly some of these writers, who used the term Aryan (but did not focus in particular on women) influenced the more specific European writing on Hindu women. Significantly, some of this writing was by women themselves.

An early example of such a work was published in 1856 by Mrs Speier who was stationed at Calcutta.[43] All we know about her is that she had access to the publications of the *Asiatic Researches*, may have attended the meetings of the Asiatic Society, and appears to have known the well known scholar H.H. Wilson whom she acknowledges in her preface.

Speier was writing what appears to be one of the many historical works by Europeans in the nineteenth century. Her book titled *Life in Ancient India* fully accepts Max Muller and the common Indo-Aryan origin theory. But she warns against associating all Indians with Rammohun Roy or Dwarkanath Tagore who were as unlike typical Hindus as Robert Burns was the British ploughman.[43] It is in her portrayal of ancient Indian womanhood that Speier is unabashedly romantic:

> A thousand years B.C. Hindu women appear to have been as free as Trojan dames or the daughters of Judaea. Hymns in the Rig Veda mention them with respect and affection . . . . Even in the succeeding phase when Brahmans contemplated the soul beneath the Himavat women attended their discourses . . . . We find in one of the Upanishads a king holding a solemn sacrifice and inviting his chief guests to state their opinions on theology. Amongst these guests a learned female named Garga is conspicuous. A more pleasing instance of women's interests in holy themes is afforded by a conversation between Yajnavalkya and Maitreyi (pp. 166-67).

Speier then goes on to transform Colebrooke's staid account of Maitreyi and Yajnavalkya (upon which her own account is admittedly based) into a more imaginative and powerful rendering in which Maitreyi *chooses* 'immortality' in place of 'mere' riches, and learns to "contemplate the soul alone since everything is soul," the aim being to merge all thought and feeling into the universal soul. It is in Speier's work that one notices Vedic women being epitomized by Gargi and Maitreyi; subsequently they were the stock favourites of the nationalist writers arguing about the 'high' status of women in ancient India.

Speier proceeds to recount the evidence of later brahminical texts, such as Manu's code, to depict the changed status of women which she characterizes as "Obedience to her husband is the beginning, and the middle, and the end of female duty," and concludes that women's rights "were wholly ignored by the Brahmanical code." Because "daughters and wives are often too happy to require rights," she argues that we tend to forget that according to the code they are without rights and get taken in by other representations of 'domestic' bliss (pp. 166-70). Though Speier is aware of the contradictory statements in the texts about women and implicitly suggests a decline in their status from the freedom and learning they enjoyed in very early times, she nevertheless goes on to paint the most romantic and glorified picture of the heroines of literature, all focussing on the beautiful 'conjugal' love among the ancient Aryans as had existed between Nala and Damyanti and Savitri and Satyavan (pp. 171-72). Speier seems to be fascinated by these models of womanhood and by the power of their love, especially the travails of couples like Nala and Damayanti who must undergo untold misery before their love is vindicated. While the Nala-Damayanti narration is titled "Wedded Love", the Savitri Satyavan story is called "Woman's Love" (pp. 171, 181). Describing Yama's attempts at taking away the dead Satyavan which are foiled by Savitri, Speier recounts what Savitri says to the God of death:

Where he goes, my path shall be,
I will follow where thou leadest,
Listen once again to me. . . .

Speier ends the story with "and at length love conquers all" (p. 183).

The fascination, even the mystique, of Hindu womanhood is much more explicit in Speier's reference to sati. Asserting that brahminical law makes woman the property of man whose fate is "death upon the funeral pyre when he dies," Speier goes on to say that nature (female nature) had not entirely succumbed to law and the "free woman's character of the Sanskrit epics has not been universally suppressed in India" (p. 454). She then cites extensively from Sleeman's account of a sati who,when prevented from mounting the pyre, refused to eat till she was permitted to fulfil her wishes and also gives the example of Ahalya Bai's daughter who argued with her mother when she tried to prevent the daughter from mounting the pyre (p. 455). Clearly, emotional accounts such as Sleeman's had left a deep impress on many European women. By this time sati had been banned for over a generation and as an issue of the past it was no longer horrifying, but rather awe inspiring, and was seen as the ultimate power that the Hindu woman had in an otherwise powerless situation.

The glorification of Hindu womanhood in the ancient past is even more noticeable in Clarisse Bader's monograph on women in ancient India. Published in 1867 when Bader was a young girl of twenty-two, it was directly inspired by Max Muller's romanticization of the past. Bader takes for granted the original connection between the Aryans be they in India or in Europe and also the moral and intellectual superiority of the Aryans in relation to the defeated Dasyus. Bader makes constant comparisons between the West and the East with the exhortation that the West should learn from the East; she bemoans the rapidly changing western society with its superficiality and materialism. Reacting to industrialized Europe she pleaded passionately, "Has not the time arrived to refresh ourselves from more life giving and generous sources? And only India has the honour of affording such sources."[44] Bader's intention in her monograph was, very simply, to seek the "part played by woman in the Hindu pantheon from the time of Aryan symbolism to the materialistic age of Krishna and his worshippers." Her enthusiasm in pursuing her mission is evident from the way she ends her preface: "May the Gangetic muse occupy her proper position on the domestic hearth, whose austere joys she has so worthily sung" (p. x).

Bader notes with approval the fact that women were not excluded from 'labouring' for the sacrifice as it was women who collected the *kusa* grass for the sacred enclosure, and the plant from which *soma* juice was extracted; they had the right of offering sacrifices in their own names as well as in composing hymns. The example of Vispala who participated in battles is cited to show that women had been the recipients of the beneficence of the gods (pp. 8-9). The account that Bader really labours over is the Maitreyi-Yajnavalkya episode in which three of her major concerns converge, namely Aryan genius, spiritualism, and women. While introducing the episode Bader says:

> In a dialogue in which the Aryan genius was displayed in all the grandeur of its spiritual tendencies and in which the great question of the immortality of the soul was debated one of the interlocutors was a woman; and it is *she* who began the solemn conversation (pp. 10-12).

Bader then proceeds to narrate the episode in the greatest detail to establish the most complete expression of belief in the universal spirit and simultaneously of the depth of the knowledge that a woman was judged capable of "receiving, and still more, of understanding" (p. 12). But alas, says Bader, the situation changed. Manu did not recognize the right of a woman to lift up her soul to God. He debased her instead by the exclusive adoration of a "creature similar to herself;" women's zeal was now to be demonstrated in the service of the husband instead of a spiritual father; in the care of the home instead of the "maintenance of the sacred fire" (pp. 17-18). The real fall for women came with the growth of the Krishna cult which was gross and materialist. The decadence continued to increase until the day came when India "debilitated and corrupted by the cult yielded to the enervating influence of Islam and showed to what depth of physical and moral degradation the most gifted of people could fall, once it had exchanged the yoke of duty to that of passion" (p. 330). In such a society the position of women naturally plunged to the depths.

Bader, like Speier, saw sati as awe-inspiring. In her view, it was an expression of woman's ability to go beyond the "bounds of requirement." As she put it, "The law commanded her to identify her life with her husband's; but she went 'further' and identified her death with his" (p. 332). For her, "Ardent piety, spiritual and ascetic tenderness, complete abnegation of herself, unlimited devotion to her family, a boundless need of love, formed the character of such women" (p. 333). And that sums up the power of 'Hindu-Aryan' womanhood as it was perceived by the Orientalist inspired women of the west.

The contribution of the second round of the Orientalists and their feminine counterparts may be summed up as the transformation of the Hindu golden age into an Aryan golden age wherein the men were free, brave, vigorous, fearless, themselves civilized and civilizing others, noble, and deeply spiritual; and the women were learned, free, and highly cultured; conjointly they offer sacrifices to the gods, listening 'sweetly' to discourses, and preferring spiritual upliftment to the pursuit of 'mere' riches. Additionally they represented the best examples of conjugal love, offering the supreme sacrifice of their lives as a demonstration of their feeling for their partners in the brief journey of life. This was to be an enduring legacy.

The researches and writings of European scholars in the second half of the nineteenth century idealizing and giving prominence to the notion of the Aryan, were a tremendous boost to the attempts by indigeneous writers to raise the morale of all Indians. The researches on philology popularized by Max Muller had highlighted the common origin of the Europeans and Indians and the theory of shared Aryan origins came to be isolated as the most significant aspect of Sanskrit studies as far as the cultural nationalists were concerned. As used by the indigeneous intelligentsia the Aryan origin theory was however, a double edged weapon. On the one hand, it gave the subjugated people a sense of self-esteem, and a means by which all Indians of the upper strata could, in opposition to their colonial rulers, gain a sense of 'national' identity; on the other, it meant that the subject people could at the same time identify with the rulers as people belonging to the same stock and therefore no different from themselves. Comparative philology thus had a political utility and provided a specific character, and a scholarly basis to modern Indian cultural nationalism.[45]

The Aryan was an important element in the nationalist construction of a sense of identity for its association with vigour, conquest, and expansion; in other words, for its connotations of political and cultural achievement. These aspects are to be seen in relation to the negative qualities of an effete, unmanly, slothful and slack people as imputed by one section of European writers on India. This characterization was in a general sense applicable to all Hindus but it had a particular association with Bengalis. Many Bengalis themselves believed this to be true since they were perceived as failing to have shown sufficient resistance to Muslim power. Since the loss of independence was associated with effeteness, regeneration required the forging of a new identity. To counteract the weakness of the Bengali or the Hindu the nationalists projected heroes from an earlier era but also constructed an alternative Hindu male. Thus a trans-regional unified Hindu identity was forged using elements from history and folklore to valorize heroic action. As conceived by the nationalists, jointly they were the inheritors of a glorious Hindu-Aryan heritage, and with renewed vigour they would succeed in asserting a new Hindu identity.[46]

The foregrounding of Aryan elements in the formation of an alternative identity was accompanied by the introduction of specifically martial qualities that were associated with particular regions and groups of people such as the Marathas, Rajputs and Sikhs. Such groups had been categorized by the British as martial races for purposes of recruitment in the army. The nationalists adapted the notion of martial races to their own ends, endowing them with the heroic character of resistance to foreign rule (primarily Muslim). The process was considerably helped by the publication, around the mid-nineteenth century, of the detailed works of British writers: Grant Duff on the Marathas, Tod on the Rajputs, and Cunningham on the Sikhs.[47] These works, although widely used by Indians later on in the century, hardly excited great enthusiasm, at least initially, among the British for whom they were meant.

But in the last quarter of the nineteenth century there was a spate of more popular historical writing where the 'heroic' communities received enthusiastic coverage. While Ranade popularized the heroism of Shivaji and the Marathas,[48] works like *Rajasthaner Iti-*

has[49] highlighted the chivalry, honour and heroism of Rajputs. Similarly *Sikh Yudher Itihasa*[50] circulated awareness of the great battles fought by the Sikhs against the British. A most popular work was *Arya-Kirtti* (The Fame of the Aryans) by Rajani Kanta Gupta which ran into fifteen editions and had sketches of the great historical figures of 'Hindu' India, the Rajputs, Marathas and Sikhs, and was intended to produce national consciousness, self respect and a feeling of pride in one's country. The same author wrote a seven hundred page book in four parts on the Mutiny called *Sipahi Yudher Itihasa* (1876) which highlighted characters like the Rani of Jhansi, Kunwar Singh, and Nana Sahib, for their heroic role in the Mutiny.[51] This process of rewriting history at a popular level provided material for novels, stories, poems and plays and contributed tremendously to the rise of a militant cultural nationalism.[52]

The roots of the martial spirit valorized by the nationalist writers could be traced back to the traditional Kshatriya values of the ancient social order as in R.C Dutt's writing.His work is important as he contributed the first major historical account of ancient Indian civilization. At Bankim's instance[53] he also wrote novels, four of which dealt with historical themes set in the medieval period, idealized a 'Hindu' past and regretted its loss.[54] They enabled Dutt to inspire patriotism as he effectively used the medium of Rajput and Maratha heroes to construct his images of patriotism. Apart from the symbolism of a heroic, unselfish, and relentless warrior, the Rajput hero in particular was cast as a hero who had never accepted — even in the face of the severest hardship including certain death — the overlordship of 'alien' rulers.

The Rajput warrior was linked to ancient Kshatriya warriors such as the Pandavas and other heroes whose valour had been preserved in the "imperishable epics."[55] The Kshatriya warrior himself was then linked to the Aryans who were the original primeval conquerors in history and whatever was good among the later Aryans, after their original vigour had declined, was associated with the Kshatriyas.[56] In part this may be explained by the belief, by now fairly strong, that it was the 'priesthood' that was responsible for the moral and material degeneration of Hindu society. Further the ideology of martial races[57] enabled a covert identification with the aggressor just as the common Aryan origin theory had done. Authentic Indianness in the regenerated Hindu thus lay in Kshatriyahood which combined in itself martial, Hindu and Aryan elements of the past. As R.C. Dutt viewed it Kshatriyahood also combined the vigour of heroic conquerors and the truly spiritual speculation and knowledge of the Upanishadic seers and philosophers.

In the wider context of cultural nationalism Bankim too was creatively involved in forging a new national identity for both men and women which highlighted the newly regenerated Hindu-Aryan male as one who combined in himself the militancy of the martial groups and the spirituality of the *sanyasi* (renouncer). In Bankim's view India was in a subject position because Indians were weak *(balhin)* and effeminate *(strisvabhav)*.[58] He bemoaned that liberty was unknown to any Indian people except the Rajputs. According to Bankim the concept of *svadhinta* (freedom) was unknown in ancient or in medieval literature.[59] The only people who had a consciousness of their nationhood were the ancient Aryan invaders of India but in course of time even they became divided into small and separate groups and lost the sense of nationhood.[60] To remedy the situation, Bankim felt it was necessary to develop a strong militant race. The prerequisite for attaining this objective was the restoration of national unity and pride through a reinterpretation of the past.[61]

It was this analysis that motivated Bankim into writing his most historically significant piece of work, the *Krishnacharita* where he constructed a Krishna for the future as a historical figure symbolizing the possibility of energetic historical action. This he achieved by cleansing the Krishna legend of its erotic dimension, and by 'recovering' the earlier rationalist figure, the Krishna who was a man of action and of serious philosophic thought.[62] Bankim's newly constructed nationalist identity, for which Krishna was the ideal model, also had other elements not contained explicitly at least in the recovery of the 'warrior'. A major element was a deep consciousness about a 'Hindu' past symbolized by the great works of art, literature and philosophy.[63]

The aggressiveness of the new cultural nationalism marked a sharp break from the universalism of the earlier phase associated with Rammohun Roy and a section of the Brahmo Samaj. The new identity of aggressive cultural nationalism valorized select features of a Hindu past; everything related to Aryan and Kshatriya values embodying vigour and militancy were central to this new identity; so was genuine spiritualism of the world-affirming kind such as that associated with the Vedas or even with Bankim's Krishna in the *Krishnacharita* or the sanyasis in *Anandmath*. But this process of selection also meant a process of exclusion in the formation of the new national identity. First, it was clearly a new 'Hindu' identity which excluded all 'foreigners' which for Bankim meant Muslims. Further, in his view, the Hindu identity also came to be explicitly associated with a specifically Aryan identity. In his analysis there was also a connection between the un-Aryan and the Muslim. In Bengal the awareness and pride in an Aryan identity had led to a simple dichotomization of the population into high castes comprising Aryan, and labouring groups comprising un-Aryan. Bankim extended this dichotomization by associating Aryan purity with the high castes, especially the Bengali Brahmin, and non-Aryan impurity with the low castes, especially those who had converted enmasse to Islam. Thus Bankim's regenerated Hindu 'national' identity excluded not only the Muslims but also the lower castes as they were of non-Aryan and 'impure' extraction. This process of exclusion and inclusion was more explicit in Bankim's case but it is important to bear in mind that it was fairly representative of the nineteenth century cultural nationalists.

What was expected of women in the context of aggressive cultural nationalism and the valorization of Kshatriya values in the new national identity for men? Men must be heroic in a country that has been subjugated but what were women to do in such a situation? What kind of heroism or what kind of role was required of them? From the disparate body of writing a sub-stratum may be extracted to throw some light on the emerging ideology of womanhood.

A point to note about the problems in the formation of a 'national' identity of women was the whole question of the continuing impetus to a reform of their status, the need for a protection of their minimum rights and a raising of their status through education. Alternative identity formation in the case of women had no single or coherent model like regenerating the Hindu male from the ignominy of effeminacy. The kind of woman required for the present and the future was much more difficult to construct, given the need for a different kind of regeneration that was necessary in her case. In such a situation it was considerably easier to construct models of womanhood in the past. The most significant historical work was R.C.Dutt's *History of Civilisation in Ancient India* where he provided a comprehensive rebuttal of James Mill's denigration of Hindu civilization and of the low position of Hindu women within it. In Dutt's work the fully worked out version of the myth of the Vedic woman as the highest symbol of Hindu womanhood, indicated by writers like Peary Chand Mitra, Speier, and Clarisse Bader, was finalized. His sketch of the Vedic woman, is penned with a keen eye to contemporary debates on women's status.[64]

Dutt takes up every debated area of the contemporary status of women and counterposes it with evidence drawn from the Vedas. women were educated, chose their partners and even contracted second marriages which according to Dutt was a 'national' custom. Dutt's work relies on the careful researches of Sanskrit scholars from the days of Jones and Colebrooke and also recounts the Gargi and Maitreyi instances in great detail to establish the 'high' status of women in the Aryan golden age.[65] He concludes:

> Do not such passages as these indicate that women were honoured in ancient India, more perhaps than among any other ancient nation in the face of the globe? Considered the intellectual companions of their husbands, as their affectionate helpers in the journey of life, and as inseparable partners in their religious duties, Hindu wives received the honour and respect due to their position. . . .[66]

Dutt also outlined the role of women in the more recent medieval past. The Vedic 'helpmate' in the sacrifice which was so important to the early nationalist historians, was easily extendable to other helpmate roles for women. The brave warriors who would not give in to the might of alien rule were supported by the female Kshatriya values of courage and bravery which made no demands on their menfolk; indeed these values enabled the men to resist to the very end. This they did in a variety of ways including the ultimate example of the major feminine counterpart of Kshatriya value — that of choosing death rather than ravishment.[67] In his novel *Pratap Singh,* all the women characters are of course brave but, pre-eminent among the exemplars of 'Kshatriyani' virtues are women like the wise Devi of the cave, a strong mother figure who acts as an oracle and inspiration to martial valour; the Amazonian figure as the biological progenitor of a heroic race; and the heroic Rajput mother who must perforce continue to live for the sake of her son. Dutt recounts an episode wherein a Rajput ruler dies while defending his fort against the foreign invader. Before the widow of the chieftain could mount the pyre a neighbouring chieftain attempted to usurp the throne of the minor son. The queen then fought tooth and nail to save the ancestral kingdom for her son. She met her end when ten men overwhelmed her but her indomitable courage and fierce resistance inspired the young son with a burning passion to avenge his parents' death.[68]

There are other instances in the narrative of 'Kshatriyani' virtues such as the resolve to mount the pyre to allow the men to go and fight without the fear of their womenfolk being ravished.[69] The high point in the narrative comes when the kingdom is surrounded by alien armies. The Rani calls all the womenfolk together and addresses them, "Friends, we shall perform the sati today; what happier fate can destiny hold for Rajput women? Let our enemies behold the sight. Our men are heroes, our women are chaste." The account concludes with a rhapsodic description of the event.[70] Rajput women, no less than their menfolk, were thus seen as providing models of widsom, indomitable courage and undying resistance.

Women of the past were valorized in two separate ways; for their spiritual potential and their role as *sahadharminis* (partners in religious duties) in ancient times, and as heroic resisters to alien rulers who cheerfully chose death rather than dishonour. From these elements out of history and folklore, constituting images of glorious women of the golden past, was fashioned a new identity for women to suit the present and the future. How much and what aspects of tradition went into the construction of a new feminine identity varied from one writer to another but on many essentials there was considerable similarity; indeed the convergence on the fundamental characteristics of Hindu womanhood cut across the liberal-revivalist divide.

The most coherent early construction of a 'national' identity for women was by Bankim. The inherent tension between the womanhood of the past and the womanhood of the present was resolved in Bankim's literary portrayal of women especially in his last novels.[71] Essentially conservative on contemporary issues relating to women his literary characters are however free to pursue non-conventional roles. He makes contemptuous jibes at the new type of worthless woman emerging in Bengal whose utter laziness was bound to have disastrous consequences on her own health and upon her children. Such a woman, who contributed to no one's happiness but her own, was little better than an animal and her birth was in vain.[72] Not surprisingly, one of his female characters argues that people who recommend widow remarriage, education for women and oppose child marriage, will not understand the "true significance of the devotion to one's husband."[73] In all his novels the wife never transgresses the notion of true wifehood. But in his last novels true wifehood extends to energizing the husband for the goal of regenerating the motherland. Actual questions of women's status including the problem of widowhood and the need for reform remained outside the ambit of Bankim's concerns.

In *Anandmath* Bankim creates, according to Bagchi, a parable of nationalist confrontation in the novel. The role of women in such a situation could not thus remain what it was, or could be, in a period of stability as the golden past had been. Thus the traditional roles of women would no longer do in a crisis of the kind that the nation had never faced in the past. Externally and internally the threatened moral and social order desperately required a new kind of woman for which the old sahadharmini model was too passive and could only apply once order had been re-established. A ravaged nation required heroic action from both men and women; if anything it was women who could actually release the potential for such action. It was therefore incumbent upon them to energize men who might easily fall into temptation otherwise. Only women, by controlling or sublimating their sexuality, could release both men and women for the selfless sacrifices required for the liberation of the ravaged motherland. Bankim thus provided a powerful image of womanhood, one that dynamized the image of a sahadharmini of the past into a force for the present and the future. In this aspect the transformed woman "defied the normal canons of femininity in order to join the resistance against the crisis in the order."[74]

Shanti in *Anandmath* is the prototype of the womanhood required by a nation in crisis. Only such a crisis justified the delinking of wifehood from the 'enclosed space' of domesticity.[75] Shanti performs her wife's role in the war of liberation by donning the guise of a male *sanyasi* (religious mendicant) and fighting by the side of her husband. The Vedic woman who performed sacrifices to the gods by the side of her husband as an equal partner in the offering of oblations (till then envisaged as the highest role for women by the early cultural nationalists) is here dynamized into a figure who fights shoulder to shoulder with her husband in liberating the Motherland from its shackles. Shanti has thus transcended both her sexuality and her domesticity and made it possible for her husband to do the same. She would provide a model of womanhood, which came closest to a 'national' feminine identity during the late nineteenth and twentieth centuries till India became independent.

The Aryan theme was developed somewhat differently by Dayananda. As a practical reformer he was less concerned with identity formation than the nationalist historian or the litterateur. Nevertheless, Dayananda too had a vision of the past — however, this past was to be actually recreated rather then merely remembered, and that accounts for the rather direct and fundamental way in which the Vedas became the foundation of his ideology. The Vedas in turn account for the centrality of the Aryan theme in Dayananda's writing and provide it with its most long term expression in the institution of the Arya Samaj. As the influence of the Arya Samaj spread throughout north India the concept of an Aryan golden age and the philosophy and social institutions of the Aryans as embodied in the *Rig Veda* became part of the general consciousness of the region. Historical awareness of the past was now fully permeated with an 'Aryan' consciousness accompanied by its attendant baggage of associations such as vitality, spirituality and high mindedness.

A core feature of Dayananda's reformed Hinduism was his insistence on the superiority of the Vedic religion over all others and this in turn made for irreconcilable differences between his thought and that of the Brahmo reformers in Bengal.[76] But there is reason to believe that it was in Calcutta that he was first exposed to the women's question which ultimately became part of his basic vision of a reformed society. He found Vidyasagar in particular a man after his own heart as someone who was steeped in tradition. Dayananda also met historians and other members of the intelligentsia who made him aware of the world of historical scholarship. Works such as Datta's *Dharma Niti,* which had attempted to answer certain questions related to the nature and function of the state, made Dayananda sensitive to the problem of statecraft in any comprehensive philosophy.[77] Subsequently in the *Satyarth Prakash* (published in 1875) he proposed an overall theory of the state, and expressed his understanding of society, history, and religion.

Dayananda, like Rammohun Roy earlier, also reinterpreted the past and rewrote history. In the reinterpreted version of the Vedic religion, on which Dayananda's Arya Samaj was based, monotheism replaced polytheism, the pantheon of gods becoming merely attributes of one universal God. Idolatory, caste, child marriage, brahminical claims of superiority and the vast bulk of popular Hindu religious practices — all disappeared along with polytheism, leaving only a rationalist monotheism. Dayananda was looking for an overall historical explanation both of contemporary conditions and of their relationship with the Golden Age of the Aryas in the past. The *Satyarth Prakash* thus starts out with a "panegyric of that Golden Age in the Aryavarta, the ancient land which overflowed with milk and honey, where even the poor grew rich. There the first men were born, Sanskrit, mother of all tongues was spoken, and not only did theoretical wisdom flourish but also the practical industrial sciences."[78]

But how was the present degeneracy of Hinduism and the fact of colonial subservience to be explained? What cataclysmic event destroyed the "Golden Age" of Vedic truth? Dayanada found a novel answer — it was the great Mahabharata war. The titanic struggle engulfed the subcontinent, beginning a decline into ignorance from which Hinduism could not escape. War and selfishness on the part of the priestly classes destroyed the vitality of Hindu culture.[79] Since Aryavarta had been ruined by Brahmins and others Dayananda, like Vivekananda later, was struck by the need in Hindu culture for vigour, self assertion and courage. The loss of masculinity and cultural regression of the Hindus was due to the loss of their original Aryan qualities which they had shared with westerners. He expected Hindus to take on European characteristics by reforming Hindu religious life through a return to Vedic faith.[80]

It was Dayananda's emphasis on a reformed Hinduism based on the *Rig Veda,* that led him to use the term "Arya" for regenerated Hinduism. While in Calcutta he had heard a great deal about the stigma attached to the term Hindu and had told his audience then that they should discard "that derogatory name imposed by foreigners" and call themselves Aryans instead.[81] While others had used the term Aryan synonymously with Hindu, with Dayananda it came to mean a purified and reformed Hindu. However, it had by now also become clearly identified with race and this aspect certainly had a bearing in popularizing it as a term; indeed it could gain widespread currency precisely because it carried within itself such a connotation.

Dayananda's references to the women of the past were part of his wider concern for a reformed Hindu society dominated by Aryan institutions. He believed that in the ideal society of the Vedic period women lived an idyllic existence, fully participated in all areas of public life, and it was Muslim influence that taught Hindus to imprison their women inside the house. These ideas were fairly common by the latter half of the nineteenth century and were not unique to Dayananda.[82]

What was central to Dayananda's thinking was his understanding of the role of women in the maintenance of race, and inter-alia, concern about their sexuality. Motherhood for Dayananda was the sole rationale of a woman's existence but what was crucial in his concept of motherhood was its specific role in the procreation and rearing of a special breed of men. For example, the *Satyarth Prakash* lays down a variety of rules and regulations for ideal conception. The birth of the child is also followed by a series of regulations on food, cleanliness, clothing etc. for both mother and child. Dayananda's concern for a healthy and pure stock of Aryas even leads him to advocate the appointment of a wet nurse for the child rather than that the mother should feed it. According to Dayananda the child's body is made up of elements derived from the body of the mother, which accounts for the mother getting weaker after each confinement. Thus he says:

> It is best therefore, for the mother not to suckle her child. Plasters should be applied to the breast that will soon dry up the milk. By following this system the woman becomes strong again in about two months. Till then the husband should have thorough control over his passions and thus preserve the reproductive element. Those that will follow this plan will have children of a superior order, enjoy long life, and continually gain in strength and energy so that their children will be of a high mental calibre, strong, energetic and devout.[83]

What really marks Dayananda's conceptualization of womanhood is the way he deals with the sexuality of women. The general concern for the propagation of race implied that both men and women were equally the objects of his attention. But since the function of the women in particular was merely to procreate healthy progeny, the sexuality of women was of fundamental importance. At one level Dayananda's thinking is related to the way in which the monastic tradition in India had perceived women's sexuality as a threat to the pursuit of salvation.[84] But Dayananda had one foot in the sanyasi ethos and another (the more active foot) in the overall regeneration of Hinduism. While Dayananda had imbibed the traditional hostility of the sanyasi to women he also had a dynamic view of the changed times and shared the nationalist ethos. The traditional suspicion of women's sexuality was thus tempered, and the sexuality of women was transformed into a force which could be constructively channelized to serve in the regeneration of the Aryas. This transformation was unique to Dayananda: of the nineteenth century thinkers he alone was to grapple squarely with the question ; whereas others had worked around the problem restricting themselves to merely resurrecting images of ancient womanhood, Dayananda had a theoretical framework within which he could confront the sexuality of women and successfully fit it into an ideology which was consistent within itself.

So deep seated was the anxiety to control sexuality that it occurs even in the conceptualization of the school system. Both boys and girls in this regenerated Hinduism were entitled to education but-they had to be physically segregated. The structures to ensure this physical segregation were of the most stringent kind. The schools themselves were to be separated by a distance of at least three miles. Further, the preceptors and the employees in the Boys school should all be male, and in the Girls school, female. Dayananda ruled:

> Not even a child of five years of the opposite sex should be allowed to enter the school. As long as they are *Brahmacaris* [in the stage of celibacy] they should abstain from the following eight kinds of sexual excitement in relation to persons of opposite sex: looking upon them with the eye of lust; embracing them; having sexual intercourse with them; intimately conversing with them; playing with them; associating with them; reading or talking of libidinous subjects; and indulging in lascivious thoughts.[85]

Dayananda's division of the traditional *ashrams* or four stages of life was suitably redesigned from the point of view of his overall ideology. There were, according to him, four stages of the human body: a period of adolescence (16-25 years), a period of manhood

(25-40 years), a period of maturity which was about the 40th year when the tissues, organs and secretions of the body reached their highest stage of perfection. Thereafter came the period of loss in which there was excess of secretions when the reproductive element began to be lost in sleep, through perspiration, and so on (p. 43). The best time for marriage was the fortieth or forty-eighth year. But since this was rather too long to wait Dayananda suggested the more flexible period of between 25 - 48 for men and 16 - 24 for women (p.90). Once marriage is decided upon, certain categories of people should be excluded from being considered as suitable partners; this was necessary from the point of view of ensuring healthy progeny. The best form of marriage — the *svayamvara* (self chosen partner) — itself is linked with the maximum probability of ensuring the best reproduction (p. 93).

While Dayananda considered that the partners to a marriage should themselves be responsible for their choice, on no condition were the two to meet alone before marriage "since such a meeting of young people may lead to bad consequences." Some amount of interaction in the presence of tutors, parents and other respectable persons was desirable (p. 105). Then, "as soon as they feel that their love for each other is strong enough to entitle them to marry" a suitable date should be fixed. Dayananda advised that the very best arrangement "should be made with regard to their diet so that their bodies that had weakened through the practice of rigid discipline may soon gain in muscles and strength just as the new moon grows into the full moon" (p. 105). Later, when they are strong enough, on the day which has been decided upon for the "purpose of generating a new life" (i.e. marriage) they should most "cheerfully go through the ceremony of *panigrahana* (clasping of the hands)" (p. 106). The ceremony should be finished by 10 or 12 p.m. and then the couple must retire to fulfil the *summum bonum* of the wife's existence, that is, to forthwith 'generate' a new life. "As far as possible they should never waste their reproductive elements, perfected and preserved by the practice of Brahmacharya because the children born of such a union *are of a very* superior order" (p. 107). If the rules laid down are not followed carefully "the reproductive element is uselessly lost, the lives of the husband and wife are shortened and they are afflicted with diverse diseases" (p. 107). For the continued needs of propagating strong and healthy children the wife and husband should be content with each other for if the wife does not love and please her husband, the husband will be unhappy; being unhappy, he will not be sexually excited and consequently no offspring will be produced. Even if they are, the children so born, are "very wicked and of a low type" (p. 109).

The management of sexuality was the key to the thorny problem of widow remarriage. Throughout the nineteenth century the most problematic category of women were widows, and reformers were attempting to resolve the problem of what to do with the widow especially since a large proportion of upper caste women were widowed, often as a consequence of early marriage. Implicit in the whole debate on widow remarriage was the recognition of women as sexual beings and the relationship of female sexuality with prevailing family and property structures. While others had tackled the problem from a humanitarian standpoint, essentially as a response to the plight of the child widow, Dayananda came to grips with the problem within his broader philosophy of a regenerated Hinduism which required a regenerated race of people. Since motherhood played a vital role, he held that remarriage for both men and women was equally valid if there were no children from the earlier marriage. Dayananda found his solution to the remarriage question and the problem of female sexuality in the institution of the *niyoga* (levirate), associated with the early Aryans.

The practice of niyoga was suggested by Dayananda in the form of a theoretical debate between an objector and Dayananda himself in the *Satyarth Prakash* (pp. 129-40). The main points in the discussion are significant in tracing the development of Dayananda's position on widow marriage. Dayananda first argued that remarriage for the twice born castes was prohibited because there would be family disputes based on property disagreements, and many families would just be blotted out of existence if a widow remarried (p. 129). The objector then pointed out that family lines would die out anyway if either party died before any male issues were born. "Besides," says the objector, bringing up the sexuality question, if remarriage is not allowed "widows and widowers will resort to fornication and adultery, procure abortion, and commit wicked deeds of kindred nature" (p. 130). For these reasons the objector suggested that remarriage was desirable. At this point, Dayananda ruled that the best practice for both men and women was *brahmacharya* (self control), followed by the adoption of a boy. However, he added that for those who could not control their passions the best recourse was niyoga. Dayananda tells the objector that when people are young, "desire for children and sexual enjoyment will drive people to the necessity of forming secret relations if the laws of the state or society disallow lawful gratification." The only proper way of preventing adultery and illicit intimacies is to let those who require it contract niyoga relationships "so that the chances of illicit intercourse may be greatly minimised, good children can be born, the human race improved, and the practice of foeticide put a stop to" (p. 133). Dayananda interpreted a variety of texts to allow the contracting parties to practice niyoga till two children are born; however, successive niyoga relationships are permitted until ten children are born (this is the number of children prescribed for normal marriages) after which the practice must be terminated (p. 132).

Both marriage and niyoga thus share the same basis in Dayananda's view, that of begetting healthy and strong children. In recommending niyoga Dayananda sought both to revive an institution that had been "shunned by Hinduism for nearly two millenia, and also to greatly extend its application. From the narrow purpose of providing a son to a deceased husband it was now to solve the much wider problem of widowhood."[86] This was one form of the nationalist resolution of women's sexuality; to use her biological potential for child bearing in the service of the physical regeneration of what was seen as a now weakened Aryan race.

III

Did these visions of womanhood relate to the workings of women's lives, to their experiences and actions as they unfolded themselves in the last quarter of the nineteenth century? There is some evidence that many women had internalized notions of the 'golden age' of the Hindus, and of the highminded and spiritual qualities of Vedic women. One of the earliest tracts written by an educated woman, Kailashbhashini Devi, in the second half of the nineteenth century, on the pitiable conditions of Hindu women is a good example of such a notion of the past.[87] After outlining the miseries faced by women which included purdah (female seclusion), child marriage, Kulin polygamy, and enforced widowhood, she argues that evils such as purdah and child marriage were "unknown in ancient times." In contrast to present times, women reached maturity and acquired learning before they were married and they continued learning even afterwards without the superstitious fear of widowhood. Hence, according to Kailashbhashini, there was better communication between husband and wife and a superior ideal of married life prevailed. Views such as these were beginning to be commonly believed, as we have seen, thanks to the increased historical consciousness of people during the first half of the nineteenth century. Awareness of the normative characteristics of the term Aryan was widespread, and its association with women and the ideal of womanhood, was strikingly noticeable in the second half of the nineteenth century. Almost every organization set up to alleviate the condition of Hindu women evoked the 'Aryanness' of women. The Ladies Union set up by Keshub Chunder Sen in 1879 was called the Arya Nari Samaj and one of its distinctive features was the adaptation of traditional Hindu *bratas* (fasts) to new objectives; aptly there was now to be a Maitreyi brata based on the Vedic Maitreyi for those who wanted to cultivate religious fellowship with their husbands.[88] Everything associated with women in the Arya Samaj exemplified the Aryan theme. Even the organization set up by Pandita Ramabai in Poona to 'improve' the degraded condition of women was known as Arya Mahila Samaj.[89] The normative model of womanhood in the second half of the nineteenth century was certainly the Aryan woman, whatever that might imply in real terms.

Just as women had begun to identify with Aryan values they also identified with other aspects of cultural nationalism and its symbols. For example, Kumudini Mitra, who graduated in 1903, wrote a number of articles one of which, published during the Swadeshi movement, was titled *Sikher Balidan* (The Sacrifice of the Sikhs) — a history of the sacrifices made by Sikhs in the defence of their religion. A review of the book published in *Bamabodhini Patrika,* a women's journal, drew the obvious conclusion that if Bengalis wanted to riseas a nation they should emulate the example of the patriotic, self sacrificing spirit of the Sikh martyrs.[90] More generally, the beginnings of nationalism acted as a major catalyst in the awareness of women. Particularly in Bengal in the days of the Swadeshi movement women became "uncharacteristically militant" (as Borthwick puts it) and, in an ethos inspired by nationalist fervour, boldness, bravery, and physical fitness, were accepted as female virtues if they served a political purpose. A lady correspondent in the *Sanjibani* appealed to all Bengalis to undergo physical training in order to repel and prevent the insults heaped on Bengali women by Europeans.[91] The need for heroic action from both men and women in the cause of the 'motherland' was clearly a value which had struck a positive response among women.

Within this broad canvas upon which history and mythology had left its impress for women, it might be useful to consider in greater depth the changed quality of women's experiences and see whether the models of womanhood, current in the late nineteenth century, were effectively able to explain real women as they were situated. We shall take up for consideration two women, one in Bengal and another in Maharashtra, who were roughly contemporary in their periods of activity and were, as well, women of unusual energy and sensitivity.

Sarala Debi was the younger of our two women but her experiences meshed fairly well with the nationalist ethos just outlined. Born in 1872 in the privileged Tagore family of Bengal, Sarala Debi decided, at the age of twenty three, to take up an appointment, despite heavy family opposition, in a girls school in far away Mysore. In her own words she had wanted to 'flee' the cage or the prison of home and establish her right to an independent livelihood like men.[92] Unfortunately, the experiment ended six months later following an incident when a young man stole into her room at night. The incident was made much of in the press and the *Bangabasi* wrote in its editorial, "What is the need for a girl from such a family to go off to distant lands for the sake of employment? There is no dearth of work here. This is just an example of blindly aping western civilization" (pp. 123-24). Her mother, Swarna Kumari Debi, then persuaded her to return in order to serve the larger cause of the nation and handed over to her the editorship of *Bharati* which she had edited until then. When Sarala Debi came back to Calcutta she was taunted with statements like "Have you satisfied your whim to work; have you satisfied your whim for independence?" Sarala's response was, "The whim to work is satisfied, but not the whim for independence." In her own understanding the whim for independence had grown to include the entire people and the nation, and finally crystallized into a cause (p. 125).

While returning home to Calcutta by train Sarala Debi noticed that the guards on the train looked very "weak" and was struck by the difference between Bengali weakness and the strength of the Punjabi and Maratha, but she noticed also that they all had one thing in common, and that was fear of the white skin (p.127). When she got back she asked the readers of the *Bharati* to communicate instances in which men had resisted insults by British soldiers or civilians heaped upon wives, sisters, daughters and upon menfolk themselves, and she published these accounts (p. 127). Sarala Debi went on to become one of the most militantly nationalist women of the period. To counteract the internalized notion of effeteness by a subject people she lauched a vigorous campaign. Initially she began with exhortations to Bengali youth to rouse themselves from their torpor and engage in physical culture which had been a favourite activity of the Hindu Mela held annually by the Tagore family. She did not attempt to become directly involved in the formal political activity of male associations but used instead the symbolic power of local history and legend to create political consciousness and so became one of the most effective proponents of Bengali nationalism.[93]

Sarala Debi's particular contribution broadly lay in the encouragement of a martial, heroic culture in Bengal that would serve the nationalist cause and, within this larger cause, Sarala Debi made imaginative use of folklore and history. Her activities included the conversion of a local king, Pratapaditya, into a Bengali hero equal in stature to Shivaji, the publication of a series of children's books on the lives of Bengali heroes, the composition of patriotic songs, and the organization of classes for increasing physical stamina (pp. 126-29).

Sarala Debi was extremely conscious of her role in creating heroic figures and so were others around her. She had noticed the power of the brave Rajput symbol upon the Bengali *bhadralok* (gentlefolk) but realized that while they were impressed with these figures, Bengal needed its own heroes; this need led her to project Pratapaditya and his son Udayaditya as larger than life characters but in doing so it was clear that she was manipulating history. When her uncle Rabindranath Tagore objected to her suppression of the criminal aspect of Pratapaditya, who was a patricide and therefore unworthy of being the hero of an entire nation, Sarala's candid reply was that she had not constructed Pratapaditya as a symbol of an "ideal moral being;" but as the sole brave and manly Hindu *zamindar* (landlord) to have resisted the Mughal king, and declared Bengali independence (p.128).

Sarala Debi's harangues, carried in the pages of the *Bharati* resulted in the formation of a *dal* (group) and in 1902 she moved from writing to action. "In the gymnasium that she ran in her father's house training in sword and *lathi* [wooden stick] play were accompanied by pledges made on the map of India that the pledgers would be prepared to sacrifice their lives for their country's independence. Each pledger would receive a *rakhi* [token of brother's protection] from Sarala Debi as a token of the vow" (p.127). They were also urged to take the Pratapaditya vow in memory of the "Bengali Hindu patriot prince who fought Imperial Muslim power" (p. 140). In 1903 Sarala Debi started a festival on the second day of Durga puja called Bir Ashtami where Sanskrit verses listing bygone heroes of India were recited. These heroes included Krishna and Rama on the one hand and Rana Pratap, Shivaji, Ranjit Singh, Pratapaditya and Sitaram on the other (p.140).

It is significant that it was at one of the Pratapaditya festivals presided over by Sarala Debi in 1905 that an attempt was made to use the words Bande Mataram as a national call, following the staging of Bankim's *Anandmath*.[94] She was also reputed to have become a member of the inner group of revolutionaries[95] and one is struck by the similarities between Sarala Debi's energizing of men before and during the Swadeshi movement and Bankim's selfless Shanti fighting alongside the men in the war of liberation. Whether Sarala Debi was consciously inspired by Bankim's model of womanhood (she was called Debi Chaudharani in her own heyday) in moments of crisis or not, it appears that the "mother-centred rhetoric of Hindu nationalism"[96] had, by its use of women as political symbols of national awakening, created a political space for women i.e. created the possibilities of a Sarala Debi's involvement in politics. Sarala Debi describes in her own memoirs that she had a favourite image of Kali placed on a table beneath her own portrait showing her with long open hair. When the Maharaja of Baroda came to tea and was shown the favourite image of Kali he remarked "Which Kali shall I look at; this one or that one?" (p.143).

In fact Sarala Debi presented a challenge to Bengali males. Beginning from a position when she exhorted young men to start a dal for self-defence, and the defence of their women from molestation by British soldiers in streets and stations (the parallel with the ravaged and humiliated motherland is unmistakable) she had ended by appearing to have taken on the role of a hero herself. Her defiance of the conventional female role did not escape notice and the *Rangalay* remarked that unlike the wives and mothers of heroes in the Sanskrit literature the "Bengali girl of the day" would be satisfied with nothing less than playing the hero herself.[97]

At the height of her active career Sarala Debi, however, lived up not to her expanded self but to the conventional role of a wife, also in keeping with the nationalist construct of womanhood. At the age of thirty three in 1905 she was persuaded, or rather emotionally blackmailed, to marry by her mother who begged her to agree since she did not want to die without seeing her daughter married. The family had chosen for her a widower, Ram Bhuj Choudhari, whom she had never seen before but who was a nationalist, a good speaker, and an Arya Samaji (although his family was not), and was known to the extended family. Sarala Debi moved to Lahore with her husband and despite having been brought up in a strictly monotheistic family she agreed to observe the idolatorous rituals which were customary in her husband's family. It is possible that none of this conflicted with the spirit and demands of nationalism as Sarala Debi understood it. She continued her programme for physical regeneration even after moving to Lahore where she and her husband introduced some of the festivals that she had initiated in Calcutta (pp. 185-86).

What is significant in the activities and concerns of Sarala Debi was the way in which the women's question never featured as an issue. Everything that Sarala Debi did was in the larger cause of nationalism. It is significant that Sarala Debi's autobiography virtually ends with her marriage. Her subsequent life is put into her book as an epilogue by someone else. Thus, despite her relatively unorthodox career, Sarala Debi was uncontroversial except for some minor criticisms originating from conservative sections or from the Anglo-Indian press. The nationalist construct of womanhood did not conflict with Sarala Debi's militancy and with her efforts at dynamizing the youth of Bengal; indeed it was in keeping with the basic design mapped out for nationalist regeneration. That the nationalist construct of womanhood could be empowering for at least some women is clear from Sarala Debi's life.

Very different in all essentials was the case of Pandita Ramabai.

Unlike Sarala Debi who belonged to a patrician-Brahmo family, Ramabai was born in a learned but indigent Brahmin household. Her father Ananta Dongre, titled Shastri, had been a student of Ramachandra Shastri who was employed by the reigning Peshwa to give Sanskrit lessons to his favourite wife. Ananta would accompany his teacher and occasionally heard the lady reciting Sanskrit poems which are said to have filled him with admiration.[98] When he returned to his village he attempted to teach his girl-wife Sanskrit but the bride was unreceptive and the elders objected so he dropped the idea. After his first wife died and when he remarried he resolved to repeat his experiment with the new bride. The elders objected once again so Ananta Shastri decided to move out with his young wife to a remote forest where he set up a house and continued to teach young Lakshmibai. By the time Ramabai, the youngest of Lakshmibai's three children, was born in 1858 her father was too old to instruct her so it was from Lakshmibai that Ramabai learnt Sanskrit (p.xi). Ramabai's reminiscences indicate the extreme affection that existed within the Dongre household particularly between mother and daughter. The lessons from her mother had to be conducted early in the morning before the mother's household chores began and these moments were cherished by Ramabai who went on to dedicate her book *The High Caste Hindu Woman* to Lakshmibai whom she described as "the light and guide of my life."

Ananta Shastri's attempt at creating a more humane world of his own did not fully succeed. The first crisis in the household came when Ananta married off his elder daughter, according to custom, when she was very young. He had tried to ensure that the marriage would be different by reversing the normal pattern of residence. The young son-in-law was persuaded to remain in the Dongre household so that he too could be exposed to learning and have a chance to break away from the "iron law of custom" (p.xii). This attempt ended in failure; the young man would not learn and returned to his father's home, and when Ramabai's sister was old enough to perform her "married duties" a demand was made for her to come and join her husband. The parents according to Ramabai's account could not bear to send "their darling daughter" to a man who would be thoroughly incompatible with her. The community however rallied to the young man's defence, collected funds and enabled him to sue her in court. The court upheld the man's right in accordance with Hindu law and the wife was "doomed" to go with him. Ramabai wrote later that fortunately her sister was soon "released from this sorrowful world by cholera" (pp. 62-64).

Financial problems in running the household even in the forest, especially because it had become something of an *ashram* (religious retreat) for other students who were fed by the Dongres, led to the shutting down of the forest household. The family now wandered from place to place with no fixed dwelling through all of which Ramabai's education continued. After the negative experience of the first daughter's marriage Ramabai's parents decided not to throw her into the "well of ignorance," by giving her in early marriage. Ramabai's parents died soon after each other in the course of these wanderings. The poverty of the family was so extreme that no Brahmins could be secured to bear the remains of her mother to the burning *ghat* (cremation ground). Finally two Brahmins took pity on them and, with their assistance, Ramabai and her brother themselves carried the bier. Ramabai had to bear her part of the bier on her head because of her small stature (p. xiii). Thereafter Ramabai and her brother continued their travels covering a distance of 2000 miles, much of it on foot. The travels gave them a good opportunity of "seeing the sufferings of Hindu women."[99]

In Calcutta the two young people, but especially Ramabai, created something of a sensation because of their learning, and the title of Saraswati was conferred on Ramabai. Soon after, Ramabai's brother died, filled with foreboding about what would happen to Ramabai after his death. Ramabai states that it was in this intense moment of loneliness that she was first comforted by the presence of God. As long as her brother had lived she had not thought of marriage but left utterly alone she agreed to marry Bipin Bihari Das, a friend of her brother whom she had known for about two years, in 1880. The marriage was brief since in 1881 her husband died, soon after the birth of a daughter. Ramabai returned to western India and decided to work for the uplift of women. She gave evidence before the Hunter Commission.along with the women of the Arya Mahila Samaj, an institution she had formed in Poona (p.xv). During this year she tried to get the help of the Hindu elite at Poona to start a home for widows but none was forthcoming. In 1883 Ramabai went to England in pursuit of a medical degree and with this her controversial career as a public figure began (p. xviii), of which we shall see more later.

Ramabai's analysis of Hindu womanhood which, unlike for Sarala Debi, remained the primary focus of all her concern, is contained in the book she wrote in America in 1886, aptly titled *The High Caste Hindu Woman*. The book itself was written to raise funds and to propagate the cause of women's reform. It was widely circulated in America selling 10,000 copies in a short while and ennabled her to collect the funds required to set up a widows home in India.[100]

Ramabai's book is an insightful account of the actual status of women in high caste Hindu households, and combines quotations from the sacred texts with personal reminiscences of instances she had witnessed of the miserable plight of women. She was able to perceive the contradiction between custom and religious precepts and the superior weight given to custom in actual practice. Because of her command over sacred texts her account was difficult to ignore as she was able to quote relevant passages in support of her own position on the low status of women. Ramabai's analysis differs from all others that preceded it in the belief that there never was a golden age for Hindu women. The glorious Aryan woman did not exist for Ramabai precisely because of her knowledge of Sanskrit. In fact she uses the term 'golden age' scornfully, associating it with a period in which a man could "take a woman [from] wherever she may be found and drag her to his house" (p.62). Having dismissed the golden age she goes on to indict the present. While in the olden days the laws enforcing a man's power over a woman were the work of the community, now under "the so-called Christian British rule" and their laws women were in no better condition. The only difference is that now a man was bound to bring a suit against a woman to claim his "marital property" as in the case of her sister (p.62).

In *The High Caste Hindu Woman* Ramabai divided the life of a woman into three stages; childhood, married life, and widowhood, with injustice and oppression getting worse in each stage. Ramabai's analysis of the miseries of Hindu womanhood begins with the agony of the mother even before a child is born:

> In no other country is the mother so laden with care and anxiety on the approach of childbirth as in India. In most cases her hope of winning

> her husband to herself hangs solely on her bearing sons. . . . [to ensure this] women pray with herbs and roots. . . . and son-giving gods are devoutly worshipped. . . .There is [even] a curious ceremony which is administered to the mother for converting the embryo [of a pregnant woman] into a boy (p.14).

In spite of all these precautions Ramabai goes on devastatingly to say that girls *do* come into Hindu households "as ill luck, or rather nature would have it" (p.17). Then, depending on how strong is the influence of social custom, and the individual's ability to withstand it, discrimination against girls begins. Ramabai praises the mother who often stands against custom, sacrificing her own happiness by braving the displeasure of "her lord" and treats her own daughter as the "best of all treasures" (p.17). Further, Ramabai provides a psychological understanding as to why mothers sometimes subject their daughters to miseries which she attributes to the internalization of the values of the community. Under such circumstances girls begin to *feel* their misery without understanding why it should be so. Ramabai recounts how often she heard the statement, "It would have been good for all of us if thou hadst died" (p.18).

Ramabai's travels in Rajasthan had exposed her to the custom of infanticide. Her description of it is as effective as Tod's descriptions of chivalry :

> After considering how many girls could safely be allowed to live, the father took good care to defend himself from caste and clan tyranny by killing the extra girls at birth which was as easily accomplished as destroying a mosquito or any other annoying insect. Who can save a baby if the parents are determined to slay her, and eagerly watch for a suitable opportunity? There are several . . . nameless methods that may be employed . . . . There are not a few child thieves who generally steal girls; even the wild animals are so intelligent and of such refined taste that they mock at British law, and almost always steal girls to satisfy their hunger . . . . The census of 1870 revealed the curious fact that 300 children were stolen in one year by wolves from within the city of Umritzar, all the children being girls (pp. 25-26).

Ramabai ends her section on childhood by pointing out the adverse sex ratio between males and females, and gives figures from the 1881 Census according to which men exceeded women by over five million.

If childhood was bad for girls, married life was infinitely worse, an area where custom was much worse than the regulations of religious texts. Ramabai points out that even the conservative Manu had enjoined that girls must be married only to good suitors but no one paid attention to such homilies. She also dwells on the romantic illusions of marriage, especially of the ceremony itself when momentarily even a girl will feel elevated, a feeling compounded by the fact that girls are married off while they are still "babies." And then all of a sudden the girl who was "like a young colt before" suddenly finds herself with a yoke put on her (pp. 42-43). Among her reminiscenses is the case of a young girl of thirteen who was beaten cruelly by her husband for telling the simple truth that she did not like to be in his house as much as being in her own home (p.48). But despite instances such as these Ramabai acknowledges that there are many happy and loving couples in India where the wives would have nothing to complain about except the "absence of freedom of thought and action" (p.48).

In Ramabai's analysis of the place of women in religion and society she argues that although women are looked upon as inferior beings, as mothers they are honoured. This honour is however countermanded by countless condemnations and restrictions placed upon them. She illustrates from a collection of proverbs from popular literature:

What is cruel?
The heart of a viper.

What is more cruel than that ?
The heart of a woman.

What is the cruellest of all?
The heart of a souless, penniless widow (p. 57).

The sharpest part of Ramabai's writing deals with the marital rights of men over their wives. Quoting from Manu she shows how the wife is classed with cows, mares, female camels, slave-girls, buffalo-cows, she-goats and ewes (p.60). The rights of a husband over a wife are so complete that the yearly epidemics that carry away women are not unwelcome to women who are persecuted by social, religious, and state laws (p.64). The courts provide no relief for women as the right of the husband upon the wife is recognized by the law. Thus the wife is hemmed in on all sides.

Much worse is widowhood which is regarded as retribution for crimes committed in an earlier life. If the widow has a son she may adjust to her degradation. But the child widow is "regarded as the greatest criminal upon whom heaven's judgement has been pronounced." Ramabai deftly exposes the hypocrisy of Manu by putting together his injunctions for widows and widowers. She quotes:

> Let her emaciate her body by living on pure flowers, roots and fruits but she must never ever mention the name of another man after her husband has died. . . . Until death let her be patient of hardships, self controlled, and chaste. . . . (p.72).

And for the widower:

> A twice born man, versed in the sacred law shall burn a wife of equal caste. . . . [and] having at the funeral given the sacred fires to his wife who dies before him, he may marry again, and again kindle the nuptial fires (pp. 72-73).

The miseries of widowhood are such that although sati is gruesome and entirely the creation of a "wicked priesthood," if it appeared to the widow that it was a sublime act it was because it was the only relief she had against a cruel world. In Ramabai's view the momentary agony of suffocation in the flames was nothing as compared to her lot as a widow (p.75). Apart from her humiliation and disfigurement, the young widow is always looked upon with suspicion and must be constantly closely guarded like a prisoner lest she bring disgrace to her family. Mortification is prescribed to repress her natural desires (pp.84-85). While Ramabai recognized the value of social reform she saw also how limited its reach was and its failure as a practical means of ending the widow's humiliation. She pours scorn on the reformers who "took oaths that they would marry widows" but no sooner were they confronted with actual situations, off they went and married "pretty little maidens" (p.91). She ends the section on widowhood by suggesting that with the one chance of ending her miseries in the sati rite taken away from her, there is now nothing to mitigate the widows sufferings (p.93).

In concluding her essay Ramabai follows the by now well established strategy of relating the effects of the condition of women upon society as a whole. But this is where she takes off from James Mill on the one hand, and R.C. Dutt on the other: while Mill had related the low status of women to the barbaric nature of the civilization, and Dutt had established the reverse, Ramabai made a remarkable correlation. If Hindu men are weak it is because their mothers were kept weak and sickly; what is more important is that because women have had years of submission behind them they have been converted into slavery-loving creatures. According to Ramabai, "They are glad to lean upon any one and be altogether dependent, and thus it has come to pass that their sons as a race, desire to depend on some other nation and not upon themselves" (p.98). Ramabai thus subverts Dayananda's argument about a strong race being the contribution of strong women by talking about psychological and not physical weakness: a subject womanhood could not be expected to produce anything better than a subject nation.

Ramabai's career as a reformer could easily have proceeded uneventfully as there was considerable support for social reforms from liberal sections by the last quarter of the nineteenth century, if she had not damned herself in the eyes of all Hindus — liberals and conservatives alike — when she decided to adopt Christianity in 1883. Hindus, who had regarded her as learned and had conferred on her the title of Saraswati were outraged at this slap in the face, especially from a woman, and everything that she was to do thereafter was controversial. Significantly Ramabai was the butt of controversy both from Hindus and the British government whom she indicted for its ineffective plague relief measures in 1897.[101] Even the Christian missionaries she worked with found her too difficult to contain in any system where she was required to submit to authority.[102] Ramabai did not fit into any stereotype of womanhood, either Hindu or Christian.

Why did Ramabai choose to cut her links with Hinduism? Was it not possible for her to have found a space for herself in the emerging reformist atmosphere in Maharashtra which was not completely insensitive to the plight of Hindu women? From her own account it appears that she wanted to set up a widow's home but funds were not forthcoming from within the Hindu community. As Ramabai saw it, the major drawback was the hypocrisy of the reformers. Ramabai's environment was dominated by Ranade and Tilak from whom not much could be expected for the cause of women.

Ranade's feeling for the Hindu widow was never in doubt but his inability to stand up to conservative pressure, even in pursuance of his own stated position was so poor, that his own colleagues and fellow reformers were disappointed in him.[103] When the opportunity to marry a widow came his way he succumbed to parental pressure. On the other side of the country Keshub Chandra Sen was doing the same. After all his progressive posturing (when it came to his own family) Sen married off his minor daughter while she was still below the age of consent. The moderate liberals were thus a total disappointment. As to Tilak, his position was clearly conservative. He was not willing to recognize the need for changing women's status until Hindus could govern themselves. As far as he was concerned the misery of women was an issue which had to wait till India became independent. He told a friend, half jokingly, that he would arrange the marriage of a thousand widows the day India became independent,[104] but the statement sums up Tilak's position on women quite well. To tell women to wait till the whole nation was free would be cold comfort for women like Ramabai who wanted to change the quality of women's lives then and there.

A classic case of the trap that women were in during this phase of aggressive cultural nationalism, now being transformed into political nationalism, was the case of Rukmabai who was also a friend of Ramabai. Rukmabai was married by her father while still a minor and after his death declined to go to her marital home. Her husband, both consumptive and illiterate, moved the court for restitution of conjugal rights to force his wife to live with him.[105] Rukmabai in turn used the argument that since the marriage was concluded without her consent it was not legally binding on her and the lower court did not consent to forcing Rukmabai to live with her husband against her will. Ramabai writes that on hearing this decision the "conservative party all over India rose as one man and girded their loins to denounce the helpless woman. . . . They encouraged the 'alleged' husband to stand his ground." They threatened the British government with public displeasure if it "failed to keep its agreement to force the woman to go to live with her husband according to Hindu law."[106] Large sums of money were collected in the husband's support to appeal against the decision, and finally the courts ordered her to join her husband. When she adamantly refused the court ordered her arrest.

Rukmabai's letter to Ramabai and the latter's comments on the case reveal what women thought of the laws of the Hindus, of British Justice, and hence of the utter inability to change the quality of their personal lives in the present circumstances. Rukmabai wrote:

> The learned and civilized judges. . . are determined to enforce, in this enlightened age, the inhuman laws enacted in barbaric times, four thousand years ago. . . . There is no hope for women in India, whether they be under Hindu rule or British rule . . . . The hard-hearted mothers-in-law will now be greatly strengthened and will induce their sons to sue the wives in British courts since they are now fully assured that under no circumstances can the British government act adversely to the Hindu law.[107]

Ramabai in her turn eloquently describes the helplessness of a lone woman pitted against the range of forces symbolized by the Rukmabai case:

> Taught by the experience of the past, we are not at all surprised at this decision of the Bombay court. Our only wonder is that a defenceless woman like Rukmabai dared to raise her voice in the face of the powerful Hindu law, the mighty British government, the one hundred and twenty nine million men and three hundred and thirty million gods of the Hindus, all . . . having conspired together to crush her to nothingness. We cannot blame the English government for not defending a helpless woman; it is only fulfilling its agreement made with the male population of India. . . .[108]

With penetrating insight Ramabai concludes her account of the Rukmabai case by connecting the relationship between British imperialism, Indian men and the subjugation of women; the British were hardly going to bother about the rights of women if "British profit and rule in India might be endangered thereby."[109]

The Rukmabai case received some support from liberal sections but characteristically Tilak found the case to be in defiance of the Shastras. In fact Tilak used the Rukmabai case to bolster his argument that education corrupted women; one reason why Rukmabai was perceived as refusing to go to live with the "husband" was because he was illiterate. Tilak defended the husband's position by insisting that a case of this kind be tried according to Hindu *Dharmashastra* instead of English common law. He also wanted the case treated as a criminal offence and not as a civil dispute. He himself would judge the case by ordering the "erring" woman to be punished. He wrote, "If a woman does not go to her husband she should be punished by the king. And if she disobeys the king's order she should be imprisoned."[110]

For Tilak the Rukmabai case was mainly a stick to beat the reformers with. According to him the reformers were using Rukmabai "to fire bullets at our ancient religion with the intention of castrating our eternal religion."[111] Rukmabai, Ramabai and countless other women were now caught in the political crossfire between liberals and conservatives, and between imperial Britain and subjugated India. While models of womanhood and a national feminine identity were being constituted with at least some women such as Sarla Debi shaping their lives in conformity to it, there were others whose life experiences did not mesh with such images. The hysterical reaction to Ramabai's conversion from Hindu nationalists echoed a hundred year old Hindu fear of the loss of national identity; numbers were not important in the conversion question. The high visibility of Ramabai's conversion swamped everything else.

Ramabai took a position against the British government, as patriotically as Tilak did, when she criticized the government for its handling of women during the plague epidemic of 1897 in a letter to the *Bombay Guardian.*[112] The Governor of Bombay dismissed Ramabai's charges as grossly inaccurate and misleading whereupon Ramabai accused him of making assertions without giving any proof of their truth. Ramabai's letter was treated by one of her Christian benefactresses as "childish, sensational and seditious."[113] This reaction indicates how impossible it was to reduce Ramabai to any kind of a stereotype. Even in far off Calcutta where nationalist heroines were in the making, one newspaper castigated Ramabai for her unwomanly behaviour in criticizing the government.[114]

In the ultimate analysis it was not Ramabai's lack of nationalism that accounted for the hostility that she generated; it was her unambiguous stand against men who were the cause of women's oppression. Her exposure of the ugly face of Hinduism made it impossible for her to be accommodated even within a reformed Hinduism. Writing in 1896 after a visit to many cities in north India she pleaded with those who were easily taken in by the high claims of Hinduism:

> I beg of my western sisters not to be satisfied with . . . the outside beauties of the grand philosophies . . . and the interested discourse of our educated men, but to open the trapdoors of the great monuments

> of the ancient Hindu intellect, and enter into the dark cellars where they will see the real working of the philosophies which they admire so much . . . [In] Jagannath Puri, Benaras, Gaya. . . and such other sacred cities, the strongholds of Hinduism and seats of sacred learning . . . where the sublime philosophies are daily taught and devoutly followed, there are thousands of priests and men who are the spiritual rulers of our people. They neglect and oppress widows, send out hundreds of emissaries to look for young widows, and bring them to the sacred cities. . . and rob them of their virtue. . . Thousands of young widows . . . are suffering untold misery . . . but not a philosopher or Mahatma has come out boldly to champion their cause and help . . . . There are many hard and bitter facts that we have to accept and feel. All is not poetry with us. . . .[115]

The prime of Ramabai's life coincided with the well developed phase of aggressive cultural nationalism and a strong urge within the Hindu community to close ranks. The women's question both theoretically and in practice was something of a casualty during this period as is evident from the tremendous reaction against the Age of Consent Bill. In Bengal and Maharashtra particularly, the polarization between supporters and opponents was not over the rightness of the bill in relation to women but over whether a foreign government had a right to legislate for a people demanding the right to govern themselves. Tilak argued that the issue was a religious one (in Bengal too the Shastras were quoted to show that the bill would violate religious injunctions) and set the tone of the whole debate which for the orthodox was an outraged cry of "Hinduism in danger."[116] In Bengal it was "Mother India" who was to be defended against calculating alien attacks; the Age of Consent Bill thus became the first social issue that was the subject of a nationwide controversy. The controversy was so fierce that the usual argument of "reinstating ancient social regulations" put forward by Ranade in this case (and a favoured strategy right from the sati debate onwards) had very little impact. Like the earlier debates here too was the implicit fear of loss of control over women's sexuality as is clear from some of the issues raised by the 'conservatives' against the Bill.[117]

*

As the nineteenth century closed, the women's question as an area of reform appeared to evoke less enthusiasm than it had done before. What appeared to be more important was the question of a feminine identity which continued to receive finishing touches throughout the twentieth century.

At the beginning of the twentieth century the experience of the nineteenth century, especially of its second half, in terms of the formation of women's identity, is reflected in Vivekananda's image of Hindu womanhood. Many of his statements on women (like Ramabai's before him) were addressed to a western audience and this might explain the context in which his picture of Hindu womanhood within the image of a spiritual East is contrasted with western women in a materialist setting. In fact there is a constant interplay between the West and East in Vivekananda's characterization of Hindu womanhood. On the ideal of womanhood Vivekananda held:

> The ideal of womanhood centres in the Aryan race of India, the most ancient in the world's history. In that race men and women were priests "Sabatimini" (Sahadharmini) or co-religionists as the Vedas call them. There, every family had its hearth or altar. There man and wife together offered their sacrifices . . . In India it was a female sage who first found the unity of God and laid down this doctrine in one of the first hymns of the Vedas . . .[118]

> The Aryan and Semitic ideals of woman have always been diametrically opposed. Amongst the Semites the presence of a woman is considered dangerous to devotion . . . According to the Aryan, man cannot perform a religious action without a wife.[119]

On the materialism of the West and the spiritualism of the East with its bearing on women he reiterated:

> On the one hand rank materialism through foreign literature has caused a tremendous stir; on the other through the confounding din of all these discordant sounds she hears in low yet unmistakable accents the heartrending cries of her ancient Gods, cutting her to the quick. There lie before her various strange luxuries . . . new manners, new fashions, dressed in which moves about the well educated girl in shameless freedom. All these are arousing . . . desires. Again the scene changes and in its place appear, with stern presence Sita, Savitri, austere religious vows, fastings, the forest retreat, the matted locks and the orange garb of the semi-naked Sannyasin, Samadhi and the search for the self. On the one side is the independence of western society, on the other the extreme self sacrifice of the Aryan society.[120]

Vivekananda also extols the mother and associates true motherhood with chastity. What fulfills a woman is motherhood. He then goes on to turn the tables on western society for its treatment of the western woman. While men in America can disinherit their wives, in India according to Vivekananda, the "whole estate of the husband must go to the wife." In the west witches were dragged and burnt amid jeering mobs, while in contrast Indian women mounted the pyre of their husbands cheerfully. Significantly in response to constant criticism about the treatment of Hindu widows Vivekananda categorically asserted that he had travelled all over India but failed to see "a single case of ill treatment."[121] The closing of ranks is now unmistakable; there is no women's question for Vivekananda. Women have always been respected and given their due. The Hindus as a race could not have produced the image of Sita without revering women and that was all that mattered. Vivekananda confidently asserted that "a race that produced Sita, even if it only dreamt of her, has a reverence for woman that is unmatched on earth. . . ."[122]

The nation's identity lay in the culture and more specifically in its womanhood. In the changed political and social environment the image of womanhood was more important than the reality. Historians and laymen would complete the process by ensuring, through continued writings in the twentieth century, that the image also came to be perceived as the reality.

Conclusion

The process that I have outlined in the preceding sections has attempted to document the 'invention' of a tradition[123] during the nineteenth century. During this phase what took place was the construction of a particular kind of past which was the context for the construction also of a particular kind of womanhood.[124] The past itself was a creation of the compulsions of the present and these compulsions determined which elements were highlighted and which receded from the conscious object of concern in historical and semi-historical writings.

In the context of the women's question the entire focus of attention in the nineteenth century had been on the high caste Hindu woman whether it was to highlight her high status in the past or in reforming her low status in the present. The emphasis on the Shastras in settling the debates of the present ensured that the only issues taken up about women in the past were those that had a bearing on legal and familial questions. Reaction to the attacks by colonial writers ensured that Indian women were almost built up as superwomen: a combination of the spiritual Maitreyi, the learned Gargi, the suffering Sita, the faithful Savitri and the heroic Lakshmibai. Spiritual power and the sahadharmini model in particular were central to the idea of womanhood because these could be transformed to play other roles in the regeneration of the nation. Nationalism itself came to occupy the same place that religion had before; it was a permitted area for women's participation. In this model of womanhood there was no difference between the perceptions of progressives and of conservatives.

The limited focus, from the days of Rammohun onwards, on a particular section of women which, in turn, led to the consideration of a particular kind of womanhood was an aspect of the nationalist project which excluded various sections from its ambit. The obsession with effeminacy for example was confined to the educated elite. The construction of a heroic identity was similarly a contribution of the intelligentsia. While the Marathas were being transformed into champions of nationalism, sections left out from participating in the creation of such myths were still voicing their perception of the Marathas as marauders.[125]

The focus on the upper sections of society to the total exclusion of all others is evident also from Dayananda's injunctions that Arya mothers should not nurse their babies, but employ wet nurses instead so that they might recover quickly and so be ready to produce strong sons once more. But what of the wet nurse? Who was she? What about her place in the system of procreation? Was she not required to produce strong sons too? Clearly Dayananda's injunctions were meant for one section at the expense of another. Vast sections of women did not exist for the nineteenth century nationalists. No one tried to read the ancient texts to see what rights the Vedic dasi and others like her had in the Vedic golden age. Recognizing her existence would have been an embarrassment to the nationalists. The twentieth century has continued to reproduce, in all essentials, the same kind of womanhood that the nineteenth century has so carefully, and so successfully constructed as an enduring legacy for us.

NOTES

1. Uma Chakravarti, "Of Dasas and Karmakaras: Servile Labour in Ancient India," in Utsa Patnaik and Manjari Dingwaney ed. *Chains of Servitude: Bondage and Slavery in India* (Delhi: Orient Longman,1985), pp. 35-75.
2. Jadunath Sarkar, *India Through the Ages* (1928; rpt. Calcutta: Orient Longman, 1979), p.84.
3. William Jones, "On the Chronology of the Hindus," In Lord Teignmouth, ed. *The Works of William Jones* (London: John Stockdale, Picadilly, and John Walkes, 1807). IV, p.64.
4. H.T. Colebrooke, "On the Duties of the Faithful Hindu Widow," *Asiatic Researches,* 4 (1895), pp.205-15.
5. Ronald W. Neufeldt, *Max Muller and the Rig Veda: A Study of its Role in his Work and Thought* (Calcutta: Minerva, 1980), p.3.
6. H.T. Colebrooke, "On the Vedas, or Sacred Writings of the Hindus," *Asiatic Researches,* 8 (1805), pp.377-498.
7. Ibid, pp.443-48.
8. David Kopf, *British Orientalism and the Bengal Renaissance* (Calcutta: Firma K.L. Mukhopadhyaya, 1969), p.149.
9. Lata Mani, "Production of an Official Discourse on Sati in Early Nineteenth Century Bengal," Review of Women Studies in the *Economic and Political Weekly,* 26, no.17 (26 April 1986), p.35.
10. Bernard Cohn, "The Command of Language and the Language of Command," in Ranajit Guha, ed. *Subaltern Studies* (Delhi: Oxford University Press, 1985),4, p.326.
11. *Parliamentary Papers on Hindu Widows,* 1821, p. 532; cited in Lata Mani, p.35.
12. Kopf, *British Orientalism,* p.8.
13. J.C. Ghose, *The English Works of Raja Rammohun Roy* (Calcutta: Oriental, 1885), p.43.
14. C.H. Philips, "James Mill, Mountstuart Elphinstone and the History of India," in C.H. Philips, ed. *Historians of India, Pakistan and Ceylon* (London: Oxford Unversity Press, 1961), p.218.
15. The casting of moral balance sheets has been called the characteristic vice of British writers on Indian history. See K.A. Ballhatchet, "Some Aspects of Historical Writing on India by Christian Missionaries," South Asia Seminar, School of Oriental and African Studies, London, May 1956.

16. James Mill, *The History of British India,* with notes by H.H. Wilson, 5th ed. (London: James Madden, 1840), pp. 312-13. Subsequent references are cited in the text.

17. Mrinalini Sinha, "Colonial Politics and the Ideal of Masculinity," Indian Association of Women's Studies, The Third National Conference of Women's Studies, Chandigarh, Oct. 1-4, 1986.

18. John Rosselli, "The Self Image of Effeteness: Physical Education and Nationalism in 19th century Bengal," *Past and Present,* 86 (Feb, 1980), p. 121.

19. One young man when asked to bow down before the goddess Kali greeted the image with a "Good morning madam." See S.C. Sarkar, "Derozio and Young Bengal," in A.C. Gupta, ed. *Studies in Bengal Renaissance* (Jadavpur: National Council of Education Bengal, 1958), p.20.

20. Kopf, *British Orientalism,* p. 125.

21. Ibid., p.124.

22. Gautam Chattopadhyaya, *Awakening in Bengal: Early Nineteenth Century Selected Documents* (Calcutta: Progressive Publishers, 1965), I, p.201.

23. Ibid., p.131.

24. Ibid., pp. 168, 176, 180-81, 94-96, 277.

25. Ibid., p.94.

26. Ibid., pp.95-96.

27. Ibid., p.277.

28. Johannes H. Voigt, *F.M.Max Muller: The Man and his Ideas* (Calcutta: Firma K.L. Mukhopadhyaya, 1967), p.xi; Georgina Max Muller, ed. *Life and Letters of F. Max Muller* (London: Longmans Green, 1902), p. 72; Voigt, *F. M. Max Muller,* pp.53-58.

29. Max Muller's romantic interest in India was awakened when at the age of ten he saw a picture of Benares in one of his school books which showed men and women on the banks of the Ganga stepping down to bathe in it. Until then he knew of India only as a place where the "people were black" and they "burnt their widows." On his book however they were represented as "tall and beautiful" certainly not like "niggers." The mosques and temples on the banks of the river were so impressive that they looked more majestic than the churches and palaces in his home-town. The young boy was moved enough by the sight to remember it almost fifty years later (Neufeldt, *Max Muller,* p.3).

30. The attention drawn to the Vedas was almost entirely due to their popularization initially by Max Muller and later by R.C. Dutt and Dayananda. When first published by Colebrooke in 1805, it was dismissed as a damp squib. See R.C. Dutt, *A History of Civilization in Ancient India* (1888; rpt. Delhi; Vishal, 1972), p.viii.
31. F. Max Muller, *India: What It Can Teach Us* (London: Longmans Green, 1892), p.57.
32. Quoted in Nirad C. Choudhari, *Scholar Extraordinary; The Life of Rt. Hon. Frederich Max Muller P.C.* (Delhi: Oxford University Press, 1974), p.90.
33. Ibid., p.135.
34. Max Muller, *India,* p.13.
35. F. Max Muller, *Chips From a German Workshop,* I, p.4, cited in Voigt, *F.M. Max Muller,* p.6.
36. F. Max Muller, *Chips From a German Workshop,* I, p.63, in ibid., p.7.
37. F. Max Muller, *A History of Sanskrit Literature* (London: Longmans Green, 1859), p.12.
38. Max Muller, *India,* p.15.
39. Ibid., p.33.
40. Max Muller, *History of Sanskrit Literature,* p.24.
41. A paternalistic concern for the misery of the widow was however evident in Max Muller's activities. He petitioned Queen Victoria on the need to alleviate the pathetic condition of child widows. See Voigt, *F. Max Muller,* p.49.
42. E.T. Stokes, "The Administrators and Historical Writing on India," In *Historians,* ed. Philips, p. 394.
43. Mrs. Speier, *Life in Ancient India,* 1856; rpt. as *Phases of Indian Civilization* (Delhi : Cosmo, 1973) p.39. Subsequent references are cited in the text.
44. Clarisse Bader, *Women in Ancient India* (London: Longmans Green, 1925), p.viii. Subsequent references are cited in the text.
45. The common origin theory worked both ways and affected British attitudes towards Indians. According to one Bengali writer "From being niggers at one time we have now become brethren". See Choudhari, *Scholar Extraordinary,* pp. 316-18.
46. As S.C. Bose put it, "The young man of the future, our heart tells us will be very different," cited in Rosselli, p.126.
47. Grant Duff, *History of the Marathas* (London : Longmans Green, 1826); James Tod, *Annals and Antiquities of Rajasthan, 1829-30,* ed.

William Crooke (London: Oxford University Press, 1920); J.D. Cunningham, *History of the Sikhs*, 1849.

48. See V.G. Hatalkar, "M.G. Ranade": in S.P. Sen, ed. *Historians and Historiography in Modern India* (Calcutta: Institute of Historical Studies, 1973).

49. A.R. Mallik, "Modern Historical Writing in Bengali" in *Historians* ed. Philips, p.451.

50. Ibid., p.449.

51. Ibid.

52. R.C. Majumdar, "Nationalist Historians" in *Historians* ed. Philips, p. 423.

53. Sunil Sen, "Romesh Chandra Dutt" in *Historians* ed. Sen, p.320.

54. Sudhir Chandra, "Lake of Palms : An Essay in Understanding Early Indian Nationalism Without the Imperialist Discourse," unpub. paper, Seminar on Communication and Society, Nehru Memorial Museum and Library, Delhi, July 22-25 1987, p.5.

55. Dutt, *History of Civilization,* p.7.

56. Ibid, pp.-8-9.

57. Ashis Nandy, *The Intimate Enemy : Loss and Recovery of the Self Under Colonialism* (Delhi : Oxford University Press, 1983), p.7.

58. T.W. Clark, "The Role of Bankimcandra in the Development of Nationalism" in *Historians,* ed. Philips, p.435.

59. Ibid., p.436.

60. Ibid., p.437.

61. According to Bankim while the British recorded even their yawns, the modesty of the Hindus meant that there was no 'Hindu' history. The writing of history was thus very important to Bankim. Ibid., p.435.

62. See Sudipto Kaviraj, "The Myth of Infinity: The Construction of the Figure of Krishna in Krishnacarita," Occasional Papers, Nehru Memorial Museum & Library, Delhi, 1987.

63. Thus apart from the assertion of a warrior figure there was also a move towards a 'specific' Hindu identity forged through a recourse to history and a constant reiteration of a link between the past, the present, and the future as in this passage by Bankim: "Who polished the stones with such delicate artistry, was he a Hindu like any one of us?. . . Who carved those female figures,were they Hindus like us? Then I remembered the Hindus, then I recollected the Upanishads, Gita, Ramayana, Mahabharata, Kumara Sambhava, Shakuntala, Panini, Katyayana, Sankhya, Patanjali, Vedanta . . . all these were the

achievements of Hindus. Then I thought blessed am I that I was born a Hindu." Cited in Aravind Poddar, *Renaissance in Bengal : Search for Identity* (Simla : Indian Institute of Advanced Study, 1976), p. 202.

64. Dutt, *History of Civilization,* p.67.
65. Ibid., pp. 73. 169-70.
66. Ibid., pp. 170-71.
67. R.C. Dutt, *Pratap Singh, The Last of the Rajputs* (Allahabad : Kitabistan, 1943).
68. Ibid., pp.8-9, 64-68.
69. The code of conduct for Rajput men in times of crisis requires that they fight to the bitter end after they have ensured that their women will not be ravished. As a young prince tells his mother, "The Rathor fears no human foe, he will fight. But before this the honour of the Rajput ladies must be secured" (Ibid., p. 124).
70. "In the morning sunlight one thousand women performed their baths, offered their prayers and assembled together. The child, the youth, the aged all stood together and with joy in their hearts chanted a prayer. And then? And then in accordance with the ancient Rajput custom the thousand women decked with jewels and ornaments with a joyful cry on their lips mounted the pyre. When defeat, dishonour, and loss of religion are inevitable Rajput women preserve their chastity in this manner." (Ibid., pp. 124-25).
71. Jashodhara Bagchi, "Positivism and Nationalism: Womanhood and Crisis in Nationalist fiction, Bankim Chandra's *Anandmath,"* in Review of Women Studies, *Economic and Political Weekly,* 20, no.43 (Oct. 1985), pp.60-61.
72. Meredith Borthwick, *The Changing Role of Women in Bengal 1849-1905* (Princeton : Princeton University Press, 1984), p. 196.
73. *Bankim Racnabali,* 5th ed. (Calcutta : Sahitya Sangsad 1968), I, p. 374; cited in Ghulam Murshid, *Reluctant Debutante* (Rajshahi : Rajshahi University, 1983), p. 195.
74. Bagchi, p.61.
75. Ibid.
76. J.T.F. Jordens, *Dayananda Saraswati, His Life and Ideas* (Delhi : Oxford University Press, 1978), p.82.
77. Ibid., pp.85-87.
78. Ibid, p.110.
79. Kenneth Jones, *Arya Dharma : Hindu Consciousness in 19th Cen-*

tury Punjab (Delhi : Manohar, 1976), p.32.

80. Nandy, *Intimate Enemy,* p.25.
81. Ibid.; there was thus a political meaning in Dayananda's decision to call his organization the Arya Samaj.
82. Jordens, *Dayananda Saraswati,* p.117.
83. Swami Dayananda, *Satyarth Prakash,* trans. Chiranjiva Bharadvaja (Agra : Arya Pratinidi Sabha, 1915), p.22
84. Uma Chakravarti, *The Social Dimension of Early Buddhism* (Delhi: Oxford University Press, 1987), p.35.
85. Dayananda, *Satyarth Prakash,* p.32; the last two are described by the helpful translator as having 'mental' intercourse. Subsequent references are cited in the text.
86. Jordens, *Dayananda,* p.119.
87. Kailashabashini Devi, *Hindu Mahilaganer Durabasth* (Calcutta: Durgacharan Gupta, 1863), p.44ff; reference and translation provided by Tanika Sarkar.
88. Borthwick, *Changing Role,* p.282.
89. Pandita Ramabai Saraswati, *The High Caste Hindu Woman* (Philadelphia; n.p., 1888), p.xv.
90. Borthwick, *Changing Role,* pp. 347-48.
91. Ibid., p.348.
92. Sarala Debi, *Jibaner Jhara Pata* (1922; rpt. Calcutta: Rupa, 1922), p. 106. I am greatly indebted to Indrani Chatterjee who translated large portions of this book for my use. Subsequent references are cited in the text.
93. Borthwick, *Changing Roles,* p.340.
94. Sumit Sarkar, *Swadeshi Movement in Bengal* (Delhi : People's Publishing House, 1973), pp.304-5.
95. Ibid.
96. Borthwick, *Changing Roles,,* p.340.
97. Sarala Debi, *Jibaner,* p.185-86.
98. Ramabai *The High Caste Hindu Woman* p.x. Subsequent references are cited in the text.
99. Sister Geraldine, comp., *The Letters and Correspondence of Pandita* (Bombay : Maharashtra State Board, 1977), p. 17.
100. Ibid. p.xx.
101. Ibid., p. xxviii.

102. Ibid., p. xxix.

103. Charles Heimsath, *Indian Nationalism and Hindu Social Reform* (Princeton : Princeton University Press, 1964), pp. 184-85.

104. D.V. Tahmankar, *Lokmanya Tilak* (London : John Murray, 1956), pp. 48-49.

105. Heimsath, *Indian Nationalism*, p. 170.

106. Ramabai, *High Caste Hindu Woman*, pp. 65-66.

107. Ibid.

108. Ibid., p.67.

109. Ibid., p.68.

110. Stanley Wolpert, *Ranade and Gokhale* (Berkeley : University of California Press, 1962), pp. 37-38.

111. Ibid., p.38.

112. *Correspondence of Pandita Ramabai*, p. xviii.

113. Ibid., p.xxix.

114. The *Bangabasi* wrote, "this is no reason to write so strongly against the government." See Borthwick, *Changing Roles*, p.339.

115. *Correspondence of Pandita Ramabai,* pp. xiii-iv.

116. Heimsath, *Indian Nationalism*, p.164.

117. Ibid., p.165.

118. Swami Vivekananda, *Complete Works* (Calcutta: Advaita Ashrama, 1958), II, pp.504-5.

119. Ibid., V, p.229.

120. Ibid., IV, p. 476.

121. Ibid., III, pp.506-8.

122. Ibid., V, p.231.

123. Eric Hobsbawm "Introduction : Inventing Traditions" in *The Invention of Tradition,* eds. Eric Hobsbawm and Terence Ranger (Cambridge : University of Cambridge Press, 1983), p.1.

124. Hobsbawm suggests that 'invented' traditions are highly relevant to that "comparatively recent historical innovation, the nation with its associated phenomena: nationalism, the nation state, national symbols, histories" (Ibid, p.13). We might add womanhood to the list. All these rest, according to them, on social engineering which is often deliberate and always innovative.

125. Mothers in Bengal continued to put their babies to sleep with the lullaby.

Chheley ghūmolo, pārā jurolo bargi elo deshey
Bulbulitey āhan kheyechhe, khajina debo kishey

(My child sleeps, the neighbourhood is peaceful, Suddenly the Bargis [Maratha horsemen] come; the birds have destroyed all the crops, with what will we pay the revenue.)
(Bengali folk song translated by Sumanta Banerjee.)

Contentious Traditions:
The Debate on Sati *in Colonial India**

LATA MANI

THE ABOLITION OF *SATI* (widow immolation) by the British in 1829 has become a founding moment in the history of women in modern India. The legislative prohibition of sati was the culmination of a debate during which 8,134 instances of sati had been recorded, mainly, though not exclusively, among upper caste Hindus, with a high concentration — 63 per cent — in the area around Calcutta city.[1] The debate, initiated primarily by colonial officials, is regarded as signifying the concern for the status of women that emerges in the nineteenth century. Colonial rule, with its moral civilizing claims, is said to have provided the context for a thoroughgoing re-evaluation of Indian 'tradition' along lines more consonant with the 'modern' economy and society believed to have been the consequence of India's incorporation into the capitalist world system.[2] In other words, even the most anti-imperialist amongst us has felt forced to acknowledge the 'positive' consequences of colonial rule for certain aspects of women's lives, if not in terms of actual practice, at least at the level of ideas about 'women's rights'.

Among such reinterpreters of Indian tradition, Rammohun Roy holds a privileged place as the first nineteenth century Indian figure to publicly undertake such a critical examination of Indian heritage, both in his stand against sati and also more generally in his attempts to reformulate Hinduism. There is an enormous body

* For their perceptive suggestions and careful reading of earlier versions of this paper, I would like to thank James Clifford, Ruth Frankenberg, Inderpal Grewal, Donna Haraway, Caren Kaplan, Katie King, Thomas Metcalf, Carla Petievich, Kumkum Sangari and Sudesh Vaid.

of literature on Rammohun as the father of the so-called 'Bengal Renaissance' ranging from adulation to denunciation, to the more measured appreciation extended him by Sumit Sarkar, Rajat Ray and others, who have argued that Rammohun should be historicized.[3] Sarkar believes that Rammohun's modernity is contradictory and as such reflects the objective conditions of colonial subjugation which, in his view, produces not a "full-blooded bourgeois modernity" but only a "weak and distorted caricature" of the same.[4] In other words Sarkar sees colonialism as a partial modernizing force and warns against the simplistic application of narratives of progressive modernization to a study of nineteenth century India. This is an important intervention in the debates on modernization. However, it leaves unproblematized the content of the concepts 'tradition' and 'modernity'.

I will argue in this paper that part of the project of historically contextualizing Rammohun and nineteenth century debates on women includes specifying the notion of tradition that they seek to reinterpret. For, as I will show through analysis of the debate on sati, the conception of tradition that Rammohun contests, and the orthodoxy defends, is one that is specifically 'colonial'. My concern with the debate on sati is thus not so much with who was for or against the practice, but rather with how these ideological positions were argued. In other words, my interest is in the discursive aspects of the debate — what various sides assumed about sati, Indian society and the place of women in it, what they understood to be tradition, what counted as evidence, and so on. I will examine official and indigenous discourses on sati focussing on three documents selected out of a larger field of texts as exemplary registers of these discourses. Walter Ewer's letter to the Judicial Department written in November 1818 will represent the official position. Rammohun Roy's 1830 tract in favour of the abolition of sati and the orthodox community's petition protesting the regulation will serve as examples of the 'progressive' and 'conservative' indigenous positions respectively.

I will also examine the constitution of official knowledge about sati. Official knowledge was generated through questioning pundits resident at the courts. The interactions between pundits and judges, pundits and magistrates, are invaluable for plotting the logic of official discourse. Analysing them clarifies how the very formulation of official questions shapes the responses of pundits and how the answers of pundits are interpreted in specific ways by officials. Such moments thus provide the grounds both for naming the discourse as 'colonial' and for questioning its premises.

Since the core argument is somewhat provocative and goes against the grain of the current historiography on social reform, I will present it first in the interest of clarity. It is crucial to add here that this paper is part of a longer project and that in the desire to further debate on the nature of the Bengal Renaissance, particularly its implications for women, I venture to include here claims that are at this stage speculative.

In this paper I will argue the following: First, that tradition is reconstituted under colonial rule and, in different ways, women and brahmanic scripture become interlocking grounds for this rearticulation. Women become emblematic of tradition, and the reworking of tradition is largely conducted through debating the rights and status of women in society. Despite this intimate connection between women and tradition, or perhaps because of it, these debates are in some sense not primarily about women but about what constitutes authentic cultural tradition. Brahmanic scriptures are increasingly seen to be the locus of this authenticity so that, for example, the legislative prohibition of sati becomes a question of scriptural interpretation. Contrary to the popular notion that the British were compelled to outlaw sati because of its barbarity, the horror of the burning of women is, as we shall see, a distinctly minor theme. Second, this privileging of brahmanic scripture and the equation of tradition with scripture is, I suggest, an effect of a 'colonial discourse' on India. By colonial discourse I mean a mode of understanding Indian society that emerged alongside colonial rule and over time was shared to a greater or lesser extent by officials, missionaries and the indigenous elite,[5] although deployed by these various groups to different, often ideologically opposite ends. This discourse did not emerge from nowhere, nor was it entirely discontinuous with pre-colonial discourses in India. Rather, it was produced through interaction with select natives; though, as I will show, officials clearly had power over the natives in question.

This greater power had several consequences. It meant that officials could insist, for instance, that brahmanic and Islamic scriptures were prescriptive texts containing rules of social behaviour, even when the evidence for this assertion was problematic. Further, they could institutionalize their assumptions as Warren Hastings did in 1772, by making these texts the basis of personal law. Official discourse thus had palpable material consequences, of which the constitution of personal law from religious texts is perhaps most significant from the point of view of women. The power underwriting official discourse also ensured its increasing normativity at least among the elite who were compelled, as we shall see, to take account of its key premises. I do not construe the elite as passive in this process, but as wresting these ideas to their own ends.

The claim that the discourse on sati is specifically colonial is approached through an examination of the internal dynamics of the discourse and also by drawing on the work done by Sumit Sarkar contrasting the radical rhetoric of Rammohun Roy in *Tuhfatul Muwahiddin* with that of his later writings.[6] Sarkar has discussed how Rammohun Roy moves from arguments based on reason in *Tuhfat* to arguments that are increasingly reliant on brahmanic scripture. I suggest that this trajectory of Rammohun might be understood as mapping the discursive shift that accompanies colonial rule. In other words, Rammohun's appeal to the scriptures in his later work might have more to do with the colonial insistence on the centrality of scripture to Indian society than on the 'feudal' or 'semi-feudal' character of early nineteenth century Bengal.[7] A claim that such a discursive shift occurred is, of course, far reaching and one that I can only begin to substantiate here. I hope, however, to make a convincing case that such an approach is fruitful and that it raises serious historiographical questions regarding the place of brahmanic scripture in pre-colonial India, the nature and functioning of pre-colonial legal systems and pre-British indigenous discourses on tradition and social reform. These issues seem to me to be especially compelling to an analysis of the consequences for women of such a discourse. For, as I will show, the equation of scripture, law and tradition, and the representation of women *as* tradition produced a specific matrix of constraints within which the question of sati was debated. This grid was fashioned out of the requirements of an expanding colonial power in need of systematic and unambiguous modes of governance, of law, for instance, and out of a particular view of Indian society. These twin features make intelligible the nature and scope of arguments about sati, and the marginality of women to a discourse ostensibly about them.

A note on the focus and method adopted here is in order. This is not a social history of sati. I am not concerned here with what the practice of sati meant to those who undertook it,[8] but with the definition of it generated by colonial officials and with its place and function in debates on the status of women. Further, my reading of the debate is not chronological but discursive, examining that which is specifically colonial and which unifies the superficially different analyses of sati and Indian society advanced by proponents and opponents of legislative intervention.

Walter Ewer: An instance of official discourse[9]

Official discourse on sati was prompted by deliberation on whether it could be safely prohibited through legislation. The concern with safety was premised on the belief that the practice had a basis in scripture and that interference in a religious matter might provoke indigenous outrage. Those opposed to abolition thus emphasized its 'religious' basis and the dangers of intervention, while those in favour of outlawing sati stressed its 'material' aspects (such as the family's desire to be rid of the financial burden of supporting the widow), and thus the safety of legislative prohibition. The two strategies were not mutually exclusive. For instance, abolitionists made use of both 'religious' and 'material' arguments for their position as did those in favour of tolerating sati. Indeed the interplay between the two strategies was often quite complex.[10]

I have demonstrated elsewhere how, even though officials differed in their attitude to sati, both those in favour of abolition and those opposed to it were united in their analysis of Indian society and sati.[11] Stated briefly, I argued that officials advanced their positions from within a common discourse on India whose chief features were the centrality of brahmanic scriptures, unreflective indigenous obedience to these texts and the religious nature of sati. Here I will draw on Walter Ewer, Superintendent of Police in the Lower Provinces, an abolitionist who epitomises the official discourse on sati.

Ewer proposed that the contemporary practice of sati bore little resemblance to its scriptural model, which he defined as a voluntary act of devotion carried out for the spiritual benefit of the widow and the deceased. In reality, he argued, widows were coerced and sati was performed for the material gain of surviving relatives. Ewer suggested that relatives might save the expense of maintaining the widow and the irritation of her legal right over the family estate. Also said to apply pressure on the widow by extolling the virtues and rewards of sati were 'hungry brahmins' greedy for the money due to them for officiating at such occasions.

Even if the widow succeeded in resisting the combined force of relatives and pundits, Ewer held that she would not be spared by the crowd. According to him, "the entire population will turn out to assist in dragging her to the bank of the river, and in keeping her down on the pile."[12] Ewer thus concludes that "the widow is scarcely ever a free agent at the performance of the suttee."[13] According to Ewer, scriptural transgressions, such as the coercion of widows or the performance of sati for material gain, could be the result of ignorance of scriptures, or might reflect conscious design on the part of relatives and pundits. In the former case sati could be abolished without provoking indigenous outrage; in the latter case, sati could not be considered a sacred act and could safely be prohibited.

Ewer's inference of the safety of abolition from instances of individuals acting by design suggests that in his view, when Hindus acted 'consciously' they could not, by definition, be acting 'religiously'. 'Religious' action is, in this perspective, synonymous with passive, unquestioning obedience. If the widow is thus construed as a victim of pundits and relatives, they in turn are seen by Ewer to act in two mutually exclusive ways: either 'consciously' that is 'irreligiously', or 'passively', that is, 'religiously.' Hence Ewer nowhere suggests that pundits and relatives could manipulate religion to their own ends. Ewer submitted that left to herself, the widow would "turn with natural instinct and horror from the thought of suttee."[14] However, in his opinion, given the widow's ignorance and weak mental and physical capacity, it took little persuasion to turn any apprehension into a reluctant consent.

Having demonstrated that the actual practice bears no semblance to a religious rite, Ewer goes on to question the assumption of a scriptural sanction for sati. He points to the heterogeneity of the scriptures on the issue, demonstrating that Manu, "the parent of Hindoo jurisprudence," did not even mention sati, but instead glorified ascetic widowhood. It is important to note that what unites both the 'temporal' and 'scriptural' aspects of Ewer's arguments is the privileging of religion and the assumption of a complete native submission to its force.

The accent on 'will' in Ewer's analysis signals the ambivalence which lies at the heart of the official attitude to sati. It suggests that within the general and avowed disapproval of the practice, there operated notions of 'good' and 'bad' satis. Good satis were those that were seen to be true to an official reading of the scriptures. It was this kind of reasoning that produced the 1813 regulation which defined sati as legal providing it met certain criteria, chief among which was that it be a voluntary act.[15] The Nizamat Adalat or criminal court accordingly instructed magistrates to pay close attention to the demeanour of the widow as she approached the pyre so that officials could intercept at the merest suggestion of coercion. As a result magistrates recorded in the annual returns on sati such remarks as the following: "the widow voluntarily sacrificed herself," "ascended the pyre of her own free will," burnt "without (sic) in any way inebriated and in conformity with the Shaster."

Official approval of sati as long as it was an act of free will was also reflected in a non-horrified announcement of two satis in the *Calcutta Gazette* in 1827, at a time when it was officially maintained that fear of political repercussions was the only reason for tolerating sati. It described the widow as "having abandoned with cheerfulness and her own free will, this perishable frame," and as "having burnt herself with him in their presence with a swelling heart and a smiling countenance."[16] Of course, many officials conceded the possibility of such voluntary satis only in the abstract. Ewer, offered here as the paradigmatic example, insisted that in actuality widows were incapable of consenting and must therefore be protected from pundits and crowds alike.

Analysis of official discourse makes it evident that arguments in favour of prohibiting sati were not primarily concerned with its cruelty or 'barbarity' although many officials did maintain that sati was horrible even as an act of volition. It is also clear that officials in favour of legislative prohibition were not, as it has generally been conceived, interventionists contemptuous of aspects of indigenous culture, advocating change in the name of 'progress' or

Christian principles. On the contrary, officials in favour of abolition were arguing that such action was in fact consistent with upholding indigenous tradition, even that a policy of religious tolerance necessitated intervention. And indeed this was how the regenerating mission of colonization was conceptualized: not as the imposition of a new Christian moral order but as the recuperation and enforcement of the truths of indigenous tradition. C.B. Elliot, Joint Magistrate of Bellah, expressed this sentiment when he suggested that the preamble to the sati regulation should include apposite quotations from the Hindu scriptures so that the indigenous subjects would:

> rejoice in the mercy and wisdom of a government which blends humanity with justice, and consults at once the interests and prejudices of its subjects, by recalling them from practices revolting, and pronounced erroneous even by their own authorities.[17]

Official conception of colonial subjects held the majority to be ignorant of their 'religion.' Religion was equated with scripture. Knowledge of the scriptures was held to be the monopoly of Brahmin pundits. Their knowledge was, however, believed to be corrupt and self-serving. The civilizing mission of colonization was thus seen to lie in protecting the 'weak' against the 'artful', in giving back to the natives the truths of their own "little read and less understood Shaster."[18]

The arguments of officials in favour of abolition were thus developed within the ambit of 'religion.' The pros and cons of sati were systematically debated as considerations of brahmanic doctrines. In employing the scriptures to support their views, the officials were dependent on the *vyawasthas* of court pundits whose exegesis of the texts made them accessible to colonial officials. Vyawasthas were the written responses of pundits to questions put to them by colonial officials on various aspects of sati. However, as I shall demonstrate below, officials interpreted vyawasthas in particular ways so that the concept of sati produced by official discourse was specifically colonial.

Official discourse on sati rested on three interlocking assumptions: the hegemony of religious texts, a total indigenous submission to their dictates, and the religious basis of sati. These assumptions shaped the nature and process of British intervention in outlawing the practice. However, a close reading of the sources, attentive to the nature of evidence advanced for these ideas as well as the social relations of their production, makes it possible to contest this official view.

To begin with, I suggest that the insistence on textual hegemony is challenged by the enormous regional variation in the mode of committing sati. The vyawasthas of pundits had elaborated differences by village and district, even caste and occupation, in the performance of sati: "In certain villages of Burdwan, a district in Bengal, the following ceremonies are observed,"[19] or, "In some villages situated in Benares, the following practices obtain among the widows of merchants and other traders."[20] Local influence predominated in every aspect of sati. For instance the pundits pointed out, "She then proceeds to the place of sacrifice . . . having previously worshipped the peculiar deities of the city or village."[21] In the face of such diversity court pundits concluded, "The ceremonies practically observed, differ as to the various tribes and districts."[22] Colonial officials acknowledged these differences and instructed magistrates to allow natives to follow local custom. However, such diversity was regarded as 'peripheral' to the 'central' principle of textual hegemony.

Similarly, regional variation in the incidence of sati did not serve to challenge the assumption of the hegemony of religion, even though it did count as evidence of a material basis for sati. Colonial officials did not ignore the fact of such variation. The regulation of 1813 had recognized that in some districts sati had almost entirely ceased, while in others it was confined almost exclusively to certain castes. Despite this, officials decided to continue tolerating it, since they believed that in most provinces "all castes of Hindoos would be extremely tenacious of its continuance."[23] Whatever the justification for concluding thus in 1813, such insistence was hardly tenable once systematic data collection was begun in 1815. For it quickly became apparent that 66 per cent of satis were carried out between the area surrounding Calcutta city and the Shahabad, Ghazipur and Sarun districts. This indicates that religion was not hegemonic. Officials however continued to make this assumption, interpreting such regional variation to imply that although 'material' factors might be at play, sati was primarily a religious practice.

If the hegemony of religious texts and its corollary, an unthinking obedience to scripture, is problematized by regional variation in the incidence and mode of performing sati, the representation of widows as perennial victims is similarly debatable. Colonial officials consistently conceptualized women as subjected, whether they were coerced or apparently willing to jump into the flames. The *Parliamentary Papers* contain several accounts of women resisting any attempt to prevent their immolation. Magistrates noted that widows would sometimes threaten relatives seeking to restrain them with the so-called legendary curse of the woman about to commit sati.

It is difficult to know how to interpret these accounts, for we have no independent access to the mental or subjective states of widows outside of these overdetermined colonial representations of them. In any case, the meaning of consent in a patriarchal context is hard to assess. Still, it is fair to assume that the mental states of widows were complex and inconsistent. Some widows were undoubtedly coerced; the decisions of others would be difficult to reduce to 'force.'

What is surprising, though, is that officials persisted in describing as victims, even women who resisted attempts to force them onto the pyre. The annual reports of sati include many instances of women being coerced. Representations of such incidents, however, do not stress the resistance of widows but the barbarity of Hindu males in their coercion. The widow thus nowhere appears as a subject. If she conceded, she was considered victimized by religion. Despite the difficulty of ascertaining the meaning of 'willing' satis, given the absence of women's voices and the historical and cultural variability of such terms as agency and subjecthood, it seems to me that the volition of some widows can justifiably be seen as equal to the resistance of others. Official response to this contradictory evidence, however, was typically to simplify it. Women were cast as either pathetic or heroic victims. The former were portrayed as beaten down, manipulated and coerced; the latter as selflessly entering the raging flames oblivious to any physical pain. Superslave or superhuman, women in this discourse remain eternal victims.

Official representations further reinforced such a view of the widow as helpless by 'infantilizing' the typical sati. The widow is quite often described as a 'tender child.' Here again, analysis of statistics on sati compiled by officials between 1815-29 fails to confirm such a picture, for a majority of satis were undertaken by women well past childhood. In 1818, for example, 64 per cent of satis were above 40 years of age.

Finally, it is important to clarify that this criticism of the absence of women's subjectivity in colonial accounts is not to argue either that women died voluntarily or in any way to condone sati. From my perspective the practice was and remains indefensible. My interest in the representation of women is in the ways official discourse forecloses any possibility of women's agency, thus providing justification for 'civilizing' colonial interventions.

Production of official knowledge on sati: interaction and interrogation

It has been noted already that abolition of sati was made difficult by official claims that it had a scriptural basis. It is now time to examine how officials concluded this. Information about sati was generated at the instance, or rather insistence, of colonial officials posing questions to pundits resident at the courts. The pundits were instructed to respond with "a reply in conformity with the scriptures."[24] The working of colonial power is nowhere more visible than in this process. It is worth examining one such interaction in detail.

In 1805, the question of scriptural sanction for sati was first put to the pundits of the Nizamat Adalat. Specifically they were asked: "whether a woman is enjoined by the Shaster voluntarily to burn herself with the body of her husband, or is prohibited; and what are the conditions prescribed by the Shaster on such occasions?"[25] The response was as follows:

> Having duly considered the question proposed by the court, I now answer it to the best of my knowledge: — every woman of the four castes (brahmin, khetry, bues and soodur) is permitted to burn herself with the body of her husband, provided she has not infant children, nor is pregnant, nor in a state of uncleanness, nor under the age of puberty; or in any of which cases she is not allowed to burn herself with her husband's body.[26]

The pundit clarified that women with infant children could burn provided they made arrangements for the care of such infants. Further, he added that coercion, overt or subtle, was forbidden. In support of his opinion, he quoted the following texts:

> This rests upon the authority of Anjira, Vijasa and Vrihaspati Mooni There are three millions and a half of hairs upon the human body, and every woman who burns herself with the body of her husband, will reside with him in heaven during a like number of years.
>
> In the same manner, as a snake-catcher drags a snake from his hole, so does a woman who burns herself, draw her husband out of hell; and she afterwards resides with him in heaven.
>
> The exceptions above cited, respecting women in a state of pregnancy or uncleanness, and adolescence, were communicated by Oorub and others to the mother of Sagar Raja.[27]

The question posed to the pundit was whether sati was enjoined by the scriptural texts. The pundit responded that the texts did not enjoin but merely permitted sati in certain instances, drawing on quotes which spoke of the rewards sati would bring to widows and their husbands. That the scriptures permit sati can only be inferred from the above passage. Nevertheless based on this response the Nizamat Adalat concluded:

> The practice, generally speaking, being thus recognized and *encouraged* by the doctrines of the Hindoo religion, it appears evident that the course which the British government should follow, according to the principle of religious tolerance . . . is to allow the practice in those cases in which it is countenanced by their religion; and to prevent it in others in which it is by the same authority prohibited. (emphasis mine)[28]

Two moves have been made in reaching this conclusion. The pundit claims that he has answered the question "to the best of my knowledge." However, his response is treated as an altogether authoritative one. Further, permission by inference is transformed into scriptural recognition and encouragement of sati. The formulation of colonial policy on sati was based on the understanding of it produced by this interaction, for this encounter generated the only legislative enactment on sati until abolition. The statement itself was also repeatedly recalled by officials arguing against abolition. Certainly, permission to commit sati was more explicit elsewhere in the scriptures. However, at issue here is not the scriptural accuracy of the pundit's response so much as the arbitrariness so typical of the official interpretation of vyawasthas.

This example embodies many of the key principles by which a body of information about sati was generated. Questions to pundits were intended to establish clarity on all aspects of sati. Thus in 1813 Nizamat Adalat pundits were asked to specify the precise meaning of the phrase "of tender years" in their vyawastha which claimed that a woman with a child 'of tender years' was not permitted sati. Clarification was sought by officials as to the age of the child and whether or not the child had to be weaned before its mother could commit sati.

Pundits were required to comb the scriptures and produce unambiguous scriptural support. Inferential conclusions or recourse to customary practice were only acceptable where explicit documentation was impossible. Thus Magistrate B.B. Gardiner appealed to the Sadr Nizamat Adalat for a clarification of the modes of burning appropriate for various castes, since the pundit at his court had referred only to customary evidence in his response to the question. The pundits at the superior court produced a vyawastha supported by scriptural evidence. Their vyawastha was forwarded to Gardiner by officials at the Sadr Nizamat Adalat with a reprimand to the district court pundit for having "referred to the custom of a country, upon a point expressly provided for by law."[29]

Official insistence on clarity was crucial to enabling the constitution of 'legal' and 'illegal' satis. Through such continual and intensive questioning, criteria for an officially sanctioned sati were generated. Sati had to be voluntary. Brahmin women were permitted only *sahamarana*, burning with the husband's corpse. Non-brahmin women could burn through sahamarana or *anoomarana* (burning with an article belonging to the husband). Sati was forbidden to women under sixteen and to women with infants less than three years. Women of the *jogi* tribe were permitted to bury themselves.

Although scriptural authority was claimed for this model, a careful reading of the *Parliamentary Papers* suggests that such authority was dubious. For example, while officials treated vyawasthas as truthful exegeses of the scriptures in an absolute sense, it is clear from reading the vyawasthas that the pundits issuing them believed them to be interpretive.

Pundits attested to the interpretive nature of their vyawasthas in a number of ways. For one thing, they often characterized their replies as textual readings: "The authorities for the above opinion are as follows." The interpretive character of the vyawasthas was also evident from the way in which the scriptures were used: "In the above sentence by using the words 'she who ascends,' the author *must have had in contemplation* those who declined to do so,"[30] and "From the above quoted passages of the Mitateshura *it would appear that* this was an act fit for all women to perform." (emphasis mine)[31] It is clear from the above that vyawasthas claimed to pronounce neither scriptural truth nor the only possible response to a given question. The corpus of texts designated 'the scriptures' made such a claim difficult to maintain. The scriptures were an enormous body of texts composed at different times. They included the *Srutis,* the *Dharmashastras* or *Smritis* and the commentaries. The fact that the texts were authored at different periods accounted for their heterogeneity on many points, not least of which was the scriptural sanction for sati. Two pundits could thus issue vyawasthas on the same point and quote different texts or different passages from the same text to support their statement.

Official response to such heterogeneity took several forms. In general the older the text the greater was assumed to be its stature. Thus vyawasthas citing *Srutis* or *Smritis* were treated more seriously than those that referred to more recent texts. I shall return to this later. Over and above this general principle, officials sometimes recognized diversity, as in the determination and enforcement of the appropriate modes of burning for Brahmin and non-Brahmin women. At other times they acknowledged textual complexity but for practical reasons did not 'resolve' it, as for example in the considered tolerance of regional variation in the mode of conducting sati: whether the widow's body was placed to the left or right of the corpse, the direction of the pyre, and so on.

A third response was to marginalize certain vyawasthas. A telling example of such strategic marginalization was the fate of Mrityunjoy Vidyalankar's vyawastha.[32] Vidyalankar systematically called into question the colonial rationale of a scriptural sanction for sati. He questioned, among other things, its status as an act of virtue, since it was a practice undertaken not in the spirit of selfless absorption in the divine but with an end to reward. Although Vidyalankar was later to become vocal in his advocacy of sati, his vyawastha contained sufficient scriptural justification for its prohibition. It was, however, ignored. Such continual reinscription of sati into a scriptural tradition despite evidence to the contrary points to the specificity of meanings imposed by official reading of the vyawasthas, and to the production of a conception of sati that is specifically 'colonial.'

The aim of official policy prior to abolition was to ensure adherence to this 'colonial' conception of a 'scripturally authentic' sati. This desire was enabled by an unambiguous definition of sati which officials sought to ensure through scrutiny of the details of its practice. Official presence was required at each sati. Magistrates were asked to tabulate data on each case; personal data on the widow, date, place, time and mode of burning. They were also given explicit instructions to "not allow the most minute particular to escape observation."[33] Such details ensured that no shastric infraction, however small, whether on the part of natives or of the functionaries policing the proceedings, could escape the official eye. Thus we have instances of the Nizamat Adalat reprimanding officers for intervening in cases where the widow and family were well within their scriptural rights in commiting sati. So much for official arguments that sati was 'horrid' and its toleration merely strategic! In addition, whatever the official claims to religious non-interference, the process by which knowledge of sati was produced was specifically 'colonial' and its vigilant enforcement thoroughly interventionist. As the examples above indicate, despite the involvement of Brahmin pundits, the privilege of the final authoritative interpretation of their vyawasthas was appropriated by colonial officials. For it was the Nizamat Adalat judges, the Governor-General and his Council who determined which vyawasthas were 'essential' and which 'peripheral.' The authority of the pundits was problematic. The fact of being native simultaneously privileged and devalued them as reliable sources. The pundits were essential to 'unlocking' the scriptures for officials. But they were also believed by officials to be the "devious minority" against which it was the mission of colonization to protect the "simple majority."

Indigenous progressive discourse on sati

Rammohun Roy's first pamphlet on sati was published in 1818, five years after the colonial administration had authorised a particular version of the practice and three years after systematic data collection on sati had begun.[34] By this time the main features of official discourse on sati had already taken shape. Between 1818 and his death in 1832, Rammohun wrote a great deal on sati. Here I will draw mainly, though not exclusively, on a tract published by him in 1830, a year after the abolition of sati, titled "Abstract of the arguments regarding the burning of widows considered as a religious rite."[35] In Rammohun's own view this pamphlet summarizes his main arguments over the years.[36]

As the title might imply, Rammohun's discussion of sati is grounded from the beginning in a discussion of scripture. As he puts it, "The first point to be ascertained is, whether or not the practice of burning widows alive on the pile and with the corpse of their husbands, is imperatively enjoined by the Hindu religion?"[37] Rammohun suggests in answer to his own rhetorical question that, "even the staunch advocates for Concremation must reluctantly give a negative reply,"[38] and offers Manu as evidence.

> Manu in plain terms enjoins a widow to *continue till death* forgiving all injuries, performing austere duties, avoiding every sensual pleasure, and cheerfully practising the incomparable rules of virtue which have been followed by such women as were devoted to only one husband. (emphasis in original)[39]

Rammohun produces similar proof from *Yajnavalkya* of the widow's right to live with her natal or marital family on the death of her husband. Having established that sati is not incumbent on the widow, Rammohun deliberates which option, sati or an ascetic life, is more meritorious. In this he draws on the Vedas whose authority, he claims, is paramount: "From a desire during life, of future fruition, life ought not to be destroyed."[40] This, most "pointed and decisive" statement, counters in his view the claims of advocates of sati who also refer to the Vedas, but to a passage that Rammohun finds abstract and open to multiple interpretations. The sentence in question is the following: "O fire, let these women, with bodies anointed with clarified butter, eyes coloured with collyrium and void of tears, enter thee, the parent of water, that they may not be separated from their husbands, themselves sinless, and jewels amongst women."[41] Rammohun points out that this passage nowhere enjoins women to commit sati and offers a reading of it as an allegory of the constellation of the moon's path. In this interpretation, butter signifies "the milky path," collyrium "the unoccupied space between one star and another," husbands "the more splendid of the heavenly bodies." Finally, allusions to ascending and entering the fire are understood as "the rise of the constellations through the south-east horizon, considered as the abode of fire."[42] Rammohun thus dismisses this, at best inferential, Vedic support for sati in favour of statements from the Vedas that explicitly recommend ascetic widowhood.

Rammohun then considers the *Smritis* which he designates as "next in authority to the Vedas."[43] The *Smritis* are seen to be ordered hierarchically, with *Manu* heading the list as the text "whose authority supercedes that of other lawgivers."[44] Since *Manu* has already been shown to approve of ascetic widowhood, Rammohun turns his attention to those *Smritis* like *Ungira* and *Hareet* that do appear to place a positive value on sati. Rammohun notes a passage from *Ungira* exalting a widow who commits sati as equal to Arundhati, but dismisses its recommendation of sati as inferior since it is avowedly a "means to obtain future carnal fruition"[45] and as such occupies a lower rung in the spiritual hierarchy of acts.

Having demonstrated that sati is not commanded by the scriptures and argued that, even where it is presented as an option, it is decidedly of inferior virtue as an act undertaken to procure rewards, Rammohun concludes his tract by considering "whether or not *the mode of* concremation prescribed by Hareet and others was ever duly observed." (emphasis in original)[46] Rammohun points out that "these expounders of law" require the widow to voluntarily ascend the pyre and enter the flames. In his opinion violation of either of these provisions "renders the act mere suicide, and implicates, in the guilt of female murder, those that assist in its perpetration."[47] Rammohun, like colonial officials, is here concerned with the thorny question of the widow's will. His view is similar to that of Ewer. He claims "no widow ever voluntarily *ascended* on and *entered* into the *flames* in the fulfilment of this rite." (emphasis in original.)[48] No wonder, he says, that those in favour of sati have been "driven to the necessity of taking refuge in *usage,* as justifying both suicide and female murder, the most heinous of crimes." (emphasis in original.)[49]

It is clear even from this brief discussion that Rammohun's discourse shared key features with official discourse on sati. His case for abolition was grounded primarily in a discussion of the scriptures. Both his first and second pamphlets on sati, in which Rammohun stages dialogues between an advocate and opponent of sati are debates on how the scriptures are to be interpreted. The opponent in both instances takes up, and seeks to demolish, the arguments put forward by advocates of the practice regarding its scriptural foundation. In January 1830, Rammohun joined together with 300 Calcutta residents in presenting a petition to Governor-General William Bentinck in support of the regulation prohibiting sati that had been enacted on December 4, 1829.[50] The petition offers further evidence that sati is not legitimized by scripture. Rammohun and the petitioners argue that sati originated in the jealousy of certain Hindu princes who, to ensure the faithfulness of their widows, "availed themselves of their arbitrary power, and under the cloak of religion, introduced the practice of burning widows alive."[51] According to them the princes then sought to legitimize the practice: "by quoting some passages from authorities of evidently inferior weight . . . as if they were offering female sacrifices in obedience to the dictates of the Shastras and not from the influence of jealousy."[52] Elsewhere in his writings, Rammohun gives further evidence for regarding sati as a material practice, relating its greater incidence in Bengal to women's property rights under Dayabhaga law.[53] Rammohun suggests that such worldly interests are responsible for women being fastened onto the pyre in "gross violation" of the *Shastras.*

At first glance Rammohun does not seem to share the ambivalence that I have argued is characteristic of official attitudes to sati. This ambivalence, I have suggested, sorts satis into good and bad ones, the former being those that are properly voluntary, the latter those involving coercion. By contrast, there is neither qualified approval nor fascination for sati in Rammohun's writings. Indeed Rammohun's analysis of Hindu women's status in society is extremely sophisticated for its understanding of what we now call male domination. For instance, in Rammohun's second conference between an advocate and opponent of sati, the opponent sharply criticises the advocate for imputing faults to women "not planted in their constitution by nature" and then persuading others "to look down upon them as contemptible and mischievous creatures, whence they have been subject to constant miseries."[54] The opponent also proposes that men have taken advantage of their greater physical strength relative to women, to deny "them those excellent merits that they are entitled to by nature, and afterwards they are apt to say that women are naturally incapable of acquiring those merits . . . ."[55] Rammohun was thus clearly cognizant of the societal basis of female subjugation.

Yet, even in this rousing defence of the character of Hindu women, there is evident a certain ambivalence towards sati. Sati functions both as the act confirming the stoicism of women and as the practice that epitomises their weakness. Thus, of the accusation that women lack resolve, the opponent has this to say:

> You charge them with want of resolution, at which I feel exceedingly surprised: for we constantly perceive, in a country where the name of death makes the male shudder, that the female from her firmness of mind offers to burn with the corpse of her deceased husband.[56]

Here Rammohun seems to concede the possibility of 'voluntary' sati. Not only that, he implies that women undertaking sati exhibit heroism and resolve; that sati exemplifies women's strength of mind and character. However, in the very next paragraph Rammohun cites the example of sati to make the opposite claim: the vulnerability of women.

> One fault they have, it must be acknowledged; which is by considering others equally void of duplicity as themselves, to give their confidence too readily, from which they suffer much misery, even so far that some of them are misled to suffer themselves to be burnt to death.[57]

In this instance sati is offered as testimony to women's naiveté, a weakness that is said to make them overly trusting of others. In pointing to the way Rammohun draws on sati to make contradictory claims about women, I am not 'accusing' Rammohun of 'approving' of sati. Rather, I suggest that, even for the staunchest abolitionist, the *idea* of sati continues to provoke ambivalence. This ambivalence is enabled by the construction of woman as either supreme being or victim. It would not have been as credible given a more complex notion of female subjectivity. This discursive construction of sati and of women makes it possible to mobilise the practice to make diametrically opposite claims.

The conservative discourse on sati : the orthodox petition to Bentinck[58]

Whatever ambivalence may have marked 'liberal' discourses on sati is strikingly absent from the conservative writings on the subject, which openly eulogize the practice as one willingly undertaken by devout Hindu widows.

> Under the sanction of immemorial usage as well as precept, Hindoo widows perform of their own accord and pleasure, and for the benefit of their husband's soul and their own, the sacrifice of self immolation called suttee, which is not merely a sacred *duty* but a high privilege to her who sincerely believes in the doctrines of their religion; and we humbly submit that any interference with a persuasion of so high and self-annihilating a nature, is . . . an unjust and intolerant dictation in matters of conscience . . . . (emphasis in original)[59]

Eulogy is, however, not the petition's main focus. The burden of the orthodox argument was to demonstrate that the East India Company's criminalizing of sati was based on an erroneous reading of the scriptures. This is hardly surprising since, as we have seen, the entire debate turned on the issue of sati's scriptural grounding. The orthodox argument did, however, differ in one respect from that of Rammohun and most colonial officials: it assigned a relatively greater weight to custom. The petition claimed that ". . . the Hindoo religion is founded, like all other religions, on usage as well as precept, and one when immemorial is held equally sacred with the other."[60] Thus while Rammohun privileges scripture over custom, criticizing his opponents for "being driven to the necessity of taking refuge in *usage*"[61] the orthodox petitioners argued that the antiquity of Hinduism implied an equal status for both. Nevertheless, despite this claim they proceed to argue their case almost exclusively in terms of scripture.

The orthodox strategy was to undermine the credibility of scriptural interpreters held in esteem by the colonial administration, among them Rammohun, as well as the validity of their interpretations regarding the textual basis for the prohibition of sati. The petition charged the government with deriving their interpretations from apostates.

> But we humbly submit that in a question so delicate as the interpretation of our sacred books, and the authority of our religious usages, none but pundits and brahmins, and teachers of holy lives, and known learning, ought to be consulted . . . not . . . men who have neither any faith nor care for the memory of their ancestors or their religion.[62]

Pundits and Brahmins are proposed as authoritative interpreters and the differences of opinion between them reduced to an opposition between believers and unbelievers. The petition was signed by 800 persons and included pundits of the Government Sanskrit

College, Supreme Court, Nizamat and Diwani Adalat. As we know, the claim that the government was dependent on unbelievers like Rammohun is without basis, since officials had relied primarily on their pundits at the civil and criminal courts where many of the signatories were employed.

The petition was accompanied by a "paper of authorities" signed by 120 pundits presenting scriptural evidence in favour of sati or, in the words of the petition, "the legal points declaring the practice of suttee lawful and expedient."[63] The enclosure sets out objections to the chief arguments of those who advocate the prohibition of sati: that asceticism has greater value than sati, that sati brings temporary rewards, while ascetic widowhood holds the promise of permanent bliss, and that Manu recommends asceticism and has priority over other *Smritis* since his text "is immediately originated from Sruti."[64]

In response to the suggestion that ascetic widowhood is more highly recommended than sati, the petition quotes *Manu* as cited in *Nirnaya Sindhu*: "On the death of her husband, if, by chance, a woman is unable to perform concremation, nevertheless she should preserve the virtue required of widows."[65] Here, the petitioners claim, "the order of meaning has preference over that of reading,"[66] in other words, that ascetic widowhood is a secondary option and one intended for women unable to perform sati. Thus they conclude, clearly overstretching their case, "It appears from the *Shastra* that the first thing which a widow ought to do is to ascend the flaming pile."[67]

The second objection to sati as producing only temporary bliss, is countered with the observation that asceticism is also a "gradual step for final beatitude" and while sati involves only "short term suffering" and delivers "heavenly blessings," ascetic widowhood subjects women to "labouring under austerities for a long time."[68] The greater 'spiritual' value of ascetic widowhood is thus contrasted negatively with what petitioners see as the greater and prolonged material suffering it implies for widows.

Finally, the following case is outlined for why the absence of a positive injunction to sati in *Manu* presents no particular problem for its scriptural status. Firstly it is pointed out that many acts currently performed in society such as Durga puja or *dola jatra* (religious performance) have no basis in *Manu* and yet their performance is not believed to be inconsistent with scripture; indeed their non-performance would be regarded as sinful. It is interesting to note that although the petition begins with a general argument for regarding custom as equally important as scripture, this is the only point on which customary support is cited. In any case, the petition continues, the absence of sati in *Manu* cannot be construed as an argument against it. The *Dattaca Chandrika* is offered as positing the opposite — that "non-prohibition constitutes sanction." Finally, the petition ingeniously proposes, if copies of the *Institutes of Manu* in Bengal neglect to mention sati, this cannot be supposed to be the case generally, for it suggests:

> *the text has been omitted by the mistake of the printers,* for the authors of the *Nirnaya Sindhu* and other works, which are most prevalent in Dravira and other countries, quoted the following text of Manu: "A widow may either practice austerities or commit herself to the flame." (emphasis in original)[69]

A printing mistake is thus made accountable for the status of sati in Manu's text in Bengal!

The petitioners wrap up their case for regarding sati as a scriptural practice, by returning to a consideration of interpretive principles. They suggest that the fragment from the *Rig Veda* "let not these women be widowed . . ." (the passage that Rammohun debunks as obscure) implies that sati was conformable to *Sruti* and proposes that where *Sruti* and *Smriti* conflict, 'the former has preference over the latter."[70] Thus they conclude that "it is unobjectionable that concremation, being enjoined by the Sruti, which is the most prevalent authority and original of all the Smritis, must be performed."[71] Where Rammohun prioritises *Manu Smriti* as a founding text containing "the whole sense of the Veda" and insists that no code be approved which contradicted it, the orthodox petition argued the absolute priority of *Sruti* in every case, although within the *Smritis, Manu Smriti* is conceded a premier position.

A common discourse on sati

It is evident from the foregoing discussion of the official and indigenous arguments for and against sati that, whatever their attitudes to the practice, all participants in the debate on abolition held in common certain key ideas about sati and Indian society, and employed rather similar procedures for arguing their case. Advocates both for and against sati grounded their case in a discussion of brahmanic scriptures, with opponents endeavouring to prove that sati had no clear scriptural status and proponents contesting these conclusions. One could analyse these arguments for logical consistency and conclude that by and large the orthodox pro-sati lobby had a weak case and resorted to disingenuous and facile arguments to make its point. One could also conclude appropriately that the use of scripture was strategic; each side read the texts in a manner that supported its ideological position. However, given my interest in the discursive aspects of the debate, I will adopt a different focus. I will elaborate the internal logic and parameters of the discourse, examine the kinds of arguments admissible within it, and the ideological implications of these for arguing for an improved status for women.

From this perspective what is interesting is the fact that the entire issue was debated within the framework of scripture. In other words, however clumsy or unconvincing the use of scripture in a particular argument, what is significant is the explicit coding of arguments as scriptural. Even Rammohun, commonly regarded as the first modern champion of women's rights, did not base his support for abolition on the grounds that sati was cruel to women. He did of course develop critical analyses of the status of women in India of a more 'secular' variety, but these are marginal to his arguments against sati.

Not only did colonial officials and the indigenous male elite consider the issue mainly in terms of religious texts, they also shared, with minor differences, remarkably similar ideas of what counted as evidence. Scriptural evidence was consistently treated as superior to evidence based on custom or usage. Thus officials ordered pundits to revise vyawasthas that depended on customary practice, and the orthodox petition abandoned customary evidence even though it claimed an equivalence between scripture and usage.

Officials and the indigenous elite also shared general principles for ordering the enormously heterogeneous and unwieldy corpus designated 'the scriptures.' These were ranked as follows: *Srutis, Smritis* or *Dharmashastras*, and commentaries. The *Srutis*, including the Vedas and the *Upanishads* were placed at the apex since they were believed to have been transcriptions of the revealed word of God. Thus the anti-sati petition describes the *Sruti* as "the most prevalent authority, and original of all the Smritis."[72] Next in line were the *Smritis* or *Dharmashastras*, texts supposed to have been written by particular sages. *Manu Smriti* is conceived as the most important among these. Thus Rammohun quotes approvingly Sir William Jones' description of *Manu* as a "system of duties, religious and civil, and of law, in all its branches, which the Hindoos firmly believe to have been promulgated in the beginning of time by Menu . . . . a system so comprehensive and so minutely exact, that it may be considered as the institutes of Hindoo law."[73] As we have seen, Ewer also regards Manu as "the parent of Hindoo Jurisprudence." The orthodox petitioners are less vociferous about the founding status of *Manu*, for their argument for sati was complicated by the text not having addressed the issue. However, they indirectly concede the importance of *Manu*, at least in this debate, by their great pains to prove that Manu's neglect of the issue does not compromise the stature of sati, even going so far as to suggest that the text outside Bengal does contain references to concremation. The problematic status of *Manu* for their perspective also prompts the orthodox community to insist on the priority of *Sruti* over *Smriti* in case of conflict. By contrast, given the value of *Manu* to his position, Rammohun holds *Manu* to override *Sruti* although elsewhere — in his reformulation of Hinduism for instance — it is to the *Upanishads* that he turns.

Another interpretive principle that marks the reading of scripture is the greater value assigned to passages that were explicit in their references to sati. The more literal a passage, the more authoritative its value as evidence. Thus, as we have seen, Rammohun rejects a passage from the *Rig Veda* for being too abstract, while colonial officials reject the testimony of pundits that is in their view based on "mere inference." The orthodox lobby is less committed to literalness since it does not serve them.

To recapitulate, whatever their stands on the prohibition of sati, colonial officials and the indigenous male elite agreed that scripture overrode custom, that explicit scriptural evidence had greater weight than evidence based on inference and that, in general, the older the text the greater its value. This privileging of the more ancient texts was tied to another discursive feature: the belief that Hindu society had fallen from a prior Golden Age. We have noted how the ideology of abolition conceived the prohibition of sati as a restorative act that returned to natives the 'truths' of their own tradition. Bentinck spells this out in his response to the orthodox petition when he claimed that the regulation, by enabling ascetic widowhood, only enforced that which was "commanded above other course [sic] in books usually considered of the highest authority . . . and stated to be adapted to a better state of society; such as by the Hindoos, is believed to have subsisted in former times."[74] Bentinck goes on to note that, by practising ascetic widowhood, widows could be true both to the laws of government and to "the purest precepts of religion."[75] Further, according to Bentinck, the widows would provide "an example to the existing generation of that good conduct which is supposed to have distinguished the earlier and better times of the Hindoo people."[76]

Rammohun also subscribed to the notion that nineteenth century Indian society represented a decline from an earlier greatness. In thanking Bentinck for the prohibition of sati he notes his satisfaction "that the heinous sin of cruelty to females may no longer be committed, and that the ancient and purest system of Hindu religion should not any longer be set at nought by the Hindus themselves."[77] This notion of a fall from grace is also manifest in the claims made, by officials and by Rammohun, that the apparent scriptural legitimacy of sati was secured by tampering with the texts, or as Rammohun put it, by "interpolations and inventions, under the name of traditions."[78] According to Rammohun this necessitated a return to the 'original' texts, in this instance *Manu*, "the only safe rule to guard against endless corruptions, absurdities, and human caprices."[79] It can be argued that this desire to restore the original texts contributed to the general neglect in the debate on sati, of the commentaries written between the eleventh and eighteenth century. The theme of glorious past/degraded present is less prominent in the writings of the orthodoxy since their claim is that sati is part of the original canon and not an 'accretion.' Even so, this idea of a fall grew to be crucial to nineteenth century indigenous discourses, 'progressive' and 'conservative,' and was to intersect with the idea that Britain rescued Hindu India from Islamic tyranny, to produce specifically 'Hindu' discourses of political and cultural regeneration. I will return to this issue below.

I would now like to relate this discussion of the details of the debate on sati to the argument set out at the beginning of this paper, namely, that the concept of tradition is reconstituted in the nineteenth century, that women and scripture are the terms of its articulation and that this development is specifically colonial. So far, I have tried to demonstrate this historical specificity with reference to the process by which knowledge about sati was produced, the ideas that were central and marginal to this process and the ways in which these ideas shaped the main arguments advanced by proponents and opponents of sati both indigenous and official.[80]

My argument regarding the historical specificity of this discourse can also be made from another angle, by contrasting Rammohun's rhetoric in *Tuhfatul Muwahiddin* with that employed by him in the sati debate. I am drawing here on the excellent work of Sumit Sarkar[81] who has argued that the Bengal Renaissance should be regarded "not as a 'torch' race . . . but as a story of retreat and decline."[82] This decline is examined by Sarkar in terms of what he sees as the increasing conservatism of Rammohun's later writings. Sarkar discusses how Rammohun's argument for monotheism in *Tuhfat* is developed rigorously in terms of reason and the criterion of social comfort.

> Only three basic tenets—common to all faiths and hence "natural" are retained: belief in a single Creator (proved by the argument from design), in the existence of the soul, and faith in an afterworld where rewards and punishments will be duly awarded — and even the two latter beliefs are found acceptable only on utilitarian grounds. Everything else — belief in particular divinities . . . faith in divinely inspired prophets and miracles . . . "the hundreds of useless hardships and privations regarding eating and drinking, purity and impurity, auspiciousness and inauspiciousness" is blown up with relentless logic.[83]

Sarkar observes that Rammohun in *Tuhfat* comes "perilously close to the vanishing point of religion,"[84] a position he draws back from in his post-1815 arguments for monotheism, which are primarily grounded in a reinterpretation of the *Upanishads.* As Sarkar puts it, "the claims of reason are now balanced and increasingly limited by Upanishadic authority as well as by a conservative use of the social comfort criterion."[85]

From my perspective, what is significant is that the shift in Rammohun's rhetoric parallels his increasing involvement with colonial presence. It is known, for instance, that Rammohun did not know much English at the time of writing *Tuhfat* in 1803-4. He was at the time employed by Thomas Woodforde in a private capacity at Murshidabad. In 1805 he is said to have formally entered East India Company service under John Digby. There is much controversy over the chronology of key events in Rammohun's life[86] and in any case problems of 'influence' are complex and do not lend themselves to dating in any simple sense. However, one can agree with Rajat K. Ray, that the evidence suggests that the "three main influences in Rammohun's thought — Persian, Vedantic and occidental — were imbibed by him successively, strictly in that chronological order."[87] I would argue that although this may have been the chronological order in which Rammohun encountered these various systems of thought, their influence on him was not cumulative but that he reinterpreted his earlier ideas in terms of the occidental. In other words, the move from a trenchant critique of religion to a strategy which argued for social reform in terms of the scriptural was related to the emerging dominance of an official western discourse on India, a discourse of moral superiority that acknowledged India's greatness but only in terms of her scriptural past.

This colonial discourse not only privileged brahmanic scriptures as the key to Indian society, it distinguished sharply between the 'Hindu' and the 'Islamic,' conceiving of these as mutually exclusive and autonomous heritages. Once again Rammohun's own history is suggestive, for as Sarkar points out, "The Hindu intelligentsia of nineteenth century Bengal (and maybe Rammohun, too, to some extent, after he had mastered English) turned their backs entirely on.... [the] secularism, rationalism, and non-conformity [of] pre-British Muslim ruled India. . . ."[88]

The centrality and importance given to brahmanic scripture by the British and the construction of 'Hindu' law from these texts raises the question of the relationship between brahmanic scripture and society in pre-British India. The British saw themselves as resurrecting an ancient tradition that had been interrupted by the corruption of preceding centuries, but was this in fact the case? Were brahmanic scriptures the basis of law in pre-colonial India? D.D. Kosambi, among others, argues otherwise.[89] Kosambi is sharply critical of the British 'brahmanising tendency' which ignored the laws enforced by caste *sabhas* (associations) and focussed exclusively on brahmanic texts for the formulation of 'Hindu' law.[90] It seems to me that we must pose the following questions: Have brahmanic texts always been prioritized as the source of law? To what extent have pundits been monopolists of scriptural knowledge as officials and Rammohun have claimed? Did this access to scripture give them social or political power? Put another way, did their access to scripture matter? What use of scripture was made by the caste councils that were said to have handled most cases? Is the development of a legal discourse on scripture a colonial phenomenon?[91]

There is interesting evidence in the materials presented here, that in the beginning at least, the responses of pundits appointed to the court did not reflect the kind of authority that colonial officials had assumed, both for the texts and the pundits. As I have discussed, the vyawasthas did not claim to state scriptural truths. Pundits qualified their responses as opinions, their readings as interpretive. In other words their authority was by their own admission circumscribed. Further, vyawasthas drew equally on custom as on scripture, although such responses were invariably treated as marginal and pundits required to revise them. By contrast there is nothing tentative about the 1830 orthodox petition, no qualifiers prefacing textual excerpts. To the petition is attached "a paper of authorities" described as "A translation of *a decision of the legal points* declaring the practice of suttee lawful and expedient." (emphasis mine)[92] The *Asiatic Journal*, in reporting the submission of this petition to William Bentinck, remarks that it is "*accompanied by legal documents.*" (emphasis mine)[93] Here the equation between scripture and law is complete.

Equally significant in its ideological consequences for women was the equation of tradition with scripture. As we have seen, colonial officials, Rammohun Roy and the orthodox Hindu community all deliberated the matter of sati in terms of religious texts. The scriptures, or rather various versions of them, provided the basis for arguments for and against the practice. Given that the debate on sati is premised on its scriptural and, consequently, its 'traditional' and 'legal' status, it is little wonder that the widow herself is marginal to its central concerns. The parameters of the discourse preclude this possibility. Instead women become sites upon which various versions of scripture/tradition/law are elaborated and contested. It is thus that the alternatives to sati are also drawn from the scriptures. There is after all nothing necessarily logical or inevitable about ascetic widowhood as an option. Why widowhood? Why *ascetic* widowhood? Why not an argument for widow remarriage?[94]

The fundamental importance given to scripture in the debate on sati raises the following question: in what ways can it be regarded as an instance of a 'modernizing' discourse? It is clear that the debate was not conducted along lines that are normally held to constitute the modern. It was not a secular discourse of reason positing a morality critical of 'outmoded' practices and a new conception of 'individual rights.' By contrast, as we have seen, at the ideological level the debate was a scriptural deliberation of the legitimacy of sati that was critical of its contemporary form for not being, in a sense, 'outmoded enough,' not true to its original principles. (One must of course insist on the equally mythic status of this so-called original sati.)

The discussion of the rights of women as individuals is also absent except insofar as it is posed indirectly in the context of the widow's will. As we have seen, this will is conceded primarily in the abstract and only reluctantly, and by a few, in practice, thus justifying interventions on the widow's behalf, whether by the European official or the indigenous male social reformer. However, whatever the scepticism regarding the widow's subjecthood, this concern with individual will may itself be read as suggesting the modernity of this discourse.

But the discourse on sati was also modern in another more important sense: it was a modern discourse on tradition. It exemplifies late eighteenth century colonial discourses that elaborated notions of modernity against their own conceptions of tradition. I suggest, in other words, that what we have here is not a discourse in which pre-existing traditions are challenged by an emergent modern consciousness, but one in which both 'tradition' and 'modernity' as we know them are contemporaneously produced. The modernity of this discourse on tradition needs to be more fully recognized.

Tradition in this discourse is posited as a timeless and structuring principle of Indian society enacted in the everyday lives of indigenous people. 'Tradition,' interchangeable for the most part with 'religion' and 'culture,' is designated as a sphere distinct from material life. It is thus that officials can speak of returning to natives the truth of traditions that had been interrupted by the 'Islamic interlude.' This conception is also evident in Ewer's arguments that when Indians acted religiously they acted passively, and in his legitimization of intervention in sati given evidence for it as a material practice.[95]

There are two consequences to this concept of culture or tradition as a transhistorical and ubiquitous force acted out by people. Firstly, it produces analyses of sati in purely 'cultural' terms that empty it of both history and politics. Secondly, this notion of culture effectively erases the agency of those involved in such practices. However, as we noted in Ewer's description of how the widow is dragged to the river, not everyone involved in a sati is seen to be equally subjected to the imperatives of culture. Family members, especially the males, and the pundits present at the pyre are given alternate subject positions. The former are often seen to be acting in their own interest, the latter almost always so. Such interest is always coded as corrupt and to the detriment of the widow. Even so, within the general subjection of all indigenous people to 'religion' or 'tradition,' men are offered some measure of will.

Not so the widow. She is consistently portrayed as either a heroine — entering the raging flames of the pyre with no display of emotion — or an abject victim — thrown upon the heap, sometimes fastened to it by unscrupulous family members or pundits. We saw both these in Rammohun's descriptions of sati. These poles, 'heroine' and 'victim' preclude the possibility of a complex female subjectivity. Indeed, given the definition of tradition operative in the discourse on sati, the portrayal of the immolated widow as heroine merely rewrites her as victim of an higher order: not of man but of God (or religion). This representation of the widow makes her particularly susceptible to discourses of salvation, whether these are articulated by officials or the indigenous elite. It thus comes as no surprise that both offer to intercede on her behalf, to save her from 'tradition,' indeed even in its name.

We can concede then, that women are not subjects in this discourse. Not only is precious little heard from them, but as I have suggested above, they are denied any agency. This does not, however, imply that women are the objects of this discourse; that this discourse is *about* them. On the contrary, I would argue that women are neither subjects nor objects, but rather the ground of the discourse on sati. For as we saw, analysis of the arguments of participants very quickly indicates that women themselves are marginal to the debate. Instead, the question of women's status in

Indian society posed by the prevalence of widow burning becomes the occasion for struggle over the divergent priorities of officials and the indigenous male elite.

Indeed, as the nineteenth century progresses, at a symbolic level, the fate of women and the fate of the emerging nation become inextricably intertwined. Debates on women, whether in context of sati, widow remarriage or *zenanas* (seclusion of women), were not merely about women, but also instances in which the moral challenge of colonial rule was confronted and negotiated. In this process women came to represent 'tradition' for all participants: whether viewed as the weak, deluded creatures who must be reformed through legislation and education, or the valiant keepers of tradition who must be protected from the first and be permitted only certain kinds of instruction. For the British, rescuing women becomes part of the civilizing mission. For the indigenous elite, protection of their status or its reform becomes an urgent necessity, in terms of the honour of the collective — religious or national. For all participants in nineteenth century debates on social reform, women represent embarrassment or potential. And given the discursive construction of women as either abject victims or heroines, they frequently represent both shame *and* promise.[96]

Tradition was thus not the ground on which the status of woman was being contested. Rather the reverse was true : women in fact became the site on which tradition was debated and reformulated. What was at stake was not women but tradition. Thus it is no wonder that even reading against the grain of a discourse ostensibly about women, one learns so little about them. To repeat an earlier formulation: neither subject, nor object, but ground — such is the status of women in the discourse on sati.

I suggest that part of what enables this intimate interlocking of women and tradition is that this was a discourse of salvation: a recuperation of authenticity and purity, a vigorous protection of the weak and subordinated aspects of culture against their corrupt manipulation by the strong and dominant. We can see how easily this conception of tradition can intersect with patriarchal notions about women as pure, weak and submissive to produce a discourse in which both are intimately interwoven.

Epilogue

We have accepted for too long and at face value, the view that colonization brings with it a more positive reappraisal of the rights of women. It is of course true that women become critical matter for public discourse in the nineteenth century. But does this signify concern for women, or do women become the currency, so to speak, in a complex set of exchanges in which several competing projects intersect? The contemporary example that illustrates an analogous situation — and one which also exemplifies the continuing persistence of colonial discourse — is the Shahbano case. On April 23, 1985 the Supreme Court of India in the *Mohammed Ahmed Khan vs Shahbano Begum* case gave divorced Muslim women the right to lifelong maintenance. Mohammed Khan, Shahbano's ex-husband had contested her claims for maintenance insisting that he had, according to Muslim personal law, supported her for three months after their divorce. The Supreme Court stressed that there was no conflict between its verdict and the provisions of Muslim personal law which, in its view, also entitled women to alimony if they were unable to maintain themselves. The judgement has sparked off nationwide controversy on the question of religious personal law and the desirability or otherwise of a uniform civil code. The Shahbano case dramatizes the working of the woman-tradition-law-scripture nexus, now complicated by a political environment that is blatantly communal.

The Shahbano affair has raised many of the same questions as the debate on sati: issues of scriptural interpretation, the relation between scripture and society, the role of protective legislation for women, the tension between Shahbano as an individual and Shahbano as a member of a community. Still current, though challenged by feminists and other progressives, is the notion of women and scripture as repositories of tradition. There are also important differences. Shahbano initiated legal action against her husband, while intercession in sati was undertaken not by widows but on their behalf. In addition, there has been active participation by women and feminists in the debate, and a successful pushing of the parameters of the discussion, so that it has not (unlike sati) developed merely, or even primarily, as a scriptural issue.

Despite this, elements of an earlier colonial discourse haunt the debate and entangle it. Communalism, whose emergence is inextricably linked with colonialism, conditions what strategies are appropriate in the case at the present time. We are required to maintain a delicate balance. On the one hand we need to counter the arguments of Muslim fundamentalists who claim that 'an attack on Muslim personal law is an attack on the Muslim community as such.' (One can see in this claim, the equation between law, scripture and the integrity of religious identity that underwrote the colonial ideology of so-called 'non-interference,' an equation that was later key to the arguments of the indigenous orthodoxy in favour of sati.) Simultaneously, we need to challenge disingenuous Hindu fundamentalists and others who, carrying on the civilizing mission, are lamenting the fate of Muslim women and demanding that they be brought 'into the twentieth century.' (The echoes of colonial rhetoric here are too obvious to labour.)

One progressive response to the Shahbano affair has been to defer the demand for a uniform civil code given current communal tensions, and to seek instead reforms in specific aspects of personal law. Other progressives have persisted in the desire for a uniform civil code, suggesting that demands for legal reforms should be rooted in political principle and that political space should not be conceded to fundamentalists in either camp — Hindu or Muslim. Whatever one's strategy, we are all inscribed in the webs of a history whose claims on us are real and pressing. If Rammohun's arguments against sati were shaped by the discursive and political context of early nineteenth century Bengal, we are faced with a situation that can be said to represent the unfolding of this same discursive and political history. And our interventions will in turn set precedents for the struggles to come.[97]

I believe it is important to write the history of colonial discourse, to trace its effects on the constitution of our systematic and commonsense knowledges of our tradition, culture and identity. Given the colonial privileging of scripture, is it any wonder that when we speak of tradition with a capital 'T' it invariably refers to a textual tradition? Similarly, how far has the nineteenth century location of culture and tradition in texts contributed to analyses that treat both as essentially unchanging? Such a perspective is implicit in statements regarding 'the antiquity of Indian culture' or 'the weight and persistence of tradition,' or in discussions of the status of women in India that begin with unqualified references to *Manu Smriti* and the scriptures. Historically grounded analyses of nineteenth century social reform that take seriously the notion of a colonial discourse on India can serve to preclude analytic complicity with this discourse, or its replication. Such work would clarify the continuities and discontinuities in the ideologies of colonial and post-colonial debates on women. Equally significant, it will problematize once and for all, any insertion of these debates into narratives of progressive modernization in which the meaning of the terms 'tradition' and 'modernity' are assumed, not specified.

NOTES

1. These figures are drawn from the *Parliamentary Papers on Hindoo Widows,* (hereafter *PP*). The 8,134 satis were recorded between 1815-28. The proportion of burning in the Calcutta region is an average for this period. Break-down of satis by caste has been tabulated in the *PP* for 1823: Brahmin 234; Kayasth 25; Vaisya 14; Sudra 292 (source *PP*, 1825). Sati was proportionately higher among Brahmins.
2. There is considerable debate among political economists as to whether or not colonial rule produced conditions that were favourable to the development of capitalism in India. For instance, A.K. Bagchi has argued that colonial rule de-industrialized India. See his "De-industrialization in India in the Nineteenth Century: Some Theoretical Implications," *Journal of Development Studies*, 12 (1975-76), pp. 135-64. This debate does not affect my argument here for, whatever their analysis of the impact of colonialism on India's transition from feudalism to capitalism, all scholars agree that colonialism held the promise of modernity and inspired a critical self-examination of indigenous society and culture.
3. See V.C. Joshi, ed. *Rammohun Roy and the Process of Modernization in India* (Delhi: Vikas, 1975), especially Sumit Sarkar, "Rammohun Roy and the Break with the Past," pp. 46-68 and Rajat K. Ray's introduction to the volume, pp. 1-20.
4. Sarkar in *Rammohun Roy*, ed. Joshi, p. 63.
5. For my purposes the elite may be defined as well-to-do, urban, mercantile and/or landed individuals whose business and social activities required them, in one way or other, to confront and negotiate the apparatus of the East India Company.
6. Sarkar in *Rammohun Roy*, ed. Joshi, pp. 47-55.
7. I do not suggest here that nineteenth century Bengal is neither feudal

nor semi-feudal, but that Rammohun's use of scriptural arguments should be understood not as a 'feudal residue,' but in terms of the emerging dominance of a colonial discourse on India.

8. For a very suggestive discussion that relates early nineteenth century sati to socio-economic changes wrought by colonial rule see, A., Nandy, "Sati: A Nineteenth Century Tale of Women, Violence and Protest," in *Rammohun Roy*, ed. Joshi, pp. 168-94.
9. This discussion of official discourse draws on the more detailed analysis presented in my article "The production of an official discourse on sati in early nineteenth century Bengal," Review of Women Studies in *Economic and Political Weekly*, 21 no 17 (26 April 1986), pp. 32-40. This article documents the legislative history of sati and includes a fuller discussion of the institutional context of the debate. Parts of it are included here since my arguments in this paper build on this earlier work. For Walter Ewer's letter, see *PP* 1821, xviii, pp. 521-23.
10. "Material" in official discourse refers to anything that can be shown to be without basis in scripture or counter to it. Given British colonial assumptions regarding the hegemony of scriptural texts and the passive relation to them of indigenous people, this category often included actions that represented will, whether of individuals or groups. To say more here, however, would be to anticipate my argument.
11. Mani, pp. 34-36.
12. *PP*, 1821, p. 521.
13. Ibid.
14. Ibid.
15. For the legislative history of sati, see Mani, pp. 33-34.
16. *PP*, 1828, xxiii, p. 169.
17. *PP*, 1830, xxviii, p. 918.
18. *PP*, 1821, p. 532.
19. Ibid., p. 410.
20. Ibid., p. 411.
21. Ibid., pp. 410-11.
22. Ibid., p. 412.
23. *PP* 1821, p. 321.
24. Ibid., p. 406.
25. Ibid., p. 322.
26. Ibid.

27. Ibid., p. 323.
28. Ibid., p. 325.
29. Ibid., p. 334.
30. Ibid., p. 407.
31. Ibid.
32. Vidyalankar's vyawastha is included in the appendix to the 1817 proceedings of the Nizamat Adalat and appears to have been written by him after becoming pundit of the Supreme Court in July 1816. It thus precedes Rammohun's first pamphlet on sati which was published in 1818. Vidyalankar and Roy furnished officials with sufficient scriptural grounds for prohibiting sati; but abolition came over ten years later. Its timing was related to political factors and not primarily, as officials had claimed, to ambiguity of the scriptures (see Mani).
33. *PP* 1821, p. 327.
34. "Translation of a conference between an advocate for and an opponent of the practice of burning widows alive," Calcutta, 1818. Two years later, Rammohun published "A second conference between an advocate for and an opponent of the practice of burning widows alive," Calcutta, 1820. See *The English Works of Raja Rammohun Roy*, vol 2, ed., J.C. Ghose (New Delhi: Cosmo, 1982).
35. Ibid., pp. 367-84.
36. Chronology is not significant here since the nature and structure of Rammohun's arguments remained essentially the same throughout his campaign against sati.
37. *English Works*, pp. 367-84.
38. Ibid.
39. Ibid.
40. Ibid.
41. Ibid.
42. Ibid.
43. ibid.
44. Ibid.
45. Ibid.
46. Ibid.
47. Ibid.
48. Ibid.
49. Ibid.

50. "Address to Lord William Bentinck," 16 January 1830, *English Works*, pp. 475-77. This petition was specifically intended to counter the mobilizing efforts of the anti-sati lobby and was believed to have been drafted by Rammohun. See, editor's note, *English Works.*
51. Ibid.
52. Ibid.
53. "A pamphlet of Rammohun Roy containing some remarks in vindication of the Resolution passed by the Government of Bengal in 1829 abolishing the practice of female sacrifices in India," 1831, in J.K. Majumdar, ed. *Raja Rammohun Roy and Progressive Movements in India* (Calcutta: Art Press, 1941), pp. 186-87.
54. *English Works*, p. 360.
55. Ibid.
56. Ibid., p. 361.
57. Ibid.
58. "The petition of the orthodox community against the Suttee regulation, together with a paper of authorities, and the reply of the Governor-General thereto," 14 January, 1830, in *Raja Rammohun*, ed. Majumdar, pp. 156-63.
59. Ibid.
60. Ibid.
61. Rammohun, "Abstract of the arguments etc.," *English Works*, p. 372.
62. "Petition of the orthodox community etc.," in *Raja Rammohun*, ed. Majumdar, p. 157.
63. Ibid., p. 159.
64. Ibid., p. 160.
65. Ibid.
66. Ibid., p. 161.
67. Ibid.
68. Ibid.
69. Ibid., p. 162.
70. Ibid.
71. Ibid.
72. Ibid.
73. "A pamphlet of Rammohun Roy containing some remarks in vindication of the resolution etc.," in *Raja Rammohun*, ed. Majumdar, p. 188.
74. "The petition of the orthodox community etc.," in *Raja Rammohun*,

ed. Majumdar, p. 162.

75. Ibid., p. 163.

76. Ibid.

77. "Address to Lord William Bentinck etc.," *English Works*, p. 477.

78. "A pamphlet of Rammohun Roy containing some remarks in vindication of the resolution etc.," in *Raja Rammohun*, ed. p. 189.

79. Ibid.

80. The argument that the scripturalizing of tradition is specifically colonial is also borne out in my analysis of Baptist missionary preaching narratives from this period. Here missionaries are to be found interrogating peasants on the scriptural authority for their 'religious' practices and responding to their inability to answer such questions with the accusation that the peasants were ignorant of their own tradition! Mani, "Early Missionary Discourse on India : The Journals of Carey, Marshman and Ward," unpublished ms.

81. Sarkar in *Rammohun Roy.*, ed. Joshi.

82. Ibid., p. 47.

83. Ibid., pp. 49-50. It is important to note that reason here is located within the tradition of Islamic rationalism.

84. Ibid., p. 50.

85. Ibid., pp. 53-54.

86. See the editors' comments in S.D. Collett, *The Life and Letters of Raja Rammohun Roy*, eds. D.K. Biswas and P.C. Ganguli (Calcutta: Sadharan Brahmo Samaj, 1962).

87. Ray in *Rammohun Roy*, ed. Joshi, p. 7.

88. Sarkar in *Rammohun Roy*, ed. Joshi, pp. 52-53.

89. D.D. Kosambi, "Combined Methods in Indology," in A.J. Syed, ed. *D.D. Kosambi on History and Society* (Bombay: University of Bombay, 1985), pp. 1-2. There is, in addition, a rich body of literature on law in colonial India. For references, see Mani, fn. 9.

90. Kosambi's criticism of such textualism also extends to reformers like R.G. Bhandarkar arguing against widow remarriage in terms of the *Rig Veda* without reference to actual social practice, and to P.V. Kane whose *History of Dharmashastras* is castigated for restricting "the discussion to *smriti* documents, avoiding any disagreeable contact with anthropology, sociology or reality" (ibid. p. 2). Kosambi's criticism, rooted in a materialist conception of history, is well taken. I would, however, suggest that in addition the strategies of Bhandarkar and Kane should be historicized.

91. Needless to say, similar questions need to be posed regarding the constitution of Islamic personal law. Such an analysis would probably find parallel processes of codification at work, as also similar ambivalences towards women.

92. "The petition of the orthodox community etc.," in *Raja Rammohun*, ed. Majumdar, p. 159.

93. *Asiatic Journal*, June 1830, in *Raja Rammohun*, ed. Majumdar, p. 172.

94. In this respect it is interesting, as Sumit Sarkar notes, how Rammohun's painstaking detailing of the merits of ascetic widowhood was to complicate Vidyasagar's case for widow remarriage! Sarkar in *Rammohun Roy* ed. Joshi, p. 53.

95. This conception of tradition finds its clearest expression in descriptions of incidents of sati and in what Mary Pratt has elsewhere termed the "manners and customs" material, discussion of which is beyond the scope of this paper. See Mary Louise Pratt, "Scratches on the Face of the Country; or What Mr. Barrow Saw in the Land of the Bushmen," *Critical Inquiry*, "Race, Writing and Difference" 12, no. 1 (Autumn 1985), pp. 119-43.

96. For an excellent analysis of the ambivalent attitudes to women of social reformers active in the debate on widow remarriage, see Sudhir Chandra, "Widow Remarriage and Later Nineteenth Century Literature," unpublished ms.

97. I do not intend to suggest that communalism today is essentially the same as communalism in pre-independent India. Nor am I interested in blaming colonialism for all our current ills. The point here is to document the way colonial history shapes the present, to question the 'post' in 'post-colonial.'

Marginalization of Women's Popular Culture in Nineteenth Century Bengal*

SUMANTA BANERJEE

> The entertainments, diversions and festivities of the common people are all disappearing one by one. There are no *jatras* now, no panchalis, not to speak of *kobis*. With what will the common folks live . . . ?
>
> BASANTIKA[1]

> Taking all matters into consideration, the poor woman of this country should be an object of compassion rather than of our contempt. The stimulus given to India by British example, and capital employed for the education of Indian females, is not among the least of her beneficial operations. The time will come when their worth shall be duly appreciated by the daughters of India; and then, should this work chance to be perused by them, they will sigh at the follies of their ancestors, smile at their own good fortune . . .
>
> CAPT. N. AUGUSTUS WILLARD[2]

CAPT. WILLARD, who wrote these lines in 1834, was appealing to his countrymen to consider sympathetically the plight of Indian women who were "perfectly ignorant of all knowledge." One sign of such ignorance, which shocked Willard and his English contemporaries, was that these women were fond of singing songs that "mostly appear to be licentious and voluptuous."[3]

Englishmen, like Willard, who came to Bengal in the eighteenth and nineteenth centuries, carried two burdens: the 'white man's burden' of educating the unenlightened natives, and the 'man's burden' of emancipating native women from what they considered to

* The present article is largely based on data collected by the author in the course of a research project (1985-86) on the popular culture of nineteenth century Calcutta, funded by the Indian Council of Social Science Research, Delhi. In translating excerpts from Bengali songs and poems into English, some liberty has been taken to convey the mood and the message, rather than merely the literal meaning.

be a socio-cultural milieu of utter ignorance and impurity. The latter burden came to be shared by the English-educated Bengali ***bhadralok*** of the nineteenth century (sons of absentee landlords, East India Company agents and traders who made fortunes in the eighteenth century, various professionals and government servants) all of whom, in spite of differences in economic and social status, were moving towards the development of certain common standards of behaviour and cultural norms. They played a leading role in implementing a model of female education in Bengal that was primarily fashioned by contemporary English missionaries, educationists and administrators. The Bengali bhadralok's concept of the emancipation of women was derived from these new teachers but was, at the same time, considerably modified by the patriarchal norms of traditional Hindu society. It was a concept shared over time by the women of their families.[4]

There were subtle differences among members of the nineteenth century Bengali urban elite over the extent to which women should be educated and allowed free movement in society. However, they all agreed on the need to eradicate what they were trained to believe was the pernicious influence of certain prevailing literary and cultural forms on Bengali women, particularly on the women belonging to their own homes. These forms, some traditionally rural, others born in the course of urbanization in nineteenth century Calcutta, emerged primarily from the lower economic social groups and represented a popular culture that ran parallel to what could be called the 'official culture' propagated by the bhadralok. Many of these forms — doggerels and poems, songs and theatrical performances — were fashioned by women who remained outside the framework of the formal education introduced by English missionaries and scholars. Significantly, in nineteenth century Bengal in general and Calcutta in particular, this popular culture had a wide female audience, ranging from the lower caste and lower class self-employed women of the marketplace, to the wives and daughters of the bhadralok in the sheltered *andarmahal* or *zenana* (secluded quarters for women).

Women of nineteenth century Bengal, like women in other regions, were not economically or socially a homogenous group. Their life styles and occupations, according to a contemporary observer, varied depending on whether they were "women of rich families," "women of the middle station," or "poor women." While women of the "rich" and "middle station" stayed in seclusion in the andarmahals, the majority were working women, either self-employed like *naptenis* (women from the barber caste who used to decorate with *alta* [red liquid] the feet of andarmahal women), sweepers, owners of stalls selling vegetables or fish, street singers and dancers, maidservants, or women employed by mercantile firms dealing in seed produce, mustard, linseed etc.[5] The poorer class of women used whatever time they had left after housework to assist the men in the traditional occupations like cultivation, pottery, spinning, basket-making etc. Such participation extended to cultural activities like community singing and dancing during festivals, as well as to *bratas* (rituals relating mainly to birth, marriage and death) meant exclusively for women and performed with a view to attaining their aspirations.

Because of the nature of their work, these women had to move in that 'dangerous society' which was considered to be a threat to their sheltered sisters who lived in the andarmahals of upper class Bengali gentlefolk. For the members of the zenana, it was often this vast multitude of working women (like naptenis, sweepers or singers) who had access to the andarmahal and so provided the only link to the outside world. Even as *Bamabodhini Patrika* and other advocates of women's emancipation were warning against the appearance of bhadralok women in public, almost every year women from the lower groups not only congregated in public, but also sang and danced during popular festivals. Describing a fair on the occasion of Raas (held to celebrate Krishna's carousel with the milkmaids), the Bengali weekly *Somaprakash* reported: "Ninety nine per cent of the participants were women, and one per cent men . . . and of this ninety nine per cent again, ninety nine per cent were young women. . . ."[6] A few months later, the same paper, describing another religious festival at Ghosepara near Calcutta said: "Of the participants, eighty per cent are women."[7]

With the decline of the village economy and the beginnings of industry in nineteenth century Bengal, there was a regular exodus of poorer men and women from the countryside to Calcutta. These were mainly artisans engaged in small scale occupations. They settled down in different parts of the 'black town' (the areas in Calcutta inhabited by the indigenous population, as opposed to the 'white town' which was the exclusive preserve of the Europeans). Each group occupied a distinct quarter in the town, which bore the name of its respective profession. Although they and their descendants have long since disappeared, these areas of Calcutta still continue to be known by those old names. Thus, Kumartuli in north Calcutta, was the settlement of the *kumars* or potters; Colootala of the *kolus* or oilpressers; Patuatola of the *patuas* or painters; Sankharitola of the *sankharis* or conch shell workers.

These Bengali villagers brought with them into Calcutta the songs they inherited from rural folk culture with their own poetic rules, their own musical scales and rhythms. Along with their women, they not only kept alive the old folk culture in the squalor of the growing metropolis of Calcutta, but enriched it with new motifs borrowed from the surrounding urban scenes. The street literature of nineteenth century Calcutta — songs, dances, doggerels, theatrical performances, recitations — became a great melting pot of tradition and topicality.

The appeal of these popular forms cut across the economic divisions among Bengali women of the nineteenth century. Folklore, from which street literature derived, was essentially a shared experience. There was no sharp distinction between high and low. In their cultural preferences and practices, women of all classes therefore shared a common interest in certain types of literature — an interest which continued almost till the beginning of the present century. This was possible because the literary creations of the lower economic groups, particularly those fashioned by the women of these groups, retained particular traditional features and used specific dialects and idioms[8] which were common to women of almost all classes of households in nineteenth century Bengal. A schism in this cultural homogeneity among Bengali women appeared with the spread of the new system of female education to the zenanas of bhadralok homes.

By the end of the nineteenth century this system of education had produced a new breed of women in bhadralok homes who, by their writings, cultivated patterns of behaviour which displaced women's popular culture from Bengali middle class society. The old popular culture which had rested on the social ties binding together women from different classes was discarded, and retained only by women of the lower social strata who did not relinquish their commitment to it as rapidly as the others. But finally, even they had to grasp the logic of an altered social world, and the old forms of women's popular culture withered.

The close proximity among the various socio-economic groups of women through their predilection for particular cultural genres in nineteenth century Bengal, often led the educated Bengali bhadralok to club together women in general (including those from elite homes) with lower social groups. Describing the contemporary cultural scene, one leading weekly reported: "Wherever there are *sangs* [pantomimes, lampooning familiar social types] and farces, you'll find the vulgar masses, children and women."[9] The same paper, referring to the decline in the popularity of *kathakata* (reading and exposition of mythological stories in the colloquial language, often in contemporary terms of reference) among the *sushikshita dal* (well-educated groups), commented: ". . . only women and the lower orders are its [i.e. kathakata's] admirers. . ."[10]

These attitudes of educated Bengali men influenced their entire concept of women's emancipation. Attempts at the cultural emancipation of women in nineteenth century Bengal often boiled down to strenuous efforts to wean away their own wives and daughters from those forms of popular culture which were beginning to be associated in the minds of the bhadralok with the "licentious and voluptuous tastes" of the *itarjan* or the 'vulgar' populace. While initiating social reforms such as women's education, widow remarriage, ban on child marriage and on kulin Brahmin polygamy, which were primarily aimed at bringing about changes in Bengali *sambhranto* (respectable upper classes and upper castes) homes where the women in many respects enjoyed less freedom than women of the 'lower orders' the male bhadralok undoubtedly paved the way for the 'emancipation' of their womenfolk — an emancipation which meant greater participation for women in the new social milieu and cultural affairs of educated society.[11] But, in the process, indigenous forms of women's popular culture were suppressed (often tarred with a brush dipped in moral values) through the imposition of cultural norms newly acquired by the male bhadralok from their English mentors. The denunciation of popular culture was simultaneous with the formation of a new bhadralok culture.

The present article argues that some of the main forms of popular culture in nineteenth century Bengal, in the composition and appreciation of which women of lower social groups took a leading part, expressed certain concerns, experiences and aspirations which appealed to most or all contemporary women. The mode of expression, the dialect and the idiom of popular cultural forms manifested a power and a robust sense of humour which were to be markedly absent in the future literary compositions of 'emancipated' and 'educated' women from bhadralok homes. Often stark and bitter in expressing the plight of women in a male-dominated society, the poems and songs popular among the lower social groups were, at the same time, tough, sensuous or bawdy, in an idiom specific to women. Further, the Bengali bhadralok, influenced by colonial education, began to look down upon the cultural products of the lower groups as manifestations of vulgar taste and often perceived them as threats to the newly emerging cultural integrity of their own domestic lives.[12]

Their concerted and consistent ideological campaign — often backed by administrative sanctions — against these popular literary productions, combined with other socio-economic factors (e.g. the diminishing number of old patrons, the rise of the book culture) led initially to the marginalization, and finally to the exile from urban society, of both these specific forms of women's culture and of their women 'practitioners'. The gradual elimination of women folk performers from Calcutta in the last decade of the nineteenth century is suggested by the following figures. According to the 1891 Bengal Census, there were 17,023 actresses, singers, dancers and their accompanists. In 1901, the number had gone down to 3,527.[13] Ironically, in this ideological crusade Bengali educated men found their biggest allies in their newly 'emancipated' wives and daughters who, from the end of the nineteenth century, began to play a leading role through a spate of women's magazines, in changing the older forms of women's popular culture.

I

Women in nineteenth century popular culture

The literary compositions of women found their way into most of the main forms of popular culture — doggerels, poems, proverbs, songs, dramatic compositions — and into their different sub-genres or types such as *kirtans, panchalis, kavi* songs, *tarjas, jhumur* songs and dances, *jatra* performances, kathakata recitals, *bashar* songs at weddings and similar songs peculiar to certain women's rituals, etc. While the bulk of such compositions are of anonymous authorship, and have been handed down to us through oral preservation (often published by enterprising collectors towards the end of the nineteenth and the beginning of the present century), it has been possible to trace the names and life stories of a few women composers. For the purpose of this inquiry, contemporary compositions by a few male representatives of popular culture have been included because their songs, in the use of feminine idioms and dialect as also in their treatment of women's problems, suggest the influence of their women colleagues. As for the content of the women's songs of this period, although conventionally academics divide them into the religious and the secular, such a division may not always be useful. An examination of the style in which religious themes are dealt with in many so-called religious songs would show how contemporary secular problems were often articulated through religious myths.

In this context, let us take two specific groups of religious songs which were popular among women in nineteenth century Bengal. The first group is the *agamani* and *vijaya* songs, the former sung on the eve of the annual Durga Puja, welcoming the arrival of the goddess, and the latter sung at the end of the four day festivities lamenting her departure. A peculiar feature of both types of songs is the imagery in which the goddess is presented. The singers, through the use of familiar descriptive terms, domesticate Uma — the goddess Durga — who is turned into a typical young Bengali bride. The arrival of Durga from the Himalayas once every year is visualized as the homecoming of the bride. In the agamani songs, the devotees' longing for an audience with the goddess becomes the palpable craving of a lonely mother for the company of her long lost daughter. The singers describe the woes that Uma suffers in the inhospitable home of her drug-addict husband Shiva,[14] and urge Uma's father to bring her back home:

Bha͡ngōre bhika͡ri ja͡ma͡i tōma͡r, sōnar bhramari Gauri a͡ma͡r
Uma͡r jatō basan-bhushan, beta ta͡o bechey bha͡ang kheyechhe! [15]

(your son-in-law is a hemp-smoking beggar,
My Gauri [another name for Uma] is a precious bumble-bee.
All the clothes and ornaments of Uma,
That bounder has sold away
To smoke his hemp!)

Similarly, the vijaya songs express the mother's sorrow at the departure of her daughter: the immersion of the goddess Durga becomes an excuse to give vent to the pangs of separation that every Bengali mother suffers when her daughter leaves for the home of her husband. The contemporary social problems of a poor Bengali home —the poverty of Uma's husband, the sufferings of the young bride,the few fleeting days of reunion between mother and daughter, the distance between the natal home of the bride and the home of her husband that makes such reunions difficult — are pushed into the foreground, relegating religious devotion to the background.[16]

The second group of religious songs of nineteenth century Bengali popular culture consists of the hosts of kirtans, panchalis, kavi songs, and similar types of compositions dealing with the love of Krishna and Radha. Here again, the divine pair is deglamourized through the imagery into a rustic young couple — often in a daring adulterous and incestuous relationship — expressing the same fears and hopes, wounded pride and blissful consummation that are the lot of ordinary mortals in love. Stripped of omnipotent divine qualities, Krishna and Radha are brought down to earth and turned into vulnerable human beings, as sensitive to pain and pleasure as any mortal.[17]

The love songs of Radha and Krishna were a rich repertoire for the different groups of women singers who used to throng the marketplaces and streets of nineteenth century Bengal villages and of Calcutta. These women singers were Vaishnavites, and were variously known as boshtamis or neries in popular parlance. The Vaishnava religion in Bengal, with its stress on the equality of man and woman among other things, provided room for Bengali women from different segments of society: widows of kulin Brahmins who had nowhere to go, women who wanted to escape prostitution after having been seduced from their homes and deserted by their lovers, prostitutes who, after becoming old, had lost their occupations, or outcastes aspiring to independence and recognition. The *Census of India, Bengal 1872* reported that the followers of Vaishnavism "open their arms to those who are rejected by all others — the outcasts, the crippled, the diseased and the unfortunate." Contemporary records abound with references to women in villages — widows, married as well as unmarried women — deserting their homes to join some Vaishnavite *akhara* or monastery.[18] Here religious norms allowed them a freedom of movement, an access to all corners of society, both high and low, and a certain liberty in their relations with men — privileges which were out of reach for rich and middle class Bengali women of the time.[19] Many of these Vaishnavite women went around singing and begging from door to door. Some, who had learnt to read and write in their homes, taught the girls in the andarmahal of the bhadralok homes. A few from among them rose to be well-known poets and singers. In 1826, we learn from a contemporary Bengali newspaper, *Samachar Darpan,* that in Kaikala village in Bengal, on the occasion of Saraswati Puja three *neri kavis* were invited from Calcutta to the house of one Krishnakanta Dutta.[20] The kavis were practitioners of a literary genre which developed in Bengal towards the end of the eighteenth century, marked by the impromptu composition of poems set to tune, and sung in poetic duels between two individual poets and their respective followers. The kavis also went around with their own troupes of musicians and sang songs on Radha and Krishna, Shiva and Parvati, and on Kali.

That these neri kavis became a force to reckon with is evident from a letter written by rival male poets in the same paper two years later. Describing themselves as "Vagrant Muchi and Dom Poetasters" (from the lower caste communities), they complained how some years ago "Neri [lit. shaven-headed] Vaishnavees" had ousted them from their occupations by singing and dancing during almost every festival at the houses of the rich. "But by devising some means with the help of the *Sudder* [which could either mean the district administrative headquarters, or the outer apartment of the male head of a Bengali household], we have succeeded in getting rid of the Neries."[21] It might be worth investigating whether these male kavis actually filed any complaint with the administration against the Vaishnavite women singers who at one time threatened their careers.

Women poets had indeed been a part of the Vaishnavite literary tradition in Bengal from the fifteenth century. While their songs expressing Radha's devotion to Krishna were similar in style to those composed by male poets, there were also some songs which ridicule male hypocrisy, irresponsibility and cowardice. A typical example is the following excerpt from a song by Rammoni, or Rami as she was popularly known, a washerwoman by caste, who was reputed to be a friend of the famous fifteenth century Bengali Vaishnavite poet Chandidas. It is a bitter reproach of her male neighbours who were spreading calumny about her relationship with Chandidas, a plight also suffered by Radha in her affair with Krishna:

What can I say, friend?
I don't have enough words!
Even as I weep when I tell you this story
My accursed face breaks into laughter!

Can you imagine the cheek of the sinister men?
They have stopped worshipping the Devi
And have started tarnishing my reputation.

Rami then ends with a curse on her detractors:

Let the thunderbolt crash on heads of those
Who from their housetops shout abuses at good people.
I won't stay any longer in this land of injustice,
I'll go to a place where there are no hell-hounds.[22]

The tradition of using the Radha-Krishna story as a vehicle for voicing women's grievances in contemporary society, continued well into the nineteenth century. Radha's complaints about an elusive Krishna dallying elsewhere with his mistresses, could be easily recognized as the bitter admonitions of a Bengali wife hurled at her profligate husband (a subject which was the staple of numerous contemporary social novels, poems, plays and farces). Let us take for instance, the following lines from a song by a well-known woman kavi called Jogyeshwari, who was a rival of Bhola Maira, Neelu Thakur and other famous male kavis in Calcutta in the early years of the nineteenth century. The song belongs to the *biraha* type, a sub-division in the repertoire of Radha-Krishna songs expressing Radha's woes at her separation from Krishna. The words of the song express the woman's dismay at her lover's infidelity:

Nobeenar prānadhan hōye tini akhōn,
Bheshechen sukhasāgare.
Bhālo sukhe thākun tini, tātey khōti nai
Āmaye phele gelen keno shānkher karāte.
Bolo Bolo pranonātherey
Bichhedke tānr deke ne jete.
Jodi thake dhār, nā hoy shudhei āshbo tar
Keno toshil kore porā moshil barāte.
Āmar holo udor bojha budhor ghārete.
Tini pran loye hey holen satantar,
Madan tābujhe nā, bolle shune nā,
Āmar thāin chābey rājkar.

He has now turned into the darling of
His new young sweetheart, and is
Floating in eternal happiness!
Well! Let him be happy.
There's no harm done.
But why did he have to leave me
On the horns of a dilemma?

The poetess goes on the explain her dilemma in terms of a contemporary socio-economic analogy, that of a revenue collector and a tax payer. Whatever she had — in this case her soul — has been taken away from her by her lover. But Madan, the god of love, keeps harassing her, like the revenue collector, reminding her of the anguish of separation. What more can she pay as tax? She then appeals to her lover to help her out of this dilemma or situation by taking the anguish away from her.[23]

While the biraha songs provided women with a form to express the feelings of a deserted wife or beloved, often in this rather mournful style, there was another category of Radha-Krishna love songs which offered an avenue to let off steam in a more uninhibited way. This was the *kheur* which dealt with the love affair in a merry, ribald manner. It was recognized as an essential part of the narrative songs on Radha and Krishna and was popular among all classes of Bengalis till the beginning of the nineteenth century. It began to be condemned as obscene by the educated Bengali gentry and was finally banished from 'respectable' society by the end of the century.

But even as late as 1892, the tradition of kheur was kept alive by both male and female singers of the lower strata in western Bengal, Burdwan and Birbhum. A contemporary report tells us that instead of using the conventional *khole,* a type of drum played during kirtans, the male and female singers of kheur stood and played on the *madal* — a tribal drum — and exchanged repartee in the form of short songs.[24] From another source, we get a specimen of such repartee. The woman singer quips:

Orey a͡ma͡r Ka͡lo͡ Bhramar,
Modhu lutbi jo͡di a͡ye!

(Come hither, my black-bee,
If you want to feast on my honey!)

The bold Radha's unabashed invitation to the black-bee, who is the unmistakable dark-skinned Krishna, is resented by the possessive husband who retorts:

Ā͡mi tha͡ktey cha͡ker mōdhu pa͡nch bhramōre khe͡ye ja͡ye!

(How is it that while I am here, all and sundry come to
taste the honeycomb!)[25]

While biraha and the other sections of the Radha-Krishna narrative deal in a serious vein with the ardent moods of the lovers, kheur in a ribald style expresses the mischievous thoughts lurking behind such moods. Often openly erotic like the above exchange, it sometimes expressed the sheer playfulness involved in a love affair as in the following:

Gopōney jatek sukh, praka͡she tato asukh,
Nanadi dekhley pare pronoy ki roy?

(There is as much happiness in having it in secret
As pain in making it public.
Will love be possible,
If the sister-in-law comes to know of it?)[26]

The themes of kheur were borrowed not only from the stories of Radha and Krishna but also from other mythological narratives. The words were put in the mouth of a woman character, although the songs might be written by men. Interspersed with serious mythological narratives about divinities, were these comic and abusive songs which parodied the heroes and heroines. Radhamadhav Kar, an old theatre personality of Calcutta, in his reminiscences in the course of an interview, gave an illustration of a kheur in a jatra performance in the middle of the nineteenth century. It was sung by Ambalika, a female character in the *Mahabharata,* as a repartee directed against her mother-in-law, Satyavati. Ambalika became a widow at an early age. Satyavati, in her desire to preserve the family line, wanted her to beget a child with the eldest son, the venerable Vyasa (a practice which was quite common in those days as is evident from numerous stories in the *Mahabharata*). In the kheur, Ambalika satirizes the leering behaviour of the old Vyasa:

Sey jey mastō derey,
Dāari nerey,
Andarey dhukey,
Giye bōshlō taal thukey!

(The whopping shaggy beast, shaking his beard, he entered my bedroom, sat on the bed slapping his arms).

As Ambalika tries to escape, old Vyasa stands in her way and pulls at her sari. When Satyavati tries to convince her daughter-in-law of the need to accept Vyasa's overtures to have a son, Ambalika retorts with a refrain:

If it has to be done,
Why don't you do it, mother?

She then reminds Satyavati of the latter's not-too-reputable past:

People say —
As a girl you used to row a boat in the river.
Seeing your beauty, tempted by your 'lotus-bud',
The great Parashar stung you, and —
There was a hue and cry:
You've done it once,
You don't have anything to fear.
Now you can do as much as you want to,
No one will say anything.
If it has to be done,
Why don't you do it, mother?[27]

The bawdy satricial wit, the frank sensuality, the hearty unashamed appetite expressed in kheurs in the language and idiom of women, could be explained at two levels. At one level, songs of this type challenged the orthodoxy embedded in brahminical religion. By ridiculing the venerable Hindu gods and goddesses, heroes and heroines, they provided an oblique criticism of the purist conventions sought to be imposed by the Brahmin priestly order. Significantly contemporary bhadralok critics, obviously ashamed of such uninhibited debunking of Hindu deities, took pains to dismiss kheurs as the domain of the itarjans or 'lower orders' whose base instincts, they said, needed to be tickled by such 'obscene' songs![28]

At the other level, such songs afforded a 'dissenting space' for women. For nineteenth century Bengali women of both classes (the sheltered upper class zenana as well as the comparatively independent working women of the lower groups, both living in a male-dominated social environment), the prevailing patriarchal values were the ruling norms. A common saying current in those days reveals the typical male attitude:

Nāō, ghōra, nāaree — jey chōrbey tāari

(The boat, the horse and the woman belong to
whoever rides them).

Among the poorer classes in the villages, during famines, women were the first to bear the brunt of the crisis, either deserted by the menfolk, or even worse, sold to touts by their husbands or fathers. In this context, it is not surprising that even women poets — who often scored over their male rivals — could not escape humiliation from fellow male poets. Thus, the early nineteenth century woman kavi Jogyeshwari (whose song has been quoted above), was once insulted during a public poetic duel by her male contender, the famous Bhola Maira; in a song in reply to her, he took her to task for daring to "bellow forth" in the presence of the babus and described her as a "shameless" woman who had lost all sense of proportion.[29] In such a social milieu, songs like kheurs seemed to temporarily liberate the women not only from the external censorship prevalent in bhadralok homes, but also from the internal censor — the traditional fear of the power wielded by men. The mockery of male depravity (as in the barbed shaft aimed at Krishna's promiscuity, or in the more openly bawdy description of the old Vyasa), based on a common recognition of tyrannical husbands or unfaithful lovers, was no doubt popular with female listeners, who found in the songs a symbolic solace or perhaps even a revenge.

Such symbolic inversions or reversions — where the dominated (the lower groups, or women in the present context) laugh at the values and shibboleths of the dominators — have often been explained by anthropologists as a means of emotional release, as symbolic expressions of underlying and normally suppressed conflicts within society, as a mechanism by which the pressures engendered by social conflict may be vented without allowing the conflict to become fully overt and threaten the survival of the social system.[30] But a quite different result could flow from such ritualistic displays of defiance in the form of female ribaldry. Instead of containing discontent within the confines of light-hearted kheurs, it could widen the behavioural options for women within or even outside marriage, or encourage disobedience among both men and women of the lower orders in a society that did not allow them formal means of protest.[31]

It was this fear that could have prompted the nineteenth century Bengali bhadralok to abandon the attitude of complacent indulgence, and to launch a campaign against women's songs in particular, and against contemporary popular and folk cultural forms in general. We should also remember in this connection that such songs did not always resort to the cover of religious themes. There was quite a substantial crop of songs, dances and theatrical performances in folk repertoires that grew around secular subjects. The pace-setter in Bengali literature was the famous romance *Vidya-Sundar* by the early eighteenth century composer Bharatchandra Ray who was the court poet of Raja Krishnachandra of Nabadwip.[32] Although *Vidya-Sundar* was written in chaste — often Sanskritized — Bengali, and was meant to please a feudal royal patron, it became a popular story which was later treated in colloquial style by urban folk singers who catered to the wider audience of the growing metropolis of Calcutta.

From the early nineteenth century, a host of popular versions of *Vidya-Sundar* flooded the market prompting the journal *Calcutta Review* to warn its readers that the particular narrative's "tendency is essentially and grossly immoral, and its perusal by native females must be injurious in the extreme," after noting that it "is the great favourite of Hindu ladies. . . ."[33] Jatras (folk and popular theatrical performances) were composed about the romantic pair Vidya and Sundar. This fed the tendency towards an increasing secularization of themes in popular songs which had begun to deal directly with contemporary events and characters without taking recourse to religious themes. Working women composed songs about their respective occupations. Their dances (like those of the *methrani* or sweeper) became stock pieces for providing comic relief in jatras, and later, on the modern Bengali stage which, from the middle of the nineteenth century, began to mount plays written in the style of European playwrights.

Certain traditional forms like tarjas (marked by an exchange of repartee) and jhumur (described in Bengali literary criticism variously as a tribal song and dance performance, or as part of the Radha-Krishna kirtan or song) became vehicles for singing about non-religious events. Women singers formed their own troupes of tarja and jhumur performers, which toured the country. We come across the name of Bhavani (also known as Bhavarani) who led one such group in the late 1850s. One of her jhumur songs parodies the conventional style used by traditional poets to describe a familiar episode in the Radha-Krishna story — Radha's frequent trips to the river, ostensibly to fill her water vessel but actually to tarry there for a glimpse of Krishna:

Chal sõi, bãndha ghatey jãi,
Aghater jaleyr mukhey chhai!
Ghōla jal pōrley petey
Gata omni guliye othhey
Pet phempey aar dhekur uthey, heu heu heu!

(Come on friends, let's go to the new bathing place,
Enough of the waters of out-of-the way tanks!
As soon as I take in the muddy waters,
I feel like throwing up.
My belly aches and I start belching — heu heu heu!

Having de-romanticized the situation by describing in bare prosaic language the physical hazards involved in such a rendezvous, the singer introduces a bitter-sad note describing her emotional state:

My tears dry up in my eyes,
I go around making merry.
I'm writhing in pain,
Yet, I act coy
Swinging my hips.
The accursed ornaments of mine
May not remain long with me,
What with the evil eyes
Cast upon them
By the wretched wenches![34]

The frequency of descriptions of prostitutes and their life styles in nineteenth century Bengali songs and sayings is striking. Apart from songs written about them by men, they themselves created their own genre, known as *bashya sangeet* (songs of prostitutes) where they ridiculed their male clients and also laughed at themselves. The rise in the number of prostitutes in nineteenth century Calcutta could be explained by several factors: the increasing migration into Calcutta of men who left their families behind in their villages, the poverty of widows and deserted women from both high and low castes, and the need of poor working women to supplement their meagre earnings. In 1853, Calcutta with a population of about 400,000 people, supported 12,419 prostitutes. Of these more than 10,000 were Hindus, including several daughters of kulin Brahmins. More than a decade later, in 1867, although the city's total population had come down to some extent, the number of prostitutes rose to more than 30,000. We are told that it was mostly women of the weaver, barber, washermen, milkmen, fishermen and other lower castes who resorted to this profession.[35]

The metaphors used in the bashya sangeet replace the traditional romantic images of flowers, rivers, moon, etc., with more substantial images of material things of daily use. The following lines from one such song are interesting:

Amar bhalobasha abaar kothaey baasha bendhechey,
Piriteyr parōta kheye mōta hoyechey.
Mashey mashey barchhey bhaara
Baariulee dichhey taara
Goylaparar moyla chhōnra praney merechhey![36]

(Love has taken me to another room, another place,
Past affairs have fattened me like rich *paranthas*
[layered fried bread]
The room rent is going up every month
The landlady is threatening to evict me
But my soul is smitten by that dark lad from the *goylaparar* [milkmen's colony].)

Or, take these lines which play on the imagery of the contemporary popular game of kite-flying:

Why are you still hanging on
After having snipped the kite of love?[37]

Bold wit emerges in a comic song, sung by gypsy women (known as ***bedeni***) who used to sell herbs and oils in the streets of Calcutta, advertised as cures for 'broken hearts',:

Ei ōshudh mōre chhuntey chhuntey,
Hurkōe bōu jāye aapni shutey,
Bāro-phatka purush jara,
Āanchal-dhara hoye uthey![38]

(As soon as these medicines of mine are touched, the truant wife will come back to sleep with her husband, the profligate will get tied down to his wife's sari.)

Doggerels which originated from the daily experiences or social situations of working women found their way into the andarmahals and became household proverbs (some of them being still in use). Many such proverbs are directed against worthless husbands, like the following:

Bhāat debar nāam nei, kil marar Gōnshai

(He can't provide me with rice, and yet is quite a mighty one in beating me with his fists.)

or:

Darbārey ñā mukh peye gharey eshey māag thengae.

(Unable to speak out in the court, he comes home and takes it out on his wife.)

Implements of daily use, and experiences in the kitchen became the central images in proverbs and doggerels. Thus:

Dhenki swarge geleo dhān bhāne

(Even when a husking machine goes to heaven, it continues to husk paddy. In other words, habits die hard.)

Teley beguney chōtey ōtha

(To explode in anger like brinjals dropped in a frying pan).

Or, take this beautiful couplet describing the fate of love:

Pirit jakhōn jōtey phul kalāi photey
Pirit jakhon chhōtey dhenkite pheley kōtey. [39]

(When love comes, it bubbles like frying peas. When love leaves, it pounds you like paddy in the husking machine.)

Strikingly enough, the five major social issues directly affecting women in nineteenth century Bengal taken up by contemporary bhadralok social reformers — *sati* (widow immolation), widow remarriage, child marriage, kulin polygamy and female education — rarely found a place in the majority of songs or doggerels composed by women from lower social groups. There is a lone doggerel describing the fate of the wife of a Kolu (belonging to the lower caste of oilmen) being forcibly burnt on the pyre of another man, while the audience shouts blessings on her in mistaken piety, drowning her complaints. It is often used as a proverb to imply that the wrong person is being praised or abused for what he/she has not done.

(kā̃ār ā̃guney ke bā̃ mare, ā̃mi jā̃tey kōlu
Mā̃ā̃ ā̃mā̃r ki punyabati, bōlchhney de ulu). [40]

Though no direct references to kulin polygamy are to be found in the street songs of women, doggerels and proverbs abound with digs at co-wives and taunts at old men wanting to marry young women.

We must hasten to add in this context that the issues of sati, widow remarriage, kulin polygamy or female education were the staple of numerous songs, poems, plays and polemical articles in nineteenth century Bengal. But they were almost always written by the educated bhadralok or by their women. Even when their authorship is anonymous, the mode of expression, the style of composition, the frequent use of chaste Sanskritized words (as distinct from the popular idiom found in the conversation of uneducated women), indicate the bhadralok origins of such literary compositions.

The lack of serious interest in these major social issues within women's popular cultural forms could have resulted from the fact that these issues had no relevance for the women involved. For instance, kulin polygamy affected mainly the upper caste and upper class Hindus. As for widows, among lower caste and lower class Bengalis (who formed the majority of the population) their re-marriage or co-habitation with a man, was often accepted in their respective communities. *Sanga* or *sangat* appeared to be a recognized form of marriage among the lower social groups, as is evident from a contemporary popular saying:

Ghar pōrley chhāgoley m͡aray
Ra͡nr hōley saba͡i eshey s͡anga͡ kōrtey cha͡y[41]

(When the hut collapses, even the goat tramples on it.
When one becomes a widow, everyone comes to arrange
a sanga with her.)

In cities like Calcutta, widows from the lower classes were often known to be co-habiting with men of their choice, as revealed by the evidence of a woman textile worker before the Indian Factory Commission, who said that she was a widow and was living with an "adopted husband".[42] The system of child marriage also might not have been as widespread among these classes as among upper caste Hindus.[43]

It is necessary to draw attention to another aspect of these popular compositions by women. Certain types of colloquial expressions and expletives, peculiar to women only, occur frequently. One can pick out some of these words at random: *abaagi* (a wretched woman); *aantkuri* (a barren woman); *bhataar* (husband); *dabka* (a girl with a youthful body); *dhoska* (aged woman); *dhumshi* (fat woman); *minshey* (man); *naang* (lover); *raanr* (widow or a prostitute). Most of these words were used in a perjorative sense, and were looked down upon by educated males in respectable Bengali households. Not only such words, but the profanities and oaths, the *double entendres* and bawdy quips that marked women's songs and proverbs were a kind of reservoir in which various speech patterns and images derived from folk humour, which were excluded from bhadralok discourse, could freely accumulate. For the Bengali male elite, which was making strenuous efforts to create new patterns of deference and patronage, such songs and expressions were perceived as products of lower class beliefs and behaviour which were doubly annoying and embarrassing because they were shared by their own women in the andarmahals. This is how a bhadralok described an andarmahal towards the end of the nineteenth century:

> It is needless to add that their [the women's] familiar conversation is not characterized by that chaste, dignified language which constitutes a prominent characteristic of a people far advanced in civilization. Objectionable modes of expression generally pass muster among them, simply because they labour under the great disadvantage of the national barrenness of intellect and the acknowledged poverty of colloquial literature.[44]

Even Bankim Chandra Chatterjee, the famous Bengali novelist of that period, who had a perceptive ear for women's dialect (he uses, for instance, the word *maagi* rather than the genteel *mahila* or *nari* quite frequently in dialogues in his novels) while reviewing a play in 1873 rebuked the playwright for having used bhataar (instead of the more refined *purush*) too often in the dialogue of a woman character, and said it reflected "vulgarity in style"[45] Often the bhadralok felt that such songs and expressions were also threatening or dangerous. Following is a typical comment by a contemporary newspaper:

> Look at the streets of Calcutta, how the vulgar lower orders right in front of thousands of bhadralok, trampling on the chests of the powerful police force, go around wherever they want to, singing extremely obscene songs and making obscene gestures![46]

Such concern for 'social discipline' and 'public order' shaped the vigorous bhadralok campaign to suppress popular cultural forms and artistes in Calcutta.

II

The bhadralok campaign against women artistes and their performances

To free the andarmahal from the contaminating culture of the lower orders, it was necessary to strike at its roots. i.e. at various cultural forms and at those who practised them, particularly the women who had free access to the zenana. From the mid-nineteenth century, educated Bengali males attempted to rouse public opinion through articles in newspapers, meetings in city halls, and often through books, against these popular forms and against their performers. By the beginning of the present century, they had succeeded, to a large extent, in driving them away from the precincts of 'respectable' urban society, pushing them either to distant villages where their descendants today still manage somehow to carry on their earlier occupations, or down into the underworld of prostitution, from where some among them fought their way out to make a place for themselves in Calcutta's theatre, and later, in the film world.

It is worth noting, however, that during the early decades of the nineteenth century, the Bengali bhadralok community did not present a homogeneous set of ideas, either in their attitude towards women, or towards many other social questions. First, there was the tendency to maintain status quo in the andarmahal, by allowing the women to continue their life style, while at the same time recognizing the need for women's education, preferably by the older methods rather than by those advocated by the Christian missionaries or their followers.[47] The second tendency was represented by the Young Bengal group and the various new educated converts to Christianity, who vigorously campaigned, often in a demonstrative fashion, for the remarriage of widows, for an end to polygamy, for the emancipation of women through the new system of education in English and other similar reforms.[48] By the last decades of the nineteenth century, both these tendencies seemed to lose their respective sharp edges and often merged into a third — that of accepting the reforms at a gradual pace and in modified forms as part of the general bhadralok inclination towards social stability based on a set of values born of a compromise between the old and the new.[49]

By the middle of the nineteenth century, contempt for popular culture was becoming a common feature of all the three tendencies.[50] This contempt was a gift from the Christian missionaries and English administrators. They were the first, in the early nineteenth century, to start a systematic attack on the popular art forms which were still being patronized by the Bengali aristocracy. In 1806, Reverend James Ward expressed his shock when, invited to attend the Durga Puja festivities in the house of Raja Rajkrishna Dev of Shovabazar, he had first to listen to kavi songs. Before two o'clock at night the place was cleared of the *nautch* girls who usually danced to the tunes of classical Hindustani music, and entertained both Bengali aristocrats and their English friends, and then the main doors were opened to the public. Ward describes the scene:

> . . . a vast crowd of natives rushed in, almost treading upon one another among whom were the vocal singers, having on long caps like sugar loaves . . . Four sets of singers . . . entertained their guests with filthy songs and danced in indecent attitudes before the goddess, holding up their hands, turning round, putting forward their heads towards the image every now and then, bending their bodies ...

Ward then describes his feelings: "The whole scene produced on my mind sensations of the greatest horror," and he felt unable to copy a single line of those songs as they were "so full of broad obscenity." He adds:

> All those actions which a sense of decency keeps out of the most indecent English songs, are here detailed, sung and laughed at, without the least sense of shame. A poor ballad singer in England, would be sent to the house of correction, and flogged, for performing the meritorious actions of these wretched idolators.[51]

E.S. Montagu, Secretary of the Calcutta School Book Society, in an 1820 memorandum on the indigenous works which had appeared from the native presses since 1805, found a large number of Bengali books "distinguished only by their flagrant violation of common decency," and added: "The avidity with which these indecent publications are sought for, and the general currency obtained for them, . . . is deeply to be lamented, as manifesting aloud the degraded state of those minds which will take such pleasure therein."[52] Mr Montagu succeeded in converting "one Pundit" to his viewpoint. "Subsequently he in conjunction with some other natives, concurred among themselves to express their dissatisfaction with such works . . ."[53] The works in question were popular versions of *Vidya Sundar* and similar romantic stories. This incident indicates how the indigenous elite (including the traditionalist pundits) were gradually being 'reformed' and taught to denounce popular cultural forms.

By the 1850s, the Bengali elite were becoming more and more

articulate against the culture of the itarjans. Writing in 1853, a bhadralok describes how "hundreds may be seen keeping up whole nights to see and listen" to jatras which treat of the "amours of the lascivious Krishna and of the beautiful shepherdess Radha, or of the liaison of Bydya and Sundar." He then warns: "It is needless to say that topics like these exercise a baneful influence on the moral character of the auditors. They harden the heart and sear the conscience . . . . The gesticulations with which many of the characters in these *yatras* recite their several parts, are vulgar and laughable."[54] Another bhadralok writing in 1855, complains that almost all the plots of the jatras are taken from the amours of Krishna and of Radhika, and asks: "Who that has any pretension to a polite taste, will not be disgusted with the vulgar mode of dancing with which our play commences; and who that has any moral tendency will not censure the immorality of the pieces that are performed?"[55]

It is clear that the objection was both to the form and to the content of these popular performances. Even when performances dealt with religious divinities like Krishna and Radha, their depiction in terms of human passions offended the newly acquired sense of morality of the bhadralok, who had to hear constantly from their English mentors that the Hindu gods and goddesses were the "personifications of a truly fiendish or infernal character."[56] Bankim Chandra Chatterjee's brother, Sanjeev Chandra, succinctly expressed the bhadralok attitude towards the popular jatras of those times:

> Anyone from among the illiterate fishermen, boatmen, potters, blacksmiths, who can rhyme, thinks that he has composed a song; singing it, the jatra performer thinks that he has sung a song; listening to it the audience think that they have heard a song. But there is nothing in these songs except rhyming . . . Thanks to the present type of jatras, Krishna and Radha look like *goalas* [milkmen]; in the past, the qualities of a good poet made them appear as divinities.[57]

What were the implications of this attitude for women performers, for their songs and for their theatres?

Women artistes specializing in certain forms of cultural performance — both religious and secular — were the first to bear the brunt. We have already referred to the Boshtomis or Vaishnavite women singers, who not only roamed around the streets singing kirtans, but also taught the members of the andarmahal, through kathakata or recitation of mythological stories. Swarnakumari Devi, the eldest sister of Rabindranath Tagore, heard from her elders how every morning

> a Vaishnavite lady — pure after a bath, dressed in white, fair-skinned — appeared in the zenana to teach. She was no mean scholar. She was well-versed in Sanskrit, and needless to say, in Bengali also. Moreover, she had a wonderful power of describing, and impressed everyone with her kathakata performance. Even those who were not in the least interested in learning, used to gather at the reading room to listen to the Vaishnavite lady's description of the dawn, of gods and goddesses.

But Swarnakumari Devi, who was born in 1855, "did not have the fortune to see the Vaishnavite lady."[58] Apparently, by then, the Tagore family's male members, eager to emancipate their women from the influence of the lascivious stories of Radha and Krishna, had barred their doors to the Vaishnavite kathakata reciters.

One must remember that kathakata was an important source, both of popular entertainment and of religious knowledge (presented in a simple narrative form, often with references to the contemporary environment) for the unlettered. Even after the elimination of women kathakata performers from respectable andarmahals, the practice continued in village fairs and religious congregations for several years, attracting huge crowds including women. Since religious fairs and congregations also provided women of the andarmahals with an opportunity to get permission to go out and attend kathakatas, the Bengali bhadralok soon became alarmed at the exposure of their women to such performances. Their fears found expression in contemporary journals. Thus, one bhadralok writer complained that during the narration of the Krishna-Leela: "It is not possible for an uneducated young woman to remain unexcited when listening to episodes like Raas [Krishna's dance with the milkmaids] or Krishna's escape with the clothes of the milkmaids." He then proposed:

> . . . since it [kathakata] has become a source of so much evil, it is not advisable for bhadraloks to encourage it. Those who allow their ladies to go to kathakata performances should be careful . . . If, during kathakata performances, women stay home and are provided

with opportunities to listen to good instructions, discussions on good books and to train themselves in artistic occupations, their religious sense will improve and their souls will become pure and they will be suitable for domestic work . . .[59]

The bhadralok fear of their women being corrupted by popular entertainments was in all probability, a result of their new 'enlightenment' by the British. One can well imagine the impact of rebukes, such as the following administered by one such enlightened educator, who was shocked to find that *Vidya-Sundar* was "the great favourite of Hindu ladies," and added: "The study of it must destroy all purity of mind and yet it cannot be doubted, that if any book is read by, and to, respectable Bengali females, this is it."[60]

Driven out from the andarmahals, the Vaishnavite singers carried on their occupations in the streets of Calcutta, and occasionally in the courtyard of some rich Bengali homes when invited for religious events, almost till the end of the nineteenth century. They specialized in a particular type of kirtan, known as *dhap* which used to be sung in a light rhythm.[61] We come across the name of one Sahachari, who was a popular kirtan singer around the 1840s, to be followed by Jaganmohini who made a name as an expert dhap singer. She was reputed to have a distinct intonation as well as a wide range.[62]

But the popularization of kirtan in the form of dhap and in easily acceptable idioms by women singers, became a target of bhadralok ridicule. Towards the end of the nineteenth century, a doggerel which ridiculed these women singers became popular in bhadralok circles. It ran thus:

Jatō chhilōe nara-buney
Sab hōlōe kirtuney;
Kaste bhengey garaley
Khole kartal[63]

(All those who were agricultural labourers or 'lower orders' working in the paddy fields, have become kirtan-singers. They have bent their sickles to fashion drums and cymbals.)

We can also sense the unmistakable bhadralok disapproval of the style of these popular female singers in other contemporary records. There is an attempt to brand them as prostitutes, so that they could be driven out from the streets under the anti-prostitution law: "Groups of kirtan and dhap singers have become indirect avenues for prostitutes to earn money. . . . They wear four or six pieces of anklets round their feet; they have a scarf around their shoulders like the *khemta* (a style of dance popular in nineteenth century Bengal) dancers; they wear whatever ornaments they can afford; and decorate their coiffure with colourful flowers. . . ."[64]

The independent lifestyle of the Vaishnavite women, and the expression of unashamed sensuality and eroticism in their songs on Krishna and Radha, now appeared as a set of alternative mores which posed a challenge to the nineteenth century Bengali bhadralok. Eager to preserve his authority over the andarmahal, and yet keen on impressing his English mentors with the progress he had achieved in educating and emancipating his womenfolk, the bhadralok was caught in a peculiar bind. The Evangelist missionaries, the English teachers from Victorian England and the English administrators trained at Haileybury College — all brought up to look down upon the 'native' customs and habits as obscene — constantly warned the bhadralok against the corrupt influence of their popular culture on their women. The Radha-Krishna kirtans celebrating the frolics of the divine pair in unabashed human terms, which had entertained both Bengali men and women all these years, suddenly assumed threatening dimensions for the bhadralok. These kirtans were not only obscene, according to the new rulers, but could also whisk away their women into the dark alleys of adultery. The colonial interpretation of Hindu religious myths in accordance with the contemporary Victorian ethical norms, drove some of the bhadralok to discard Hinduism and embrace Christianity, some to evolve Brahmo morality, and almost all the bhadralok to disown or ban those forms of popular culture which expressed human passions in a down-to-earth manner and indulged in raillery at the expense of the sacrosanct Hindu divinities. What used to be innocent fun, now held a threat to domestic stability, thanks to the 'enlightenment.'

Vaishnavite women became the main target of attack because they sought to continue a tradition — both social and literary

—which was uncomfortable for the bhadralok. They were literally hounded out from bhadralok society. After being ostracized from the andarmahals and persecuted in the streets of Calcutta, they tried to carve out a place for themselves within the new female education system. In the late 1860s normal schools were set up to train Bengali women teachers who were expected to visit the andarmahals and teach those women who were not willing to come out and attend public schools. We find from contemporary records that Vaishnavite women — who, as we have seen, were accustomed to imparting lessons to andarmahal women in the traditional style — offered themselves for training in the new system. The Bengali bhadralok however objected to their entry into these training schools. A letter in a contemporary journal complains:

> . . . there is a 'normal school' in Dhaka; but the majority of the trainees are Vaishnavites. We are not insulting them, but let us remember that people have no respect for Vaishnavite women . . . . if they therefore do not send their daughters to be taught by such women, we should not be surprised. Women of this type cannot educate girls who are expected to grow up to embellish their homes, provide happiness to their husbands and become ideals for their children. . . .[65]

The bhadralok offensive was directed against the various popular forms as well as against women's participation in them. Thus, while jatra remained an object of such attacks almost throughout the nineteenth century, women performers in jatras were singled out for special criticism. Mahendranath Dutt (a brother of Swami Vivekananda) in his reminiscences about his childhood in Calcutta in 1873-74 describes the female jatra groups: "They themselves acted (in different roles) and also played the parts of clowns. As a child, I saw jatra-plays like *Daksha-yagna* and Parvati's marriage. . . . They could not play on *tanpura* or violin; but managed with cymbals, clapping of hands and kettledrums, and they sang in chorus." Dutt then added: "But female jatra could not continue for long. The educated people began to denounce them, and they disappeared."[66]

When the educated bhadralok started to stage Bengali plays written in the style of European theatrical pieces, women from the lower strata tried to make their way into this new cultural medium.

For example, in October 1835 Nobinchunder Bose mounted a play adapted from *Vidya-Sundar* at a spacious hall belonging to another rich Bengali, Ramtonu Bosu (popularly known in Calcutta in those days as Tonu Mag, since he worked as an agent of Mag, a Burmese-Arakanese merchant house). In a rare instance of bhadralok appreciation of the artistic merits of the women performers, a contemporary Bengali correspondent wrote:

> The female characters in particular were excellent. The part of Bidya . . . played by Radha Moni (generally called Moni), a girl of nearly sixteen years of age, was very ably sustained; her graceful motions, her sweet voice and her love tricks with Sundar filled the minds of the audience with rapture and delight. . . . The other female characters were equally well performed, and amongst the rest we must not omit to mention the part of the Rani, or wife of Raja Bir Singha, and that of Malini . . . were acted by an elderly woman Jay Durga, who did justice to both characters in the two-fold capacity. . . .

He then added: "The proprietor, Babu Nobinchander Bose deserves our highest praise for endeavouring to raise the character of our mistaken though truely praiseworthy women."[67] As expected, both the play (being an adaptation from *Vidya-Sundar*) and the actresses, drew derogatory comments from the Bengali bhadralok community as well as from their English mentors. It however goes to the credit of the Bengali correspondent who originally reviewed the play that he stuck to his guns despite the barrage of criticism.[68] But it seems that the opposition to the introduction of actresses (who primarily came from the Vaishnavite community from lower strata, or most often, from the red light areas of Calcutta) by the bhadralok was so vehement, that the Bengali theatre movement could not dare to induct actresses again (after the rough weather which the October 1835 *Vidya-Sundar* play ran into) till the early 1870s when the poet-playwright Michael Madhusudan Dutt campaigned for the right to allow women to act in female roles.

Even in the 1870s, however, when actresses like Binodini, Golapi, Jagattarini, Elokeshi and Shyama were making their mark on the Bengali stage, sections of the bhadralok continued to resent their presence. Manomohan Bosu, a well known literary figure who was equally proficient in the folk kavi form as well as in the modernized form of Bengali theatre, came out vehemently against the intrusion of these actresses onto the contemporary theatre: "To get actresses, one has to collect prostitutes from the red-light areas. Young bhadraloks carousing with prostitutes in their midst, dancing and acting on stage, in public with prostitutes — can we see and listen to all this? How can we suffer it?"[69] In his animosity towards women artistes, Manomohan Bosu was even prepared to overcome the bhadralok prejudice against jatra artists. He said: "It is even better to have the abominable acting of the *jatra-wallahs* [male performers] which goes against the grain of our existence. But still, our national theatre community or other acting communities should not adopt this shameful system [of introducing actresses] which encourages vices and destroys our religious principles."[70]

Behind the bhadralok opposition to the introduction of actresses in the bhadralok theatre, was the prejudice against prostitutes. As we have seen, prostitutes came to constitute a major section of the female population in nineteenth century Bengal, sometimes even creating their own cultural genres, and they posed a constant threat to the bhadralok confidence about their own wives and daughters. The educated Bengali male's fears emerge clearly in an unusually frank article in a leading contemporary Bengali journal. After referring to the evil influence of prostitutes on Bengali men, the journal said:

> It is not only men who are led astray. Many women of the andarmahal deviate from a religious life under such influence. When they, being imprisoned [in their andarmahals] see how free the prostitutes are, when many among them find their own husbands addicted to frolics with prostitutes, is it surprising that they also would be fired with the desire for such vices, mistaking them for delights? We learn that many such women have left their homes to join the ranks of prostitutes. . . .[71]

It was not only Vaishnavite women actresses and prostitutes who were singled out for such attacks. Any class of women following an independent lifestyle and likely to influence the norms of the andarmahal through cultural activities was suspect. In the effort to fashion the respectable woman into a shape that would suit their newly acquired tastes and demands, the bhadralok sought to insulate their women from these traditional cultural forms — songs and jatras, kathakatas and doggerels — composed and performed by women from outside respectable society. Since many of these popular 'events' took place in the open — in streets, marketplaces, fairs and at religious festivals — the bhadralok had to step up their campaign against these open displays. One of the casualties of this campaign was the jhumur. We have mentioned earlier how in the 1850s the juhumur singer Bhavani toured Calcutta and other parts of Bengal with her own troupe. We find from Mahendranath Dutt's reminiscences that till the 1870s, women jhumur troupes were still to be seen in the streets of Calcutta. His description of their performances is tinged with typical bhadralok contempt:

> They were *chhotolok* [the uneducated lower orders], dark skinned wenches who stank when they passed by. They used to wear anklets round their feet when they sang. In those days during wedding ceremonies, *jhumurwalis* [female performers] used to dance on peacock-shaped papier-mache boats set up on bullock-carts. As they danced a man from behind used to beat a drum, or strike a bell-metal plate. . . . Their language was extremely coarse, but some among them had talents as poets.

Dutt adds: "But later these jhumurwalis became objects of virulent censure."[72] By the beginning of the twentieth century jhumur troupes had practically disappeared. A collector of these songs, writing in 1905 said: "The number of tarja and jhumur troupes is going down day by day in this country. It is doubtful whether we can come across even twenty tarja and jhumur troupes all over Bengal now. *Because of the police, in many places their clubs have been closed down.*"[73] (emphasis mine)

To ilustrate how 'obscene' their songs were, Mahendranath Dutt quotes a couplet from a jhumur song which describes the familiar image of goddess Kali standing on the supine Shiva:

Mā͡agi minsheyke chit kōrey phele diye buke diyechey pā͡a;
Ā͡r chōkhta karey julur julur, mukhey neiko rā͡a.[74]

> (The hussy has thrown the bloke flat on his back, with her foot on his chest; wordless she stands glaring in anger.)

The bhadralok reaction to such language describing the goddess in a facetious style suggesting the earthy image of an Amazon bestriding a suppliant male, rather than any religious devotion, doubtless was one of hurt and outrage. We should also remember that during this period the Bengali bhadralok were trying to salvage Kali from her tribal associations. In order to demarcate their own compositions from the popular songs on Kali (composed by Ramprasad and by folk poets of earlier centuries) the bhadralok were creating their own image of a goddess endowed with ethereal qualities, and expressing it in songs full of emotional frenzy. The gross, rustic shrew of Ramprasad's songs was being replaced by the divine Mother, whose ugly nakedness was to be glossed over by chaste Bengali expressions. Typical of the bhadralok version of Kali are the following lines from a song:

> Who is she walking on the heart of Hara [Shiva]?
> Who is the enchantress who has stolen the heart of Hara?[75]

While jhumur was banned from the marketplace, another performative genre of women artistes — the panchali — was exiled from the andarmahals. Women singers of panchali narrated stories from mythology in doggerels. A contemporary writer describes a panchali session in an andarmahal:

> They [the women] sit on benches or chairs, or squat down barefooted on *farash bichhana* [a clean white sheet] and enjoy the *tamasha* [entertainment] to their hearts' content. These amusements continue till evening, entertaining the guests with songs on gods and goddesses (Durga, Krishna and his mistress Radha); those relating to Durga have a reference to the ill-treatment she experienced at the hands of her parents, but those pertaining to Krishna and Radha tell of his juvenile frolics with his mother and the milkmaids, and amorous songs on disappointed love, which though they may appear harmless to their worshippers, have nevertheless a partial tendency to debase the mind.

The writer then assures his readers that such songs "which were shamefully characterized by the worst species of obscenity and immorality" were on their way out from the andarmahal thanks to the "progress of enlightenment" which has "of late years, wrought a salutary change in their [women's] minds."[76]

Another form of women's entertainment in the andarmahal also retreated in the face of increasing bhadralok criticism. This was known as the *basharghar* jokes or songs. The basharghar was the bridal chamber in the Bengali household where, after the wedding, the bride, her female relatives and her girl friends spent the night with the bridegroom (he being the only male in the gathering), cracking jokes at his expense and singing songs. The ceremony not only freed the members of the andarmahal from the censorious frowns of the male patriarchs, but also offered them an opportunity to wreak a sort of vengeance on male superiority. The newly-married husband, who for the rest of his life would dominate the wife, on this particular evening had to play a reverse role — that of the beleagured male. What follows is a faithful description of the plight of a bhadralok (who was marrying for the second time) on his entry into the basharghar:

> There were only women all around . . . First they received me with much welcome, but gradually they began to use their hands. . . . They slapped me, they pulled my ears, and my beard and moustache were about to be plucked out. The war ended after some time. Then, the ladies asked me to take my wife on my lap, and they began to hurl taunts at me. I cannot reproduce them. You, and the readers can well imagine what sort of jokes they were. I somehow managed to escape and was thanking my stars, when the younger ladies asked me to sing. I had learnt a few songs when I was a student. Remembering one such song, I began to sing a Brahmo Samaj song. Immediately there were shouts of "Shut up! Shut up!" I then began to sing a song by Ramprasad. But that didn't please them either.

After being unable to meet the ladies' demands for songs like *tappa* and kheur, the bridegroom had to suffer another round of taunts: "Stupid ass! Dullard! The lout doesn't know anything but books, books and books!"[77]

While the writer of the above letter described his woes in a half-humorous style, the editor — a dyed-in-the-wool bhadralok — who published it in his newspaper was in no mood for such indulgence. In a strongly worded editorial he condemned the behaviour of the women, and asked: "Is this a specimen of our women's natural mildness? Is this an expression of their modesty? Is this a sign of their bashfulness?" He then warned:

> When things have gone beyond the bounds of polite norms and reached the stage of intemperance, it is not advisable to allow indulgence any longer. . . Let every master of the house, after reading this letter, warn his wife, daughters and daughters-in-law. Since they [the women] are incapable of making proper use of their freedom in this regard, they cannot have any right to freedom.[78]

The ceremonial basharghar managed to maintain a precarious existence even as late as the 1950s in Calcutta. Although the rituals of traditional Hindu marriage are followed faithfully by many, even among the most westernized Bengali bhadralok of Calcutta today, one rarely comes across basharghar songs and raillery. They may, however, still be alive in rural areas.

One by one, the independent forms practised by women disappeared by the turn of the present century; under attack by the Christian missionaries, English administrators and the Bengali bhadralok, they had to give in to a hostile male world. Even fellow male artistes — who were being equally hounded out from respectable society — did not always lose the chance to denounce these women.[79] Though they could enjoy patronage in the andarmahal till almost the end of the nineteenth century, as a new generation of educated 'ladies' began to replace the older generation, the ties of the andarmahal with popular forms of culture were snapped.

III

Conclusion: The rise of the *bhadramahila*

By the end of the third quarter of the nineteenth century, the products of Bethune School, other women's educational institutions and of various forms of zenana teaching (either through trained women teachers or private coaching by husbands) were making their presence felt in the Bengali cultural field. It is estimated that 190 odd women authors from 1856 to 1910 produced about 400 works, including poems, novels, plays, essays and autobiographies. During the same period, 21 periodicals with which women were associated editorially, and which were primarily devoted to women's issues were in circulation in Bengal.[80]

The majority of the women authors of this period came from respectable homes, usually from upper-caste, well-to-do bhadralok families. The leading names are those of Swarnakumari Devi (1855-1932) of the Tagore family who was Rabindranath's elder sister; Prasannamoyi Devi (1857-1939), daughter of an East Bengal *zamindar* (landlord) who was educated in her home; Girindramohini Dasi (1858-1925), who learnt English first from her father and later from her husband, a scion of the family of the well-known millionaire Akrur Dutt; Mankumari Basu (1863-1943), a niece of the poet Michael Madhusudan Dutt; and Kamini Ray (1864-1933), who was educated in a school, and later became a teacher at the Bethune School.

The aim of this section is not to assess the literary merits of the compositions of these women — some of which were definitely of a high standard — but to indicate the new style and content that set them apart from women's popular cultural forms. The style of their compositions — poems, stories, novels, articles — showed signs of the training that they had undergone. The earthy dialect, the witty, homely idioms that marked the sayings of their predecessors were replaced by chaste, Sanskrit-derived compound Bengali words and expressions. Metaphors and images were now borrowed from the classics, the stress more often being on the distant, the romantic, and the ethereal. Reviewing Prasannamoyi Devi's collection of poems *Banalata* in 1880, the *Calcutta Review* commented:

> It consists of several short poems on a variety of subjects which bear the impress of a mind emancipated from the thraldom of . . . Juthi, Mallika, Malati [names of flowers commons in Bengali households] of bygone ages, and awakening to an appreciative perception of the beautiful, the grand and the sublime not simply in terrestrial objects, but likewise in the phenomenal aspects of Nature, in all her immensity.[81]

The minds of the imprisoned andarmahal women were indeed opened to a world different from and wider than the domesticated scene of the panchalis, kathakatas, dhap kirtans and similar other popular cultural forms to which they had been accustomed to in the past. While editing the magazine *Bharati* (from 1884 to1894), Swarnakumari Devi introduced a variety of social and political topics as well as reports from abroad. Prasannamoyi Devi composed poems on the plight of women who were married to unworthy husbands, as well as on the Rani of Jhansi, and on the visit of the

Prince of Wales to Calcutta in 1876.

Their treatment of these various issues — personal as well as social — was often marked by a soft sentimentality, in sharp contrast to the forthright, aggressive and ribald tone of women's popular cultural forms. The portrayal of saintly, virtuous and dutiful women, so often found in their poems and novels, must, in part, have been influenced by the 'text books' they studied. An eighteenth century pastoral romance — *Paul and Virginia* by Bernardin de St Pierre — was one such book recommended for the women of the andarmahal. Girindramohini Dasi learnt it by heart from her father. The book tells the story of the respectful love of Paul, the poor, illegitimate child of a deserted woman, for Virginia, the daughter of an aristocrat, and ends with the death of Virginia when her ship is wrecked in a storm. She could have been saved but for her maidenly modesty which made her refuse the proferred assistance of a naked sailor!

The model of female education, which influenced the compositions of the women authors of bhadralok families, stressed the cultivation of genteel norms and domestic virtues among respectable women. Speaking in 1856, a Young Bengal radical said:

> Females are not required to be educated by the standard which is adapted to men. . . . Woman has but one resource — Home. The end and aim of her life is to cultivate the domestic affections, to minister to the comfort and happiness of her husband, to look after and tend her children, and exercise her little supervision over domestic economies. . . .

He then pointed out how best to train the Bengali woman to serve this purpose: "She must be refined, reorganized, recast, regenerated. . . ."[82] More than two decades later, a Brahmo magazine reiterated the same model for women's education:

> A woman's nature is generally emotional while a man's is rational. Only that therefore can be termed authentic female education which primarily aims at improving the heart of a woman, and only secondarily at improving her mind. . . . The main aim of real female education is to train, improve and nourish the gentle and noble qualities of her heart . . . Under such a system [of education], attempts should be made through means of religious education, moral education, reading of poems which inspire noble feelings,

> and training in music which rouses pure thoughts, so that women can become tenderhearted, affectionate, compassionate and genuinely devout to be able to be virtuous and religious-minded. . . .[83]

The woman's magazine *Bamabodhini Patrika* emphasized a similar need for *naram-naram* or gentle and tender education for women.[84]

The lesson indicated for andarmahal women in these suggestions was clear. The coarse, 'untutored' expletives and expressions that they shared with the women of the streets, had to be expurgated from their vocabulary. Any sign of assertiveness or of departure from their domestic roles that might be inspired by stories about the adulterous Radha, or the assertive Vidya, had to be suppressed. *Bamabodhini Patrika* warned against the tendency to subvert the objective of female education by some women who still read *Vidya-Sundar* and panchalis in the andarmahal.[85]

The model of the new "refined, reorganized, recast, regenerated" Bengali woman, however, was reinforced from an unsuspected quarter. Quite a few women, from those professions looked down upon by the bhadralok, succeeded in trespassing into the field of educated women's literature with their own original compositions written in the refined, chaste Bengali required by the bhadralok. Earlier, in the 1840s, and 1850s, some Bengali newspapers had dared to carry letters signed by "prostitutes who have been ousted from their houses."[86] These letters described the circumstances that had forced the women into prostitution: desertion by husbands or lovers, economic necessities, and so on. But now literary compositions began to emerge from these very 'red light' areas of Calcutta. In 1870, a book came out entitled *Kamini Kalanka* written by one Nabinkali Devi, which purported to be the autobiography of a prostitute.[87] A theatre actress Golap (who was one of the first women to be recruited for acting in Michael Madhusudan Dutt's *Sharmishtha* in 1873, and later, after her marriage to a bhadralok came to be known as Sukumari Dutta), published in 1875, a play called *Apurva Sati.* Another actress, Tinkari, (who acted in a Bengali version of Shakespeare's *Macbeth* at the Minerva Theatre in Calcutta, and became so rich that on her death, she gifted two houses to a hospital in the city, and willed the sale proceeds from her ornaments to needy tenants in her neighbourhood) published a collection of stories in 1894. The best known among these actresses was Binodini who joined the stage when she was nine years old, and retired at quite an early age after 14 years, wishing to escape from the compulsions of prostitution which the life of an actress entailed in those days. Her collection of poems *Kanak O Nalinee* came out in 1905 and her autobiography *Amar Katha* in 1912.[88]

These actresses learnt to communicate in the new literary language by taking on roles in which they played heroines who had to utter dialogues often in high-flown, ornate Bengali. Some among them also learnt from their bhadralok patrons in the world of Bengali theatre, or from those educated Bengali gentlemen who kept them as their mistresses—a common practice in nineteenth century Bengal. But, in spite of their success in breaking through the barrier of language, they still seemed to remain untouchables to both the bhadralok and their newly emerging *bhadramahila* (educated wives and daughters of the bhadralok) sisters.

How did the bhadralok intellectuals react to these efforts by socially oppressed women? When Nabinkali Devi's *Kamini Kalanka* was reviewed in *Hindoo Patriot,* the progressive Brahmos in their journal *Indian Mirror* came out with bitter comments: "Imagine a public woman depicting in her peculiar language the scenes of her early life and the strange vicissitudes which a career like hers necessarily presented . . . . The repentance was all a sham for we are told the authoress was still pursuing her ignominous course. . . ."[89] The courage of a young liberal bhadralok from an upper caste family to marry the actress Golap, evoked only bitter contempt from his peers. Manomohan Bosu, a noted theatre personality of those days, composed a sarcastic song in 1874, which was meant to be sung as a *nagar sankeertan* (a popular urban form of street singing in procession, initiated by the Vaishnavite preacher Chaitanya in fifteenth century Nadia in Bengal, and which still continues today). The song lampoons Golap reminding her that when she was a public woman, she had a hundred husbands and that fate had brought to her a gem of a husband through the theatre green room. It describes Golap "dressed as a chaste woman, but looking for sport."[90]

Thus, the acquirement of and proficiency in the new literary forms was not necessarily a passport for entry into the society of the bhadramahila. The bhadralok insistence on membership of the andarmahal, on the total dependence of the woman on the male head of the family, on strict adherence to the traditional responsibilities of a respectable home, was an important pre-condition for a woman's literary apprenticeship.

As a result, when they started writing, the bhadramahilas internalized the male concepts of the new womanhood. Thus Kailashbashini Devi's *Hindu Mahilaganer Heenabastha,* which was published in 1863 and favourably reviewed in contemporary newspapers, though stressing the need for the education of women to free them from superstition, finally accepted this position: "From the particular nature and capacities with which God had endowed women, it is quite clear that the subservience of women is God's will. By becoming strong therefore, women can never become independent.... It does not become a woman to be without protection. An unprotected woman will not be respected anywhere. . . ."[91] Another woman writer, Hamangini Choudhury, writing in *Antahpur,* a women's magazine, advises Bengali wives in these words: "Even if the husband uses abusive language out of blind anger and behaves rudely, the wife's duty is to accept it in silence. It is extremely improper to show disobedience before the husband. Even if you are at the point of death, you should never speak ill of your husband to others. . . ."[92]

In these literary activities which arose from within the framework of a strictly defined domestic role, one could not expect any expression of women's independent aspiration. The literature of the bhadramahila was constrained by their obligation to be refined, to cultivate those tastes which their husbands liked, to speak in a language which did not come spontaneously but had to be learnt painstakingly. The women artistes of the market place and streets also lived in a male-dominated society. But their economic self-reliance, their independent life style and non-conformity to the morals of bhadralok society allowed them some freedom which often found expression in the derisive defiance of patriarchal norms, irreverent drollery at the expense of the divinities, and bolder assertion of their own desires, although often under the somewhat transparent veil of allegory.

Why did they fail to sustain their culture? We can hazard a few guesses. The popular culture of nineteenth century Calcutta was derived in part from the rural traditions which arrived in the metropolis and were modified in the new environs. The women who migrated to Calcutta in the early nineteenth century were mainly the wives and daughters of artisans and cottage-industry workers, who sought to replicate their economic and cultural life-styles in the new setting. But with the growth of modern industries in Bengal and the emergence of a new generation (their own sons and daughters) cut off from their rural roots — who joined these industries as workers — the rural cultural traditions were eroded to a great extent. Migrants from other parts of India — eastern Uttar Pradesh and Bihar — came to swell the ranks of these workers. The change in occupations affected their cultural output. The linguistic homogeneity of the working class in Bengal was fragmented. Could this be one of the reasons why the industrial proletariat of Bengal has come out with few songs, compared to the rich heritage of the nineteenth century working class songs of the industrialized nations of the West, or even of Bombay in the present century? This is a subject beyond the purview of the present article which is primarily concerned with the impact of the newly-acquired culture of the bhadralok of nineteenth century Calcutta, upon contemporary forms of women's popular culture in particular, and upon popular culture in general.

The cultural values imbibed by the bhadralok from Victorian England changed the character of the patrons of art. We have already seen how they drove a wedge into the relatively homogeneous cultural world of the women of nineteenth century Bengal. In the general context of popular culture, though the bulk of their audience were common people, the jatrawallas, the kavis and other folk artistes of Calcutta depended on rich patrons for their actual livelihood. In the early nineteenth century, patronage was offered by the descendants of the old zamindars or landed gentry, the *parvenu banias* (traders and brokers) and the East India Company agents, who were yet to give up their traditional attachment to these forms of entertainment, and were yet to be enlightened by English education. However, by the late nineteenth century, their sons and grandsons had grown up to look down upon these forms as licentious and voluptuous, thanks to the education that they had received in Hindu College and other institutions. By the end of the century, as 'enlightenment' closed in blotting out the familiar world with education, industrialization, new cultural tastes and activities, the popular culture that developed in nineteenth century Calcutta had to retreat and seek refuge in the Bengal countryside, perhaps in the hope of rediscovering the ties that had led to its birth. As one perceptive observer of the history of Bengali kavis describes the retreat:

> . . . Faced by the powerful onslaught of English education, prudery camouflaged by Brahmo Samaj fastidiousness, and the mid-Victorian morals of the Bankim [Chatterjee] group . . . the kavi songs with their tumult, jugglery of tunes and rustic slanging matches had to wind up from Calcutta. Deserting the gas-lit urban atmosphere, the kavi songs, tarjas and panchalis descended on the dimly-lit village stage in evenings ringing with the cricket's chirp. . . .[93]

But even in the Bengal villages, the women among these folk artistes had to fight the same sort of discrimination that they had suffered in Calcutta. We hear about one Kusumkumari at the turn of the present century who, during a kavi song performance in a village in the East Bengal district of Barisal, was abused by her male contender. The latter's aspersions, curiously enough, echo the same attitude which a hundred years ago Bhola Maira betrayed when attacking Jogyeshwari: "How dare you sing with us being a woman? You are only good for cooking!"[94] But the poetic rules of these folk cultural forms — like the practice of poetic duels in kavi songs — did allow the women singers to retaliate. Public performances, where the audience also often participated, — an integral aspect of folk performance — helped these women to draw upon a fund of imagery which belonged not to the mind of a single poet, but to the hidden collective life of the entire audience. Their retorts in a kavi duel, their amazingly imaginative interpretations of a mythological story in a panchali session, could therefore still evoke appreciative responses from the audience.

On the other hand, in the environment of a nuclear family (which was developing towards the end of the nineteenth century as opposed to the traditional Hindu joint family), the bhadramahila's cultural pursuits acquired a private chamber character. The collective gaiety of a panchali session or a basharghar was narrowed into individual compositions to be appreciated by the husband and his friends, or to be printed in magazines to be read by the educated few. The language itself of these compositions became the code of a private and defensive world insulated from the mainstream of life in the streets.

There were of course some exceptions. Mankumari Basu wrote

satirical verses on westernized Bengali men and women. Swarnakumari Devi's farces sometimes incorporated traditional women's dialect into the dialogues of her female characters. An interesting departure from conventional, effete bhadramahila literature was poem entitled "Bangaleer Babu" (the Bengali Babu) composed in 1882 by Mokhadayinee Mukhopadhyaya, a sister of W.C. Bonerjee, one of the founders of the Indian National Congress. She composed the poem as a retaliation against another poem entitled "Bangaleer Meye" (The Bengali Girl), written by the famous poet, Hem Chandra Bandyopadhyaya, who made fun of Bengali women describing them as shrews who were fond of Dashu Ray's doggerels and jhumur songs and had no serious interests. Mokshadayinee in a parody of the poem, replaced the Bengali woman with the Bengali babu — the lawyers, the deputy magistrates, the school teachers, the sub-judges, the clerks, the overseers — who from "ten in the morning till four in the afternoon work as slaves" and yet brag about their positions, and end up "blustering over pegs" of whisky in their homes in the evening.[95]

But the bulk of the literature produced by the newly educated women at the end of the nineteenth century, consisted of poems which expressed in refined, chaste Bengali a wide range of private sentiments — undying faith in the husband; grief at separation from or on the death of the husband; affection for children; love for nature and — often in a didactic tone — the need to educate their sisters who were still awaiting emancipation.

Education no doubt helped the bhadramahila to gain access to the sophisticated literature which was being produced by her male peers, to the debates that were raging on social reforms in intellectual circles, to the new concepts of white-collar domestic bliss and the accomplishments necessary to keep the husband in good humour. But in the process she lost something else — the potent and vigorous language of women's popular and folk cultural forms, the nimble-witted drollery and gusto that her mothers and grandmothers shared with the panchali singers and the jhumur dancers of the past. Bankim Chandra Chatterjee half-humorously summed up the situation. While acknowledging that the "new woman's" tastes were better than her predecessor's he said: "Her voice has ceased to rend the air like the cuckoo, and has become instead the mew of a pussy."[96]

NOTES

1. Basantika is a woman character in a skit in a Bengali journal, *Basantak*, 2, no. 10 (1874).
2. N. Augustus Willard, *A Treatise of the Music of India* (1834) in William Jones and N.A. Willard, *Music of India* (Calcutta: Sushil Gupta, 1962), p. 76.
3. Ibid.
4. The attitude comes out clearly in the following speech by a Young Bengali advocate of female education:

   > Hindoo girls may be permitted to attend public schools so long as they are infants, or, when ripened into womanhood, to receive a finished education at home: but for them to come out into society, it will be foolish to fear or expect the consummation of such a result, constituted as Hindu society at present is, as it will be, on the other hand, equally foolish on the part of any among our orthodox countrymen now to think of debarring our women from the light of knowledge, which has already struggled its way into their chambers of darkness. Educated, our women will certainly become more amiable and high-principled, more faithful and devoted to our service, but will by no means rebel against the sense of their rightful guardians.

   Koylaschunder Bose, "On the Education of Hindu Females," Medical College Theatre, Calcutta, 14 August 1846 in *Nineteenth Century Studies*, ed. Alok Roy (Calcutta: Bibliographical Research Centre, 1975), p. 198. The same sentiments were expressed in 1864, curiously enough, by a women's magazine which championed female education:

   > As long as the minds of men and women do not become pure, it will not be advisable to let them [women] out in this dangerous society....To bring out women in the open, the first requirement is to make them change their uncouth dress and steady their fragile minds by religious advice....

   Bamabodhini Patrika, c. 1864 (Sravan, B.S. 1271), p. 163.
5. See speech by Babu Greesh Chandra Ghosh, "Female Occupations in Bengal," Bengal Social Science Association, Calcutta, 30 Jan. 1868, in Bela Dutt Gupta, *Sociology in India* (Calcutta: Centre for Sociological Research, 1972), app., pp. 60-61.
6. *Somaprakash,* 7 Dec., 1863.
7. *Somaprakash,* c. 1864 (Chaitra 23, B.S. 1270).
8. Sukumar Sen, *Women's Dialect in Bengali* (Calcutta: Jijnasa, 1979). See also Sushil Kumar De, ed. *Bangla Prabad* (1945; rpt. Calcutta: A. Mukherjee, 1986). An exhaustive collection of Bengali proverbs, this

contains an invaluable introduction by De which devotes considerable space to women's proverbs, popular in the past, but now lost (pp. 26-32).

9. *Somaprakash*, 23 Nov. 1863.
10. *Somaprakash*, April 1864 (Chaitra, 23, B.S. 1270).
    The bhadralok tendency to equate women with the 'lower orders' can also be seen in the following statement of another Bengali intellectual who draws sanction from the scriptures: "There has been a discipline effected by the Rishis and the Brahmans in the heart and mind of the women and masses of Hindu society." Refuting the criticism that the "Sudras lay under a special suppression" in India, he claims that this was simply "on par with matters like the disabilities of woman and child." He then adds, "The Sudras knew it, and have never gone to Western savants for a redress of grievances in which it seems, ***common cause might as well be made with the Hindu womankind from the topmost down to be lowest castes***" (emphasis mine). Jogendra Chandra Ghosh, *Brahmanism and the Sudra* (Calcutta, 1901), pp. 50-52.
11. When speaking of the reforms for 'emancipating' women in nineteenth century Bengal, we often tend to ignore the possibility that the issues around which the debates on 'emancipation' revolved might have concerned only the andarmahal women of respectable bhadralok homes who constituted a minority of Bengali women.
12. Meredith Borthwick, "Bhadramahila and Changing Conjugal Relations in Bengal, 1850-1900," in Michael Allen and S.N. Mukherjee, *Women in India and Nepal*, Australian National University Monographs on South Asia, No. 8 (Delhi: Oxford University Press, 1982), pp. 108–9. Borthwick analyses how both the new anglicized education and the colonial avenues of employment made it desirable for the English educated bhadralok to have a wife who had some understanding of this new milieu.
13. Usha Chakrabarty, *Condition of Bengali Women Around the Second Half of the Nineteenth Century* (Calcutta: Published by the author 1963), p. 97.
14. The transformation of the mighty Shiva of Aryan mythology into a corpulent and indolent hemp-smoker in Bengali folkfore (found both in popular Bengali folk songs as well as in folk paintings) needs some explanation. Kosambi suggests pre-Aryan gods or godlings who were incorporated into and identified with the established Aryan Hindu pantheon, like Shiva and Vishnu. While retaining their primitive features in the local imagination, these gods were rechristened under new names. (See D.D. Kosambi, *The Culture and Civilization of India in Historical Outline* (Delhi: Vikas, 1977), pp. 48. 179.) It is quite possible that a similar local god associated with a cultivator's life style,

marked by labour in the fields during the sowing and harvesting seasons, and by a sort of languor during the off season, was incorporated into the Shiva image. A modern Bengali critic seeks to explain the popular image of Shiva in Bengal by suggesting that there was a deliberate attempt on the part of the upper caste Bengalis, after the Muslim invasion, to woo lower caste Hindus by co-opting the local gods into the Aryan pantheon. According to him:

> The Muslims came and conquered the country. The Hindus lost their kings and kingdoms. As a result, cracks developed among the warrior communities — the Bagdis, Doms, Hadis, Lohars, Khoiras, Tiors, etc. (who belonged to the lower castes). Temptations for royal patronage, for conversion to the religion of the conquerors, struck at the roots of society. At that moment, there was no other way available to bind them together except some religious identity. They had to be told: they were blessed by the gods, there was nothing ignoble in their occupations. Even if they did not have jobs of paid warriors, they could live with dignity by following their respective occupations.... They had to be told that the great Mahadeva (Shiva) himself at one time worked on the fields as an ordinary peasant. Annapoorna (another form of the goddess Durga, Shiva's consort), who gives rice to the entire world, once had to take on the appearance of a low caste Bagdi woman to catch fish. For a nation which believes in rebirth, consequences of one's misdeeds and in gods, these assurances were of no mean value.

(Harekrishna Mukhopadhyaya, *Gaudabanga Sanskriti* (Calcutta, 1972), pp. 117-18.)

15. Vaishnavcharan Basak, comp., *Bharatiya Sahasra Sangeet* (Calcutta, Basak and, Sons, n.d.).
16. Debiprasad-Sarbadhikary's reminiscences of his childhood in a Bengali village give us a glimpse into the easy indentification by Bengali women of the immersion of the goddess Durga with the departure of the newly-wed daughter for the home of the husband. He describes a typical scene on the day of the immersion, "...when the village housewife with tears in her eyes, and in a choked voice, bade goodbye to the Mother (Durga), no one seemed to remember the great omnipotent goddess. It was as if the sad scene of seeing off a village bride on her way to her father-in-law's house, had just been reenacted." See *Smritirekha* (Calcutta: Nikhil Chandra Sarbadhikary, 1933), p. 83.
17. The legends and anecdotes that had grown around Krishna in Bengal are at variance with the ancient Sanskrit texts. Krishna in Bengali folklore is a cowherd prince, who falls in love with Radha. Radha is married to Ayan Ghosh, who happens to be an uncle of Krishna. Ghosh is a Bengali surname, not usually found in any other part of India. Ayan's

mother, Jotila, and sister Kutila (literally meaning wily and crooked) are always waiting to catch unaware the two lovers who go to great lengths in secretly arranging their rendezvous. Radha as a Bengali village housewife, involved in an adulterous relationship, going to the river on the plea of filling her water vessel, but actually to meet Krishna, or pining in her home for the return of Krishna, or starting at the sound of his flute: these images have inspired Bengali folk poets for centuries.

18. Panchan Mandal, *Chithi-patre Samajchitra*, 2 vols. (Calcutta: Vishwabharati, 1953).
19. See reports in *Somaprakash,* c. 1863 (Chaitra 12, B.S. 1270) and in *Samvad Pravakar*, c. 1847 (Poush 18, B.S. 1254) in Benoy Ghosh, ed. *Samayik Patre Banglar Samajchitra* (Calcutta: Papyrus, 1978), 1.
20. Their names were Golokmani, Dayamani and Ratnamani. *Samachar Darpan*, 11 March 1826; quoted in Brojen Bandyopadhyay, ed. *Samvadpatre Sekaler Katha*, 2 vols. (Calcutta: Bangiya Sahitya Parishad, 1932, 1935).
21. *Samachar Darpan,* 22 Nov. 1828 in ibid.
22. Ramani Mohan Mullick, *Pracheena Stree Kavi* (Calcutta, 1863). The Devi here is a local Bengali goddess called Vashuli who was worshipped by Chandidas. The poetess Rami was employed as a sweeper in the temple of Vashuli.
23. Durgadas Lahiri, comp., *Bangleer Gaan* (Calcutta, 1905), p. 186. Madan is the god of love in Hindu mythology.
24. *Vishwakosh* (Calcutta, 1892). A reference to kheur is found under the entry kavi.
25. Prafulla Chandra Pal, *Pracheen Kabiwalar Gaan* (Calcutta: Calcutta University, 1958), p. 36.
26. Quoted in Mukhopadhyay, *Goudabanga Sanskriti*, p. 130. The last line is a variation on the perennial theme of keeping the affair secret from Jotila and Kutila, the two in-laws. See note 17.
27. Bepin Bihari Gupta, *Puratan Prasanga* (Calcutta: Vidyabharti, 1966), pp. 254-60. Ambalika, the daughter of Kashi Raja, was married to Vichitraveerjya, the son of King Shantanu and his wife Satyavati. Vichitraveerjya died young, and Satyavati sent her eldest son, Vyasa (composer of the epic poem *Mahabharata*) who was born out of her pre-marital union with the sage Parasara, to beget a child with Ambalika. The result was the birth of Pandu, the father of the five Pandava heroes. ("Adi Parva," *Mahabharata*).
28. Even Ishwar Chandra Gupta, the well-known poet and journalist, who was sympathetic towards kavis and other folk poets, seemed to be ashamed of the liberty they often took in jatras in ridiculing Hindu deities. He wrote: "Except the merry-making *itar* [vulgar or unedu-

cated] people no one from respectable society can find any pleasure in their compositions." *Samvad Pravakar*, 28 June 1848; quoted in Gaurishankar Bhattacharya, *Bangla Lokanatya Sameeksha* (Calcutta: Rabindra Bharati University, 1972), p. 188. Explaining the gradual dissociation of the bhadralok from these traditional popular cultural forms, Sivanath Shastri, the Brahmo reformer wrote later: "As English education spread in the country, educated people developed a sense of disgust towards these forms. Many felt ashamed to be present at kavi or jatra performances." See Sivanath Shastri, *Ramtonu Lahiri, O Tatkaleen Bango Samaj* (Calcutta: New Age, 1957), p. 57.

29. Pal, *Pracheen Kabiwalar Gaan*, 80.
30. M. Gluckman, *Closed Systems and Political Disorder in Early Modern Europe* (Edinburgh: Oliver and Boyd, 1964) and *Order and Rebellion in Tribal Society* (London: Cohen and West, 1963).
31. See Natalie Zimmon Davis, "Women on Top: Symbolic Sexual Inversion and Political Disorder in Early Modern Europe," in Barbara A. Babcock, ed. *The Reversible World: Symbolic Inversion in Art and Society* (Ithaca: Cornell University Press, 1978).
32. The story of Vidya-Sundar has been treated by many Bengali poets, the earliest being a composition by the sixteenth century poet Govinda Das of Chittagong (now a part of Bangladesh). But the best, in terms of poetic images, is that composed by Bharatchandra (1712-60). The story revolves round Vidya (which literally means knowledge), daughter of the king of Bardhaman; Sundar (literally meaning beautiful), son of the king of Kanchi; and Malini (an elderly woman selling flowers) who acts as a sort of go-between in arranging secret rendezvous for the lovers. The lovers get married according to Gandharva rites by exchanging garlands, unknown to their parents. Much of the poem is taken up by rather uninhibited descriptions of the various stages of their love making, couched in beautiful imagery. Sundar is finally caught when Vidya is found to be pregnant. On the eve of his execution, he prays to Kali who appears and saves him by revealing his identity. The King of Bardhaman welcomes him as his son-in-law, and everything ends happily.

    We should add however that in Bengali folk literature there was an old oral tradition of romantic songs about ordinary human characters (as distinct from the romantic songs about the divine pair Radha and Krishna). In Mymensingh (now in Bangladesh) there were two such popular songs: one on Andha-Bondhu, a blind flute-player with whom the wife of a prince fell in love, and the other on Shyam Ray, a prince who wanted to marry a low caste Dom woman. See Dinesh Sen, *Banglar Pura Naree* (Calcutta, 1939).
33. *Calcutta Review,* 13, no. 26 (1850), pp. 257-83.

34. *Bangaleer Gaan,* comp. Lahiri, p. 1041.
35. *Report of Chief Magistrate of Calcutta* and *Calcutta Municipal Corporation Health Report,* quoted in Chakrabarty, *Condition of Bengali Women.*
36. Meghnad Gupta, *Rater Kolkata* (Calcutta: Hemanta K. Roy, 1923), p. 10. The last line is an imaginative localized version of the Krishna legend sung in flippant vein.
37. Ibid.
38. *Bharatiya Sahasra Sangeet,* comp. Basak, p. 553.
39. All the proverbs quoted here are taken from *Bangla Prabad,* ed. De.
40. There was occasional interaction between popular and bhadralok forms, as well as between men and women artists, on the issue of widow remarriage.

    An anonymous, well known song on widow remarriage, which adopts the voice of a woman, was popular in the streets of Calcutta in the nineteenth century. It begins thus:

    Benchey thāk Vidyasagar chirōjeebee hōye
    Sadarey kōrechhey report bidhōbader hobey biye.

    (Long live Vidyasagar! He has submitted a report to the headquarters recommending marriage for widows.)

    After describing how they will live happily with their husbands following the passing of the legislation, the widows sing:

    Ālochāley, kanchkalāye, mālshār mukhey diye chhāi
    Eō bōey jābo shabey barondāla māthāye lōye.

    (Fie on sunned rice [the staple food which Bengali widows were supposed to have], green plantains and earthen pots! [used by widows in their daily worship]. With our husbands alive, we shall carry on our heads baskets welcoming them.)

    Quoted in *Bharatiya Sahasra,* comp. Basak, p. 455.

    Another anonymous folk song describes in a lilting tune:

    Orey Vidyasagar dibey biye
    Bidhōbāder dhōrey,
    Tāra āar phelbhey nā chul
    Bāndhbey benee gunjbe rey phul
    Sānkha sāri pōrbey nōtun kōrey.

    (Vidyasagar is getting widows to remarry. They'll no longer shave their heads. From now on, they'll tie their hair in tresses, tuck in flowers, and wear shell bangles and saris again.)

    Quoted in Barun Kumar Chakravarty, *Loka Sanskriti: Nana Prasanga* (Calcutta: Booktrust, 1981), pp. 20-21.

    A male folk poet, Dasarathi Ray, popularly known as Dasu Ray, whose panchali songs were sung all over nineteenth century Bengal, composed a song on widow remarriage, putting the words in the mouth of a woman who expresses her happiness at the prospect of remarriage.

In fact, many of Dasu Ray's songs use the popular idiom common among women. Born in 1805, he was probably influenced in the composition of his songs by a woman kavi of his village, Akshaya Patni. She had her own troupe which Dasu Ray joined as a young man. His relatives and the upper caste villagers did not approve of his attachment to Akshaya (who as her surname suggests, may have belonged to the lower caste of ferrymen). Dasu Ray was compelled to quit her troupe and set up his own troupe of panchali singeers in 1835. One of his songs, put in the mouth of women 'sinners' (*kula-kalankinis*) narrates the exploits of some of the much revered 'virtuous' women of the Hindu epics —Kunti, Ahalya, Mandodari, Satyavati and others — all of whom had children out of wedlock. The 'sinners' then ruefully complain:

They all fell in love and still got the reputation of being chaste women;
They easily came into possession of piety, wealth and love.
But in our love, there is only immense agony.
We can't bear it any more.
What else can we say?

See, Harimohan Mukhopadhyay, *Dashu Rayer Panchali,* p. 639.

41. *Bangla Prabad,* ed. De, p. 73.
42. *The Report of the Indian Factory Commission 1890* (Calcutta: Government of India, 1890).
43. Chakrabarty, *Condition of Bengali Women,* p. 63.
44. Shib Chander Bose, *The Hindoos As They Are* (London: Edward Stanford 1881; rpt. Calcutta, 1883), p. 8.
45. Review of *Naesho Rupeya* in *Bangardarshan* c. 1873 (Vaishak, B.S. 1280).
46. *Sulabh Samachar,* c. 1871 (Bhadra 28, B.S. 1278).
47. This tendency is represented by people like Radhakanta Deb (1784-1867) of the Shobhabazar royal family; the writer Bhabanicharan Bandyopadhyaya (1787-1848) who founded the Dharmasabha to fight the Act banning sati, and edited the newspaper *Samachar Chandrika;* and later by the poet journalist Ishwar Chandra Gupta, who ran the popular newspaper *Samvad Prabhakar.*
48. For the views of this section of the bhadralok, see Gautam Chattopadhyay, ed. *Awakening in Bengal in Early Nineteenth Century* (Calcutta: Research India, 1965). This is a compilation of speeches and articles submitted to the Society for the Acquisition of General Knowledge, an organization of the Young Bengal group.
49. In spite of the differences of opinion which often divided them, the Brahmo Samaj movement on the one hand, and intellectuals like Bankim

Chandra Chatterjee on the other, could both be taken as representatives of this trend. See, Pradip Sinha, *Nineteenth Century Bengal: Aspects of Social History* (Calcutta: Punthi Pustak, 1965).

50. See note 28 for Ishwar Chandra Gupta's views. As for the Young Bengal group, their attitude towards popular culture was set by their preceptor, H. Derozio (1819-42) whose journal *The Kaleidoscope* condemned the kavi songs which are "most esteemed by the natives" as "so disgustingly obscene and vulgar that they would shock the ears of any but a native to hear them." See The Kaleidoscope, no. 5 (Dec. 1829) quoted in *Awakening in Bengal*, ed. Chattopadhyay, p.79. Journals like the *Tattvabodhini Patrika* edited by the Brahmos, or *Bangadarshan* edited by men like Bankim Chandra Chatterjee, which shaped the views of the bhadralok to a great extent, took a similar stand on the popular cultural forms of nineteenth century Bengal.
51. Quoted in Bose, *The Hindoos As They Are,* pp. 118-19.
52. *Third Report of the Calcutta School Book Society* (1819-20), app. no. 2, p. 47.
53. Ibid.
54. Hur Chunder Dutt, *Bengali Life and Society* (Calcutta, 1853), pp. 10-11.
55. "A Hindoo on the Drama," Letter, *Morning Chronicle,* Jan. 1855.
56. *Calcutta Review,* 23, no. 26 (1850), pp. 257-83.
57. *Bangadarshan,* c. 1873 (Kartik, B.S. 1280).
58. See Swarnakumari Devi's article on education in the andarmahal in *Pradeep*, c. 1899 (Bhadra, B.S. 1306), quoted in Brojen Bandyopadhyay, *Sahitya Sadhak Charitmala,* No. 28 (Calcutta: Bangiya Sahitya Parishad, 1948). We get a glimpse of the Vaishnavite woman singer's immense popularity in the nineteenth century Bengali andarmahal from an amusing incident in Bankim Chandra Chatterjee's novel *Bisha-Briksha* (1873) set in the early part of the century. The villain dressed as a Vaishnavite female singer enters the andarmahal and is immediately flooded with requests for songs. The nature of the requests indicates the wide range of the taste of the andarmahal women in those days. Some ask for songs by Gobinda Adhikari and Gopal Urey, popular kavis of early nineteenth century Calcutta. Others want to hear Dashu Ray's panchali. A few elderly women order songs on Krishna, following which some middle-aged women start an argument about which section of the Krishna kirtan should be sung — the *sakhi-samvad* (dialogue between Radha and her women friends) or the viraha. In the midst of all this a "shameless young girl" demands a "tappa by Nidhu." The tappa or love song, marked by a rhythmical swing and composed by Ramnidhi Gupta, popularly known as Nidhu Babu, were great hits in Bengal at that time, but were often looked down upon by the orthodox and the puritanical, who felt that they belonged to the immoral environs of the brothel.

59. *Somaprakash,* c. 1863 (Chaitra 23. B.S. 1270).
60. *Calcutta Review,* 13, no. 26 (1850), pp. 257-83.
61. Dhap, invented by Rupchand Chattopadhyay of Murshidabad (1722-92), was later embellished by Madhusudan Kan (1818-63) of Jessore. Women singers came to monopolize this style. See Harimohan Mukhopadhyay, *Banglar Kirtan O Kirtaniya* (Calcutta: Calcutta Sahitya Sansad, 1971).
62. *Vishwakosh.*
63. Ibid.
64. Ibid.
65. *Somaprakash,* c. 1866 (Paush 3, B.S. 1273).
66. Mahendranath Dutt, *Kolikatar Puratan Kahinee O Pratha* (1929; rpt. Calcutta: Mahendra Publishing Committee, 1983), p. 29. Daksha-yagna is an episode in Hindu mythology, which describes a sacrifice organized by Daksha, the father of Parvati. Parvati cannot bear to hear her father speak ill of her absent husband, Shiva, and dies on the spot from grief. Shiva arrives with his followers, kills Daksha and spoils his *yagna* (fire sacrifice).
67. Bhuban Mohun Mitra, "The Native Theatre," *Hindu Pioneer,* 1, no. 2 (Oct. 1835), in *Nineteenth Century Studies,* ed. Ray. See also entry under 'rangalaya' in *Vishwakosh.*
68. "Much has been said by the correspondent of the *Hurkaru* about *Bidya Sundar's* being a very indecent play. Is it indecent because it is a Bengali work? Is it devoid of novelty and utility because it is a play composed in the vernacular language of the country? . . . The play of *Romeo and Juliet* and that of *Bidya Sundar* are much alike; he who thinks differently does not understand the spirit of Bharat Chandar's writings. . . . The Native Theatre is immoral because women of a public character are seen on this stage! Look . . . to the theatres of Italy, France, Germany etc., and tell me what you can object to the Native Theatre which you do not disapprove in others?" (Bhuban Mohun Mittra, Letter, *Hindu Pioneer,* 1, no. 3 (Nov. 1835) in *Nineteenth Century Studies,* ed. Ray). Attempts to defend indigenous popular culture and to appreciate lower class women performers were few and far between in nineteenth century bhadralok literature. We come across a review of jatra performance sponsored by "some respectable gentlemen well-versed in music" in Jorasanko, Calcutta, where we learn about a girl "over thirteen years old" called Chiddam (a rustic distortion of the name Sreedam, suggesting the plebian origins of the girl) whose songs charmed the audience. The reviewer writes: ". . . the girl is not very beautiful, but there is a certain gracefulness in her and one is moved to like her. I have never heard such a sweet voice ..." *Samvad Bhaskar,* 30 March, 1849.
69. *Madhyastha,* c. 1873 (Paush, B.S. 1280), pp. 621-23. Even the liberal minded journal *Hindoo Patriot* grudgingly accepted the introduction of

actresses into the public urban theatre. While reporting the performance of Michael Madhusudan Dutt's *Sharmishtha*, the paper said, "We wish this dramatic corps had done without the actresses," (18 Aug. 1873).

70. *Madhyastha*, ibid.
71. *Tattvabodhini Patrika*, 36 (1846) in *Samayik Patre*, ed. Ghosh, IV, p. 106. As part of their campaign against prostitution, bhadralok correspondents in newspapers repeatedly urged that they should not be allowed entry into musical gatherings, jatra performances and similar cultural events. See *Samvad Bhaskar*, 30 March 1849 and *Somaprakash*, c. 1863 (Chaitra 20, B.S. 1270). Even a paper like *Sulabh Samachar*, brought out by liberal bhadralok to educate the poor, demanded that prostitutes be debarred from entering the precincts of the Hindu Mela festival c. 1870 (Falgun 10, B.S. 1277).
72. Dutt, *Kolikatar Puratan Kahinee*, pp. 29-30.
73. *Bangaleer Gaan*, comp. Lahiri, p. 1041
74. Dutt, *Kolikatar Puratan Kahinee*, p. 30.
75. Composed by Kalidas Chattopadhyay (popularly known as Kali Mirza), quoted in *Bharatiya Sahasra Sangeet*, comp. Basak, p. 218. Although composed towards the end of the eighteenth or the beginning of the nineteenth century, the use of Sanskrit-derived Bengali words and the frequency of alliteration found in the poem became almost a mannerism with the bhadralok poets who followed him, whenever they composed songs in praise of Kali.
76. Bose, *The Hindoos As They Are*, p. 309.
77. *Somaprakash*, 30 Nov. 1863, p. 47.
78. Ibid., p. 38. Twenty years later, bashargar songs were still in vogue as is evident from the contemporary account of an English educated bhadralok who describes how the women entertained the bridegroom with "amorous songs, having reference to the diversions of Krishna with his mistress, and the numerous milkmaids," He then warned: "Frail as women naturally are, the example of such a god, combined with the sanction of religion, has undoubtedly a tendency to impair their virtue," See Bose, *The Hindoos As They Are*, p. 66.
79. See note 21.
80. Chakrabarty, *Condition of Bengali Women*, pp. 147-93.
81. Quoted in Jogendra Nath Gupta, *Bangeyr Mahila Kabi* (Calcutta: Ramkumar Machine Press, 1930) p. 59.
82. Bose, "On the Education of Hindoo Females" in *Nineteenth Century Studies*, ed. Ray. pp. 200, 214.
83. *Tattvabodhini Patrika*, 1880 in *Samayik Patre*, ed. Ghosh, V. p. 75.
84. *Bamabodhini Patrika*, c. 1864 (Kartik, B.S. 1271) in ibid., III p. 143.
85. Ibid., p. 152.
86. See *Samvad Pravakar*, Sept. 1854, quoted in ibid., I, pp. 184-86 and "A

Prostitute Residing in Calcutta" in ibid., III, pp. 20-21.

87. Chakrabarty, *Condition of Bengali Women*, pp. 147-93.
88. Ibid.
89. Quoted in *Hindoo Patriot*, 13 Oct. 1873.
90. Manmohan Bosu, *Manmohan Geetabali* (Calcutta: Gurudas Chattopadhyay, 1886), pp. 241-42.
91. Kailashbashinee Devi, *Hindu Mahilaganer Heenabostha* (Calcutta, 1863), p. 66.
92. *Antahpur*, May 1899.
93. Asit Kumar Bandhopadhyaya, Introd., *Kabial Kabigan* by Dinesh Chandra Sinha (Calcutta, 1977), p. 1.
94. Ibid., p. 2.
95. Gupta, *Bangeyr Mahila Kabi*, pp. 222-24.
96. Bankim Chandra Chatterjee, "Pracheena O Nabeena" in *Bibidha Prabandha* (1879; rpt. Calcutta: Basumati Sahitya Mandir, 1930).

That Magic Time:

*Women in the Telangana People's Struggle**

VASANTHA KANNABIRAN
and
K. LALITHA

The struggle was for land. Black soil. It was Sarkar land lying uncultivated . . . Five hundred acres . . . Why should the poor be without land?

Pesaru Sathamma

Sangham, Sangham folk I thought and served . . . I serve everyone. Because of the love I bear. Not because they fought for the land. Even if they fought for land do I have land now?

Chityala Ailamma

I was the only woman who went. I — Salamma. The sound of Salamma was like the roar of a lion, I fought like that . . . I fought in the movement and collapsed. That's all that counts. Nothing else. Not a cow in the herd; not a rupee in my waistcloth; not even a copper chain on my neck. Look at my life now.

Dudala Salamma

It was the magic of that time.

Acchamamba

THE TELANGANA PEOPLE'S STRUGGLE which began in 1946 and lasted till 1951 [1] is one of the two major post-war insurrectionary peasant struggles in India. Paradigmatic, both for the theoretical and the ideological questions that it raises for the left, it also raises several issues specific to women who were in the struggle. One reason for this is that by all accounts, both oral and written, women poured into the struggle in large numbers. Two differing perceptions of

* Much of the understanding that helped us write this paper is a result of the collective effort of the Telangana Working Group of Stree Shakti Sanghatana and the Group's work on editing and compiling histories of women in the Telangana People's Struggle for publication in Telugu.

their participation tend to emerge, especially from written accounts. Women are either seen as passive, secondary, supportive, inert, or they are glorified as heroines in revolt. Neither of these perceptions has the capacity to encompass completely the curious contradictoriness that emerges through the accounts of the women for whom the struggle was a lived experience. We find that there were many different kinds of activity and levels of consciousness coexisting among these women. Often we feel a kind of wonder at the whole complex of attitudes, ranging from subordination to rebellion, thrown up among the women from time to time. It is these attitudes as they surfaced in relation to specific problems, issues, or interpersonal grievances that rendered the women a subordinate group — possessed of its own dynamic and its own tensions — within the larger group of struggling peasants. While it is not our intention to deny that in a certain sense women arose along with the men in the struggle for land and against feudal exploitation, such statements in isolation tend to gloss over and erase the specificity of their participation. It was not merely the worsening conditions of existence affecting their practical interests, that was the cause of women joining the struggle. Perhaps the rumours of a change that was imminent or the fact that old values were crumbling, and that women were on the threshold of a new order, moved them in a manner that was qualitatively different from the way in which it moved the men. While to the men the breakdown of feudal authority meant an end to extortion and compulsory free labour, to the women it added the promise of a life where there would be greater equality, both within and outside the home. The awakening consciousness of these women does not appear as a simple and direct result of their participation in the struggle. It was a gradually increasing awareness mediated by the socio-economic situation, by tradition and by the very processes through which they struggled. While it is undeniable that the movement was ideologically committed to equality between the sexes, what emerges in retrospect is that the Party (or at least the persons in leadership positions) seemed to relate to the women, however unconsciously, through the hierarchy of gender. The hierarchy of this relationship as it was reproduced and experienced throughout the struggle, and their own self conception as it mediated the awareness of these women produced complex and contradictory accounts. We find that women poured into the movement seizing eagerly an opportunity that opened up for them the possibility of response to a world in which they were hitherto powerless and invisible. They soon discovered, as we realize looking back today, that the mechanisms of power which had held them back physically and overtly in the past had been transformed gradually into a mode of social control. As we analyse their experiences in this paper we discover how older mechanisms were replaced by an invisible policing which used microscopic measures. We see the hundred different ways through which control is experienced and exercised: the silences, the nuances of speech, the body language. Expressions of power internalized and built not only into the attitudes of the men but even more importantly into the very bodies of the women so that their subordination was constantly and subtly reinforced. A subordination so apparently tenuous, yet so pervasive, that it was difficult to articulate.

The conditions affecting the women of this time were doubly oppressive because of the additional burden they were forced to bear. Crucially affected by the oppression of landlord and moneylender, women who were a large section of the agricultural labour and tobacco leaf pickers, moved militantly into the struggle for land, better wages, fair rent, reasonable interest on cash and grain loans. They were subjected to *vetti* (compulsory services and exactions), bonded to the landlord, and exploited physically and sexually. Rape was an everyday reality, the undenied right of landlord or moneylender. *Adi bapa* or concubinage was prevalent. Adi bapa was a form of concubinage peculiar to Telangana, where a young girl usually from a bonded family, had to accompany the bride to her husband's house to tend her mistress, and to provide sexual service to the master. Her virginity was therefore as important as the bride's. The fact that girls had already been raped or seduced by a man in the house they were attached to by birth often saved them from this fate.

The oppression of the upper class women was qualitatively different in the sense that the violence they faced was not visible and physical but invisible and structural. *Purdah* (seclusion) was strictly observed both by high caste Hindu and Muslim families. Child marriage and early widowhood were common. Education for women was unheard of. Outside the Nizam's state social reform movements had already touched women's lives and the nationalist movement had brought women into public life. In Telangana the cultural dominance of Muslim feudal rule kept women out of the mainstream much longer. Fora, such as the Andhra Maha Sabha which sprang up to assert the cultural identity of the people, added women's education to their agenda of constitutional reform and civil liberties. Thus many women who were drawn into the cultural movements, drew closer to the Communist Party which was working through the Andhra Maha Sabha. When the Andhra Maha Sabha added basic agrarian reforms to its programme of action these women also plunged into the struggle.

What was the response of women to the new horizons opening up before them? Suddenly, the four walls of the household seemed to fall apart and structures of feudal oppression, so unchanging and permanent in the past, were not only being questioned but were also challenged in practice. A new society, a socialist society was on the horizon. Women were being exhorted and required to come out and share the responsibility of building this new society where men and women would be equal. Paradoxically enough, although women are perceived as the guardians and preservers of traditional culture and although the very stability of any given society is perceived as resting on the purity and orthodoxy of its women, in practice women have achieved major gains during periods of war or revolution. It is only in such periods of social dysfunction, with the breakdown of constant surveillance and the mechanisms of discipline that normally objectify them, that women rush forth to grasp the opportunities for response and growth that become possible.

Let us look at what the women tell us of their life before the struggle. (For additional information about the women see list at the end of the paper.) Sugunamma tells us how her first contact with the outside world occurred when her brother insisted on her serving tea personally to their visitors. The brother also objected to his sister's marriage to an old, already married, rich man and tutored her to say no to the marriage. Listening to Sugunamma's account of how the whole village gathered to gasp at the unprecedented sight of a girl actually saying no, we learn how for a woman even the possibility of consent or choice in marriage was radical in its implications.

Lalitha, who was married at the age of five, tells us how after coming into the movement, when her husband was in jail, she went to her parent's home to deliver a child. She had no choice but to subject herself to a purification ceremony where her "*inner tongue*" (uvula) was burnt with a hot golden wire. It is interesting how the punishment seeks to purify and discipline by fire her "*inner tongue*" for the abuse of her brahmin taste through mixed eating (as a Brahmin she had lost her caste by eating with other castes). Lalitha shrugs off the physical pain of the incident but it is evident that it has had the desired effect of searing her own humiliation and powerlessness into her memory. The punishment is also an example of how quickly deviant women can be reclaimed and disciplined by tradition at moments of physical helplessness.

The peasant women from Vempati told us how in those days they did not dare to wear a flower in their hair, or to wear a good sari. It was not simply a question of seeming attractive and thus inviting sexual harassment. The harassment was already there. But the added fear of seeming to step beyond their station in life and the fear of what punishment it might bring was inhibiting enough. They asked us whether *before the Sanghams* (lit. associations, here local branches of Andhra Maha Sabha) *came* they could have sat down with us all together and talked as they did now.

Kamalamma, who came from a *devadasi* background, tells us how her sister escaped being sent as an Adi bapa with the girl of the house since she had been seduced by one of the other men in the family. Koteshwaramma tells us how she was married at four and widowed at five or six. When she was married again at eighteen, the groom came hiding in a heavily curtained cart, so that villagers would not attack him and prevent the marriage. Examples like this abound. Upper class women had to observe purdah in Telangana. Mallu Swarajyam describes how her mother could not be seen even by the washer-woman except at a fixed hour on a fixed day. When bangle-sellers came to the house the women thrust their hands out from under the curtain to have the bangles fitted. Dayani Kausalya tells us how they had never stepped out of the courtyard of the house into the fields before the struggle. Details such as these establish for us the norms which circumscribed and defined women just a few years before the struggle but are so distanced from the present to belong, as it were, to another age. The changes that have come after the struggle are tangible and easy to see.

In most societies there has been a fairly clear demarcation of the public domain — of war, production and politics — and the private domain: of the family, domestic labour, reproduction and sexuality. While men have moved fairly easily between the two, women, by and large, have been confined to the private domain. Peasant women have no doubt always had access into the public sphere of production, but have remained at a level that is marginal and powerless. Further even the woman who is a wage-labourer has, with few exceptions, internalized and accepted the sexual division of labour. They have always culturally and ideologically accepted the power and control of their men however powerless or oppressed the latter may be outside the home. From such a situation women were catapulted, as it were, into a moment when everything entered the realm of possibility. It was "the magic of that time" many women said to us. They were asked to come and attend meetings. They were taught to read and write and discuss political questions. Political classes were held for them and they were told about their own country as well as about distant countries. The knowledge they gained as a result of these classes gave them the tools to understand their own social reality. For example, Kamalamma says: "It was because of the Communist Party that my learning stood me in good stead and I knew at least this much. But my sister has just forgotten everything and it's all just wasted." The ideological framework provided by the Party helped the women to analyse their situation, process their knowledge and make sense of their surroundings. Priyamvada says, "It was the Party that made human beings of us." Kondapalli Koteswaramma says, "It was the Party that gave us the enthusiasm and said to us 'come!'." Peasant women like Salamma said: "One should work in the Sangham and die. One should be born to life with strength, the strength of our shoulders. How did my wisdom grow out of this? . . . I used to graze buffaloes but its all at the tip of my tongue. . . . The struggle for gruel and water — I lived in such strength and power for it." The opportunity to act, the power to fight for control over their own lives gave the women an identity, a sense of enormous strength and wisdom. Chakali Ailamma, a figure of significance because one of the earliest struggles was for her land says; "My husband was nobody, my sons, they are nobody. Wherever you go, whatever you do it is my name they will mention first . . . you must be like Ailamma they say." All the women refer to the Party or the Sangham as the basis and the cause of their liberation.

Koteswaramma describes her fear of marrying again, afraid that her ill luck would kill the man who married her; she also spoke of the support and encouragement of the men in the Party. Later she went on stage, acting and singing as part of the cultural squad of the Party. She talks of her misgivings and anxiety when she had to go on stage. She explains that it was the assurance that the Party would protect the women who acted, that finally gave them the confidence. Respectable women, after all, did not act in those days. Crossing the barrier of respectability, although eventually liberating in its effect, is painful and frightening for women initially. The time, she says, was so *right.*

As the women became active in the Sanghams they were asked to take up issues specific to women and organize the peasant women around these issues. Two different reasons emerge for the mobilization of women, from the accounts of the women themselves. Manikonda Suryavathi tells us: "The members of the Sanghams sent their wives and sisters to the classes. They believed that if men were to be emancipated, if they were to become highly conscious then the consciousness should also spread to the home. This was elementary to their education." She speaks of how, when the educated women formed clubs, they did not allow ordinary women to join. And so they wanted to start Sanghams for women who were peasants or agricultural labourers. Kondapalli Koteswaramma asks: "How could they manage without women? Suppose there is a den — if there were four men there, it would be suspicious. A family would not be suspicious. Children would make it less suspicious and so they took us away." Priyamvada gives yet another reason.

> It was then decided that if women were trained and sent out among the villages it would be useful for the Party. It would be easier to get help during times of severe repression and underground life. If women didn't came forward and work that kind of help would not be possible. So the party gave us such programmes.

And Mallu Swarajyam says,

> In those days we women came forward, we had an aim, were filled with an enthusiasm . . . . We felt firmly that we were equal to the men. That was so important. A time when there was purdah, when they used to oppress women terribly . . . men had total authority over women . . . . If they spoke up they were beaten more . . . except for a few all houses were the same. So women had to be brought out of this condition.

Thus there was a deliberate attempt to mobilize women and to take up campaigns that would affect their practical interest. Priyamvada tells us how the discussions included issues like wages, wife beating, child care, hygiene and the right to breast feed infants during work. Both Suryavathi and Udayam tell us of a campaign called "model housewife," where the women were taught to cook nutritious food, bring up healthy infants, keep their environment clean, and which also included conducting various sports and games for women. One campaign, in Andhra, which was extremely popular was constructing lavatories for women. The Navjivan Mahila Mandal, situated in Hyderabad, took up the distribution of ration cards, cheap grain coupons and ran cheap milk centres. The women who came to these centres were eventually politicized to oppose the atrocities of the Razakars. Pramila Tai's work in the Navjivan Mahila Mandal gave her such a network of sympathetic contacts that she was able to arrange for the shelter and the support of many underground Party comrades during periods of acute repression. Both the Navjivan Mahila Mandal and the Mahila Sanghams (women's organizations) were successful in reaching out to women because they took up issues of practical gender interest to women i.e., issues arising from their concrete conditions of existence and women's specific place in the existing division of labour. One of the reasons the Party found it necessary to mobilize women was also because it would be easier to get support during periods of repression. But while such problems were taken up in an attempt to involve women, we do not find that there was an awareness of these gender specific areas as valid sites of political struggle. And so we find that although the interest of women in such issues arose from their subordination, mobilization around these issues drew their loyalty and support without leading to an increased awareness of the nature or source of that subordination.

The peasant women who formed the backbone of the resistance

undoubtedly came into the struggle for land, for better wages, abolition of vetti, and against exorbitant interest on grain and cash loans. In the thick of the struggle and bearing the brunt of repression their interests were bound to the cause in a way which made their participation inevitable. Accounts tell us how two hundred peasant women stood together in Penukonda and chased the police out of the village. In Appajipet, women encircled a police van, attacked the police with pestles and chilli powder and secured the release of their Sangham activists. Women from villages like Akkirajupalli were constantly beaten, tortured and raped by Razakars in an attempt to crush the resistance. They refused to reveal the whereabouts of the Sangham activists in spite of severe torture. Gajjela Ballamma of Akkirajupalli says: "My husband was also in the Party. That's why the Razakars were so furious — because he was there. . . . The whole of Akkirajupalli became famous. The whole village should be one —united they said." And Saidamma describes how the Sangham activist would come:

> As we were going — they said, "Sister we are your slaves — it is four days since we ate!" . . . "Where have I been able to cook? I have only a little bread" — then they said, "Please give us a piece of bread." I had only three *rotis*, one came, and I gave him one, then another one came, and I gave him the other and another one came, and I gave it all away. All three of them jumped over the wall. . . . They ate the bread there. What sin was this? They drank the water from the pot and blessed me saying, "Thank you, it is four days since we ate" —and went their way. Now they were Communists. . . .

And Vajramma describes: "In those days when the Razakars asked us to dance *Bathakamma* (dance performed at the festival of Bathakamma, a local mother goddess) we danced. We stripped when they asked us to strip. In those times where was honour, where was shame?"

But for their staunch support and commitment the movement could not have survived for nearly six years. In dire want themselves, they shared the little food they had with the Sangham activists. Fully aware that supplying food and shelter would bring more repression they evolved their own systems of passing messages and relaying food to the squads in the forests.

Women from all classes who were thus drawn into the movement not only responded with energy and commitment, but moved with a new found deliberate skill both into the urban middle class as well as into the peasant sections of the population, drawing their support slowly but surely into the movement. The Communist Party which seriously took up issues of social reforms for women like widow marriage, prohibition of child marriage, education for women, and better opportunities, also began to identify women of ability and draw them into the movement. It quickly realized that these women were crucial for the continuation of the struggle.

When we look at the way in which women generally perceived their own work, we find two marked trends. On the one hand, a kind of pride at their ability to travel alone, to travel at night, transport guns, arrange and run shelters, travel through forests and address meetings. Even where they were constantly expected to cook and provide food for the party comrades they seldom resented it. They probably shared the conviction that in a new society with the revolution, women would be emancipated as a matter of course. We hear glowing accounts of Bullemma, who was referred to as Gorky's "Mother". She took great pride in extending her gentle mothering care to all the young people in the movement. And her reward was the gratitude and love showered on her. Ailamma said: "I serve everyone. Because of the love I bear." Lalitha, who was in the Telangana area in the thick of struggle, does not sound any different.

> Although I was young, I took all the responsibilities here — in the Party. The cooking and serving meals were all my responsibility. Swarajyam and the others used to help a little but the responsibility was mine. They were not so interested in the work. The men would often say, "Look Lalitha is working alone. That shouldn't happen." But I never created problems or compared the work done. *I was an example to all of them.* Swarajyam and the others called me *Akka* (elder sister) and were very respectful to me. Since I came from a traditionally cultured family my word was always final on many things. How to behave with men, how to wear the sari over their shoulders. At a glance from me they would adjust their saris over their breasts. I never said anything much to anyone. I used to just work till my patience lasted. *The men never helped in these chores. . . .* I never insisted on companions. *It was the men who chided the other women for not doing enough.* (emphasis added)

Significantly, Lalitha's tone carries no note of criticism for the men who were not doing anything. The implied criticism is for the women who did not share the work, and a certain pride at the recognition of her work. Related to the tone of responsibility is the sense of authority. How to dress, how to behave with men, there is pride in the fact that she was an example. Thus, by according silent approval and authority to the women who reinforced and maintained middle class norms, it was possible to herd women into culturally acceptable patterns of behaviour.

Koteswaramma gives us an instance that is interesting. She tells us how in the beginning they were encouraged to come to the meetings but later as their enthusiasm grew the men would say: "There are comrades coming, you all do the cooking. It doesn't matter if you don't come for the procession, so many others are coming, you have to do the cooking for them." The women would then protest saying: "Why should we cook? Why don't you go to a hotel and eat? Why don't we need to come?"

Repeatedly when we asked women about domestic chores in the dens and shelters they would claim that such work was shared equally —but in their accounts we never came across instances of the work actually being shared. Housework, by its very invisibility, adds to the devaluation and marginalization of women. Further the assumption that it is naturally women's work not only reinforces the division of public and private domains but keeps women in supportive, secondary roles. We find that while during the struggle there was some ideological recognition of this, it was in practice limited to the extent of statements being generally made that all work should be shared and shared equally. Everyday behaviour invariably relegated domestic chores to the women. Understandably enough, the women took all this work in their stride. Even if their role in the movement was an extension of their familial role, the fact that it was for a cause brought a sufficient sense of fulfilment. The extension of the private sphere into these areas of the public domain which were barred to women was itself a release. But the code within which these women defined themselves and were defined emerges in some of the descriptions of their work. Acchamamba, one of the earliest barefoot doctors known to us, narrates her ability to suture and dress wounds, give injections, treat bullet wounds and deliver children as if it were nothing. She describes in detail her capacity to procure edible fruits and meat to provide food for the squad. But as she narrates her story it is evident that the problem of catering to individual tastes without seeming partial and her pain at being accused of an immoral relationship allowed her no space to consider the radical dimensions of her medical practice.

Evidently, the women resisted being relegated to cooking and often demanded more. Dudala Salamma says: "Where did I cook? May your mother . . . . Damn cooking! No I never cooked! I wore a *dhoti* [garment tied around the waist, usually by men] like a man, wore a shirt and shorts, bound a kerchief round my head. I was disguised as a man. One should serve the people." Dronavali Anasuya says: "I told them that nowhere in the world has a revolution taken place without women. At the most we may take five minutes to do what they do in three minutes." Narasamma in her letter to the Party asks fiercely why women were not being taken into the guerilla squads. Swarajyam who says defiantly that she didn't even know how to cook during the struggle, adds wryly that she has not had much choice after the struggle was called off! Leaders mention that while a few women carried guns they were generally helpful in other ways — cooking, taking messages, nursing wounded comrades, etc. While claiming that the women were emancipated *as far as the struggle was concerned* there is a quick qualification that they did not have the consciousness to fight with rifles and all that: "*After all they are women is it not?* After all they are women, we did not like that women should be taken into the battlefields." [2]

This figure of the traditionally *backward* woman who would display endurance and heroism in secondary supportive roles but who could not be expected to fight with rifles is central to our whole understanding of the problem of women in the struggle. The Party sought to organize these women through political classes where certain types of knowledge, which included a degree of literacy and selected readings, were made available to them. Women grasped the knowledge offered in these classes hoping to gain thereby the tools which would eventually liberate them. They hoped perhaps to find a solution to what they experienced as a paradox in their own situation. Koteswaramma, talking of the political education, says: "I wonder whether they went on without seeing if we understood anything. Maybe we did not understand or digest anything. It was like feeding *avakai* [hot mango pickle] on the *annaprasan* day [first ceremonial feed of solids, usually soft rice and sweet lentils]." She also adds that the matter was as difficult to swallow as boiled iron pellets.

What we begin to sense here is the problematic of seeing the whole question of organizing women as a matter of political education. Discussing the global situation, the Russian revolution and socialist society may have extended the frontiers of their knowledge. But what bearing did it have on the issues of power and authority that constantly came into prominence where the women were concerned? How did it touch upon the tensions that marked the traditional gap between the women who flocked into the movement and the feudal attitudes of the leadership, so deeply rooted in the culturally established relationships of power? How could such a political education clarify for the women the possibility that the very demands of organizational discipline could prevent and discourage them from sharing or discussing problems specific to them? Both Swarajyam and Anasuya tell us of specific instances when they were warned not to support or defend women (who were under attack), merely out of a sense of partiality to their own sex. It was this same organizational discipline applicable to both men and women, we are assured repeatedly, which left the women feeling marginal, inadequate and problematic. Women always have and still continue to locate the social problems in their environment within themselves and in their own shortcomings. Men in the leadership often having been the emancipating factor in their lives, women have found it delicate or awkward to articulate, or even perceive, at what precise point the patriarchal assumptions of the men grew into obstacles to women's own growing awareness. Recruiting women into the Party was always seen as fraught with problems. The fact that the Party took up questions of social reform for women, undoubtedly threw it open to public attack on grounds of morality. Priyamvada mentions how women flocked to the Party in search of a better life.

> They probably felt that if they came to the Party their lives would change for the better. They couldn't say all this very clearly but they felt they could experience another life, live as they chose to. But the Party could not support them as it did not have a clear understanding of how to tackle the problem of women who left their husbands and came away. They were afraid the Party would lose its reputation. It would

> have been good to support those women. . . . There was possibility then for the Party to have strong roots in the women. But they failed. . . .

At the same time we find that there is an anxiety in the leadership to maintain a 'pure' image. Sundarayya for instance says:

> At the same time *we did not encourage licence or anarchic sexual behaviour*, even though we did not look at sex relations or lapses and mistakes from the ascetic angle or from the angle of sin. But before a decision was given and implemented, it was necessary to explain to the person concerned, as well as to the public, how the decision helped towards *a cleaner and frank life*. It contributed to a better development of the people's movement and of social relations. *No decision was to be given which would put mass opinion against us.*[3] (emphasis added)

We find that as a result of the social reforms that the Party took up, women were released for political action from the structures that confined them. Women who had lost their husbands in the struggle, women who found it impossible to continue working within marriages that had turned oppressive — divorces and remarriage had to be arranged for some of them. In order to release the women for political action and ensure their continued support through the arduous periods of struggle some of the feudal ideologies that confined and oppressed them had to be attacked. But how deeply the leadership itself was enmeshed and held by the very structures it sought to attack is reflected in the quickness with which the boundaries were re-established. Women continued to suffer the burden of surveillance that being the bearers of tradition entailed. The changing times and the changed requirements of the period placed certain demands on the women. At the same time, the deep rooted prejudices that were so difficult to eradicate laid a different set of expectations on them. The dual requirements often clashed and were quite contradictory. It is difficult to analyse exactly how these attitudes defined the social relationships of that period. But taking these attitudes into consideration is crucial to any understanding of women's struggle since they so effectively restrict women's lives and affect their conception of themselves. What the women found was that while entry into the movement had released them into the public domain for political action, the code by which they were judged and assessed was still the code of the private domain.

Pramila Tai narrates the story of a young woman, an active worker at one of the centres, who had to run away from home. *All* the comrades insisted on sending her back to her mother. Tai was alone in objecting and she was overruled. Her comment on this is interesting:

> *What I found insulting* is that they thought that if this girl is detained, then there may be scandals in the Party, that this girl is carrying on with someone and all that, so they objected. *Men always think like that and leadership especially.*

Time and again we hear in their voices an undertone of harassment. In spite of the nostalgia and warmth with which they relive those magic times there is a note of pain, of a vision betrayed. Kamalamma left one child behind and joined a squad. She delivered another child in the forest and was ordered to give away the six month old child as the safety of the squad was at stake. She was told she would *be making history*, that her name would go down in history if she sacrificed the child for the movement. She begged for a few days time to wait for her husband before giving away the child. She felt deeply wounded when accused of not having a correct proletarian consciousness. She gave the child away but the rawness of that experience remains with her today. She was not the only woman to give up a child. Dronavali Anasuya left a twenty-day old infant with a couple who came to visit her, went for a procession, got arrested and ran a high temperature (milk fever) for days because she was unable to feed her infant. Her fellow prisoners describe how they looked after her, fomenting her breasts and drawing out the milk. And most of the women did it with courage and out of a resoluteness which showed that the exigencies of the movement took precedence over all 'natural', 'maternal', or 'familial' ties.

Acchamamba talks of the gossip and scandal she had to face. She tells us how she was expelled merely because a man in another squad claimed a relationship with her. Her protestations of innocence were to no effect. It was her word against his. Narsamma, a peasant activist, writing to Sundarayya raises the question clearly:

> We women are still being looked upon with the old outlook that we are inferior. Any slip or mistake we commit, our leaders come down on us heavily. It becomes a subject of open gossip and scandal. We must be

guided and improved and not derided. If we move a little freely we are watched with suspicion. Why have you not allowed any women to participate in actual guerilla raids on the enemy ? [4]

Narsamma's accusation that the old outlook still prevails is echoed in many of the accounts women give of those days. Another woman tells of her shock when men in the den tried to use her. "I felt that the only protection I could get would be through marriage. There was no one to talk it over with." There was an implicit but definite pressure to marry that operated on the women. Single unattached women were an uncertain factor. It was so much easier then, in the movement, as now, to contain and define women through marriage. In spite of all this it is evident that women took their work in the struggle for granted. They accepted without question the need to give up children, put up with 'inconveniences' uncomplainingly, adjust to situations and to people. The *visible* battle that they fought was so simple that it left them with a sense of exhilaration. The scarring that is visible today, the note of suffering, the sense of betrayal is the result of the invisible battle that they constantly had to fight. Their anguish springs from the fact that women are traditionally held responsible for the desires they excite, and end up paying dearly for this, apologizing for their very existence from a deeprooted sense of guilt and insecurity. Koteswaramma murmurs: "Women are like untouchables is it not? Then or now?" and Pramila Tai says, "Whatever you may say it is still there." Sugunamma provides an even more moving example. She tells us of her horror when several years after the struggle was called off, she asked Swarajyam's husband what Swarajyam was doing, "Cooking and eating, what else?" he retorted. If someone like Swarajyam, the legendary heroine of Telangana, could be dismissed in such terms, she felt, what of lesser mortals like herself?

Given this background of dismissive contempt it is hardly surprising that many of the women we met often began with: "What did we do? nothing much." It was only as they began to narrate their experiences, reliving those days with a nostalgia and warmth that marked them as the best period of their lives, that the range and quality of their participation came through. Swarajyam describes how her mother invoked a provision of the Nizam's law to protect the custom of purdah which prohibited the police from either entering a house at night or without sufficient notice. Quoting that law, she kept the police outside till daybreak while her son escaped at night through the back door. No traditional account documents the creativity and ingenuity with which women drew on group support, exploiting its structure to ward off danger. Antici pating an attack from the Razakars, they often sat together pretending that a woman was in labour, or that an old woman was dead, or that a girl had just reached puberty. Time and again they drew on such ritual occasions, displayed cunning strategies of survival and exploited traditionally held taboos, taboos which even the enemy would be wary of violating. All this and more.

The issue that troubles us today is why is it that in all these accounts there is a note of pain, the sense of a vision betrayed? Why is it that a movement that was undeniably exhilarating for the women, so rich an experience that their voices and faces came alive as they spoke of those days, left them so isolated and vulnerable? Salamma who said her name was like the sound of a lion says: "Not a rupee in my waistcloth, not even a copper chain on my neck. Look at my life now." One concern that constantly surfaces for us is that in attempting to analyse the political dimensions of that isolation and vulnerability we do not erase the creativity, the commitment, or the will that women brought into the struggle.

Ailamma says:

Our bangles broken
Our pots broken
Not a pot to beg in
Not a pot to cook in
No pot even to drink in.

Speaking of life after the struggle was called off Priyamvada says, "I felt like committing suicide," and Sugunamma says, "That was my first taste of suffering." Swarajyam tells of how she waited, working in her fields, in the hope that the Party would certainly require her talent for public speaking and call her back. Both Pramila Tai and Narasamma are so clear in their assessment that one hardly needs a sterner indictment of the patriarchal attitudes that prevailed in the Party. It is fairly easy to see that the isolation and vulnerability that women felt, and their experience of being marginalized after the struggle was called off, are rooted in two factors. The first is a feudal patriarchal attitude which felt that women are problematic in the movement because of their 'tendency' to attract men, get pregnant, need abortions or child care, and create conflicts within the ranks of men. The second is a marxist resistance to accord emotions or subjective experiences any objective or critical significance, coupled with the assumption that the basis of all these conflicts and struggles can be ultimately traced to the economic sphere. This results in the conviction that areas of personal experience are neither legitimate areas of debate nor of critical value. These factors resulted in relegating women to the private domain, in continuing to see problems of sexuality, of children and of the family as personal problems, and in an emphasis on a code of morality that often resulted in oppressing women further and policing them socially. The whole problematic of women in the movement is further complicated by the fact that the ideological claims of a socialist equality, which included equality between sexes, kept clashing with the culturally given relationship of subordination and domination coded into their everyday behaviour. The failure of the leadership to see how trapped they were within the very culture they sought to destroy, their inability to see that the socialist message of equality was ultimately assimilated into the patriarchal and moralistic terms of the older culture, resulted in the situation women were faced with. When did the women become aware of the fact that their subordination — sanctified by religion, made desirable by tradition and materialized by the very structure of society — was not going to disappear with classes in political education? We hear so much about the problem both from what has been written of the period and from what the participants say, but we learn even more from their silences. And it is these areas of silence that shift the question from the sphere of ideology into the realm of culture. We wonder what it meant to these women to pour into a movement so rebelliously? After a lifetime of training, women learn to decipher and manipulate the familiar signs around them and try to make sense of their surroundings. Having learnt the slow hard way to extract some meaning from their harsh reality, would they really throw it all away in a moment of emotion? Is it possible, we must ask, for women who perfect their strategies for survival, whose greatest expertise has been to eke an existence out of practically nothing, creating a semblance of comfort, to risk their family, home and security and flock into a struggle so impulsively? And yet why were they treated as if this was the case? Why did the family as a sacrosanct unit with all its traditional associations, loom so large before the leadership? But even so in acute or crisis conditions, the exigencies of the struggle required of women that they "create history" by deserting or giving up their children or husbands. The question that confronts us here is how the women were perceived in this struggle. Were they seen as mere agents or was there any sense in which they were also seen as subjects? Was their will and their reason perceived as constitutive of their readiness to rebel? Or were they like wilful children rushing out to join in an event which stood clearly outside the flow of daily life and threatened to displace existing power structures? Was it perhaps an incipient political consciousness which saw, however faintly, the possibility of an inversion of the relationships of subordination and domination that had seemed hitherto inviolable? Such as the power relationships which were part of the very character of village life — the vetti, the levies, the taxes —and also the power relations that characterize what we would define today as patriarchy?

One of the issues that we see constantly being raised is the problematic of political organization. Organizational discipline (and every woman we spoke to referred to its strictness and neutrality) becomes the means of solving all questions of power and authority. It can lay down the blue-print for what can be discussed and what cannot. No doubt when there is a crisis, solutions will be sought towards establishing what Sundarayya calls a cleaner and franker life. But the perspective from which one decides what is clean and what is licentious does not enter the area of debate. In turning away from issues of culture and consciousness and viewing organization purely as a matter of political organization the old relationships of power and authority are not only reproduced but even reinforced. The fact that women then were unable to push this forward, or, if at all, to do so apologetically, is not a function of their dependence or traditional backwardness. To interpret it as such would be to ignore the two-sidedness of this relationship. It would be to miss the loud silence with which authority sedulously policed the sphere of the personal where the subjugation of women is situated. To expect that the women of that time could have spoken out, to take their silence on certain issues at face value without reading its meaning, is to forget how completely the subjugated person reproduces and participates in the systems of power which subjugate her. And so all that we can hear is a murmur, "Women are like untouchables is it not? Then or now." We find that when these women tried to raise issues as women they were dealt with either through firm authority or a kind paternalism. When key questions of authority and power came up, women were warned in the interests of organizational discipline not to support other women who were under criticism. And so there was in fact an unstated, but nonetheless clearly understood, prohibition on women raising or rallying around issues that were gender specific. While 'social problems' like child marriage, widow marriage and divorce had a legitimacy and were widely discussed, there was an uneasy sense that the crucial areas where power operates (for women) — the family, marriage and sexuality —were outside the scope of debate. Thus the assumption that problems arising from the personal or private domain were problems to which individual solutions had to be found, was really rooted in the culturally given relationships of power. The refusal to see the political significance of these issues for women, the exclusion of the private domain from the area of political debate resulted in erecting the four walls of the household again. It was not merely, as we see now, the objective conditions prevailing, nor the course of history, but the inability to *hear* what the women were saying that resulted in their being sent two steps back. It was the satisfaction arising out of taking the correct ideological position without the capacity to link it to an understanding of the roots of their own cultural attitudes that left the leadership trapped unquestioningly in old feudal assumptions and banished the women from the unknown dangers of forest and battlefield to the old familiar site of their oppression and their security — the family and the fireside.

The women

All the women interviewed by us were in their late fifties or mid-sixties and most of them lead semi-retired lives today. Dates of birth were difficult to gather as women mark the passage of time with their marriages, the birth of their children and different calamities, rather than through exact dates.

1. *Pesaru Sathamma:* peasant woman from Addagudam where a police and Razakar camp was set up.
2. *Chityala/Chakali Ailamma:* significant figure in the struggle. Her land was the first to be seized. She died in 1985.
3. *Dudala Salamma:* peasant woman from Quila Shapur, an active worker, tortured greatly by the police.
4. *Regalla Acchamamba:* real name, Susheela. Was a barefoot doctor in the forests. Now lives in a village called Kunum near Warangal.
5. *S. Sugunamma:* an active and articulate woman from a bonded family who spent much of her time in dens. Now lives on a farm in Mianpur about 30 km. from Hyderabad.
6. *Chakilam Lalithamma:* from a *deshmukh* (hereditary revenue officers who became landowners over time) family in Suryapet, travelled extensively and worked during the movement. Now teaches at a Zilla Parishad school in Suryapet.
7. *Ch. Kamalamma:* from a *devadasi* family, active political worker in the cultural squad. Still does cultural work and lives near Warangal.
8. *Kondapalli Koteswaramma:* from an Andhra middle class family, active in the cultural squad. Well known writer. Now leads a retired life and works as a warden in a hostel.
9. *Mallu Swarajyam:* from a landlord's family, still active with the CPI(M). Legendary heroine of the Telangana struggle.
10. *Dayani Kausalya:* from a wealthy landlord family in Vempali, near Suryapet.
11. *Dayani Priyamvada:* very articulate and active during the movement. Close to the CPI. Lives in Turpugudem, a village near Suryapet. Retired, though still interested in politics.
12. *Manikonda Suryavathi:* middle class woman, an active member of CPI(M) from Vijayawada.
13. *Pramila Tai:* an active member of Navjivan Mahila Mandal. Very well known and with a wide circle of contacts. Arranged shelters and supplies during the struggle. Now a retired teacher.
14. *Gajjela Balamma:*
15. *Saidamma:*
16. *Vajramma:*

Peasant women — in a group discussion —from a village called Akkirajupalli, known for the repression and mass rapes perpetrated there.

17. *Bullema:* from Andhra, Surayavathi's mother-in-law. She ran a commune and was called "Amma" after Gorky's "Mother." Many women refer to her. (not interviewed)
18. *Dronavali Anasuya:* from Andhra. Her husband was shot in an encounter. Militant and articulate. Lives a semi-retired life now.
19. *Narasamma:* peasant activist whose letter appears in Sundarayya's book. (not interviewed)

NOTES

BACKGROUND NOTE:

The Telangana People's Struggle (1948-51) was the armed resistance of the peasants to the feudal oppression of the Nizam and the Hindu landlords in Hyderabad state. The state formed by the Nizam at the close of the Mughal empire, was reduced to a subsidiary feudatory state under the British. Consisting of three linguistic areas — eight districts of Telangana, five districts of Marathwada and three Kannada speaking districts — its official language was Urdu. Telangana formed fifty per cent of the area. Any new schools that were started to teach the mother tongue of the people required the permission of the Nizam. The setting up of libraries or literary and cultural associations also required his permission. Thus the struggle against the cultural dominance of the Muslim ruler was also an integral part of the struggle against the Nizam.

The basic feature of the life of people in Hyderabad state under the Nizam was the feudal exploitation that persisted till the uprising of the Telangana peasants. The peasants on the Nizam's personal estate were practically bonded to the ruler. Under the *jagirdari* (tenurial system in which lands and/or revenues were granted by the State either for services rendered or in lieu of debts and advances) system various illegal taxes and forced labour were exacted from peasants by the landlords. Apart from this there were the *deshmukhs* and *deshpandes* (principal revenue officers of a district who became landowners over time), or tax collectors of the Nizam who grabbed thousands of acres of land and made it their own property. Peasants thus became tenants-at-will.

One common social phenomenon was the vetti system of forced labour and exactions imposed on all peasant sections in varying degrees. Each family had to send one person to collect wood for fuel, carry post to other villages, carry supplies, etc. Footwear, agricultural implements, pots or cloth had to be supplied free to landlords. Another system that prevailed was keeping of peasant girls as slaves in the landlord's house. When the landlord's daughters were married these girls were often sent with them to serve as concubines.

When the exactions of the landlords reached the point of evicting peasants from their land, the peasants began to resist. Sporadic struggles were launched in 1946 against the deshmukhs of Visunur, Suryapet, Babasahebpet, and Kalluru. The beginning of the Telangana People's Struggle in 1946 was against the Visunur deshmukh when his hirelings murdered Doddi Kumarayya, an Andhra Maha Sabha worker.

Various intellectuals and liberals influenced by the national movement elsewhere organized the Andhra Maha Sabha in 1928. The Andhra Maha Sabha, initially a forum for the democratic aspirations of the people, developed under the pressure of militant youth in the state into a broad political organization. By 1940-42 the Andhra Maha Sabha changed from a liberal organization to a united militant mass organization against the Nizam, and began to demand abolition of vetti, of illegal exactions, reduced taxes, confirmation of title deeds for the peasants, reduction of usurious rates of interest and so on. In 1944 there was a split between the right and left wings of the Sabha.

Meanwhile the repression in the state increased and was accompanied by the Nizam's decision to set up Hyderabad as an independent state. The Majlis Itthad-ul-Muslimeen (formed in 1927) had now a paramilitary wing — the Razakars. The brutality of their attacks on the people was hard to parallel. Organized by the Sangham, as the Andhra Maha Sabha was known in the villages, and led by its workers, thousands of peasants marched against Visunur Ramachandra Reddy in the first of many such pitched battles. People's courts were set up to try the culprits. The guerilla warfare waged by the peasants of Telangana forced the landlords and Razakars to retreat. The struggle spread over the areas of Nalgonda, Warangal, Khammam, Adilabad and Medak.

The Communist Party in Andhra served as a rear base for the Telangana Struggle, arranging for relief and supplies and keeping in touch with the struggle areas. The entry of the Indian Army into Hyderabad in September 1948, the police action as it was called, brought about the surrender of the Nizam and the disbanding of the Razakars. The force of the Army was now turned on the peasants, the Communist Party was banned and repression increased. The rich peasantry withdrew its support once the Nizam was gone and the squads had to retreat into the forests. Finally, the struggle was withdrawn in 1951.

In 1951 when the struggle was withdrawn some changes had come in. Forced labour was abolished, village committees continued to be active, and people resisted the return of the old jagirdari system. The demand for division along linguistic zones to facilitate all round political, social and cultural development of the people was also subsequently pushed forward. More important was the fact that it had set a revolutionary tradition among the Telugu people.

2. Ravi Narayan Reddy, interview, quoted in Peter Custers, *Women in the Tebhaga Uprising: Rural Poor Women and Revolutionary Leadership 1946-47* (Calcutta: Naya Prokash, 1987).
3. P. Sundarayya, *Telangana People's Struggle and its Lessons* (Calcutta: CPI(M) Publications, 1972), p. 351.
4. Sundarayya, *Telangana*, pp. 347-48.

Feminist Consciousness in Women's Journals in Hindi, 1910-20

VIR BHARAT TALWAR

Translated from the Hindi by Manisha Chaudhry, Neeraj Malik and Badri Raina

FOR THE PAST two hundred years the west has been seen as a major source of new ideas for the so-called 'backward' nations such as India. Indeed, many of our contemporaries continue to exhort us to look at the new movements in Europe and America in order to learn how to further the cause of progressive movements in India. However, while not denying the importance of this view, especially for left movements, I feel that for us it is equally important that we also look towards the history of the Indian nationalist struggle. An understanding of various movements, in different provinces, in which women were involved during the nationalist struggle which also borrowed from the west, will demonstrate whether or not inspiration and ideas from the west can satisfy the material needs and aspirations of Indian women. The history of the remarkable century-long women's movement in India is connected with the growth of worker's and peasant's movements, movements against untouchability, cultural and literary movements, and, of course, their parent movement —the anti-colonial struggle — which bound them. An understanding of these interlocking histories will be of great use to the contemporary feminist movement.

The Hindi region has a lesser record of awareness and agitation on women's issues as compared to Maharashtra, Bengal and Madras during the nationalist movement. However, I have chosen to deal with this area precisely because it has been a relatively neglected area of concern.

I

In the same way as feudal landlords first organized Kisan Sabhas for the uplift of peasants, the movement for the uplift of women was initiated by their oppressors — the men. From the time of Raja Ram Mohun Roy's protest against widow immolation until the end of the nineteenth century, there were a number of agitators and reformers who spoke on behalf of women. The central issues they raised were education, widow remarriage, abolition of *purdah* (veil and seclusion of women) and agitation against child marriage. These movements because they were dominated and run by men, were fundamentally different from the women's movements of today. A more significant difference was that the nineteenth century women's movement did not attack the prevalent patriarchal system in any way. Rather, the attempt was to improve the condition of women *within* the frame of patriarchy. The term patriarchy is used to mean not only the system of familial organization in which the father as head is vested with primary rights, but also to mean *all* the extant economic, social, political and cultural systems which 'naturally' grant the first place to men rather than to women. Nineteenth century reformers wished to give some importance to women without at any time challenging the position or power enjoyed by men within a male dominated society. The social reform movement was perhaps aptly termed a movement for the 'uplift' of women — uplift is indeed effected by an outsider. Attempts to improve their own situation by women themselves would not be perceived as uplift or reform but as the assertion of a *right* — especially by feminists today. An awareness of their rights was lacking, by comparison, in women in the nineteenth century who were, by and large, at the receiving end of male patronage. However, efforts were made to improve the lot of women within the framework of patriarchy so that as wives, mothers and daughters they could have a better deal inside the family. This was not a result of some sudden outbreak of generosity on the part of men. The social reform movements arose out of the conflict between the needs of an emergent 'educated' urban middle class and the norms of the older, feudal joint-family system — in fact the reforms were an attempt to change the older patriarchal system and bring it in line with the material needs of the urban middle class. Certain changes within the patriarchal system appeared desirable and some of the more ugly and unpalatable forms of oppression and 'backwardness' for women were sought to be eliminated. Further, the family was no longer a productive unit amongst the urban educated middle class; exposure to western values also led to the perception of the family as a space for emotional fulfilment, and as a consequence the role of women had to be readjusted. These were some of the reasons for the movements being confined mainly to urban areas — they found few propagators in small towns and rural areas.

The women's movement in the Hindi provinces around the time of World War I is significantly different from the nineteenth century reform movements, in the fact that it was led by women, and in that it raised questions from the standpoint of women rather than that of men. Another important difference has been the growth of women's own organizations and groups. Women active in this movement wrote sharp criticisms of the self-centred egotistic behaviour of men, their privileged position in society, their disparaging attitude towards women and their predilection to exploit and rule over women. Though today's feminist movement is once again different (in fact it is recognized now more as an ideological perspective) it is interesting to note that the special features of today's movement were nascent in the movement even then.

Feminist consciousness around World War I in the Hindi provinces is more closely linked to the woman-led movements of the last decades of the nineteenth century than the earlier male-led reform movements. It can be said to have begun in the last decades of the nineteenth century when Pandita Ramabai, Ramabai Ranade, Anandibai Joshi, Frenana Sorabjee, Annie Jagannathan, Rukmabai and others crossed the bounds of familial and cultural restrictions of a patriarchal society and went abroad to study. They returned with a new awareness of their rights and immediately became involved in raising women's issues in the country. For the first time women formed independent organizations. In 1886 Swarna Kumari Devi started the Ladies Association. Pandita Ramabai started Sharda Sadan in Pune in 1892 to provide employment and education for women. Ramabai Ranade started the Hindu Ladies Social and Literary Club in 1902 and Seva Sadan in 1909 in Pune. Around the same time *Stree Bodh,* a journal about women, was released from Bombay in 1901. A similar women's journal was founded in Madras. In Calcutta in 1905 Sumati started Mahila Samiti; 1908 saw the beginning of a Gujarati Ṣtree Mandal in Ahmedabad and Mahila Seva Samaj was founded in Mysore in 1913. Bhagini Samaj started in Pune in 1916 and became a key organization in the movement. 1914 saw the emergence of Annie Besant as a leading figure in the national movement. She started the Women's India Association with Margaret Cousins in 1917. This had most of its branches in the Madras Presidency and its objective was to demand women's rights and increase their participation in the national movement; it also brought out a journal called *Stree-Dharm*. In an attempt to establish an all-India organization for women, the National Council of Women in India was initiated in 1925. In 1926 the Women's India Association brought together several scattered women's groups in the country at a convention and many of them united under the banner of the All India Women's Conference. Thus, like the burgeoning number of peasants and workers' organizations all over the country, women's own organizations developed as part of the anti-imperialist movement.

II

Bhartendu Harishchandra of Benares was the first to raise women's issues in the Hindi region. Not only did he focus on these in his own writing but he also brought out a Hindi journal for women called *Bala Bodhini* in 1874. Although he managed to raise some consciousness about emerging democratic ideas and nationalism, the women's movement did not coalesce until 35 years after the first publication of *Bala Bodhini*. Then the upsurge of the movement in Maharashtra, Madras, Gujarat and Bengal made its impact not only on the provinces of the Hindi belt in the late nineteenth century but also acquired a national character.

Rameshwari Nehru established the Prayag Mahila Samiti in Allahabad in 1909 and began a serious journal for women called *Stree Darpan*. A closely linked journal, *Kumari Darpan* was brought out under the editorship of Roop Kumari Nehru. *Stree Darpan* became the most important instrument in the women's movement in the Hindi provinces. There was no other magazine which brought such gravity and depth to the examination of women's issues. During and after World War I much women's literature was written with the same intent as peasant literature: questions important to women were raised and women took the lead in writing and arguing about them. Some women's organizations were also formed at local levels though none covered the entire Hindi region. Many magazines, journals and books pertaining to women's issues began to be published.

Another important magazine for women was *Grihalakshmi.* The issues being debated in *Stree Darpan* were echoed in *Grihalakshmi* and many debates were simultaneous; often rebuttals and rejoinders to questions raised in one could be found in the other. The third women-oriented magazine was *Arya Mahila* from Benares. These magazines drew support for women's rights not only from the west but also from India's past. *Arya Mahila* of the Sanatan Dharma Mahamandal subscribed to the tendency which demanded education and status for women on the basis of Vedic ideals. The urban educated middle class which drew support from ancient Indian history had to go a little further since, by itself, recourse to the past alone was insufficient. Some evidence of this can be found in the 2 June 1919 issue of Ganesh Shankar Vidyarthi's nationalist paper *Pratap* (Kanpur). While reviewing *Arya Mahila,* it suggested ways in which the magazine could bring women's issues into a wider, mainstream perspective.

> We feel that not only skilled handicraft workers but also other such accomplished artisans should be given a place in our community. Not only this, it is necessary to start a regular feature called Videshi Stree Mandal so that the views of women from other parts of the world and women's movements elsewhere should be evaluated and represented.

This critical comment suggests that some of the most politically aware of the educated middle class wished to consider and place the problems of Indian women in a larger context and in an international frame of reference. Two major Hindi literary magazines, *Saraswati* and *Madhuri,* carried descriptive accounts of women from other parts of the world complete with photographs. The intention, however, was only to acquaint readers with matters of sociological interest and to give them access to varied materials.

The fourth important journal for the women's movement, which carried material of use to women, *Mahila Sarvasv,* was published from Aligarh by Pandit Devdutt Sharma. The January 1919 issue of *Stree Darpan* carried a critique of this journal which said: "This journal needs to improve itself by trying harder." The fifth magazine, a monthly called *Kamasth Mahila Hitaishi* was brought out by two women, wives of lawyers. 1922 saw the publication of an illustrated magazine for women from Allahabad called *Chand*; the editors were Ramrikh Sehgal and Ramkrishna Mukund Laghate and the manager was Vidyavati Sehgal. *Chand* was a popular magazine and it was through its columns that the talented young Mahadevi Verma emerged into the literary world. The number of journals published for women during this period of anti-imperialist struggle, is unsurpassed even today.

The September 1917 issue of *Stree Darpan* carried an introduction to the "best sociological novel on women's education" entitled *Sadacharini* by Kumudbala of Calcutta. The preface to the book asserted: "This book is not a translation from any other language. It is an original work." Original work in Hindi was not often done at the time; translations from other languages, especially Bengali, were more common. *Stree Darpan* went on to observe: "It is indeed the good fortune of Hindi that women now write original novels in it" (*Hindi bhasha ka ahobhagya hai ki deviyan bhi bilkul swatantra upanyaas likhne lagi hain*). The initial crop of women writers in Hindi had, in fact, made women's issues the subject of their work. *Pratap* carried an advertisement for *Grihalakshmi* in the 15 March 1920 issue calling it "the most unparalleled narrative on women's education." In September 1917 *Stree Darpan* carried an article on a book called *Om Sahriday Bhaiyon se Nyaya Yachna* by Srimati Damyanti Devi of Shikarpur (Sindh). This book contained the speech Damyanti Devi had made in a public meeting full of men in defence of herself and in answer to slanderous allegations spread about her by some men in Shikarpur. The April 1918 issue carried an introduction to *Nari Ratna*, a book written by the wife of Pandit Chandrabhalji Vajpayee, the *taluqdar* (landlord) of Kardaha (Unnao): "In her little book the learned author expresses some original views on women's education." (At this time it was customary to mention whose wife or daughter the writer was.) A January 1919 issue which reviewed Vidyalankar's book *Stree Dharm ka Vedic Adarsh* said: "Those people who think that women occupied as low a status in ancient India as they do at present, their misconception will be removed on reading this book." *Stree Darpan* itself published *Nari Ratna Mala*, a book which introduced the work and biographies of famous women.

The profusion of literature on women's issues written by women was the special feature of this period. *Stree Darpan* published stories and poems by women on women's education, on purdah and on the degradation and exploitation of women by men. In 1918 a Hindi Sahitya Sammelan on literature was organized at Indore. Among the topics on which papers were solicited was "Literature suitable for women in the Hindi language." Gandhi chaired this conference in which, for the first time, 700 women took part and discussed literature in Hindi. Smt. Gangabai, Smt. Hemant Kumari Chaudhrani, Pandita Manoramabai, Smt. Renubai and Smt. Maganbai, spoke on women's education and other women's issues.

Out of the numerous women's journals of the period, the three important ones are *Gribalakshmi, Stree Darpan* and *Chand.* All three were published from Allahabad which was also the centre for the middle class nationalist movement. *Gribalakshmi* was edited by a man and a woman, *Stree Darpan* was edited only by a woman, and *Chand* had only male editors though the manager was a woman. *Gribalakshmi* and *Stree Darpan* both began in 1909; *Chand* was first published in November 1922 and therefore falls a little outside the period I am examining. From the point of view of subject matter and feminist consciousness, *Stree Darpan* was a little ahead of *Gribalakshmi*, and *Chand* a little ahead of both. Despite the fact that both *Gribalakshmi* and *Stree Darpan* raised women's issues and problems from a similar viewpoint, *Gribalakshmi* continued to emphasize the traditional roles of mother, sister, and daughter-in-law. The desired ideal relationship between a mother-in-law and daughter-in-law, the ideal behaviour for a wife, the demeanour and conduct towards the family expected from a 'good' daughter-in-law, and the behaviour of other family members towards her, were all subjects covered in articles in *Gribalakshmi. Stree Darpan* did not carry such articles. However, exploitation and injustice against women was repudiated in both journals. *Chand*, which was also supported by major writers in Hindi, was larger than these, both in size and perspective. In the year of its inception, it brought out three special issues: on widows, on education and on child marriage.

The 1922 Hindu Mahasabha was bitterly criticized in *Chand* because it ignored the question of Hindu widows. *Chand* did not restrict itself to treating women's issues only from the viewpoint of problematic gender relationships or from an anti-male point of view. Rather its approach was to look upon such problems as social questions, and to seek 'reforms' in the interests of revolution. The first editorial stated the objectives of the journal:

> To remove social evils such as ignorance among women, the custom of purdah etc.; to acquaint women on a sustained basis with information of use and benefit to them; to equip them with skill and proficiency in essential household tasks or in other words make the Indian woman into an ideal housewife.

But, as often happens, the shape of the magazine became quite different from its stated aims. In particular, the making of Indian women into ideal housewives was an objective that in practice soon became secondary to changing social attitudes towards women, and achieving the denied rights of women in the context of new ideas and the nationalist movement. *Chand* did, however, carry articles on the health of women and children in every issue. Equally, it informed its readers about the social and cultural status of women in other parts of the world. *Nirmala,* Premchand's most sympathetic novel about women's problems, was written at the behest of *Chand* and serialized in the magazine in 1926. *Chand* also published the early poems of Mahadevi Verma. However, since this magazine belongs to the period after the World War, *Stree Darpan* is a better basis for examining feminist awareness among women between 1910-20.

III

Every issue of *Stree Darpan* carried editorial commentaries, plays, short stories, poems, articles and book reviews. In addition to women's problems which formed the subject matter of most of these, there were articles on topics which the editors felt women should be informed about such as the World War in Europe. In order to understand the nature of the magazine it is helpful to examine the contents of a 'typical' issue. The January 1919 issue carried the following: War News; Influenza; Air Travel; Forced Widowhood; Water of the Ganga as a Danger to Health; Right to Vote for Women; The Peasant and the Congress. The issue carried two stories: Someshwari Nehru's "Jale Dev ka Punarjagran" which centred around a woman character and was being serialized, and

Girijakumar Ghosh's historical tale "Kannauj Sundari" based on 'womanly' love. Also included was an episode from the play "Daya Ka Khoon" which concerned itself with male attitudes and which was being serialized. The other contributions included "Bharat Geet", a patriotic poem by the famous Hindi poet Sridhar Pathak, and "Swadeshabhiman", an essay by Vishweshwari Devi exhorting women to love and serve their nation. The book review column carried reviews of the book *Stree Dharma ka Vedic Adarsh,* and of two women's journals: *Kayasth Mahila Hitaishi* and *Mahila Sarvochh.* Not only the articles but also the writers were fairly varied. Although the majority of articles were by women and the magazine was largely the result of the efforts of women, there were also articles by men, including prominent left wing writers such as Satyabhakt and Ramashankar Awasthy.

In her article entitled, "Striyan aur Purdah" (Women and Purdah), Smt. Satyawati stated that purdah was not an ancient Indian custom. It became popular during Muslim rule. Those parts of the country which did not have Muslim rule or where such rule was weak, as in the south, did not have the practice. Purdah is most widely prevalent in the Hindi region which was the stronghold of the Muslim rulers. An article by Smt. Saubhagyavati on the history of purdah, "Aadhunik Purdah Pranali Tatha us se Haniyan" (The Practice of Purdah Today and its Harmful Effects), reiterated this in the August 1918 issue. For these women writers the main argument against purdah was that it was an obstacle to women's education. However, while nineteenth century reformers opposed purdah in isolation, these women saw it in connection with various other problems and further identified it as a part of the larger vicious pattern which oppressed women. Satyavati uncovers this pattern when she writes: "Neither power, nor real knowledge, nor education, nor freedom, then what point will the mere removal of purdah serve?" She clearly linked the abolition of purdah with the doing away of all oppressive social practices. Saubhagyavati in her article had strongly refuted the slanderous accusation that unveiled women become depraved, while Satyavati also cited the health of women as a reason for doing away with purdah. The issue of health had, in fact, been part of the concern of the women's movement since the later nineteenth century. But all the debates and discussions by women on child marriage and purdah did not include the right of a woman to have control over her own body, something which is a major issue for the movement today. Writing against purdah, Satyawati says, "Women should be entitled to the full freedom to enjoy personal good health." This was a difficult proposition especially for ordinary women at the time. Satyawati also made an interesting suggestion: that the rich should open their grounds and gardens for less privileged and poor women to walk in the fresh air in the mornings; no men should be allowed at this time and gardeners should keep a watch at the gates, and this would encourage friendship and interaction among women. This novel suggestion is notable for advocating increased sisterhood among women and recognizing the importance of increasing contact between women — a perspective which is a significant part of the women's movement today.

The question of widowers remarrying greatly excercised the minds of aware women. It was common for widowers to remarry three, even four times. Women felt that given this sanction, men did not value and esteem their wives. Hukma Devi's article in the August 1917 issue of *Stree Darpan*, "Stree Unnati Kaise Ho" (How can Progress for Women be Brought About), cited widowers remarrying as the single biggest reason for the devaluation of women. Hukma Devi wrote that men were far more grieved if their pet animals and birds died or flew away than if their wives fell ill and died, because a woman's status is of as little consequence as a man's shoe — if it wears out you can always replace it. A blameless, devout young virgin is married off to a widower without taking the rights and wrongs of the situation into account. When a woman falls ill, however beautiful, accomplished and devoted to her husband (*pativrata*) she may be, the man thinks that if she can be got rid of, he can marry again and enjoy life with a new bride.

The remarriage of widowers was an issue which agitated the educated women of the Hindi provinces around the time of World War I. *Stree Darpan* carried the largest number of sharply critical articles on this issue than on any other. The February 1918 issue carried a letter to the editor on widower remarriage from Smt. Gulab Devi Chaturvedi of Kota. The importance of the letter is evident from the fact that the editor thought fit to add a postscript to it which said: "All other sisters should read and reflect on this." The writer said:

> Widowers are highly eligible and sought after matches for young girls.

The girl is a mere fifteen years of age and the venerable groom is sixty. Can such a beautifully matched ideal couple ever be the subject for reproach? Bless them! Bless them!

(Mritstreek purushon ko dhūnd dhūnd kar kanyain byāhi jāti hain. Kanyā hai pandreh varsh ki aur hamāre var yā dulhāji saath varsh ke. Kyā aisi sundar jodi bhi kabhi kharāb mālūm hoti hai? Dhanya hai! Dhanya hai!)

The writer goes on to call this a new form of assault on women. The editor added a footnote: "This is nothing new; self-centred men have been practising such oppression for a long time." It appears from this that although this practice existed earlier, it had now assumed frightening proportions and was almost as disturbing an issue as bride burning is today. After a lively and satirical description of the practice, the letter suggests in conclusion: "A Kanya Hitkarini Sabha or an association for the welfare of young girls should be established in Prayag and its main objective be to stop young unmarried girls from being wedded to widowers." Urban, educated middle class women in the Hindi speaking areas had also become aware of the need to have their own organizations as did workers and peasants. It is noteworthy that Gulab Devi Chaturvedi appealed only to women, not to men, to step forth and organize themselves on this issue. This was a special quality of her consciousness as a woman.

Smt. Hukma Devi of Dehradun began a campaign against widowers remarrying in various journals including *Grihalakshmi.* In her article, "Stree Jati ki Avnati ka Mukhya Karan — Anmel Vivah" The Main Reason for the Decline of Womankind — Mismatched Marriages) in the March 1918 issue of *Stree Darpan,* she recounts the indignities suffered by women in a touching account:

A young girl, pure as the waters of the Ganga, is married off to a sixty-seventy year old widower who not only has several grown up sons and daughters but is also a grandfather. Such marriages have become customary in society, and it is on the strength of such a practice that men can designate women as discardable, and say that if the old shoe is broken we will wear another, or why wash a ragged garment, why lament a woman.

Gangā jal jaisī nirmal kanyā ke saath 60–70 varsh ke budhe duheju, dādā, nānā, putr putrī vāle manushya kā vivāh hotā hai. Is tareh ke vivah kī pratha samāj me chal rahi hai, iseeke bal par purush

> *kehte hain ki purāni jootī toot gayī, nai pahir lenge. Athvā, choli ka kyā dhona, aurat ka kyā ronā.*

The next issue had another article by her, "Ardhangini ya Paon ki Jooti" (Woman: Man's Equal Partner or an Old Shoe?) She wrote:

> In the present time India is plagued by the atrocities within the institution of marriage. Not a single household is exempt from this. You lose one wife, you marry another, the second dies and a third is ready .... Isn't this evil custom inimical to women in the extreme? Is it not this custom which has reduced woman to the status of a shoe?

> *Vartmān samay me Bhāratvarsh me burī tareh se vaivahik atyāchar phailā huā hai. Koi ghar is prathā se shunya nahin hai kī ek stree mari, doosri se vivah kar liyā, doosri mari, teesri tayaar hai ... Kya yeh dusht prathā strijatī ke liye maha apattikarak nahin hai? Kya stree jatī ko jootī ki padvi dene vaali yahi prathā nahin hai?*

The expression — a woman is like a shoe — recurs in several essays of that period. The phrase both reveals and encapsulates the inferior status given to women in society and for women, especially for those with a feminist consciousness, it became a symbol of the realities of a woman's existence in a patriarchal system. Hukma Devi was the headmistress of a school for girls in Dehradun; an ordinary middle class woman, she called upon women, not men, in her appeal to stop the exploitation of women:

> Sisters! you have slumbered long enough — awake! Dignity, honour, duty — all is taken away. Open your eyes and see what is going on in the world....When the whole world sings of freedom then is it right in such a world that Indian women should lie inert and not make an effort to regain their lost freedom, defend themselves against the oppression of men and rise above the level of a shoe.

> *Bahino, bahut kaal vyateet ho gayā, ab nidrā ko tyaag do. Maan, maryaada, dharma, sab kuch lut gayā; aankh khol kar dekho, sansār me kyā ho rahā hai? ... Jab sarā sansar swatantratā kā raag alaap rahā hai, to kyā bhartiya stree jātī ko apni ḳhoi hui swatantratā ko prapt karne, purush jatī ke ghor atyāchar se bachne, joote ki padvi se muktī prapt karne ke vāste kuch prayatna nā kar, is swatantratā ke yug me chupchaap paḍi rehnā uchit hai?*

Hukma Devi asked women to organize and find solutions to their problems. In the April 1918 issue she proposed that a Kanya Hitkarini Sabha (a society for the welfare of young girls) be set up and also put forth a list of fourteen objectives. These included a united front of women for "active resistance" ("sakriya pratirodh") against the mismatched marriages of widowers. Other suggestions were that the Sabha should bring out a newsletter called *Kumar aur Kumari*, and that the Government of India should be petitioned by women to declare mismatched marriages as illegal. *Stree Darpan* and *Gribalakshmi* did not stop at raising consciousness through the medium of articles, stories and poems. They in fact contributed actively in consolidating the women's movement and in organizing women. Rameshwari Nehru, the editor of *Stree Darpan* was an active participant in the women's movement and in its organization. In 1917 women from Rangoon invited Rameshwari to help start their own organization. Hukma Devi's suggestions on the movement and its organizations in *Stree Darpan* and *Gribalakshmi* evoked responses in the form of letters and helped to establish contact with twelve women across the country. Although this number is too small to seem inspiring, there is no denying that these magazines were to some extent becoming instrumental in uniting women. For example, when Hukma Devi wrote a book, entitled *Goodh Bhav Prakash* on widowers remarrying, the readers of and writers for *Stree Darpan* raised funds for its publication.

It is of considerable interest that around the time of World War I, the women's movement in the Hindi region opposed child marriage, emphasized the need for the education of young girls, but did not raise the issue of widow remarriage in either a direct or a forceful fashion. Rather, the articulate and active women focussed more on the need to find ways to keep widows busy or to find other creative outlets to mitigate the loneliness and emptiness of their lives. Ashrams for widows and education and learning of new skills by widows were encouraged but the demand for widow remarriage does not figure anywhere in their articles. Again it is of interest to note that it was the men, rather than women, who openly advocated widow remarriage in their writings. The January 1919 issue of *Stree Darpan* carried an editorial commentary on enforced widowhood entitled "Zabardasti Vaidhavya." This commentary gives a glimpse of the awful life widows led at the time in the Hindi speaking areas. In a conference of social reformers held on 5 October 1918 at Aligarh, the male chairperson presented the following statistics on the number of widows in U.P.

Age (Years)	Number of Widows
0-1	113
1-2	70
2-3	151
3-4	603
4-5	1,131
5-10	13,069
10-15	38,849
15-20	49,555

Setting forth this example of 'justice' in patriarchal society the chairperson said that when people do not hesitate to marry a second time if the first wife dies, what right do they have to preach that widows should not marry again? And this from a male chairperson. But in a report on this conference the editor of *Stree Darpan* did not demand widow remarriage openly, she only made an appeal for raising the legal age limit of marriage for girls: "In our opinion, if there are genuine difficulties in suddenly introducing the practice of remarrying widows then at least the custom of marrying girls between one to fifteen years can be immediately stopped." It seems a little odd that one of the chief spokeswomen for the women's movement did not openly demand acceptance of widow remarriage whereas male reformers had been advocating it since the nineteenth century.

The women who were part of the movement were not against widow remarriage, but unlike male reformers, they were not vehement about demanding it. In actual fact men took a saviour like attitude on the question of widows. For men to advocate remarriage for widows was to work for their 'uplift' and 'deliverance.' In an article by a male writer in the April 1919 issue of *Stree Darpan* an impassioned appeal was made to the young men of India to save "fallen widows." The question arose whether the widows themselves should take any initiative in this matter. The writer states emotionally: "Can they ever overcome their natural reserve and modesty and ask to be married again?" And what if they dare to do so? Considering this possibility the writer gets quite carried away:

> The day this happens, the day the Hindu widow, like a European widow, openly sets out on her own to seek a second husband for herself, do you know what will happen on that day?... That very day the

> heart of Mother India will split asunder in anguish and all of us men will be engulfed in it. Remember, that will be the day of the final destruction of the world; when all the stars in the sky will break, the sun and moon will collide and fall on Bharat, and this our green and prosperous land will on the instant be burnt to ash.

> *Jis din aisa hogā, jis din Hindu vidhwā khulebandi ek European vidhwā stree kī tareh doosre patī ko swayam talaash karn'e niklegī, us din jaante ho kyā hogā? Us din Bharat maiya kī chaatī phatkar do tukr'e ho jaayegī aur hum sab purush usme samā jayenge. Yaad rakhnā us din vaastvik pralay hogā, tab ākaash ke sab taare toot kar, chand suraj laḍ kar, isī Bharat par girenge aur yeh harā bharā Bharat dam ke dam me jal kar khāk syah ho jayegā.*

This then was the point of view of a reformist male on the question of widow remarriage, and clearly demonstrates that for men women do not have the right to fulfil their sexual needs — this is the right and prerogative of men alone. Moreover, men firmly believed that women naturally accepted this arrangement and would not under any circumstance transgress its rules.

The perspective of some women differed from this patriarchal 'uplifting' attitude of men. Rameshwari Nehru wrote in the editorial commentary of *Stree Darpan* in the May-June 1919 issue:

> Those revered widows who like goddesses embodied a life of selfless asceticism, are fit to be worshipped by us and by all the world. But the problem is really about those helpless women who cannot control their desires and yearn for marriage. There are young girls as well as young women who are in this predicament. What we cannot understand is why the leaders of our country consent to the idea of remarriage for one set of women but not for the other?

> *Jo vidhvayain devī pad par sushobhit reh kar nishkaam dharma ki moortimatī devī bani hain ve hamari aur sansār ki poojniya hain. Par prashn hai un bechariyon ka jo laalsā daman nahin kar saktin aur vivah ke liye tarasti hain. Ve bālāyen bhi hain aur yuvtiyan bhi hain. Hamāri samājh me yahi baat nahin aati ki hamāre desh ke netā ek ke vivāh ke liye sammati dete hain to doosri ke liye kyon nahin dete?*

Gandhi and some other national leaders were in favour of the remarriage of child widows but did not deem it correct for young women. The awareness of the women's movement at the time did not extend to repudiating socially prescribed values and standards of moral behaviour expected of widows. Praising the concept of purity in a widow's life Rameshwari Nehru writes in the same commentary:

> There are some widows who have dedicated their entire life to selfless devotion and have determinedly taken a vow of chastity and piety; by the grace of God, they are unmoved by the lowly desires of this world, and so sanctify Mother India by their presence.
>
> *Kuch vidhwāyen bhi aisi hain jo apnā sarā jeevan nishkaamvrat me arpan kar pavitra devi jeevan kaatne ke liye sab prakar se mansoobā pakkā kar baithi hain aur bhagwatkripa se asar sansar ki tucch laal saon se avichlit rehkar bharatmatā ko dhanya kar rahi hain.*

Two stories written by women and published, interestingly, in *Stree Darpan* — "Prembindu" in the June 1917 issue and "Aradhna" in the May-June 1919 issue — can be used to understand the level of women's consciousness on the question of widow remarriage. The plot of "Prembindu" is as follows: A beautiful, virtuous, and accomplished young woman from a *zamindar* (landlord) family is forbidden to marry the man she loves, and instead is married to a sickly young man who dies soon after. The young woman starts work as a teacher in a widow's home in Poona. Her first lover is wounded in the World War and admitted to a hospital in Bombay where she happens to be working; here, the two meet and recognize each other. He leaves on recovery after donating a lakh of rupees to the hospital for having given refuge to his now widowed beloved. He also writes a letter of appreciation for organizations which give support to helpless widowed women. The story ends here.

In the second story, "Aradhna," Bhoopati Bhusan, the son of a prosperous family, chooses to marry Champa, the daughter of an indigent widow. He goes to the mountains for a holiday with his friends and does not return. His friends return and report that he has died of cholera. Champa spends her life as a widow and devotedly serves her in-laws. She happens to go with them to Benares on a pilgrimage and on Shivratri spots her husband in the guise of a *sadhu* (holy man). Both of them recognize each other; subsequently, Bhoopati returns to his family (or to *girihasta ashram*) with the permission of his *guru* (preceptor). Neither story shows the remarriage of a widow: one praises the protective shelter offered to widows, the other evades the issue by simply keeping the husband alive. In this they show a certain cowardice on the issue of widows. About 12-13 years earlier, Premchand, whose literary career was yet to take off, had strongly supported widow remarriage in his novel, *Humkhurma va Humsawab*, in which the widowed heroine is shown marrying again. This novel was published in 1906 and its Hindi version, *Prema*, came out in 1907. It is true though, that the hero, Amrit Rai, who eventually marries the widowed heroine, has a reformer's zeal.

Both the stories on the life of widows in *Stree Darpan* indicate an acceptance and endorsement of traditional attitudes in the way in which the future of widows has been 'contained.' This makes one feel that the role of male reformers on the issue of widow remarriage was a historical necessity, a necessity which continued during the period under review.

The question of education for women was the most important issue for the women's movement. *Stree Darpan* had many articles on this between 1917-20. In the changing socio-cultural context the wide gulf between the educated man and the uneducated woman created difficulties in the social and family structure. The social and family structure was (and still is) such that while the idea of change was easily accepted and absorbed by men, they became a major hindrance and prevented it from percolating down to their women. The reason for this lay in the gender specific roles of men and women within the family and society. The changing social, political and cultural situation transformed this gulf into a deeper contradiction. Educated men were often not able to have a satisfactory relationship with their uneducated wives, and their humiliating and insulting behaviour towards their wives became another part of the lives of women. The Hindi literature of the time is laden with images of women who are humiliated and devalued only because they are uneducated.

The nationalist movement also helped the issue of women's education to become important. Women identified lack of education as a major reason for their oppression and humiliation. They opposed child marriage and purdah on the ground that these were obstacles in the way of education. In the Hindi provinces in 1917 the argument was not whether women should be educated or not. This point had been won a long time ago and most male leaders of the nationalist movement were with women on this. The debate was rather on the kind of education that was deemed suitable for women — only practical or also liberal? Only that related to domestic affairs or also social and political education? Ought education to be indigenous or western or both? *Stree Darpan* advocated an education that was geared to meeting the needs of the nationalist movement, in other words, a social and politically sound education. The question of which subjects women should study was linked to the status and role of women in the family and in society. It was a question that was concerned not only with the field of education but also with a social attitude and recognition of women by society. The women's movement of the time recognized this fact and linked the issue of women's education to that of women's liberation. Therefore women's education came to be seen as a means of creating a new balance of power between men and women. Arguments to keep women ignorant were viewed as ignoble attempts by men to safeguard their special interests and power over women. The famous writer Padam Singh Sharma wrote an article for *Gribalakshmi* called "Stree Shiksha Par Akbar ke Vichaar" (The Views of Akbar on Women's Education). Padam Singh Sharma supported the views of Akbar, an Urdu poet, who was opposed to women's education. A rebuttal of this by Hridayamohini was published in June 1917 in *Stree Darpan.* Hridayamohini was not awed by the reputation and fame of Akbar. She writes: "Mr. Akbar's views are like old weevil-infested wheat. They are so narrow and orthodox that one should not pay any heed to them." *(Akbar mahashay ke vichar ghune hue purane gehun hain. Yeh itne sankirna hain ki kadapi manne yogya nahin.)* She sarcastically commented on the learned Hindi litterateur, "Sharmaji is great! Like guru, like disciple," and mocked Akbar who was opposed to the idea of social and political education of women. There was an interesting exchange of sarcastic couplets between Akbar and Hridayamohini — Akbar asks women, "Why is it necessary for you to assert yourself in public/why can't you acquire knowledge and be an angel by the hearth?" (*Public me kya zaroor ki ja kar tani raho/padh likh ke apne ghar hi mein devi bani raho*). Hridaymohini parodically turned the tables and asked men to do the same saying that if they stayed at home women would "worship" them and the 'lats' or British sahibs would certainly not miss them.

Rather why is it necessary for you to be public men
Acquire knowledge and stay like gods at home
We shall set you up as idols on the shelf and worship you
If you confine yourself to the pleasures of the home
You will spare the Lats all anxiety and tribulation.

> *Public mein kyā zaroor ki ja kar tane raho/paḍh likh ke apne ghar hi main ishwar bane raho/Tum ko bithā ke taak par poojā karenge hum/Bhogō jo ghar mein baith, na laton kō hōve gam.*

She challenged men who opposed women's education and said:

> Selfish men! you gave us no opportunity to engage in significant or noteworthy work. You have deceived us, but now we are wise to your game. We are not just women, we are also members and citizens of Indian society.
>
> *Swaarthi purushon! tumne humkō kuch ucch kārya karne kā avkaash nahin diyā. Bahut dhokhā diyā; kintu ab tumhaari daal na galegi. Hum keval striyan hi nahin hain kintu bhartiya samaaj ki sadasya aur naagrik bhi hain.*

The issue of women's education was not important at the level of debate alone; it took the form of a social agitation. From the turn of the century, women's organizations had begun to set up schools for girls. During the World War I period Annie Besant started an institution for girls in Benares which is today known as Besant Kanya Mahavidyalaya. One of the problems faced by pioneers at this time was that female teachers were hard to find. In a fairly backward place, Mirzapur, a women's organization called the Bharat Mahila Parishad, was formed. The November 1918 issue of *Stree Darpan* had an appeal made by this organization asking educated women to come forward and teach in schools. The most important centre for women's education in the Hindi speaking areas was Allahabad, which was also one of the political centres of the nationalist movement. Crosswaithe Girls High School in Allahabad became particularly important in the movement for women's education. This is evident from the article and pictures of the school in prestigious magazines like *Saraswati* and *Maryada*. *Stree Darpan*, November 1917, also had a write up on the school. Girls from far off places such as Calcutta, Santhal Parganas, Lahore, Jalandar, Lucknow, Saharanpur, Multan, Quetta, Delhi, Agra, Saran, Gaya and Rangoon came to study here as the school had boarding facilities. Sakori Bai Shyam Rao Mankar was the headmistress. The editor of *Kumari Darpan*, a journal closely linked to *Stree Darpan*, taught in the school on an honorary basis. Apart from formal studies the school held classes in crafts such as stitching; there was provision for athletics, sports and exercises. There was also a branch of

Scouts. Crosswaithe Girls School was an important part of the middle class nationalist women's movement. Mahadevi Verma, the celebrated Hindi poet, was a product of this school. Interestingly, she was married at the age of ten after which her mother kept her in purdah. Her father, however, continued her education. While at school Mahadevi wrote an article on the system of purdah for which she was awarded a prize in an essay competition. She also wrote a play called *Bhartiya Nari* (Indian Woman) which was enacted at the school. After completing school Mahadevi rejected for all time the marriage which was performed when she was ten years old. This step, which showed rare courage, needs to be viewed not only as a personal event but also against the backdrop of the ongoing women's movement.

The women's movement in the period of the World War gathered support on three counts. One was on the basis of history and the Puranas. The August 1917 issue of *Stree Darpan* published Rameshwari Nehru's speech delivered at the Rangoon Mahila Samiti. She sought examples from the Hindu Puranas and history to support her arguments for the liberation of women. "Sita, Savitri, Damyanti, Shakuntala were not women who lived within the confines of purdah. The brave Rajput women who fought and died on the battlefield for their country were likewise not women who could be confined by purdah." Women often used such arguments for supporting their demands for women's liberation. One writer sympathetic to the movements was Satyabhakt. He wrote an article that ran for four issues (January to April 1918) in *Stree Darpan* called "Prachin Bharat mein Striyon ke Adhikar" (The Rights of Women in Ancient India) which gave support to the movement and cited examples from history. It is significant that Satyabhakt, one of the first to help organize the communist movement in the Hindi region, had earlier taken initiative to help organize the women's movement. Many years later, when he was sidelined by the international communists, he again turned towards the women's movement and became the editor of *Chand*. Another major personality of the Communist Party in the Hindi region (who had inspired Bhagat Singh's group to study socialism), Radha Mohan Gokulji, had also been involved in the women's movement before he joined the communist movement. The first biographer of Lenin in Hindi, Ramashankar Awasthy, was a frequent contributor to *Stree Darpan*.

The next major source of support that the movement drew upon was the European women's movement. In 1905 in Europe women were agitating for rights for political participation. The ongoing debate on the role of women in society was put to an effective end by the World War, when all able-bodied men were away at the warfront and women took on men's responsibilities with complete success. As a result, in England, when the war came to an end the government had to concede the demands of the women's movement. Educated upper middle class Indian women were instrumental in publicizing the role and achievements of European women. The October 1918 issue of *Stree Darpan* traced the history of the suffragette movement in England. Uma Nehru drew attention to the change in the status of women in the aftermath of the economic and moral upheaval of the World War in European society in her write-up.

The third form of significant support for the women's movement came from the national movement for swarajya (self-rule). The August, September and October 1917 issues of *Stree Darpan* had an article called "Striyan aur Swarajya" (Women and Swarajya) which raised the question that if women are equal to men in every respect then how can there be true swarajya without the full participation of women. Annie Besant, a major figure in the agitation for Home Rule, had become a symbol for the involvement of women in the nationalist movement. Referring to Annie Besant, the article underscored that today it was a woman after all who was fighting for the freedom of men and women alike; in view of this how is the reluctance of men to give equal rights to women within family and society to be explained. Male leaders were asked which demands for women they were putting forward in their demand for swarajya. Would they accept women as shareholders in power in the government? This is similar to the situation today in western Europe where, as part of the movements for socialism, women are saying that instead of figuring gender relations after a socialist revolution they should be prefigured in the process itself. In the same way, the women's movement in the Hindi provinces in 1917-18 put forth a demand that after swarajya the equal rights envisaged for men and women should be evident in the process of attainment as well: "You can grant us equal rights in the Swarajya of the future by first giving us equal rights in the present struggle for Swarajya." The question of women clashed with the national movement in the same way as that of peasants, workers and untouchables. The zamindars and lawyers who were leaders and spokespersons for the national movement and demanding rights for themselves were not prepared to give any rights to the peasants. Leaders, many of whom were orthodox Brahmins by caste, cried themselves hoarse on freedom from the British but they themselves had branded millions of people untouchable and subjected them to all forms of bondage. This very contradiction existed between male leaders of the national movement and the women's groups. Uma Nehru in the May 1918 issue of *Stree Darpan* wrote to nationalist men in a sharply ironical vein:

> Just the loss of national freedom has made you so depressed, so anxious, and so sorrowful. Consider then the enslavement of those who have lost not just political freedom but whose body, soul, and spirit have been enchained. How can their hearts ever be joyful?

> *Keval rashtriya swatantratā ke jane ne tumhe kaisā malin, kaisā vyakul, kaisā dukhit banā diya hai? Phir swayam socho, jiske shareer ki, jiski atma ki, jiske hriday ki saari swatantratā lut gayi ho, uska hardik bhav anandmay kaise ho sakta hai?*

But given the contradictions within the national movement, the issues of the women's movement took a different direction from that taken by peasants' and workers' issues as well as those relating to untouchables. For various reasons the national movement was successfully able to absorb and neutralize the issues raised by the women's movement, including those contradictions which arose between the national movement on the one hand and the women's movement on the other, during the World War.

A delegation of Indian women led by Sarojini Naidu met the Minister for India, Edwin Montagu in November 1917. The delegation made known its support for swarajya as demanded by the Congress, Muslim League, and the non-official members of the Council. They sought the inclusion of women in the impending government reforms. In addition they asked for compulsory free education for boys and girls, training for women teachers, a medical college for women, and improved health care facilities for women and children so that the increasing mortality rate among them could be checked. The women's delegation was constrained to raise all these issues separately because the national leadership had failed to do so, precisely as in the case of issues crucial to untouchables, labourers and peasants.

When in 1918 under the government's programmes of reforms, elections to the councils took place, women lost no time in demanding the right to vote. In the 26-31 August 1918 Bombay Congress session, Sarojini Naidu put forward the proposal of the women's right to vote and it was passed despite opposition from Madan Mohan Malviya. When the same proposal was put in the Aligarh Congress session, Madan Mohan Malviya raised no objection and it was passed. This event was distinctly different from the struggle by women in Europe for the achievement of political rights. There was strong opposition to the right to vote and women had to keep up a sustained struggle for several decades before they won any significant victory. Whereas in a comparatively backward country like India women gained the right to vote without having to overcome any great opposition. There was a debate in the country on the issue but the few narrow, conservative opponent's views were rejected by the nationalist educated middle classes as well as by the common people.

A 1918 issue of *Maryada* had a strong article "Striyon ke Adhikar" (Rights of Women) by Uma Nehru where she made short work of all the dissenting opinions. Those with left leanings in the nationalist movement openly supported the right to vote for women. Ganesh Shanker Vidyarthi wrote an editorial on 17 May 1920 titled "Nayi Council" (New Council) in favour of the vote for women.

IV

The role of the Nehru family in Allahabad in the women's movement in this region is an important one. The three women involved with the management and editing of *Stree Darpan,* Rameshwari Nehru, Roop Kumari Nehru and Kamla Nehru, all belonged to this family. Uma Nehru, married in 1901, was the daughter-in-law of Motilal Nehru's elder brother, Nandlal Nehru. She was the most progressive of the feminists of the period. She wrote a provocative article in the March 1918 issue of *Stree Darpan* called "Hamare Samaj Sudharak" (Our Social Reformers). She lampooned those reformers who sought to reimpose the old ideals of Sati, Sita and Savitri on contemporary women. She examined the problems of the movement in depth. She placed the issues of the women's movements in the context of the changing material conditions of India and Europe and the consequent socio-economic forces which came into play. "The same social forces which have led subjects to confront their king, craftsmen to confront their patrons and workers to stand up against their employers have also brought women face to face with men." She goes on to say that India has been backward in dealing with national and political questions which have arisen as a result of these social changes; instead, reformers dream of bringing back the age of the Ramayana and the Mahabharata. What are the historical forces pushing us even further away from the glorious past? Do we have the strength and resources to withstand these forces: "Tell the worshippers of tradition to beat their theological drums even louder" (*Apni paramparā pujakon ki bhajan-mandali se yeh kahna ki apni mridang aur bhi zor se bajao).* During the World War, the women of France and England commendably upheld the honour of their country when the men were away on the battlefront. The women of India meanwhile are far from any meaningful role in safeguarding the country's honour, because they are obliged to save their own honour from predatory men. She then adds:

> Our Hamlet-like young Indian male finds himself grappling not with the question 'To be or not to be' but with the more intractable question-Whether to lift the veil or not to lift the veil, and if lifted then how far must it be lifted?
>
> *Hamara Hamlet roopi bhartiya yuvak* to be or not to be *ke sthan par, Pardā uthaun ya nā uthauñ, aur uthaun to kitnā uthaun, ki ghōr samasyā me pada hua hai.*

Uma Nehru's style and tone were not only far more acerbic than that of her contemporaries, but she also raised women's issues within a new perspective. All other middle and upper class women from the Hindi region who were not in direct contact with western thought were opposed to the imposition of western values on Indian women. Uma Nehru however, argued that the changes in the status of European women were a consequence of the European economic and political systems. Since India seeks to organize itself by replicating those very principles of economic and political life it is impossible to escape the historical consequences. Indian men, on the one hand, are busily colouring Indian social life in western shades, and on the other, wish their women should continue to be seen to belong to an eastern way of life. What strange logic is this? Making an ironical comment on this paradoxical attitude of educated middle class nationalist men, Uma Nehru wrote:

> A Sita or a Savitri is conceivable only in the context of a Ramchandra, a Krishna, a Bharat and a Yudhisthir. But for men attired in coat, pant, collar and necktie with a lilting ambition for western economic ideals, the desire to produce such ideal Indian women is like wanting to find the proverbial but mythical flower in the sky.
>
> *Sita or Savitri banāne ke liye Ramchandra,Krishna, Bharat aur Yudhistir ki aavashyaktā hoti hai. Coat, patloon aur necktie collar shareer par our pashchimi aarthik adarshon ki tarange dil me lekar aisi strī jaatī ke utpann karne ki abhilaasha ākaashpushp dhundne ke samaan hai.*

The April 1918 issue of the magazine had Uma Nehru's second article; "Hamare Samajik Dhanche" (Our Social Structures). It has a heart rending description of the crushing of a dependent woman's identity. Men show little sensitivity in gauging a woman's feeling and needs and push women into self-willed and arbitrary structures for their purposes. She identified and labelled three pernicious moulds usually employed to control women — the Ancient Hindu mould, the Turkish (Muslim influenced) mould, and the modern western mould and described the wretchedness of women in all three. She sketched familiar and believable pictures of what women undergo within the family in contemporary society. In the event of a girl with a modern western education marrying into a traditional Hindu family or vice versa, it can cause immense psychological tension and lead to a cruel annihilation of her own identity. She ended the article with the fable of Procrustes, the dacoit, who had a bed on which he would put to sleep any lost wayfarers. "Any traveller whose height happened to be shorter than the bed was simply pulled by Procrustes till he fitted the bed. If a traveller was larger than the bed Procrustes simply chopped off the extra bit from his body. In this ingenious way he robbed and killed men." She comments, "Indian society is like a cruel Procrustean bed for women."

Stree Darpan May 1918 had Uma Nehru's third article "Hamare Hridya" (Our Hearts; the same article was later reprinted in *Aaj,* a daily from Benares) in which she criticized the hallowed ideal of self sacrifice as a woman's *dharma* (duty). "Such self sacrifice which clearly destroys one's own body and soul makes others greedy, selfish, unjust and tyrannical is not self sacrifice, it is suicide." This article, which demanded women's rights on the basis of their selfhood, their natural feelings and needs, was moving and courageous for the times. Forthrightly exposing the false consciousness of men about women Uma Nehru wrote: "Think for yourself about it. If you were dependent on us, if your spirit, body and heart were subject to our control and if we ruthlessly expropriated all your cherished freedoms, what state might you then be in." She said that the prevailing traditional relationship between men and women was akin to a hateful master slave relationship and made a plea for a relationship based on friendship. "Love between a master and slave is revolting, unstable and unnatural. Where companionship takes the place of servitude the man woman relationship becomes nobler, purer and more encompassing." (*Dasi aur swāmi ka prem ghrinamaya, asthir aur aprākritik hai. Dasi bhav ke sthan par mitrabhav ka utpann ho jana stree purush ke parasparik sambandh ko adhiktar vishaal, ucch aur pavitra banā degā.*)

There was an article in two parts in the July-August 1918 issues called "Hamari Soorten" (Our Faces). In this she contested the male patriarchal belief which designated strength as the essence of masculinity and beauty as the essence of femininity. To say that beauty is the most important ideal for every woman is to promote an anti-woman value which deliberately ignores the qualities of learning, independence and strength in women. It is a part of deliberate male hypocrisy to overvalue the importance of beauty, because the greedy self-serving male customer for and appropriator of woman's beauty, at the same time, forces this supposedly 'divine pleasure giver' to perform the tasks and duties of a slave. According to him learning, independence and strength are detrimental to a woman's good looks but working on the grindstone, pounding rice, lighting a *chulha* (earthern stove), sweeping, disposing garbage, cleaning dishes, sorting out clothes and removing cow dung is not. In bitter opposition, Uma Nehru wrote, "If it were possible we would also for a time worship man in the spirit in which he worships us 'Lakshmis' and thereby lay bare to him the ugly reality camouflaged by such worship."

Uma Nehru's acute feminist consciousness is closer to the present day feminist movement than to the movement in her times. The women's movement of 1917-20 in the Hindi region was supported by the educated middle and upper middle classes. There are two perspectives among the upper middle class supporters of the movement. One saw the women's movement not only in the Indian context but also in the context of the women's movement in Europe. This was largely propagated by that section of the upper middle-class which came into contact with European society and ways of thinking — Uma Nehru represented this group. The other drew support from the European context but viewed it keeping in mind its specificity to India. The middle class group with this perspective did not have much contact with European life. However, women who did have contact with European society also held this latter view. This difference in perspectives was a genuine difference in terms of ideology rather than simply a division based on class between those who had access to western thought and those who did not have such direct contact with it. For instance, Rameshwari Nehru, the editor of *Stree Darpan,* in spite of belonging to the upper middle class, held the latter point to view. This clash in perspectives was evident in the upper middle class which led the women's movement. The middle class women who were involved in the movement largely saw women's issues in the Indian context. Most women within an underdeveloped and colonized social order did not endorse Uma Nehru's progressive feminist views precisely as the early Indian communists did not accept M.N. Roy's politics of socialist revolution. Uma Nehru's feminism and M.N. Roy's revolutionary ideas were not in accord with the material conditions of Indian society, the needs of the nationalist movement and the general level of popular consciousness. In fact the questions that Uma Nehru was struggling to answer were not those taken up by the Indian women's movement but were raised abroad. The questions she took up and the answers she gave were part of the discourse of the British women's movement. Indian middle class nationalist women did not attack gender discrimination in a way which would make a dent in male domination and patriarchy. Instead they confined themselves to reformist issues, and laid greater stress on opposition to widower's remarrying, child marriages, support for widow remarriage, women's education and greater participation in the national movement. They demanded greater selfhood, freedom and respect for women without, however, disowning the ideals of self denial and self sacrifice for women. In March 1919 the editor of *Stree Darpan* criticized the very idea of rejecting the Sati-Savitri ideal:

> Let Sita, Damyanti and Savitri always be venerated by us, and may our women of today have the great good fortune of achieving the kind of independence and freedom they enjoyed, even as they brought glory to this ancient motherland. This is our heartfelt prayer to the omnipresent, all-knowing, merciful Lord.
>
> *Sita, Damyanti aur Savitri sada hamari poojya bani rahen aur jis prakar ki swatantratā swadheentā kā sukh bhogti hui ve hamari budḥiyā bharatmatā kā naam ajar amar banā gayi hain usi prakar ka saubhagya vartmaan yug ki mahilaon ko bhi prapt ho. Yahi ghat ghat vaasi antaryaami dayamay se hamari hriday khol kar prarthnā hai*

In spite of her progressive feminism Uma Nehru was not able to contribute to the movement in 1917-20 to the same extent as Gandhi did, even though he was much less of a feminist. Gandhi studied law in Europe and though he was all for the improvement of the lot of women, he still upheld Sita, Draupadi, and Damyanti as ideals. This stand found great favour with lower and ordinary middle class women. Bhagini Samaj, a Poona women's organization, invited Gandhi to speak at one of their meetings. His speech was printed in the March 1918 issue of *Stree Darpan.* He attacked the feminist stand of upper class women who viewed the Indian women's movement against a European context: "The present day movement is limited to a very small section of people." He stressed the need to take into account the conditions and thinking of 85 per cent of the women in the country: "If my Bhagini Samaj sisters examine the lives of India's millions they will be enabled to find many creative and profitable ways of making themselves useful in our society." Gandhi said:

> Men have laid down the principles of social organisation, which are flawed in many ways. In order to rectify social inequities... we shall have to reimbue women with the purity, firmness, resolve and the spirit of self-sacrifice of Sita, Damyanti and Draupadi. If only we are able to produce such women, then today's women, pure as satis, would begin to command the same respect in Hindu society as was enjoyed by their ancient prototypes.

Gandhi stated that men and women are equal. Women have the right to freedom and to achieving as high office as men. He said that the point of view that held women unworthy of these rights because they were not educated was unjust. More important than education was an awareness of their situation. It was unfair on the part of men not to consider women as their equals because of their lack of education. This was not to say that women should not be educated. But it was not essential that women should receive the same education. Indeed both men and women should stay away from the prevalent system of education. A knowledge of English was not necessary for either. He said: "I do not believe in women taking up jobs or business after an education." Gandhi also opposed child marriages and said that men marrying young girls should educate their young brides before consummating the marriage.

Gandhi took a compromising stand on the women's question. He supported many traditional ideas but to a certain extent openly favoured rights for women. It is worth noting that this support is in no way anti-male, and that his support for the women's movement was not informed by a feminist perspective, but from the point of view of the needs of the nationalist movement for swarajya. This support was qualified by the same ideational limits as his notion of swarajya. But Gandhi's support did help to further the movement, as well as increase women's participation in the national movement. The editorial comment in *Stree Darpan* after Gandhi's speech at Bhagini Samaj commended his perspective on the women's question as against Uma Nehru's.

Some contemporary feminists claim that Gandhi not only cited a suffering and self sacrificing woman as the ideal 'Satyagrahi' but also gave importance to non-violence, passive resistance and fasting as strategies and this imparted a feminist character to the national movement. This is an echo of the revival of Gandhism in our time. The claim being made here is that Gandhism is feminism and feminism is Gandhism. This however is an ideological stand and cannot be considered a factual evaluation of Gandhi's role in the women's movement. Today some of our companions, disillusioned and frustrated with the mistakes of the revolutionary left movements, have taken refuge in Gandhism. Gandhi did help to raise consciousness among women but this was itself shaped by the specific ideological and philosophical structure of his thought. If one subscribes to this structure then one is most likely to be favourably disposed towards Gandhi's efforts at consciousness raising. But if our assumptions about social organization and change are different then we cannot but go beyond the ambit of Gandhi's ideas on the women's movement. The women's movement must inevitably form part of an ongoing ideological struggle.

The Nationalist Resolution of the Women's Question

PARTHA CHATTERJEE

I

THE 'WOMEN'S QUESTION' was a central issue in some of the most controversial debates over social reform in early and mid-nineteenth century Bengal — the period of the so-called 'renaissance'. Rammohun Roy's historical fame is largely built around his campaign against *satidaha* (widow immolation), Vidyasagar's around his efforts to legalize widow remarriage and abolish Kulin polygamy; the Brahmo Samaj was split twice in the 1870s over questions of marriage laws and the 'age of consent.' What has perplexed historians is the rather sudden disappearance of such issues from the agenda of public debate towards the close of the century. From then onwards, questions regarding the position of women in society do not arouse the same degree of passion and acrimony as they did only a few decades before. The overwhelming issues now are directly political ones —concerning the politics of nationalism.

Was this because the women's question had been resolved in a way satisfactory to most sections of opinion in Bengal? Critical historians today find it difficult to accept this answer. Indeed, the hypothesis of critical social history today is that nationalism could not have resolved those issues; rather, the relation between nationalism and the women's question must have been problematical.

Ghulam Murshid states the problem in its most obvious, straightforward, form.[1] If one takes seriously, i.e. in their liberal rationalist and egalitarian content, the mid-nineteenth century attempts in Bengal to "modernize" the condition of women, then what follows in the period of nationalism must be regarded as a clear retrogression. "Modernization" began in the first half of the nineteenth century because of the "penetration" of western ideas. After some limited success, there was a perceptible decline in the reform movements as "popular attitudes" towards them "hardened." The new politics of nationalism "glorified India's past and tended to defend everything traditional;" all attempts to change customs and life-styles began to be seen as the aping of western manners and thereby regarded with suspicion. Consequently, nationalism fostered a distinctly conservative attitude towards social beliefs and practices. The movement towards modernization was stalled by nationalist politics.

This critique of the social implications of nationalism follows from rather simple and linear historical assumptions. Murshid not only accepts that the early attempts at social reform were impelled by the new nationalist and progressive ideas imported from Europe, he also presumes that the necessary historical culmination of such reforms in India ought to have been, as in the West, the full articulation of liberal values in social institutions and practices. From these assumptions, a critique of nationalist ideology and practices is inevitable. It would be the same sort of critique as that of the so-called 'neo-imperialist' historians who argue that Indian nationalism was nothing but a scramble for sharing political power with the colonial rulers, its mass following only the successful activization of traditional patron-client relationships, its internal debates the squabbles of parochial factions, its ideology a garb for xenophobia and racial exclusiveness. The point to note is that the problem lies in the original structure of assumptions. Murshid's study is a telling example of the fact, now increasingly evident, that if one only scrapes away the gloss, it is hard to defend many ideas and practices of nationalism in terms of rationalist and liberal values.

Of course, that original structure of assumptions has not gone unchallenged in recent critical history. The most important critique in our field is that of the Bengal renaissance.[2] Not only have questions been raised about the strictness and consistency of the liberal ideas propagated by the 'renaissance' leaders of Bengal, it has also been asked whether the fruition of liberal reforms was at all possible under conditions of colonial rule. In other words, the incompleteness and contradictions of 'renaissance' ideology were shown to be the necessary result of the impossibility of thoroughgoing liberal reform under colonial conditions.

From that perspective, the problem of the diminished importance of the women's question in the period of nationalism deserves a different answer from the one given by Murshid. Sumit Sarkar has considered this problem in a recent article.[3] His argument is that the limitations of nationalist ideology in pushing forward a campaign for liberal and egalitarian social change cannot be seen as a retrogression from an earlier radical reformist phase. Those limitations were in fact present in the earlier phase as well. The 'renaissance' reformers, he shows, were highly selective in their acceptance of liberal ideas from Europe. Fundamental elements of social conservatism such as the maintenance of caste distinctions and patriarchal forms of authority in the family, acceptance of the sanctity of the *shastra* (ancient scriptures), preference for symbolic rather than substantive change in social practices — all of them were conspicuous in the reform movements of the early and mid-nineteenth century. Specifically on the question of the social position of women, he shows the fundamental absence in every phase of any significant autonomous struggle by women themselves to change relations within or outside the family. In fact, Sarkar throws doubt upon the very assumption that the early attempts at reform were principally guided by any ideological acceptance of liberal or rationalist values imported from the West. He suggests that the concern with the social condition of women was far less an indicator of such ideological preference for liberalism and more an expression of certain "acute problems of interpersonal adjustments within the family" on the part of the early generation of western educated males. Faced with "social ostracism and isolation," their attempts at "a limited and controlled emancipation of wives" were "a personal necessity for survival in a hostile social world." Whatever changes have come about since that time in the social and legal position of women have been "through objective socio-economic pressures, some post-independence legislation, rather than clear-cut ideology or really autonomous struggle. Mental attitudes, and values have consequently changed very much less." The pattern, therefore, is not, as Murshid suggests, one of radical liberalism in the beginning followed by a conservative backlash in the period of nationalism; Sarkar argues that in fact the fault lies with the very inception of our modernity.

The curious thing, however, is that Sarkar too regards the social reform movements of the last century and a half as a failure — failure to match up to the liberal ideals of equality and reason. It is from this standpoint that he can show, quite legitimately, the falsity of any attempt to paint a picture of starry eyed radicalism muzzled by a censorious nationalist ideology. But a new problem crops up. If we are to say that the nineteenth century reform movements did not arise out of an ideological acceptance of western liberalism, it could fairly be asked: from what then did they originate? The answer that they stemmed from problems of personal adjustment within the family can hardly be adequate. After all, the nineteenth century debates about social reform generally, and the women's question in particular, were intensely ideological. If the paradigm for those debates was not that of western liberalism, what was it? Moreover, if we cannot describe that paradigm in its own terms, can we legitimately apply once again the western standards of liberalism to proclaim the reform movements, pre-nationalist as well as nationalist, as historical failures? Surely the new critical historiography will be grossly one-sided if we are unable to represent the nineteenth-century ideology in its relation to itself, i.e. in its self-identity.

It seems to me that Sumit Sarkar's argument can be taken much further. We need not shy away from the fact that the nationalist ideology did indeed tackle the women's question in the nineteenth century. To expect the contrary would be surprising. It is inconceivable that an ideology which claimed to offer a total alternative to the 'traditional' social order as well as to the western way of life should fail to have something distinctive to say about such a fundamental aspect of social institutions and practices as the position of women. We should direct our search within the nationalist ideology itself.

We might, for a start, pursue Sarkar's entirely valid observation that the nineteenth century ideologues were highly selective in their adoption of liberal slogans. How did they select what they wanted? What, in other words, was the ideological sieve through which they put the newly imported ideas from Europe? Once we have reconstructed this framework of the nationalist ideology, we will be in a far better position to locate where exactly the women's question fitted in with the claims of nationalism. We will find, if I may anticipate my argument in the following sections of this paper, that nationalism did in fact face up to the new social and cultural problems concerning the position of women in 'modern' society and that it did provide an answer to the problems in terms of its own ideological paradigm. I will claim, therefore, that the relative unimportance of the women's question in the last decades of the nineteenth century is not to be explained by the fact that it had been censored out of the reform agenda or overtaken by the more pressing and emotive issues of political struggle. It was because nationalism had in fact resolved 'the women's question' in complete accordance with its preferred goals.

II

I have elaborated elsewhere[4] a framework for analysing the contradictory pulls on nationalist ideology in its struggle against the dominance of colonialism and the resolution it offered to these contradictions. In the main, this resolution was built around a separation of the domain of culture into two spheres — the material and the spiritual. It was in the material sphere that the claims of western civilization were the most powerful. Science, technology, rational forms of economic organization, modern methods of statecraft, these had given the European countries the strength to subjugate non-European peoples and to impose their dominance over the whole world. To overcome this domination, the colonized people must learn these superior techniques of organizing material life and incorporate them within their own cultures. This was one aspect of the nationalist project of rationalizing and reforming the 'traditional' culture of their people. But this could not mean the imitation of the West in every aspect of life, for then the very distinction between the West and the East would vanish — the self-identity of national culture would itself be threatened. In fact, as Indian nationalists in the late nineteenth century argued, not only was it not desirable to imitate the West in anything other than the material aspects of life, it was not even necessary to do so, because in the spiritual domain the East was superior to the West.

What was necessary was to cultivate the material techniques of modern western civilization while retaining and strengthening the distinctive spiritual essence of the national culture. This completed the formulation of the nationalist project, and as an ideological justification for the selective appropriation of western modernity it continues to hold sway to this day (*pace* Rajiv Gandhi's juvenile fascination for space-age technology).

We need not concern ourselves here with the details of how this ideological framework shaped the course of nationalist politics in India. What is important is to note that nationalism was not simply about a political struggle for power; it related the question of political independence of the nation to virtually every aspect of the material and spiritual life of the people. In every case, there was a problem of selecting what to take from the West and what to reject. And in every case, the questions were asked: is it desirable? Is it necessary? The answers to these questions are the material of the debates about social reform in the nineteenth century. To understand the self-identity of nationalist ideology in concrete terms, we must look more closely at the way in which these questions were answered.

The discourse of nationalism shows that the material/spiritual distinction was condensed into an analogous, but ideologically far more powerful, dichotomy : that between the outer and the inner. The material domain lies outside us — a mere external, which influences us, conditions us, and to which we are forced to adjust. But ultimately it is unimportant. It is the spiritual which lies within, which is our true self; it is that which is genuinely essential. It follows that as long as we take care to retain the spiritual distinctiveness of our culture, we could make all the compromises and adjustments necessary to adapt ourselves to the requirements of a modern material world without losing our true identity. This was the key which nationalism supplied for resolving the ticklish problems posed by issues of social reform in the nineteenth century.

Now apply the inner/outer distinction to the matter of concrete day-to-day living and you get a separation of the social space into *ghar* and *bahir*, the home and the world. The world is the external, the domain of the material; the home represents our inner spiritual self, our true identity. The world is a treacherous terrain of the pursuit of material interests, where practical considerations reign supreme. It is also typically the domain of the male. The home in its essence must remain unaffected by the profane activities of the material world — and woman is its representation. And so we get an identification of social roles by gender to correspond with the separation of the social space into ghar and bahir.

Thus far we have not obtained anything that is different from the typical conception of gender roles in any 'traditional' patriarchy. If we now find continuities in these social attitudes in the phase of social reforms in the nineteenth century, we are tempted to put this down as 'conservatism', a mere defence of 'traditional' norms. But this would be a mistake. The colonial situation, and the ideological response of nationalism, introduced an entirely new substance to these terms and effected their transformation. The material/spiritual dichotomy, to which the terms 'world' and 'home' corresponded, had acquired, as we have noted before, a very special significance in the nationalist mind. The world was where the European power had challenged the non-European peoples and, by virtue of its superior material culture, had subjugated them. But it had failed to colonize the inner, essential, identity of the East which lay in its distinctive, and superior, spiritual culture. That is where the East was undominated, sovereign, master of its own fate. For a colonized people, the world was a distressing constraint, forced upon it by the fact of its material weakness. It was a place of oppression and daily humiliation, a place where the norms of the colonizer had perforce to be accepted. It was also the place, as nationalists were soon to argue, where the battle would be waged for national independence. The requirement for this was for the subjugated to learn from the West the modern sciences and arts of the material world. Then their strengths would be matched and ultimately the colonizer overthrown. But in the entire phase of the national struggle, the crucial need was to protect, preserve and strengthen the inner core of the national culture, its spiritual essence. No encroachments by the colonizer must be allowed in that inner sanctum. In the world, imitation of and adaptation to western norms was a necessity; at home, they were tantamount to annihilation of one's very identity.

Once we match this new meaning of the home/world dichotomy with the identification of social roles by gender, we get the ideological framework within which nationalism answered the women's question. It would be a grave error to see in this, as we are apt to in our despair at the many marks of social conservatism in nationalist practice, a total rejection of the West. Quite the contrary. The nationalist paradigm in fact supplied an ideological principle of *selection.* It was not a dismissal of modernity; the attempt was rather to make modernity consistent with the nationalist project.

III

It is striking how much of the literature on women in the nineteenth century was concerned with the theme of the threatened westernization of Bengali women. It was taken up in virtually every form of written, oral and visual communication, from the ponderous essays of nineteenth-century moralists, to novels, farces, skits and jingles, to the paintings of the *patua* (scroll painter). Social parody was the most popular and effective medium of this ideological propagation. From Iswarchandra Gupta and the *kabiyal* (popular versifiers) of the early nineteenth century to the celebrated pioneers of modern Bengali theatre — Michael Madhusudan Dutt, Dinabandhu Mitra, Jyotirindranath Tagore, Upendranath Das, Amritalal Bose —everyone picked up the theme. To ridicule the idea of a Bengali woman trying to imitate the way of a European woman or *memsahib* (and it was very much an idea, for it is hard to find historical evidence that even in the most westernized families of Calcutta in the mid-nineteenth century there were actually any women who even remotely resembled these gross caricatures) was a sure recipe calculated to evoke raucous laughter and moral condemnation in both male and female audiences. It was, of course, a criticism of manners: of new items of clothing such as the blouse, the petticoat and shoes (all, curiously, considered vulgar, although they clothed the body far better than the single length of fabric or sari which was customary for Bengali women, irrespective of wealth and social status, until the middle of the nineteenth century), of the use of western cosmetics and jewellery, of the reading of novels (the educated Haimabati in Jyotirindranath's *Alikbabu* speaks, thinks and acts like the heroines of historical romances), of needlework (considered a useless and expensive pastime), of riding in open carriages. What made the ridicule stronger was the constant suggestion that the westernized woman was fond of useless luxury and cared little for the well-being of the home. One can hardly miss in all this a criticism —reproach mixed with envy

— of the wealth and luxury of the new social elite emerging around the institutions of colonial administration and trade.

This literature of parody and satire in the first half of the nineteenth century clearly contained much that was prompted by a straightforward defence of 'tradition' and outright rejection of the new. The nationalist paradigm had still not emerged in clear outline. On hindsight, this — the period from Rammohun to Vidyasagar — appears as one of great social turmoil and ideological confusion among the literati. And then, drawing from various sources, a new discourse began to be formed in the second half of the century — the discourse of nationalism. Now the attempt was made to define the social and moral principles for locating the position of women in the 'modern' world of the nation.

Let us take as an example one of the most clearly formulated tracts on the subject : Bhudev Mukhopadhyay's *Paribarik Prabandha* (essays on the family) published in 1882. Bhudev states the problem in his characteristic matter-of-fact style:

> Because of our hankering for the external glitter and ostentation of the English way of life . . . an upheaval is under way within our homes. The men learn English and become sahibs. The women do not learn English but nevertheless try to become bibis. In households which manage on an income of a hundred rupees, the women no longer cook, sweep or make the bed . . . everything is done by servants and maids; [the women] only read books, sew carpets and play cards. What is the result? The house and furniture get untidy, the meals poor, the health of every member of the family is ruined; children are born weak and rickety, constantly plagued by illness — they die early.
>
> Many reform movements are being conducted today; the education of women, in particular, is constantly talked about. But we rarely hear of those great arts in which women were once trained — a training which if it had still been in vogue would have enabled us to tide over this crisis caused by injudicious imitation. I suppose we will never hear of this training again.[5]

The problem is put here in the empirical terms of a positive sociology, a genre much favoured by serious Bengali writers of Bhudev's time. But the sense of crisis which he expresses was very much a reality. Bhudev is voicing the feelings of large sections of the newly emergent middle class in Bengal when he says that the very institutions of home and family were threatened under the peculiar conditions of colonial rule. A quite unprecedented external condition had been thrust upon us; we were being forced to adjust to those conditions, for which a certain degree of imitation of alien ways was unavoidable. But could this wave of imitation be allowed to enter our homes? Would that not destroy our inner identity? Yet it was clear that a mere restatement of the old norms of family life would not suffice : they were breaking down by the inexorable force of circumstance. New norms were needed, which would be more appropriate to the external conditions of the modern world and yet not a mere imitation of the West. What were the principles by which these new norms could be constructed?

Bhudev supplies the characteristic nationalist answer. In an essay on modesty entitled "Lajjasilata," he talks of the natural and social principles which provide the basis for the "feminine" virtues.[6] Modesty, or decorum in manner and conduct, he says, is a specifically human trait; it does not exist in animal nature. It is human aversion to the purely animal traits which gives rise to virtues such as modesty. In this aspect, human beings seek to cultivate in themselves, and in their civilization, spiritual or god-like qualities wholly opposed to forms of behaviour which prevail in animal nature. Further, within the human species, women cultivate and cherish these god-like qualities far more than men. Protected to a certain extent from the purely material pursuits of securing a livelihood in the external world, women express in their appearance and behaviour the spiritual qualities which are characteristic of civilized and refined human society.

The relevant dichotomies and analogues are all here. The material/spiritual dichotomy corresponds to that between animal/god-like qualities, which in turn corresponds to masculine/feminine virtues. Bhudev then invests this ideological form with its specifically nationalist content:

> In a society where men and women meet together, converse together at all times, eat and drink together, travel together, the manners of women are likely to be somewhat coarse, devoid of spiritual qualities and relatively prominent in animal traits. For this reason, I do not think the customs of such a society are free from all defect. Some argue that because of such close association with women, the characters of men acquire certain tender and spiritual qualities. Let me concede the point. But can the loss caused by coarseness and degeneration in the female character be compensated by the acquisition of a certain degree of tenderness in the male? [7]

The point is then hammered home.

> Those who laid down our religious codes discovered the inner spirituality which resides within even the most animal pursuits which humans must perform, and thus removed the animal qualities from those actions. This has not happened in Europe. Religion there is completely divorced from [material] life. Europeans do not feel inclined to regulate all aspects of their life by the norms of religion; they condemn it as clericalism . . . . In the Arya system there is a preponderance of spriritualism, in the European system a preponderance of material pleasure. In the Arya system, the wife is a goddess. In the European system, she is a partner and companion.[8]

The new norm for organizing family life and determining the right conduct for women in the conditions of the 'modern' world could now be deduced with ease. Adjustments would have to be made in the external world of material activity, and men would bear the brunt of this task. To the extent that the family was itself entangled in wider social relations, it too could not be insulated from the influence of changes in the outside world. Consequently, the organization and ways of life at home would also have to be changed. But the crucial requirement was to retain the inner spirituality of indigenous social life. The home was the principal site for expressing the spiritual quality of the national culture, and women must take the main responsibility of protecting and nurturing this quality. No matter what the changes in the external conditions of life for women, they must not lose their essentially spiritual (i.e. feminine) virtues; they must not, in other words, become *essentially* westernized. It followed, as a simple criterion for judging the desirability of reform, that the essential distinction between the social roles of men and women in terms of material and spiritual virtues must at all times be maintained. There would have to be a marked *difference* in the degree and manner of westernization of women, as distinct from men, in the modern world of the nation.

IV

This was the central principle by which nationalism resolved the women's question in terms of its own historical project. The details were not, of course, worked out immediately. In fact, from the middle of the nineteenth century right up to the present day, there have been many controversies about the precise application of the home/world, spiritual/material, feminine/masculine dichotomies in various matters concerning the everyday life of the 'modern' woman — her dress, food, manners, education, her role in organizing life at home, her role outside the home. The concrete problems arose out of the rapidly changing situation — both external and internal — in which the new middle class family found itself; the specific solutions were drawn from a variety of sources — a reconstructed 'classical' tradition, modernized folk forms, the utilitarian logic of bureaucratic and industrial practices, the legal idea of equality in a liberal democratic state. The content of the resolution was neither predetermined nor unchanging, but its form had to be consistent with the system of dichotomies which shaped and contained the nationalist project.

The 'new' woman defined in this way was subjected to a *new* patriarchy. In fact, the social order connecting the home and the world in which nationalism placed the new woman was contrasted not only with that of modern western society; it was explicitly distinguished from the patriarchy of indigenous tradition. Sure enough, nationalism adopted several elements from 'tradition' as marks of its native cultural identity, but this was a deliberately 'classicized' tradition — reformed, reconstructed. Even Gandhi said of the patriarchal rules laid down by the scriptures:

> . . . it is sad to think that the *Smritis* contain texts which can command no respect from men who cherish the liberty of woman as their own and who regard her as the mother of the race. . . The question arises as to what to do with the *Smritis* that contain texts . . . that are repugnant to the moral sense. I have already suggested . . . that all that is printed in the name of scriptures need not be taken as the word of God or the inspired word.[9]

The new patriarchy was also sharply distinguished from the immediate social and cultural condition in which the majority of the people lived, for the 'new' woman was quite the reverse of the 'common' woman who was coarse, vulgar, loud, quarrelsome, devoid of superior moral sense, sexually promiscuous, subjected to brutal physical oppression by males. Alongside the parody of the westernized woman, this other construct is repeatedly emphasized in the literature of the nineteenth century through a host of lower-class female characters who make their appearance in the social milieu of the new middle class — maidservants, washerwomen, barbers, pedlars, procuresses, prostitutes. It was precisely this degenerate condition of women which nationalism claimed it would reform, and it was through these contrasts that the new woman of nationalist ideology was accorded a status of cultural superiority to the westernized women of the wealthy parvenu families spawned by the colonial connection as well as the common women of the lower classes. Attainment by her own efforts of a superior national culture was the mark of woman's newly acquired freedom. This was the central ideological strength of the nationalist resolution of the women's question.

We can follow the form of this resolution in several specific aspects in which the lives and conditions of middle-class women have changed over the last hundred years or so. Take the case of 'female education', that contentious subject which engaged so much of the attention of social reformers in the nineteenth century.[10] Some of the early opposition to the opening of schools for women was backed by an appeal to 'tradition' which supposedly prohibited women from being introduced to bookish learning, but this argument hardly gained much support. The threat was seen to lie in the fact that the early schools, and arrangements for teaching women at home, were organized by Christian missionaries; there was thus the fear of both proselytization and the exposure of women to harmful western influences. The threat was removed when from the 1850s Indians themselves began to open schools for girls. The spread of formal education among middle-class women in Bengal in the second half of the nineteenth century was remarkable. From 95 girls' schools with an attendance of 2,500 in 1863, the figures went up to 2,238 schools in 1890 with a total of more than 80,000 students.[11]

The quite general acceptance of formal education among middle-class women was undoubtedly made possible by the development of an educative literature and teaching materials in the Bengali language. The long debates of the nineteenth century on a proper 'feminine curriculum' now seem to us somewhat quaint, but it is not difficult to identify the real point of concern. Much of the content of the modern school education was seen as important for the 'new' woman, but to administer it in the English language was difficult in practical terms, irrelevant in view of the fact that the central place of the educated woman was still at home, and threatening because it might devalue and displace that central site where the social position of women was located. The problem was resolved through the efforts of the intelligentsia who made it a fundamental task of the nationalist project to create a modern language and literature suitable for a widening readership which would include newly educated women. Through text books, periodicals and creative works, an important force which shaped the new literature of Bengal was the urge to make it accessible to women who could read only one language — their mother-tongue.

Formal education became not only acceptable, but in fact a requirement for the new *bhadramahila* (respectable woman), when it was demonstrated that it was possible for a woman to acquire the cultural refinements afforded by modern education without jeopardizing her place at home. Indeed, the nationalist construct of the new woman derived its ideological strength from the fact that it was able to make the goal of cultural refinement through education a personal challenge for every woman, thus opening up a domain where woman was an autonomous subject. This explains to a large extent the remarkable degree of enthusiasm among middle class women to acquire and use for themselves the benefits of formal learning. It was a purpose which they set for themselves in their personal lives as the object of their will; to achieve it was to achieve freedom. Indeed, the achievement was marked by claims of cultural superiority in several different aspects: superiority over the western woman for whom, it was believed, education meant only the acquisition of material skills in order to compete with men in the outside world and hence a loss of feminine (spiritual) virtues; superiority over the preceding generation of women in their own homes who had been denied the opportunity for freedom by an oppressive and degenerate social tradition; and superiority over women of the lower classes who were culturally incapable of appreciating the virtues of freedom.

It is this particular nationalist construction of reform as a project of both emancipation and self-emancipation of women (and hence a project in which both men and women must participate) which also explains why the early generation of educated women themselves so keenly propagated the nationalist idea of the 'new woman'. Recent historians of a liberal persuasion have often been somewhat embarrassed by the profuse evidence of women writers of the nineteenth century, including those at the forefront of the reform movements in middle-class homes, justifying the importance of the so-called 'feminine virtues'. Radharani Lahiri, for instance, wrote in 1875: "Of all the subjects that women might learn, housework is the most important . . . whatever knowledge she may acquire, she cannot claim any reputation unless she is proficient in housework."[12] Others spoke of the need for an educated woman to 'develop' such womanly virtues as chastity, self-sacrifice, submission, devotion, kindness, patience and the labours of love.[13] The ideological point of view from which such protestations of 'femininity' (and hence the acceptance of a new patriarchal order) were made inevitable was given precisely by the *nationalist* resolution of the problem, and Kundamala Debi, writing in 1870, expressed this well when she advised other women:

> If you have acquired real knowledge, then give no place in your heart to *mem-sahib* like behaviour. That is not becoming in a Bengali housewife. See how an educated woman can do housework thoughtfully and systematically in a way unknown to an ignorant, uneducated woman. And see how if God had not appointed us to this place in the home, how unhappy a place the world would be![14]

Education then was meant to inculcate in women the virtues — the typically 'bourgeois' virtues characteristic of the new social forms of 'disciplining' — of orderliness, thrift, cleanliness, and a personal sense of responsibility, the practical skills of literacy, accounting and hygiene, and the ability to run the household according to the new physical and economic conditions set by the outside world. For this, she would also need to have some idea of the world outside the home into which she could even venture as long as it did not threaten her 'femininity'. It is this latter criterion, now invested with a characteristically nationalist content, which made possible the displacement of the boundaries of 'the home' from the physical confines earlier defined by the rules of *purdah* (seclusion) to a more flexible, but culturally nonetheless determinate, domain set by the *differences* between socially approved male and female conduct. Once the essential 'femininity' of women was fixed in terms of certain culturally visible 'spiritual' qualities, they could go to schools, travel in public conveyances, watch public entertainment programmes, and in time even take up employment outside the home. But the 'spiritual' signs of her femininity were now clearly marked: in her dress, her eating habits, her social demeanour, her religiosity. The specific markers were obtained from diverse sources, and in terms of their origins each had its specific history. The dress of the bhadramahila, for instance, went through a whole phase of experimentation before what was known as the *brahmika* sari (a form of wearing the sari in combination with blouse, petticoat and shoes made fashionable in Brahmo households) became accepted as standard for middle class women.[15] Here too the necessary differences were signified in terms of national identity, social emancipation and cultural refinement, differences, that is to say, with the memsahib, with women of earlier generations and with women of the lower classes. Further, in this as in other aspects of her life, the 'spirituality' of her character had also to be stressed in contrast with the innumerable surrenders which men were having to make to the pressures of the material world. The need to adjust to the new conditions outside the home had forced upon men a whole series of changes in their dress, food habits, religious observances and social relations. Each of these capitulations now had to be compensated by an assertion of spiritual purity on the part of women. They must not eat, drink or smoke in the same way as men; they must continue the observance of religious rituals which men were finding it difficult to carry out; they must maintain the cohesiveness of family life and solidarity with the kin to which men could not now devote much attention. The new patriarchy advocated by nationalism conferred upon women the honour of a new social responsibility, and by associating the task of 'female emancipation' with the historical goal of sovereign nationhood, bound them to a new, and yet entirely legitimate, subordination.

As with all hegemonic forms of exercise of dominance, this patriarchy combined coercive authority with the subtle force of persuasion. This was expressed most generally in an inverted ideological form of the relation of power between the sexes: the adulation of woman as goddess or as mother. Whatever be its sources in the classical religions of India or in medieval religious practices, it is undeniable that the specific ideological form in which we know the Sati-Savitri-Sita construct in the modern literature and arts of India today is wholly a product of the development of a dominant middle class culture coeval with the era of nationalism. It served to emphasize with all the force of mythological inspiration what had in any case become a dominant characteristic of femininity in the new woman, viz. the 'spiritual' qualities of self-sacrifice, benevolence, devotion, religiosity, etc. This spirituality did not, as we have seen, impede the chances of the woman moving out of the physical confines of the home; on the contrary, it facilitated it, making it possible for her to go out into the world under conditions that would not threaten her femininity. In fact, the image of woman as goddess or mother served to erase her sexuality in the world outside the home.

V

I conclude this essay by pointing out another significant feature of the way in which nationalism sought to resolve the women's question in accordance with its historical project. This has to do with the one aspect of the question which was directly political, concerning relations with the State. Nationalism, as I have said before, located its own subjectivity in the spiritual domain of culture, where it considered itself superior to the West and hence undominated and sovereign. It could not permit an encroachment by the colonial power into that domain. This determined the characteristically nationalist response to proposals for effecting social reform through the legislative enactments of the colonial state. Unlike the early reformers from Rammohun to Vidyasagar, nationalists of the late nineteenth century were in general opposed to such proposals, for such a method of reform seemed to deny the ability of the 'nation' to act for itself even in a domain where it was sovereign. In the specific case of reforming the lives of women, consequently, the nationalist position was firmly based on the premise that this was an area where the nation was acting on its own, outside the purview of the guidance and intervention of the colonial state.

We now get the full answer to the historical problem I raised at the beginning of this essay. The reason why the issue of 'female emancipation' seems to disappear from the public agenda of nationalist agitation in the late nineteenth century is not because it was overtaken by the more emotive issues concerning political power. Rather, the reason lies in the refusal of nationalism to make the women's question an issue of political negotiation with the colonial state. The simple historical fact is that the lives of middle-class women, coming from that demographic section which effectively constituted the 'nation' in late colonial India, changed most rapidly precisely during the period of the nationalist movement — indeed, so rapidly that women from each generation in the last hundred years could say quite truthfully that their lives were strikingly different from those led by the preceding generation. These changes took place in the colonial period mostly outside the arena of political agitation, in a domain where the nation thought of itself as already free. It was after independence, when the nation had acquired political sovereignty, that it became legitimate to embody the ideas of reform in legislative enactments about marriage rules, property rights, suffrage, equal pay, equality of opportunity, etc.

Another problem on which we can now obtain a clearer perspective is that of the seeming absence of any autonomous struggle by women themselves for equality and freedom. We would be mistaken to look for evidence of such a struggle in the public archives of political affairs, for unlike the women's movement in nineteenth and twentieth century Europe, that is not where the battle was waged here in the era of nationalism. The domain where the new idea of womanhood was sought to be actualized was the home, and the real history of that change can be constructed only out of evidence left behind in autobiographies, family histories, religious tracts, literature, theatre, songs, paintings and such other cultural artefacts that depict life in middle-class homes. It is impossible that in the considerable transformation of the middle-class home in India in the last hundred years, women played a wholly passive part, for even the most severe system of domination seeks the consent of the subordinate as an autonomous being.

The location of the State in the nationalist resolution of the women's question in the colonial period has yet another implication. For sections of the middle-class which felt themselves culturally left out of the specific process of formation of the 'nation', and which then organized themselves as politically distinct groups, the relative exclusion from the new nation-state would act as a further means of displacement of the legitimate agency of reform. In the case of Muslims in Bengal, for instance, the formation of a middle-class occurred with a lag, for reasons which we need not go into here. Exactly the same sorts of ideological concerns typical of a nationalist response to issues of social reform in a colonial situation can be seen to operate among Muslims as well, with a difference in chronological time.[16] Nationalist reform does not, however, reach political fruition in the case of Muslims in independent

India, since to the extent that the dominant cultural formation among them considers the community excluded from the state, a new colonial relation is brought into being. The system of dichotomies of inner/outer, home/world, feminine/masculine is once again activated. Reforms which touch upon the 'inner essence' of the identity of the community can only be carried out by the community itself, not by the State. It is instructive to note here how little institutional change has been allowed in the civil life of Indian Muslims since independence and compare it with Muslim countries where nationalist cultural reform was a part of the successful formation of an independent nation-state. The contrast is striking if one compares the position of middle-class Muslim women in West Bengal today with that in neighbouring Bangladesh.

The continuance of a distinct cultural 'problem' of the minorities is an index of the failure of the Indian nation to effectively include within its body the whole of the demographic mass which it claimed to represent. The failure assumes massive proportions when we note, as I have tried to do throughout this discussion, that the formation of a hegemonic 'national culture' was *necessarily* built upon a system of exclusions. Ideas of freedom, equality and cultural refinement went hand in hand with a set of dichotomies which systematically excluded from the new life of the nation the vast masses of people whom the dominant elite would represent and lead, but who could never be culturally integrated with their leaders. Both colonial rulers and their nationalist opponents conspired to displace in the colonial world the original structure of meanings associated with western bourgeois notions of right, freedom, equality, etc. The inauguration of the national state in India could not mean a universalization of the bourgeois notion of 'man'.

The new patriarchy which nationalist discourse set up as a hegemonic construct culturally distinguished itself not only from the West but also from the mass of its own people. It has generalized itself among the new middle class, admittedly a widening class and large enough in absolute numbers to be self-reproducing, but is irrelevant to the large mass of subordinate classes. This raises important questions regarding the issue of women's rights today. We are all aware that the forms and demands of the women's movement in the West are not generally applicable in India. This often leads us to slip back into a nationalist framework for resolving such problems. A critical historical understanding will show that this path will only bring us to the dead end which the nationalist resolution of the women's question has already reached. The historical possibilities here have already been exhausted. A renewal of the struggle for the equality and freedom of women must, as with all democratic issues in countries like India, imply a struggle against the humanistic construct of 'rights' set up in Europe in the post-enlightenment era and include within it a struggle against the false essentialisms of home/world, spiritual/material, feminine/masculine propagated by nationalist ideology.

NOTES

1. See Ghulam Murshid, *Reluctant Debutante: Response of Bengali Women to Modernization, 1849-1905* (Rajshahi: Rajshahi University Press, 1983).
2. See for example, Sumit Sarkar, "The Complexities of Young Bengal," *Nineteenth Century Studies,* 4(1973), pp. 504-34, and "Rammohun Roy and the Break with the Past" in *Rammohun Roy and the Process of Modernization in India,* ed. V.C. Joshi (Delhi: Vikas, 1975); Ashok Sen, "The Bengal Economy and Rammohun Roy," in *Rammohun Roy,* ed. Joshi, and *Ishwar Chandra Vidyasagar and his Elusive Milestones* (Calcutta: Riddhi India, 1977); and Ranajit Guha, "Neel Darpan: The Image of the Peasant Revolt in a Liberal Mirror," *Journal of Peasant Studies,* 2, no.1 (1974), pp.1-46.
3. Sumit Sarkar, "The Women's Question in Nineteenth Century Bengal" in *Women and Culture,* eds. Kumkum Sangari and Sudesh Vaid (Bombay: SNDT Women's University, 1985), pp. 157-72.
4. See Partha Chatterjee, *Nationalist Thought and the Colonial World* (Delhi: Oxford University Press, 1986).
5. Bhudev Mukhopadhyay, "Grhakaryer vyavastha," in *Bhudev-racanasambhar,* ed. Pramathanath Bisi (Calcutta: Mitra and Ghosh, 1969), p.480.
6. "Lajjasilata" in ibid., pp.445-48.
7. Ibid., p.446.
8. Ibid., p.447.
9. M.K. Gandhi, *Collected Works,* 64 (Delhi: Publications Division, 1970), p.85.

10. See the survey of these debates in Murshid, *Reluctant Debutante,* pp.19-62, and Meredith Borthwick, *The Changing Role of Women in Bengal, 1849-1905* (Princeton N.J.: Princeton University Press, 1984).

11. Murshid, *Reluctant Debutante,* p.43. In the area of higher education, Chandramukhi Bose and Kadambini Ganguli were celebrated as examples of what Bengali women could achieve in formal learning: they took their B.A. degrees from the University of Calcutta in 1883, before any British university agreed to accept women on their examination rolls. On Chandramukhi and Kadambini's application, the University of Calcutta granted full recognition to women candidates at the First of Arts examination in 1878. London University admitted women to its degrees later that year (Borthwick, *Changing Role of Women,* p.94). Kadambini then went on to medical college and became the first professionally schooled woman doctor.

12. Cited in Murshid, *Reluctant Debutante,* p.60.

13. See for instance, Kulabala Debi, *Hindu Mahilar Hinabastha,* cited in Murshid, *Reluctant Debutante,* p.60.

14. Cited in Borthwick, *Changing Role of Women,* p.105.

15. Ibid., pp.245-56.

16. See Murshid, *Reluctant Debutante.*

Tracing Savitri's Pedigree:

*Victorian Racism and the Image of Women in Indo-Anglian Literature**

SUSIE THARU

IF WE CONSIDER the task of a feminist criticism to be a "revision, the act of looking back, of seeing with fresh eyes, of entering an old text from a new critical direction — for us more than a chapter in cultural history . . . an act of survival,"[1] then we recognize its originary impulse as the need to understand the assumptions and value-orientations that define our worlds and determine imaginative self images, and its goal, usually a refusal to be accomplice-victim to the self-destructiveness of our culture. Articulated thus, the feminist project becomes strangely pardigmatic of the one I believe faces the study of Indo-Anglian literature today. If the onus for women is to read against the sex inflection of the work, to make palpable and lay open to discussion the impalpable designs[2] these texts have on us, our burden as Indians is to search the texts that arose out of an encounter which sought to render feminine an entire nation. Inevitably, to read these texts as women in our country today demands also that we read them as a colonized race or vice-versa. The question of which victimization takes precedence is only academic.

The immediate resistance as we set out on this journey is from a critical orthodoxy, enshrined both in the curriculum and in scholarship; an orthodoxy which denies such action legitimacy. The text, this authority proclaims, is an autotelic whole. Its scope, if not the eternal, at least the universal. It must therefore be prised loose

* An earlier version of this article, "Tracing Savitri's Cross-Cultural Ancestry (Or the Origins of Victorian Racism in the Image of Women in Indo-Anglian Literature)," was published in *Women and Culture*, eds. Kumkum Sangari and Sudesh Vaid (Bombay: SNDT Women's University, 1985).

of its context (which includes both writer and reader) and regarded as an autonomous object if its literary quality (a function principally of its verbal patterning and consequent formal excellence) is to be grasped. To identify and demonstrate this quality, to *evaluate* the text as literary object, becomes the legitimate end of the critical venture.

It would not be correct, however, to imply that in its preoccupation with form and language, such criticism disregards content. On the contrary, till the middle of this century, an Arnoldian sense of art as the only remaining source of human order and moral value in a world bereft of God, elaborated itself. But, as Derrida's deconstructions so colourfully demonstrate, what continued to be searched for was an 'universal' or 'human' meaning, made in the same absolutist, ahistorical mould as the religious order it replaced. Derrida speaks of the dream of the transcendental signified that subterraneously determines the history of western metaphysics;[3] the work, Ransom tells us, is an "elemental cosmic and eternal object."[4]

We are up against another wall: one that reveals the necrophilic gleam of this epistemology as it affects us in a 'colonial' or 'third' world. Deprived of the doctrinal word, there was now no way of deciding what these universal, human values were, or of proving when the literary work had arrived at them, though critics seldom doubted the 'self-evident' universality of their responses. The sociology of this confidence is not hard to locate.[5] Within the criticism itself, however, the problem is solved with a ruse as old as Descartes himself. The well-formed work, or the well-wrought urn, it is assumed, precisely because of what Cleanth Brooks called the equilibrium of forces it held, also carried these universal truths. Aesthetic perfection, defined in its turn by the even more elusive norms of aesthetic taste, becomes the new guarantor of truth and morality.

It is not surprising, given the circularity of the argument, that the universal values critics located in what they now considered, or what had already been canonized as great works, were precisely the values that upheld European Society since the Renaissance: individualist, Protestant, bourgeois, white, male —the values that made for what Eliot had called, in that much lauded phrase, the mind of Europe. And the art-work, imaged as a hermetic transcendental object, free of social determination, became the new means by which these values were reaffirmed and upheld. But this is not all. Within this tradition the writer was regarded a sort of spiritual medium, a seer, who in some mysterious way (often beyond his or her *conscious* awareness) had access to the gift of form, and through it, miraculously, to the values that were to preserve humanity. The 'ideal' reader, like the writer, was also considered a member of a small intellectual, or rather, imaginative, elite entrusted with a similar function. Even Leavis (that rebel in the academy) saw this group as carrying the burden of preserving culture and directing taste in an increasingly philistine society. What is important here is not just the aesthetic mandarinism but the fact that such a bias (its emphasis on 'preservation'; the need for a reader who is steeped, or rather trained into, the established norms and values of this culture) makes for a present-past relation rather than a present-future one. Despite all the fanfare which announced it as avant-garde, art, as such criticism imaged it, was something that *preserved* the status quo, maintained stability and ensured the continuing hold of the past.

Obviously this has crucial importance, not just in India but in all ex-colonial countries where the main literature teaching/learning shop is the English Literature one. For what the student or the reader is co-opted into 'preserving' as he or she is carefully schooled into a sensibility and taste that befits the 'ideal reader', is not just an alien culture and the socio-economic or political systems it endorses, but an alien culture that historically related (and continues to relate) to us along an axis of power. When we consider that this cultural complex was invested with an idea of the Orient[6] and an ideology of racism which upheld white norms as standard and denigrated our deviance from them, the self destructive core of this venture for the Indian reader is clear. But what such a commitment also effectively ensured was a critical activity so crippled, so locked in with an Euro-centric Absolute, that we could do little more with the literature that arose out of our own ground than rate or explicate it in relation to the established canon.

I am concerned, in this paper, then with the regeneration of criticism and the rehabilitation of a critical voice. For what I search is not the aesthetic object and its privileged meaning. I am, rather, interested in the psycho-social economy that gives rise to a text, and in turn, in the limits of the imaginative self images we inherit.

That I have chosen to do this through a study, not just of that vestigial curiosity[7] (often tagged on in the curriculum as an option to the more scientific linguistics or the more glamorous American literature), Indo-Anglian literature, but (one step further into the prison-house), of women in Indo-Anglian literature, is not accidental.

Indo-Anglian literature is really a literary sub-culture that owes its existence to the British presence in India. Stated as baldly as this, it must appear a truism, based on a disproportionate emphasis on the linguistic medium employed and a devaluation of its content. This is not so. One locates this point of origin, precisely because a principal burden of this literature can be regarded a working out of the urgencies that arise from the Indo-British encounter. To do so is not to exclude other important strains in the literature, but to emphasize what I see as the dominant one. If we regard culture in its living sense as the forms, the institutions, the knowledge that arise as a people struggle to come to terms with their environment, it is clear that over the past two hundred years or so, our culture has grown, and continues to grow against the stunting, even deforming background of European imperialism and colonialism. Existing social and economic structures were crudely broken up and the political system undermined, first by the mercantile incursions of the Company and then by the imperial government. In the process, traditional institutions and values were divested of their vital function in society. Along with this came the developments (I use the word here in a value-neutral sense) in education and in religious attitudes that changed the cultural texture of that world. What we have come to recognize as Indo-Anglian literature, arises, I believe, from the resulting pressures on the Bengali *bhadralok* (respectable people).

Colonial presence gave rise to a torturous psycho-cultural situation for Indians, more so for those who came into close contact with it. British imperialism justified its continued, and after 1857, militaristic, presence in India (both to its own liberal conscience and to our muted questioning) through an elaborately developed ideology of racism, designed to prove Indians (especially the urban upper castes) as weak and immoral, incapable of just government. Imperial presence was projected as necessary, benign, restraining, parental. Obviously this ideology helped entrench colonial presence by convincing the colonized of their fundamental inhumanity and the consequent need for the colonizers' permanent presence.

Confronted with the image the West provided them with, Indian intellectuals of that time reacted in two related ways.[8] They identified positively with the British diagnosis of 'the Indian condition' and the consequent prescription for our redemption. Indeed, often, like Rammohun Roy, they refined that diagnosis with great erudition. They plunged into the reform of our people, our religion and our customs with a zeal that surpassed that of the British liberals. But at the same time they felt constrained at a personal level to *prove* their humanity in the eyes of those who doubted it. It was necessary for them to demonstrate that Indians were not innately or naturally bestial, and that with stern application we could attain an intellectual standing as well as a strength of character and purpose that was self-evidently on par with that of white men. As Frantz Fanon suggests, these intellectuals "provided proof that they had assimilated the culture of the occupying power"[9] and could manipulate its categories with ease, even write creatively in it.

Consider Toru Dutt (1856-77), who stands out in the assessment of contemporary critics as the major talent of that time. Her first book, published when she was only nineteen, is a translation from the French. *A Sheaf Gleaned in French Fields* gained acclaim both in England and in France. Being both Indian and female, she has not just to match, but to *outdo*, the British who found French notoriously difficult.[10] But as we search her poems today, more interesting formations emerge. I would like to quote a few stanzas from her long poem "Savitri".

What was her own peculiar charm?
The soft black eyes, the raven hair,
The curving neck, the rounded arm,
All these are common everywhere.
Her charm was this — upon her face
Childlike and innocent and fair,
No man with thought impure or base
Could ever look; — the glory there,
The sweet simplicity and grace,
Abashed the boldest; but the good
God's purity there loved to trace,
Mirrored in dawning womanhood.

In those far-off primeval days
Fair India's daughters were not pent
In closed zenanas. On her ways
Savitri at her pleasure went
Whither she chose, — and hour by hour
With young companions of her age,
She roamed the woods for fruit or flower,
Or loitered in some hermitage,
For to the Munis gray and old
Her presence was as sunshine glad,
They taught her wonders manifold
And gave her of the best they had.

Her father let her have her way
In all things, whether high or low;
He feared no harm; he knew no ill
Could touch a nature pure as snow.
Long childless, as a priceless boon
He had obtained this child at last
By prayers, made morning, night, and noon
With many a vigil, many a fast;
Would Shiva his own gift recall,
Or mar its perfect beauty ever —
No, he had faith, — he gave her all
She wished, and feared and doubted never.

And so she wandered where she pleased
In boyish freedom. Happy time!
No small vexations ever teased,
Nor crushing sorrows dimmed her prime.
One care alone, her father felt —
Whither should he find a fitting mate.
For one so pure? — His thoughts long dwelt
On this as with his queen he sate.
'Ah, whom, dear wife, should we select?"
"Leave it to God," she answering cried,
"Savitri may herself elect
Someday, her future lord and guide."[11]

We have here part of a narrative poem that reads as well as any nineteenth century British lyric; its metric competence almost impeccable. But, given the colonial context and the British criticism of the position of women in our society, the emblem of freedom takes on a complex signification. The writer's main anxiety is indeed to project Savitri as a *free* woman; she has a boyish freedom to wander, to choose her friends, and even, under a Calvinistic God's personal guidance, the freedom to choose her own husband. This, the poem insists, was true of all Indian women in an uncorrupted past where there were no *zenanas* (secluded quarters for women). The effort, obviously, is to rebutt the negative image the British projected, and redeem, if not the present, at least the past. But more important is the way the poet's imagination, her longings, her straining for freedom, the limits of what she sees as habitable space, and even its forms have been domesticated. In fact, what has been so efficiently controlled are the very terms in which freedom may be *imagined*, not just by the writer but also by the reader.[12]

One need hardly point out that Savitri's 'virtue' closely matches the strangely convoluted Victorian myth of sexual purity in woman. The Victorians laid great stress on sexual restraint and moral uprightness in women, for without systematic control, women's sexual powers and appetites were considered dangerous to 'civic' society as a whole. The still familiar logic of the myth runs something like this proposition; 'a pure woman excites no sexual response'. Its corollaries: a woman who arouses a man is not pure, and second, a woman's infallible protection against male aggression, is her 'virtue'.[13] There is another aspect to the construction. For the Victorians, women, like the Indians, were really children. Only, white women were not "half-devil, half-child" like the orientals were, but "half-angel, half-child." Savitri, the real, uncorrupted Indian woman is like her white counterpart, "child-like" and angelic. Her purity is "God's purity." She spreads a "divine radiance" around, for her "conduct as a wife was such/As to illumine all the place." It soon becomes evident that the writer is claiming for her Savitri the very sexual refinement, the purity, held, as always, in the virtue of women, that the British insisted Hindu society lacked. And the Satyavan she must redeem through this feat of reculturalization is India itself.

In many ways Sarojini Naidu (1879-1949) belongs to the same phase in Indo-Anglian writing. Her verse echoes the lyric forms of her contemporary *fin-de-siecle* British poets; the mood is lyrical, passionate, sentimental, as the heart compels, though the local colour is Indian.[14] Naidu's poems paint the land of Romance and Mystery, the India of the common western imagination, with its colourful bangle sellers, graceful palanquin bearers, and princely Rajput lovers. The definitive taste is British, although the subjects, ostensibly at least, are Indian, Significantly, the hub of Naidu's world is a cultured, refined upper class. What happens to women (or for that matter those who work: the weavers, the fishermen, the palanquin bearers) within this world? To see them as they are is discomfiting, so they are transformed into a romance that will fit the requirements of European taste, but which at the same time absorbs both suffering and labour into the quietism of its lilting form. If she speaks of a life in *purdah* (seclusion) as the perfect repose of protection: "a revolving dream/Of languid and sequestered ease/Her girdles and her fillets gleam/Like changing fires on sunset seas. . .;"[15] she sees the weavers as participating in the colourful, cyclic dance of life, the palanquin bearers' work as a joyful gesture; their burden weightless. "Gaily, O gaily we glide and we sing/We bear her long like a pearl on a string."[16] In the poem "Suttee" the widow is distraught: "Love must I dwell in the living dark?" she asks, and again "Shall the blossom live when the tree is dead?"[17] *Sati* (widow immolation) seems the only real answer. Again in "Dirge" we find a romantic justification of stripping the young widow of her hair and jewels. One could go on, but the point has been made, I think. Naidu's burden is to project, to explain, *to justify*, just as much as to show around. That this makes for a distortion of the landscape and of those who inhabit it, is evident. But it also makes for the peculiar formation of the Indian intellectual engaged in this relation. Not only must s/he remain servile to another order, s/he must erase, and will gradually grow to hate, all which cannot be moulded into that cultural form: witness the anger so evident when the 'image' of India projected in a book or a film is not positive.[18] As accomplished poet, Naidu is not only an exhibit herself, she becomes, through her subject matter, also exhibitor. Our country is the spectacle, our lives a masquerade, and the poet must strain to keep it so.

But what we find here in embryonic form is also a crossbreeding that was to develop and take stronger hold during the later phases of the nationalist movement. If Toru Dutt, in the anxiety to present a pure, uncorrupted India transforms the Indian landscape morally into a western one, and her heroines into virtuous Victorians, Naidu composes a land and a people that fits into a different, more exotic area in the western imagination. She feeds essentially feudal, Vedic and Islamic cultural formations into what was the structure of Victorian sentiment. And where women were concerned, these diverse patriarchal cultures were surprisingly accommodative and reinforcing of each other. This is a pattern that shows up repeatedly in Indo-Anglian writing, as, say, in Kamala Markandaya's *Nectar in a Sieve*, or in Rama Mehta's *Inside the Haveli*, but the mode acquires its distinction in another area that is determining of women's imaginative worlds today: in contemporary 'decor', and clothing styles, the use that has been made of traditional crafts, the return of the 'ethnic', where the object and the detail is Indian, but the taste is western. The discourse elaborates itself as it moves beyond the limits of a high culture to include the folk. We have succeeded in recovering an almost unbearably tasteful past and an exquisite tradition. But what, we must necessarily ask, is the effect of these inert decorative recreations of formerly fertile institutions?

Naidu's poetry marks a transition. For what was to come with an emergent nationalism (it is interesting that much of her verse dates back to the period before her involvement with the Congress Party) is a revivalism that had a new image of Savitri to project. No doubt partially in response to the British focus on women, the movement chose to create an image of the Indian woman who was not socially victimized, but voluntarily *chose* the path of suffering and death in order to save her people. Indeed, she became a heraldic device. I am not thinking merely of the Hindu Mahasabha and the nationalistic revival of sati that took place as a result of its being banned by the British. Or even of the way in which the idea of freedom from colonial domination was infused and ballasted by one of a newly resplendent traditional Hindu society, although these things *are* related. The new form is epic in scope: the new icon elaborately embodied in Aurobindo's *Savitri,* where Savitri's purity, her powerlessness, her selfless love, her suffering, her very commitment to being a *wife*, is itself divine, and will save Satyavan (who is here not just the nation but the human condition itself) from the 'death' of ignorance and evil, indeed from the constriction of time itself. Similarly in Raja Rao's *Serpent and the Rope,* Ramaswamy is brought back to a real 'Indianness' through the dignity and strength his young, widowed stepmother achieves in her careful ritual; through his awareness of his growing sister; and finally through Savitri, who is modern and even in some ways westernized, but is truly Indian. It is this Savitri who magically reunites a spiritually wandering Rama with the real India (not a country, or a history, but a *metaphysic*, Raja Rao tells us). "Woman," the novel proclaims "is earth, air, ether, sound,"[19] womanhood "a deep and reverential mystery"[20] and so on. The burden of saving the nation: politically (Gandhi), spiritually (Aurobindo) and aesthetically/metaphysically (Raja Rao) is not just on women, but on the feminine.[21] Women are no longer people, but goddess-spirits. And as such, not alive or growing, but sculpted by the requirement of the emerging power. The composition is elaborate, but also typical. What we do find here, however, unlike say in Buddhism or Christianity, is a symbolic figure-head who is *female*. And consequently, a sacrificial complex that involves humility, passivity, suffering; the recognition of the mystic strength of tradition together with a strictness of moral purpose; and the establishment of a psycho-spiritual as against a material plane for confrontation. "I hope you have not missed the women in me" Gandhiji once wrote to Sarojini Naidu, and he spoke as one who was later to reiterate the femininity of an entire approach to liberation. And in this we regarded ourselves the moral torch-bearers for the world.

This nationalist colour to what is really a common trend — glorifying women who fulfill their wife and mother roles with exceptional ardour — placed an enormous burden on the women who came within its defining scope. It was the women, their commitment, their purity, their sacrifice, who were to ensure the moral, even spiritual power of the nation and hold it together. But even as we point this out, we must not forget that this phase also made for a positive evaluation of femininity that did allow for a limited growth. And no parallel phenomenon exists in the West. Individual women, especially those who came from families that had risen economically and socially during the colonial regime, were able to develop, to move close to and sometimes even achieve leadership and power (often held tenaciously), for a very old and deeply rooted ideological sanction had been obtained for the growth. However, the women who emerged from this phase often were (and those who remain, continue to be) vociferous about the traditional role of women, of the need to fulfil domestic demands and the requirements of femininity before moving on to 'serve the nation'. These women rarely admit the real oppression of women in our society, for they believe the way out of it is open to any who has the strength and the talent to try, and of course the virtue to succeed. Such women issue dire warnings against those who reject or break the sacrosanct traditional idea of woman. And in this they are supported by Aurobindo and Tagore as much as they are by Gandhi.

Frantz Fanon considers the next major phase in such a cultural evolution to be a revolutionary one. But he identifies as prior to that, the dying cadences of revivalism. A note, I think, that marks nearly all Indo-Anglian writing today. Repulsed by the squalor and depravity they see around, a present reality that in no way matches the perfection of the recreated past, and disturbed, because for all their nationalistic fervour they are left clutching the bloated particulars of a decadent culture and remain as exiled as ever from the lives of the people, writer-intellectuals withdraw. They become cynical, engrossed in their interior landscapes and the oppressive lack of a future that defines their experience. Their work is proper, the themes small, their hands clean. The keynote is of disease, of graveyards inhabited by lizards, of backwardness, of decay.

And women? If we were the heralds of a vision yesterday, today we are the betrayers, for the dream has failed. One holds instead yesterday's soiled underwear, quintessential slime, rotting leprous limbs, and one is lost in a half-light. Images are distorted by the drunken yellow flames of an oil lamp. Mothers extend clawed hands; love is only a sort of relief. Both the hatred and the inevitable disgust is projected onto women who surprisingly often still symbolize the land. We are the ones who just "smile and smile and never say no,"[22] who "like empty pitchers,"[23] wait, or rather, indolent, insensitive, unmoved by history, 'The good wife/lies in my bed/through the long afternoon/dreaming still, unexhausted/by the deep roar of funeral pyres."[24] Poems are of separation, and even the whore in the Calcutta street who manages at last to bring out "the statue of the man within/you've believed in through the years," is a sham, because "the walls you wanted to pull down/mirror only of things mortal, and passing by. . . ."[25] The misogyny begins to match the one we are familiar with in western literature, but its roots are not identical.

I wrote as I started, of the designs literature has on us, of the way it forms and controls our imaginative self images and of the regeneration of a critical voice. As women we are certainly formed into the schemes of a patriarchal society but as Indian women today we have to understand how, in terms of struggles and counter struggles, these schemes evolved to serve the needs of an emerging nationalism. To critically investigate women in Indo-Anglian writing, then, is necessarily to expose and question the twin structuring of the field as it has come to exist in society and is confirmed by literature. It is to arrive through history at a ramified and penetrating understanding of the present and lay the systems of power embodied there open to discussion, perhaps change.

Postscript

This paper was originally read at the seminar on "Women and Culture," held at Indraprastha College, Delhi University, in November, 1981. Over the last few years there has been a growing body of work on the question of women in nineteenth century thought and on intellectual formations at the interface between colonialism and a growing nationalism. I refer particularly to the work of Jashodhara Bagchi on Bankim Chandra and Rabindranath Tagore,[26] and to Partha Chatterjee's analyses of nationalist thought.[27]

If I were to write this paper today I would perhaps have tried to identify more of the inter-textual strains that go into Indo-Anglian writing (Comte, Mill, Ruskin, Jones and the entire Orientalist tradition) and place it within the specific problematic, defined not just by British racism, but by the Orientalist enterprise as a whole. This would undoubtedly have added to the texture and scope of the argument. The principal direction of this paper, which traces the history of woman as an imaginative construct in the literature of an emerging nationalism, however, would remain unchanged.

NOTES

1. Adrienne Rich, "When We Dead Awaken — Writing as Re-vision," *College English*, 34 (1972), pp. 18-30.
2. I echo Judith Fetterley, who argues: "The major works of American

fiction constitute a series of designs on the female reader, all the more potent in their effect because they are 'impalpable' . . . . To examine American fictions in the light of how attitudes to women shape their form and content is to make available to consciousness that which has been largely left unconscious and thus to change our understanding of these fictions, our relation to them and their effect on us. It is to make palpable their designs." Judith Fetterley, *The Resisting Reader* (Bloomington: Indiana University Press, 1978) pp. xi-ii.

3. Jacques Derrida, *Writing and Difference*, trans. Alan Bass (Chicago: University of Chicago Press, 1978), p. 194.
4. This sentiment can be located in many texts. I have, however, chosen to quote from John Crowe Ransom's "Humanism in Chicago," *Kenyon Review*, 14, no. 4 (Autumn 1952), pp. 647-52.
5. For some indication of the scope of the current sociological critique of English Studies as a discipline see Peter Widdowson, ed. *Re-Reading English* (London: Methuen, 1982).
6. For a scholarly and fascinating account of the political import of this imaginative complex, see Edward Said, *Orientalism* (New York: Pantheon Books, 1978). See also Susie Tharu, "Constructing the Orient," *New Quest*, 43 (Jan-Feb. 1984), pp. 53-58.
7. Is it not significant, that despite loud manifestos proclaiming the contrary, Indian writing in English is always taught as part of English Literature and never as an *Indian* Literature?
8. The acknowledgement here is to Frantz Fanon, who in *The Wretched of the Earth* (Harmondsworth: Penguin, 1967) demonstrates that the culture of a nation emerging from colonialism evolves in response to the determining ideological interpretation of the field, in certain predictable phases. Fanon's phases have now been generally accepted as paradigmatic of the process all literary sub-cultures go through. See also Elaine Showalter, *A Literature of Their Own: British Women Novelists from Bronte to Lessing* (Princeton: Princeton University Press, 1977).
9. Fanon, *Wretched*, p. 178.
10. That Toru Dutt had in her genius completely transcended her 'natural' limitations is quite evident. Edmund Gosse wrote in a review: "when poetry is as good as this, it does not matter whether Rouveryre prints it upon Watman paper or whether it steals to light in blurred type from some press in Bhowanipore." Quoted in C.D. Narasimhaiah, *The Swan and the Eagle* (Simla: Indian Institute of Advanced Study, 1969), p. 24.
11. Toru Dutt, *Ancient Ballads and Poems of Hindustan* (Allahabad: Kitabistan, 1941), p. 37.

12. For a critique of the way imperial presence and racist ideology infects even 'progressive' humanisms see Susie Tharu, "Decoding Anand's Humanism," *Kunapipi*, 4, no. 2 (1982), pp. 30-41.

13. This Victorian sense of the need to restrain women's sexuality as well as the notion of the redeeming power of feminine virtue, is enshrined in the writings of that nineteenth century champion of the cause of women — Rammohun Roy — and, as a consequence, built into the institutions concerned with the upliftment of women that derive from those enthusiasms. He rages against sati, but argues that it is far more virtuous and even courageous for a widow to live the more ascetic, penitential life of a recluse than to throw herself onto the burning pyre. Similarly the remarriage of child widows was invariably advocated because unbridled, their sexual energies were a threat to civilized society. For a critique of these institutions as they are today, see Rama Melkote and Susie Tharu "Shelter, at what cost?", *Manushi* 9 (1980), pp. 30-33.

14. A similar formation may be detected in the work of the Mushirabad painters of the mid-nineteenth century. Those painters taught themselves to use perspective and the sombre tones of western water colour to paint subjects that were totally new to Indian art: sets of 'occupations' and 'views' that the British bought to keep in albums or send back home as evidence of Indian life.

15. Sarojini Naidu, "The Pardaanashin" in *The Sceptered Flute* (Allahabad: Kitabistan, 1958), p. 53.

16. Ibid., p. 3.

17. Ibid., p. 18.

18. The best exploration of this hidden underside of hate that ballasts efforts such as Saronini Naidu's — or indeed Festivals of India — that I have come across, is in Sembene Ousmane's novel *God's Bits of Wood* (London: Heinemann, 1970). N'Deye sets herself apart from the struggle of her people for liberation. She dreams of love and is really ashamed of her people — and of herself:

    One day she had made a mistake on the date of a film she wanted to see and gone into a theatre where a documentary film on a tribe of Pygmies was being shown. She had felt as if she was being hurled backwards and down to the level of these dwarfs, and had an insane desire to run out of the theatre, crying aloud, "No, no! These are not the real Africans!" And on another day, when a film of the ruins of the Parthenon appeared on the screen, two men seated behind her had begun talking loudly. N'Deye had turned on them like an avenging fury and cried in French, "Be quiet, you ignorant fools! If you don't understand, get out!" N'Deye herself knew far more about Europe than she did about Africa; she had won the prize in geography several times in the years when she was going to school. But she had never read a book by an African author — she was quite sure that they could teach her nothing. (p. 170)

19. Raja Rao, *The Serpent and the Rope* (London: John Murray, 1960), p. 352.
20. Ibid., p. 52.
21. For a contemporary reading of this myth see Ashish Nandy, *The Intimate Enemy: Loss and Recovery of Self Under Colonialism* (Delhi: Oxford University Press, 1983).
22. Nissim Ezekiel in R. Parthasarathy, ed. *Ten Twentieth Century Indian Poets* (Delhi: Oxford University Press, 1976), p. 37.
23. Shiv Kumar, ibid., p. 54.
24. Jayant Mahapatra, ibid, p. 60.
25. Jayant Mahapatra, ibid., p. 61.
26. Jashodhara Bagchi, "Positivism and Nationalism: Womanhood in Bankim Chandra's *Anandmath* and Rabindranath Tagore's *Ghare Baire*," seminar on "Forms of Narrative," Hyderabad University, Jan. 1985. Part of the paper has been published in Review of Women Studies in *Economic and Political Weekly*, 20, no. 43 (26 Oct. 1985), pp. 58-62.
27. Partha Chatterjee, "Gandhi and the Critique of Civil Society," in Ranajit Guha, ed. *Subaltern Studies, III* (Delhi: Oxford University Press, 1984), and *Nationalist Thought and the Colonial World: A Derivative Discourse* (Delhi: Oxford University Press, 1986).

Working Women in Colonial Bengal: *Modernization and Marginalization**

NIRMALA BANERJEE

A WELL-KNOWN FACT about the first industrial revolution that took place in Britain was the widespread participation in it by women and children in the industrial workforce. This was especially true of its early phases. They had crowded into the "dark and satanic mills" in such large numbers that, at the time of the 1851 population Census of Great Britain, women and girls in the textile and clothing industries constituted over half the total manufacturing employment and over one fifth of the entire non-agricultural workforce of the country.[1] Women's participation in modern industry appeared to be such an integral part of the new industrial technology and organization that Marx remarked: "In so far as machinery dispenses with muscular power it becomes a means of employing labourers of slight muscular strength and those whose bodily development is incomplete but whose limbs are all the more supple. The labour of women and children was, therefore, the first thing sought for by capitalists who used machinery."[2]

Another important and novel change in the British economy after the onset of the industrial revolution was the fast expansion of an independent, non-agricultural, non-industrial, service sector of employment. Industries and agriculture had always existed side by side in the British economy; but the growth of such a service sector to an extent that it employed just under half the British labour force by 1911 was an entirely new phenomenon.[3] The service sec-

* An earlier version of this article "Modernization and Marginalization," was published in *Social Scientist,* 13, no. 10-11 (Oct-Nov 1985), pp. 48-71.

tor included wholesale and retail trade, financial and commercial institutions, personal and professional services, transport and communications, as well as public administration and welfare services. In the earlier stages, women in the service sector were confined mainly to domestic service, an occupation which had expanded fast in the nineteenth century along with the growth of a new urban bourgeoisie. After 1911, however, women moved out of domestic service to other sections of the service sector and, by the 1960s, they held over half the total number of all service sector jobs in the United Kingdom.[4]

As a result of women's large-scale participation in modern activities both in the industrial as well as the service occupations, there was an increasing dominance of women in rural to urban migration through the nineteenth century. By the end of that century, the urban areas of Great Britain showed a higher proportion of females to males at all ages than in rural areas.[5]

This British pattern more or less formed the classic model for all countries of the west in their process of development towards a modern industrialized economy. However, the experience of women in the limited version of modern industrial growth that began to take place towards the last quarter of the nineteenth century in colonial Bengal, was of an essentially different quality. Female workers formed only a small part of the workforce in large-scale industries and in the service sector that developed as a part of this modern economy. Ultimately the only expanding occupation for women in the modern sector came to be domestic service. At the same time, these developments deeply affected the vast mass of the traditional village-based economy which had continued to employ the majority of the workers. In the process, a significant section of women's non-agricultural occupations in the traditional sector were destroyed. As a result, women workers increasingly came to crowd into agricultural occupations. Their share in the urban population fell steadily till the end of the period under consideration.

This paper briefly attempts to analyse the reason why the impact on female workers of modernization of the Bengal economy was sharply different from that of their male counterparts and also from the model set by Britain in its early phases of industrial revolution.

Modernization in the Indian context was more of an artificial graft on the body of the traditional economy than a metamorphosis of the latter through its own innate compulsions. It began when the British, after the establishment of their political hegemony over the region, started to invest in selected industries for processing local raw materials and agricultural products into commodities mainly for overseas markets. Simultaneously, in order to promote their political, administrative and economic interests, they were building a network of transport and communications and establishing institutions for imposing the British system of administration, finance, commerce, and judiciary as well as of medicine and education. In order to promote these activities, they established support industries as well as facilities for training and building up professional services.

In pursuing their sectarian interests, the British showed little inclination to invest in or modernize the vast bulk of traditional economic activities which continued to serve the needs of the ordinary people. However, since the modern institutions and activities were infinitely more powerful not only because of their use of large-scale capital, mechanized technology and modern organizations, but also because of the state support given to them, they made strong inroads in the sphere of the traditional economy. In the process, sections of the latter were destroyed or altered to suit the purpose of the modern economy. Over time therefore, the structure and organization of occupations in the traditional sector were also materially altered.

That women's economic activities were relatively more affected in this entire process appears to be the result mainly of the traditionally assigned role of women in this society which limited their mobility and confined them to skills and occupations susceptible to swift obsoletion. Moreover, the growth of the modern sector was so fast and so unplanned that its environment became unwholesome for the migration of women whether in families or singly. This too inhibited women from participating in the modern sector to a greater extent.

The developments in the Bengal Presidency during the period 1881 to 1931 provide an especially interesting study because of several reasons:

a) Before 1881, Bengal was one of the more industrialized regions of India. Although most of its traditional industry had already been destroyed in the de-industrialization process during the early nineteenth century, over 20 per cent of its workforce was still working on 'making and selling' of industrial goods. The all-India comparable figure for 1881 was 15 per cent.[6]

b) In the period under consideration, almost all of the modern activities of the region were established and expanded quickly, in some cases to close to their maximum size upto date.

c) By the end of this period, Bengal housed a major section of the modern industrial employment of India. The Royal Commission of Labour in India in its report of 1931 remarked that, "When the distribution of perennial factories is examined by centres, the predominance of Hooghly area surrounding Calcutta is noted."[7] In 1929, the total factory labour of India was 15.5 lakhs; of this, Bengal had the largest single contingent of factory workers which stood at 5.9 lakhs.[8]

d) In Bengal, women workers had traditionally participated actively in non-agricultural activities. In 1881 only a third of the women workers of Bengal proper (as against the Presidency as a whole, which also included Bihar and Orissa) had worked on agriculture. For the Presidency as a whole, about 41 per cent of the workers in operations of 'making and selling' were women even in 1911.

e) As a result of the modernization process, women of Bengal ultimately lost more heavily than perhaps anywhere else in the country. By 1961, West Bengal's workforce participation rates for women were some of the lowest in the country. In Bihar and Orissa, women workers became almost totally confined to agriculture.[9]

The main data used in this paper for analysis of changes in the economy relate to employment figures by occupations and gender. These have been culled from the decadal population census reports. In order to analyse the relative impact of the various forces at work, these data have been classified into two broad categories — the modern and the traditional sectors. The modern sector is not a very precise concept but includes all activities that were directly affected by British influence. The latter is supposed to have altered either the scope of their markets, or their technology, organization and content. As such it includes all production for extended markets. It also includes a service sector consisting of administrative, judicial, commercial and financial institutions as well as of transport and communication networks. From the total employment in trade, however, trade in food, fuel and fodder as well as local construction materials has been excluded. The rest is included in the modern service sector. From the agriculture sector, it includes the growing of special crops in plantations. Domestic service is a part of it but caste-based personal services have been excluded.

The definition is rather arbitrary since it includes for example, the entire textile industry, though a large component of it was handlooms which were often producing mainly for local markets. It leaves out production of crops like jute, meant specifically for extended markets but employment for which could not be separated from other cultivation. Professions such as medicine continued throughout to include a traditional sector but have been fully allotted to the modern sector. The only advantage of such a loose definition is that it serves as an indicator of the relative dimensions of the various forces at work and changes in them over time, though it is probably an overestimate of the non-agricultural sector.

The modern sector

During the period under consideration, the state machinery of Bengal was constantly watching over the progress of modern industries and services that were developing in the region. In the earlier half, their main concern was whether or not these occupations were getting an adequate supply of reasonable labour. Reports of their various committees and commissions as well as of individual experts (some of which are mentioned here) give an overall impression that the Bengal economy was in a tremendous upheaval. The Bengal Labour Enquiry Commission of 1896 categorically stated: "Europeans all agree that there is a scarcity of labour and regular imports are necessary." The Commission considered suggestions for importing labour to Bengal from North West provinces, Benares, Oudh, Lucknow and Fyzabad. They even talked about importing Chinese labour for coal mines.[10] Even in 1908, there was some scarcity of skilled labour as for example in the cotton spinning mills of Calcutta.[11]

This impression of a great flurry in the economy accompanied by a fear of scarcity of labour looming over it was chiefly because modern activities were confined to only a few pockets where the local supply of and demand for labour were not always in balance.

Also, modern activities did grow very fast within a short period from 1890 to 1911 and after World War I upto 1929. Three major industries developed in this region during this period — jute, tea and coal. Of these, the jute industry had started in 1860 and in 1880 it employed about 28,000 factory workers. In the next three decades, its employment nearly doubled every ten years. Similarly employment in collieries more than doubled between 1891 to 1901 and went up by a further 175 per cent between 1901 and 1911. Employment in Bengal's tea gardens nearly trebled between 1881 and again went up by an additional 270 per cent in the next decade. It also grew very fast during the 1920s.

As can be seen from Table 1, these three industries together accounted for an increasing part of the labour force in the registered industries of the Bengal Presidency. In 1911 their share was 68 per cent. This rose to 77 per cent by 1921. Amongst the rest were several metal-based industries including railway workshops, the armament industry and light engineering industries. Also of significant size were glass and pottery works, cotton spinning, silk filatures and leather tanning. As Table 1 indicates, women's employment in the modern industries was, however, overwhelmingly confined to the three major industries. In 1911, this figure had gone up to 91 per cent. In other words, women played a very minor role in any of the other modern industries.

It is to be noted that within these three industries, women's share in the total employment declined steeply towards 1931. In the jute industry, women's share in total employment fell from 29 per cent in 1901 to 17 per cent in 1911 and 12 per cent in 1921. In collieries, women lost their initial advantage after 1901 but their share fell particularly steeply in a short period after 1928 when they were banned from underground work. Even in tea plantations, women's employment lost its momentum during the depression years.

It is interesting to note that in each of the three industries different factors were at work to produce fairly similar results over time. In the jute industry, women simply failed to get their due share in the work force in the period after 1901 when the industry was expanding fast. In the collieries, on the other hand, women were literally pushed out of the industry after underground work by women and children became prohibited in 1928. It is also signifi-

Table 1
Employment in registered factory industries in '000s

	Year	Coal industry			Jute industry			Tea plantations			All registered industries		
		M	F	Total	M	F	Total	M	F	Total	M	F	Total
Bengal	1879-80			14.4			27.5			n.a.			
Bihar	1881			18.8			35.2			15.5			
Orissa	1891			24.8			62.7			42.9			
	1896-97			61.37			91.6			n.a.			
	1901	26	25	51	87	36	123	83	76	159			
	1906			106			133			n.a.			
	1911	97	46	143	178	37	215	98	94	192	588	209	797
	1911-15			129			n.a.			n.a.			n.a.
	1921	107	43	150	335	48	383	88	102	190	685	232	917
	1928	114	50	164						n.a.			n.a.
	1931	115	30	145	229	32	261	186	120	306			n.a.
Bengal	1901	11	12	23	87	36	123	83	76	159			n.a.
Proper	1911	27	11	38	178	37	215	98	94	192	454	163	617
	1921	34	13	47	335	48	383	88	102	190	578	179	757
	1931	24	9	36	229	32	261	174	288				n.a.

SOURCE: Coal Industry figures for the years before 1901 are from the *Bengal Labour Enquiry Commission, 1896*, p.2.

For the years after that *The Royal Commission of 1931*, p. 113.

For Jute Industry, B. Foley, *Report on Labour in Bengal*, 1906, chap. 2 B, pp. 14-47.

For Tea Industry figures for 1891, the *Bengal Labour Enquiry Commission, 1896*.

For Census Years, from the *Census Reports*.

For 1911 and 1921 there are special tables No. 22 giving Industrial Statistics in *Census Reports* vol. 6, Part 2.

cant that the ban on underground work by women became operative only in 1928 though the legal powers to do so were available to the State since 1901. In the first two decades of this century, female and child labour was in demand for carrying coal underground, since no substitute male labour was available as cheaply. In 1928, when the economy was already slowing down and male labour was cheaply available, the law was made operative. Even then, in view of the large numbers of women working underground in collieries, the State had recommended that their removal from work should be phased out over a period of ten years. In 1928, 29 per cent of underground coal labour was female; each year 3 per cent of these were to be retired. In actual fact, within the next year a quarter of the underground women workers were eased out their jobs.[12]

So, in the collieries women were pushed out of their jobs by men when they needed women's jobs. In the tea industry, women's labour has always been considered essential; but even there in the depression years of 1931, women lost their advantage and for the time being, the balance of employment tilted steeply in favour of men, presumably because men were available in greater numbers for want of other jobs.

Modern services

The other new avenues of employment in the modern sector were in the new kind of services being created in India. It was particularly after 1881 that the earlier dithering about investment in Indian railways was resolved,[13] and there was a fast expansion of railway lines. In Bengal Presidency, their length increased from 2,072 km in 1881 to 4,542 km in 1901 and 8,403 km by 1931.[14] Similarly, the government also went in in a big way for building metalled roads in the country. British India as a whole had nearly 100,000 kms of roads in 1929 and, along with them, motor transport as well as public buses had become a common sight in all parts of the country including Bengal.[15] However, despite all these developments, employment in the category of transport, communications and storage showed a stagnant or declining trend mainly because the growth of mechanized transport displaced more people from traditional water and road transport industries than it itself employed (Table 2).

Table 2
Modern service sector in '000s

		1901				1911				1921				1931			
		Bengal		*Bihar & Orissa*		*Bengal*		*Bihar & Orissa*		*Bengal*		*Bihar & Orissa*		*Bengal*		*Bihar & Orissa*	
		M	*F*	*M*	*F*	*M*	*F*	*M*	*F*	*M*	*F*	*M*	*F*	*M*	*F*	*M*	*F*
I.	Administration, liberal arts and learned professions (except priests and midwives)	241	6	136	5	257	14	134	7	253	6	101	11	288	9	117	6
II.	Domestic service	177	83	121	125	255	112	227	215	334	116	184	124	389	361	99	107
III.	Trade, commerce and finance (except local trades)	201	14	60	18	262	47	150	71	193	23	155	70	394	27	183	52
IV.	Transport, communication and storage	317	9	101	5	469	31	240	13	355	18	98	17	270	12	91	—
IV-A	Railways	34	1	20	1	74	2	34	2	43	2	35	2	67	2	32	1
	Total	936	112	418	153	1243	204	751	306	1235	163	538	292	1341	409	490	165

Figures are approximate since the census scope of trade activities kept changing over time.

Modern transport facilities had opened up more and more areas for trade. For instance, Cummins remarks: "Often people found it more lucrative to take an agency for distribution of some imported commodity rather than go in for industrial enterprise."[16] However, once again the displacement in traditional trade occupations was not fully compensated by these new openings.

Of the various occupations included in the modern services,[17] the only one to expand fast over this period for both men and women was domestic service. However, for men, the occupation at its maximum employed no more than a third of the total employed in the modern service sector. For women, both in Bengal and Bihar, domestic service was a much more important avenue. Especially in Bengal, after a brief respite in 1911, it generally accounted for over 70 per cent of women workers in modern services. And in 1931, when they had been pushed out of their industrial employment, domestic service became about the only important non-agricultural occupation. Interestingly in Bihar and Orissa, the occupation could give little respite to job seekers even during depression years. This was presumably connected with the general decline of urban areas in those regions which we discuss later on. This position continued unchanged till recently.

Traditional sector

Table 3 shows some rough estimates of the relative sizes of the various categories of employment. The modern sector consists of the two groups, *D*: production and trade for extended markets, and *E*: modern services as defined earlier. The traditional sector consists of *A*: agricultural and general labour, *B*: traditional personal services consisting of numerous caste-based occupations such as barbers, washermen, sweepers, priests, midwives, and *C*: production and trade for local markets. It is to be noted that the category *E* is larger than both the group of the registered industries and large-scale trade. It also includes several traditional industries, especially textiles which had always been traded in extensive markets from Bengal. Of these, cotton handlooms had lost their international markets since the 1830s, but they still found markets outside their immediate locality. Markets for silk spinning waxed and waned but were still spread over a large area. Production and trade in these

Table 3

Male and Female workers*[1] as percentage of population (WFPR) and percentage distribution of workers by broad occupational categories: Bengal Presidency

Year	Workforce participation rates (WFPR)		Percentage shares in total work force: Agriculture and general labour		Traditional personal service		Production and trade for local markets		Production and trade for extended markets		Modern services	
	M	F	M	F	M	F	M	F	M	F	M	F
			A		B		C		D		E	
Bengal Proper												
1881	58.3	8.7	70.3	32.2	10.4	13.3	16.2	43.2*[2]	3.1	11.2		
1901	58.6	8.8	75.3	40.9	3.9	9.9	9.5	33.3	3.2	10.4	8.1	5.5
1911	59.0	9.0	78.8	48.7	2.0	8.7	8.3	28.2	3.2	11.5	7.6	2.9
1921	57.1	8.5	78.2	54.1	1.6	6.0	8.6	21.0	4.3	11.9	7.3	6.1
1931	46.7	7.0	79.0	55.9	1.6	4.6	7.2	11.8	7.3	8.7	5.0	19.0
Bihar & Orissa												
1881	66.5	25.4	77.0	70.5	7.1	3.9	31.3	17.9*[2]	2.6	7.7	2.3	2.4
1901	63.0	28.3	82.8	74.1	3.2	4.5	7.9	16.6	1.8	2.4	2.3	2.4
1911	62.2	33.0	83.2	78.6	1.9	2.3	5.3	13.1	2.3	2.4	3.5	4.0
1921	63.3	35.0	84.7	81.7	2.8	2.0	5.2	11.2	3.7	3.0	3.6	2.2
1931	57.3	25.1	86.2	83.9	4.3	2.2	5.1	10.5	2.5	1.0	1.9	2.3

SOURCE: *Census Reports* for Bengal, Bihar and Orissa, Volumes-Part 2, Tables-Summary of Occupations

NOTES : *[1] Workforce estimates exclude persons with independent means, rent earners and also persons in "disreputable occupation" (including vagrants and prostitutes).

*[2] For 1881, all services are included under category C.

industries is also included under *D*, on grounds that western interests had altered their international organization to some degree.

In spite of the official preoccupation with modern activities, the overwhelming bulk of Bengal's workforce remained in its traditional activities. Even when the modern sector reached its maximum size within this period, it employed less than 15 per cent of the total workforce and less than 5 per cent of the total population.

It was also in the traditional sector that the more dramatic changes of this period were taking place. The most remarkable development was the increasing concentration of the workforce into agriculture. The share of agriculture in total employment of both men and women kept on rising even though population was growing very slowly. Between 1901 and 1921, the total population of the Bengal Presidency grew by only about 9 per cent. In Bihar and Orissa, there was a fall in the population between 1911 and 1921 (Table 5). In spite of that, the share of agriculture and general labour generally kept on increasing throughout this period. For women workers, especially in Bengal proper, this was a very significant change from their traditional role. Again, this trend continued unchanged till 1961, when the percentage share of women workers in agriculture in the total female work force was 58 per cent in West Bengal, 84 per cent in Bihar and 71 per cent in Orissa.

The concentration of women workers in agriculture was a direct result of a sharp fall in their traditional activity of making and selling goods, whether in the modern or in the traditional sector.

For both men and women there was an initial fall from 1881 to 1911 in the number of workers and the share in the total workforce of this category; but thereafter, as the modern sector expanded, the total number of jobs for men and the share of this sector in the total male workforce was maintained at more or less an unchanged level. For women, on the other hand, there was more or less a continuous fall from 1881 onwards in both the absolute number of jobs and their share in the workforce (Table 4).

Moreover, within the category 'making and selling', women workers were concentrated more heavily in the traditional sector where their domain was confined to local markets (column *C* of Table 3). For men, this was never a very important occupation and their losses also were, percentage-wise, relatively smaller.

Table 4
Employment in industrial production and trade (making and selling) in '000s

Year	*Bengal*		*Bihar & Orissa*	
	Male	*Female*	*Male*	*Female*
1881	2182 (20.16)	1018 (56.97)	1479 (15.85)	1010 (25.10)
1901	1510 (12.65)	707 (43.69)	1064 (9.64)	1028 (18.96)
1911	1490 (11.50)	700 (40.34)	820 (7.53)	960 (15.56)
1921	1681 (12.89)	661 (33.13)	905 (7.91)	887 (14.13)
1931	1737 (14.54)	501 (26.46)	850 (7.49)	675 (14.08)

Figures in brackets are percentages to total workforce.
SOURCE: *Census of India*, General Tables, 1881-1931.

Urbanization

Change in the composition of urban settlements was another development of this period which significantly affected women's position. The overall rate of urbanization was by no means fast but it was spread extremely unevenly between different regions. In general, the urban population of Bihar and Orissa fell in absolute numbers till 1911. Thereafter it rose very slowly and in 1931 it stood at a level higher than the 1881 level by only one sixth. The fall in urban population was mainly on account of the falling female population but nevertheless, the sex ratio in urban population of Bihar and Orissa was never as adverse to women as in Bengal.

In Bengal proper, the male urban population rose throughout; the female population, after a small dip between 1881 and 1891, rose steadily but at a much slower rate so that the urban sex ratio fell continuously till 1931. The urban sex ratio for the Presidency as a whole also fell continuously (Table 5).

The various developments noted so far together meant that women were increasingly marginalized in the Bengal economy.

Table 5

Total and urban populations and sex ratios of population (females per 1000 Males) in Bengal, Bihar and Orissa and Bengal Presidency as a whole: 1881 to 1931

Year	*Bengal proper population*		*Bihar & Orissa population*		*Sex ratio in total population*		*Urban population as percentage of total population*			
	M	*F*	*M*	*F*	*Bengal, Bihar and Orissa*		*Bengal Presidency*	*Bengal*	*Bihar and Orissa*	*Bengal Presidency*
(1)	(2)	(3)	(4)	(5)	(6)	(7)	(8)	(9)	(10)	(11)
1881	18570	18451	16499	16894	993	1023	1008			
Total								5.9	4.38	5.24
Urban	1199	986	728	736	822	1011	893			
1891	20175	14637	17597	18301	726	1040	872			
Total								6.39	3.66	4.92
Urban	1297	927	634	679	715	1071	831			
1901	21885	21003	17852	18698	959	1047	999			
Total								6.06	3.63	5.00
Urban	1563	1036	668	659	662	986	759			
1911	23804	22502	18851	19616	945	1041	987			
Total								6.41	3.44	5.06
Urban	1820	1148	685	638	630	931	713			
1921	24628	22964	18707	19248	932	1029	974			
Total								6.75	3.71	5.42
Urban	1992	1220	751	659	612	877	685			
1931	26558	24529	21082	21247	923	1008	960			
Total								7.27	3.47	6.01
Urban	2318	1394	768	700	601	911	678			

SOURCE: *Census of India*, Population, General Tables, 1881 to 1931.

They became confined to a very limited set of occupations, chiefly in agriculture and domestic service. These trends became deeply entrenched so that for the next fifty years or more women remained at a disadvantage in the economy of this region. How did this come about?

Women's role in the economy

Two sets of factors contributed to the worsening of women's economic position; their traditional role in the economy slowly became redundant while their gains in the modern sector remained negligible. The occupations assigned to women in the traditional gender-wise division of labour proved to be specially vulnerable to obsoletion through modernization. Their participation in the modern sector, on the other hand, was constrained particularly by the character of the modern sector as it developed in Bengal

Traditionally women worked in three kinds of occupations. First, in superior crafts for extended markets where they worked either in household units as helpers or on their own selling their products to agents. By this period, hand spinning of cotton yarn had become almost obsolete. The 1881 Census had recorded only 200,000 spinners in the whole of Bengal.[18] In 1812-13 there had been 330,000 spinners in Patna and Gaya districts alone.[19] By 1901, the total number of women of Bengal Presidency working in the cotton textile industry (consisting of spinning, weaving and dyeing of cotton cloth) had gone down further to 135,000.[20] Interestingly, while women's work in most sections of the cotton textile industry was usually in the role of helpers in the household industry, cotton spinning had always been one occupation where women of almost all castes and income levels worked for a cash income.[21] By the middle of the nineteenth century spinning as a cash earning occupation for women had lost its pre-eminence. Nevertheless, one does come across later references to destitute women of high castes earning a living, although of a very low level, from spinning cotton for sacred threads.[22] Also, even high caste women spun cotton yarn for weavers to weave cloths for their families.[23]

Second, women worked in other caste-specific occupations as potters, washerwomen, sweepers etc. In 1901 these caste-based occupations employed about 200,000 women in the Presidency as a whole. In most of these caste occupations, women had no independent role or income but worked as part of the household team. Only midwives and barber women had specific functions for which they got separate payment. These caste occupations included some superior crafts as in the case of cotton weavers or of silk cocoon rearers.

The third and most important set of occupations for women, however, was in a number of subsistence crafts. These consisted of tasks that women generally performed for their own families but occasionally extended for sale in markets. They included animal husbandry, making and selling of milk products like ghee or butter, preserving and processing grains and pulses, making of simple food products like *moori* or *chire* (puffed and flattened rice), preparing vegetable oil for lighting and collecting, and processing and selling forest produce. More specific examples are rice pounding, flour grinding, making leaf plates, baskets, mats, nets, brooms, producing rock salt and collecting and selling fuel and fodder.

In 1881 as against 1.2 million women working in agriculture, about 725,000 had worked on food processing and selling. Of these, about 500,000 had worked on grain processing. Another 200,000 worked in collecting, processing and selling forest produce, 340,000 worked on caste specific occupations exclusive of superior crafts. In 1901, about 462,000 women still worked on grain processing and another 200,000 on collecting, processing and selling forest produce. Altogether about 1.4 million women worked in occupations connected with traditional industries and sale of their products.

The distinguishing characteristics of all these occupations were: a) the use of only locally available cheap materials, b) the use of crude and locally made tools in production, c) very little regional specialization, d) no requirement of special training and little capital investment. The advantage of this kind of employment in subsistence crafts had been that, since the occupations were generally no different from standard household chores, any woman of any caste or community could resort to one of them in case of distress. There were no barriers, social taboos or *purdah* (seclusion) to prevent her since the dealings were mostly between women.

In their own perception, women saw these tasks not only as part of their daily drudgery but also as a backdrop to their life cycle, their longings and their celebrations. Their traditional songs, a few of which are quoted here from the original Bengali, reflect this constant interweaving of tasks and moods.[24]

Oh Mini nāi kānd gā,
Ghare duāre ko to jabrā
Gāhāl pelyāteyeē holyā belā

(Oh Mini do not cry.
There is so much work at home.
Just looking after the cattle has taken most of my time.)

For a young girl, the choices are limited.

Māthe māthe gainta kudā
Se barang bhālo
Shasur gharer hāndi mājya
Gā holyā kālo

(It is better to go around collecting cow-dung
from one field to another in one's father's village
than to waste yourself scrubbing pots
in the in-law's house.)

The work begins before daybreak and goes on till late at night.

Oh diyā jā re bhais
Dhān bāker heilō
Bānsher godāt tārā
Chāul jāo mor kārā

(Oh buffalo, go the other way.
Here, I am pounding paddy. The morning star is
already at low horizon behind the bamboo trunks.
I have to finish the work.)

Or

Charkā kātchhu
Ninde go tukchhu
Ulatiyā palatiyā go padichhu
Bārir pāch pākhat kay bā bājāy sudsudi
Mantā hoilo chhatuchhān
Aulayelo mor sutār khyābkhān

(I am spinning on the *charkhā* (spinning wheel)
late in the night. I am so sleepy, that I keep falling over.
Somebody is whistling behind the house. My mind starts
wandering and my thread gets all tangled up.)

Going off to work together with other women is a kind of relaxation.

Āai chal chal jāi go bāi
Chal jāi Pāngār nadi
Pāngār nadir dighal go jangalé
Bāi Muniyā kāten khari
Khari katigo béchā béchi
Béchādi mo bat pākhili

(Let us go to cut wood near the Pangar river.
In the large forest near Pangar river, Bai Muniya is
cutting wood. Let us cut wood selectively and leave out
bat and *pākhil* trees.)

All the tasks of preserving and processing rice were women's tasks.

Kolere pate bāndhi dhān
Kāti uthāchu ghare
Bhariyā aho māgé bhein
Bhariyā golār madhyé
Dhariyā bāndhi, nandur bāndhi,
Bāndhi āāji néké Bāi
Bāro māshe tero pārban
Tomār baré pāi

(After cutting paddy we tie the sheaves with a thread
from banana leaf. We then prepare the thick rope from coir,
grass and hay and wind it round to make a store.
Then we put paddy in it. We hold it and tie it lightly.
This way your blessings (oh new crop) will give us
thirteen festivals in twelve months.)

However, in order to sustain this sector of employment on such a large scale, the economy on the one hand needed a sufficient supply of local, freely available materials and on the other, some degree of isolation from the competition of outside goods. Towards the latter half of our period, these conditions began to weaken for the major part of Bengal's economy. The new transport network exposed ever-widening areas to outside competition and increasing commercialization. By 1931, women's employment in these subsistence crafts and trade had fallen by over a third of its level in 1911.[25] Their biggest losses were in food processing and in occupations dealing with forest products. For example, rice milling had largely become a factory industry by the 1920s. In 1929 there were only 12,500 persons working in rice milling factories in Bengal and amongst these, women were employed only in the drying process.[26] Caste occupations in general were also disintegrating fast. In 1921 only about 130,000 women worked in these caste specific occupations including traditional services as well as some occupations of 'making and selling'. These were potters, blacksmiths, goldsmiths, bangle makers, tailors, metal workers. In the case of Bengal, however, tailors now included a large section of men who were working in the readymade garment industry in Calcutta.[27]

The main reasons for these losses were: a) because women's crafts were basically for common day-to-day necessities, there was potentially a large market for such commodities in the region as a whole. Therefore, once the areas were opened up for modern transport, there were tremendous profits to be made in trade in ordinary commodities like sea salt, coal or kerosene which replaced the earlier crude, local goods made by women. The trade in these commodities involved substantial capital as well as information and mobility over large areas. Hence, it passed on to men. b) Because of their simple tools and low capital input, women's productivity in these crafts had been very low, c) the operations were by and large simple and could be easily mechanized. As a result of these factors — the wide and regular demand and the simple character of the processes — it paid to mechanize operations like rice pounding, grain milling or oil crushing and women could not compete with machine made products because of their initial low productivity, d) at the same time increasing commercialization and pressure on land resources meant that the free availability of products of forests and common lands was being sharply curtailed. These factors also led to a quick decline in the practice of payment by land grant or a fixed annual amount of grain to the workers in caste occupations. It was now being replaced by payment by product. This meant that fewer people could rely on these occupations for a living. Women's employment in these kinds of occupations also declined by nearly a third from 1921 to 1931.

Restrictions on women's workforce participation

The decline in subsistence crafts left women all the more helpless because earlier they had not fully shared in the gains made by men in the modern sector. Employment in this latter sector probably could never have fully compensated for the decline of traditional occupations. But the fact still remains that although in the first half of this period there were pockets of local shortages in the supply of women's labour to modern occupations, a sufficient number of women did not make the transition from the traditional to the modern sectors. According to contemporary reports, Bengal's cotton spinning mills could not expand fast because of want of labour, especially women's and skilled labour, even when endogenous weaving had got a fresh lease of life in the wake of the Swadeshi movement.[28] The same was the case in the collieries in the 1890s and from time to time in the tea industry.[29] In the jute industry it was shown earlier that in the first fifteen years of the twentieth century when the industry expanded fastest, women failed to claim their due share in the employment. It was reported that even in 1923, any woman could, if she wanted, work simultaneously in two mills in two consecutive shifts on the same day and many did.[30]

One important factor contributing to this state of affairs was the fact that unlike traditional economic activities, modern occupations were not evenly spread everywhere; they were concentrated in a few small pockets. Those small pockets moreover were precisely in areas where women's workforce participation rates (WFPRS) had traditionally been very low. The most important nodes of modern activities were: Calcutta and its surrounding districts for jute and engineering factories as well as modern services; north and east Bengal for cultivation, processing and trade in tea and other commercial crops; and Burdwan division for collieries.

As can be seen in Table 2, in the first five administrative divisions which constituted Bengal proper, female WFPRS were remarkably low. What is more, this was not a result of the low share allotted to women in modern activities, but a consistent trend throughout the period as can be seen from Table 3. Events seemed to work the other way round: the traditionally low WFPRs of women in these areas meant that women did not seek out jobs in the modern activities or, more precisely, social and cultural taboos constrained their responses to market forces much more so than they affected men.

Table 6

Region-wise sex ratios and women's workforce participation rates 1911 and 1931

	1911		*1931*	
Administrative division	*Sex ratio*	*Women's workforce participation rate (WFPR)*	*Sex ratio*	*Women's workforce participation rate (WFPR)*
Burdwan	980	11.2	978	9.1
Presidency	962	7.6	951	6.5
Rajshahi	971	6.3	963	5.8
Dacca	979	5.7	968	5.6
Chittagong	983	7.3	980	6.3
Patna	1041	35.2	1062	31.7
Bhagalpore	1053	32.8	1071	30.1
Orissa	1021	8.3	1030	7.4
Chota Nagpur	1039	25.7	1042	24.0

In their decisions as to whether or not to participate in economic activities and if so in which occupations, women were not free agents; they were severely constrained by the conventions and taboos accepted by the particular social group, caste or community to which they belonged. These rules were by no means uniform but varied widely from one area to another as well as between different social groups, castes or communities. The conventions governing each group were historically determined by the interaction of many factors, not the least among which were the social status and the past record of well-being of that group as a whole. Women from groups with higher social status and/or higher incomes were subject to more restrictions. In areas where there was a general feeling of prosperity, the conventions were all the more binding on women. In other areas and groups where there was a long history of general distress, the system faced a continuous challenge from within and the rules were gradually eroded.

The Dufferin *Report on the Conditions of the Lower Classes of People in Bengal* submitted to the Viceroy in 1888 [31] brings out admirably this play of factors determining women's workforce participation rates. For the report, officers in charge of each district or administrative subdivision submitted a review of the area under their charge detailing the general economic conditions of the population, the relative fortunes of different traditional occupations, their wage rates and prospects, and the availability or otherwise of alternative jobs for them. What is more, almost all officers included in their reports a quick review of women's occupations and the extent of workforce participation by women of different groups in their locality. They also made an effort to link these local conventions regarding women's work with the immediate economic conditions and prospects of the group concerned. For example, it was remarked about the Burdwan Division that "the wives and children of a poor cultivator or labourer who is in ordinary health are not required to resort to outdoor work."[32] Similarly, A. Smith, reporting on the Presidency Division mentioned that in Khulna, with increasing prosperity all families had rice for every meal, and with the exception perhaps of the women of potter families, no woman, either in cultivator or in artisan families, worked outside.[33] Mr Lyall, the Commissioner of Chittagong Division noted that unlike in most other districts, the women of Chittagong district were not to be seen even in *hats* or markets.[34] On the other hand, Mr Stevens, Commissioner of the Chota Nagpur Division, reported that although the population was fairly well off since collieries were absorbing labour from that region, nevertheless, locally there was still one woman worker for every two of men.[35] In Patna and Gaya districts, where distress was most acute and people could eat rice only once a day, men and women both worked on their own agricultural holdings and also as wage labourers for others.[36] In Bhagalpore, women of lower classes helped in cultivation of their own plots.[37] Mr C. Worsley, Commissioner of the Poori Division, mentioned that even after three years of crop failure, few women were to be found to work on road or earth cutting.[38]

In each case, the rules were determined for the groups as a whole. Individual women in isolated cases of poverty or distress could not defy them. For those women, the only way was to crowd into the two occupations in which participation was permitted for most sections of women. Domestic service was one such. (Even Brahmin women could work as cooks in other families.) The most common occupation of course was food processing, especially rice pounding. In fact Mr Ritchie, Magistrate of Howrah District, had reported that "rice pounding plays an important role in the village economy." [39]

It is important to note that work in modern mills was probably not taboo in the early part of this period; nevertheless, only poor women and women of low castes joined the mills and considered it generally as a last resort in case of distress. The Bengali women workers in Calcutta's jute and cotton mills who gave evidence to the Indian Factory Commission of 1890 were all widows or deserted women without children to support them. They all claimed that no Bengali woman would work in the factories unless she was truly "unfortunate".[40]

Women's migration

This brings us to another interesting question; even if the location of modern activities happened to be in regions of low female WFPRs, the Presidency as a whole included other areas viz., most of Bihar, where female WFPRs were high by any standards. Moreover, in the period under consideration, women of those areas underwent severe losses in their traditional economic activities as discussed earlier (See Table 4). Men had also suffered similar losses; but that had triggered off a tremendous wave of male migration from Bihar and Orissa to Bengal in search of work. As a result, there were increasingly more men as compared to women in Bengal, especially urban Bengal and more women than men in Bihar and Orissa (Table 5). There were several strands of migration as noted by the 1896 Labour Enquiry Commission:

a) from the Santhal Parganas, mainly from Ranchi and Singbhum to the tea gardens;

b) from the eastern districts of North West Provinces and the western districts of Bihar to East Bengal and Assam for harvesting or road and railway building;

c) from Ranchi and other places in Hazaribag area to Calcutta for drainage work, gardening etc;

d) from North West Provinces and Bihar to Calcutta for the jute mills;

e) from Chota Nagpur area to collieries in the Burdwan division and to Sylhet for the tea gardens;

f) tribals from Oudh and Jabalpur to the coal mines in Jharia and Ranigunge.

Already in 1895, about half of Calcutta's mill workers were upcountry people.[41]

These migrations were not random movements for seeking any kind of work but specific, point-to-point movements triggered off by changes in relative wage rates and by the opening up of new work opportunities in different areas. For example, the Ranigunge coal mining industry was expanding fast in early 1890s and daily wages had gone up from 7-1/3 annas to 8-1/3 annas in 1892. However, immediately there was an influx of labour mainly from Hazaribag area and Santhal Parganas which brought down the daily wage rate to 6 annas in 1894. In the meanwhile, the daily rate of unskilled agricultural labour in Hazaribag went up by 50 per cent between 1890 to 1894. On the other hand, although there was always talk about scarcity of skilled labour in Calcutta, their daily wage rate remained steady at about 15 annas from 1885 to 1894[42] and did not go up significantly even by 1905-06.[43] Nor did there appear to be any reluctance on the part of men to change occupations or to live in the novel environment of urban industrial locations.

As against this remarkable degree of mobility shown by men in response to changing economic conditions, women of the Bengal Presidency by and large remained in their own villages. It was only tribal women who joined these various strands of migration in significant numbers. They moreover went mainly in families to tea gardens of North and East Bengal as well as of Assam. To a much lesser extent tribal families also moved to collieries in the Ranigunge and Jharia areas: but very few women, whether tribal or otherwise, joined their menfolk in migrating to urban areas.

This immobility on the part of women has often been explained in terms of the attitudes of the newly forming urban industrial workforce. This labour was said to be less than fully committed to the modern sector and so wanting to keep intact its rural linkages and economic base.[44] For this purpose, a worker's best way to retain his rights to the family land and dwelling was to keep his wife and children on the family property, participating in the family activities no matter how low their productivity in it.[45]

This explanation was probably valid in the case of the first wave of upcountry migrants who came to Calcutta's factories. The city was unknown and their notions about work and working conditions in factories still unclear; so single males came to the city as adventurers. The first batch of migrants could very well belong to the class of cultivators and artisans of the village who were not totally rootless. However, this logic cannot fully explain the trends in the period following the initial wave of migration of upcountry workers. The workers had developed a regular pattern by which they went home for a few months but came back to the same mill area. Presumably the same *sardar* (foreman or recruiting agent) was their link to mill areas. Also, it has been shown quite clearly that by 1911 about 30 per cent of the jute mill workers came from low caste or artisan occupations which no longer had any role in the village economy. Another 30 per cent were Muslims who probably also belonged to the category of uprooted artisans.[46] In general, quite a large section of the workers had no commitment in the form of land or a livelihood in their native villages. In principle, they could have settled in urban areas with their families, rather than continuously trying to retain their rural base by remitting a portion of their earnings to maintain their families or trying to build up rural assets. Also, though the wages of single workers were probably not sufficient to maintain a family in urban surroundings, Calcutta's jute mill workers could have worked there *en famille*. As mentioned before, there was considerable demand for women and child labour in jute mills till their rationalization in the late 1920s.

The reasons why workers did not bring their wives and children to work in jute mills as they did in the Bombay cotton mills are not easy to divine. Folklore appears to have identified Calcutta and the jute industry with single men. Songs of village women from Bihar described the mills and Calcutta as the villains who separated them from their husbands and lovers.[47]

One song says:

Railiyā nā bairī, jahājiya nā bairī

Naukariyā bairībo

(Neither the railways nor the ships are our enemies;
it is the job that is our enemy taking our husbands away.)

Or this Bhojpur song:

Amwān mojāri jāilen
Mahowa tapaki jāilan
Kekrā sé pathaon sandés
Re nirmohia chhor dé nokaria

(The mango trees are blooming,
and so are the *mahua* trees.
With whom shall I send my message?
Oh cruel one, leave your job.)

Going to jute mills or coal mines was regarded rather like going to the battlefield. If your man came back triumphant, he would cover you with gold. A husband tells his wife:

Poorab ke deshwā mé kaiti nokariā
Te kari sonwān ké rojigār janiā ho

(One who gets a job in the east
can fill his house with gold.)

or

Pyāri désh Bangalwā jāieb
Tuh ké acchā sari lāib

(Beloved, I will go to Bengal and bring you fine saris.)

However, there was always the danger that Bengal's soil may suck him in or he may be seduced by some woman there.

Pia mor gaiīī Hoogly saharwā se
Le āiley nā ék Bangali sawatiā,
Le āiley na.

(My lover went to Hoogly city and has brought
a Bengali concubine.)

Altogether one waited and hoped but could never dream of following him there.

A possible reason for regarding Calcutta as clearly another and totally alien world could be the extremely unpleasant environment that had evolved around Calcutta's jute area by that time. This environment has been described with great objectivity in a report submitted by Dr Dagmar Curjel of the Women's Medical Service of India to the Government of Bengal in 1923.[48] Her report is written in an extremely low key but nevertheless reads like a horror story. In the mill area almost none of the women lived in regular families. Each woman had to live under the protection of some man but was not married to him. Upcountry men did not bring their wives but lived with local Bengali women. Dr Curjel succinctly reported: "Respectable Bengali women do not undertake industrial work and practically all such Bengalis found in the mills are degraded women or prostitutes."[49] The Assistant Director of Public Health giving evidence to the Royal Commission of Labour in 1930 also said about the jute areas that: "There is practically open prostitution near the workers' homes and most of the workers do not bring their women folk for that reason — No privacy is possible under present conditions of housing. Amongst female workers, one out of four admits to being a prostitute."[50]

A major contingent of migrant workers were called Madrasis though they were mainly Telugu and Oriya speaking. The Telugu workers brought women of their own communities with them but were seldom married to them. These women were shared between themselves and sometimes with Oriya men but if any one of them took up with an upcountry man, there was trouble. The woman had no choice in this.[51]

Each woman had to support herself by working in the mills and had to hand over the earnings, often supplemented by prostitution on the side, to the man with whom she lived.[52] Often a woman had to work in two mills in two shifts because her earnings in one job were extremely meagre.[53] Mill managers felt that giving cash benefits or paid leave for maternity would not help women because they would only have to hand over the money to the man and would probably be sent to work elsewhere. Dr Curjel agreed with their reading.[54]

The Bengali women were specially sickly and disease-ridden.[55] The rates of venereal diseases, sterility, child mortality and even infanticide[56] were very high. One mill manager reported that 50 per cent of his workers were suffering from syphilis[57] and the mill had refused to treat them because it worked out to be very expensive.

The saddest comment was "none of the women who once come to the jute mills ever go back to their own country."[58] Men went back from time to time and retired to their native villages when old or sick. They sent money to their relatives; but none of the women even sent any money to anybody.[59] In other words, for women, the jute lines were the end of the road.

This is to be contrasted with the position in 1890 when, according to the evidence given to the Indian Factory Commission, women in jute mills were distressed but not social outcastes. For example, Taroni, a Bagdi woman working in Baranagore Branch Jute Mill had claimed that she visited her relatives once or twice a year. Another witness, Rajoni (of the weaver caste) working in Calcutta Jute Mill, had told the Commission that a lot of little girls and also married women with children worked in jute mills.[60]

The main reason for this state of affairs was the terrible housing conditions in the jute mill area since the beginning of the twentieth century. Dr Curjel mentions this. Radhakamal Mukherjee specially emphasized the point that the Hoogly riverain around Calcutta showed some of the heaviest concentration of workers dwellings (*bustees*). The fast growth of various mill towns between 1911 and 1931 had given a bonus to local landlords who had leased out the land to mill employers and sardars to build unplanned bustees "to utilise the available space to maximum extent; such is the way in which these single huts are built up at all angles that there is little of the privacy which the Indian woman requires for her daily routine of household duties."[61] The situation in mill lines built by employers where the total area available per worker was 29 sq.ft. to 79 sq.ft. was little better than in the bustees.[62]

It was only a few upcountry Muslim women who came to jute mills in families. The entire family would work on the hand sewing of gunny bags. Often women worked within the mills but as unregistered labour. Muslim weaver women came to the factory lines but did not work. Their husbands' superior position as skilled workers enabled them to rig up some privacy even within the worker's quarters.[63]

The male dominance of the cities thus became a self-sustaining process. Initially it was mainly men who came to the city because migrants were unsure of the new surroundings and wanted to keep their links with the familiar surroundings of the village. But since Calcutta could draw on a vast hinterland stretching up to North-West provinces at one end and the Telugu speaking region at the other, more and more men found their way into the city to meet the very fast expanding demand for labour there. As plentiful migrant labour was available inspite of the terrible housing and sanitary conditions of the mill lines and bustees, employers made no attempt to improve those conditions. And as this process of male dominance and crowding in awful housing continued, it became more and more unthinkable for workers to bring their own families into the mill areas. A chronicle of life around mill areas in this period would read rather like the history of Dodge city or Wyoming except that we have no record of a wild Bill Hickock.[64]

Conclusion

Modernization, as it came to Bengal, was essentially an extremely limited process superimposed by outside forces. In its wake however, it changed the traditional economy in a material way. In general this meant that workers of the region, both men and women, were made increasingly dependent on agriculture for their livelihood. Men were somewhat more fortunate: the bulk of the employment opportunities in the modern sector went to them. After 1931 the share of agriculture in the male workforce declined steadily. For women, the process meant a permanent shift towards the periphery of the economy. Their non-agricultural occupations in the traditional sector suffered a serious setback mainly because of the intervention of the modern sector into the village economy. Women had neither the skills nor the capital to resist these changes.

Nor were they in a position to claim their share in the modern sector though, at least initially, employment opportunities had been created for them in those activities. The traditional society had always imposed stringent constraints on their mobility between regions and occupations.

Therefore, the mere fact that jobs were available did not always bring forth an immediate response from the local female population. However, the reluctance of local women to join the mills in larger numbers did not really create any problems for the mills. The demand of the modern sector was in fact so small compared to the negative impact it had created in the traditional sector that any fresh increase in demand was quickly met by more and more very needy workers pouring into the city from further and further afield.

NOTES

1. Phyllis Deane and W.A. Cole, *British Economic Growth, 1688-1954*, 2nd ed. (Cambridge: Cambridge University Press, 1969), pp. 143, 190, 111.
2. Karl Marx, *Capital* (Moscow: Progress Publishers, 1974), I, p. 372.
3. Deane and Cole, *British Economic Growth*, p. 146.
4. R.M. Hartwell, "The Service Revolution: The Growth of Services in the Modern Economy, 1700-1914," in C.M. Cipolla, ed. *The Industrial Revolution*, 2nd ed. (London: Collins, 1975), pp. 361-62.
5. John Saville, quoted by T.G. McGee in *The Urbanization Process in the Third World: Explorations in Search of a Theory* (London: Bell and Sons, 1979), p. 101.
6. Alice Thorner, "Women's Work in Colonial India: 1881-1931," Seventh European Conference on Modern South Asian Studies, London, July 1981, Tables C and D.
7. *The Report of the Royal Commission on Labour in India, 1929-31* (Delhi: Government of India, 1932), vol. 2, p. 603; henceforth referred to as *Royal Commission of 1931.*
8. R.N. Gilchrist, *Indian Labour and Land* (Calcutta: Government of Bengal Press, 1932), p. 3.
9. See Table 3 and Table 4. Also J.N. Sinha, *The Indian Work Force*, Monograph no. 11, *Census of India 1961* (Delhi: Ministry of Home Affairs, 1972), vol. I, Table 8, pp. 24-25.
10. *Report of Bengal Labour Enquiry Commission 1896* (Calcutta; Bengal Secretariat, 1896), pp. 15-17; henceforth referred to as *1896 Labour Commission.*
11. J.G. Cummins, *Review of the Industrial Position and Prospects in Bengal in 1908*, Special Report (Calcutta, 1908), pt. 2.
12. *The Report of the Indian Factory Commission 1890*, vol. 2, gives the evidence of H.M. Scott of the Hastings Jute Mill (witness no. 162) who

claimed that labour in his mill was very short in April, May and June; *Royal Commission of 1931*, vol. I, pp. 113-15.

13. Daniel Thorner, *The Shaping of Modern India* (Delhi: Allied Publishers, 1980), pp. 107-24.

14. *History of the Indian Railways: Constructed and in Progress corrected upto March 31, 1964* (Delhi: Ministry of Railways, 1966), p. 2.

15. *Royal Commission of 1931*, p. 197.

16. Cummins, *Review of Industrial Position*, p. 4.

17. *Census of India 1961*, (Delhi 1964). Economic Tables, pt. 2B (i), Table no. BI, pp. 86-99.

18. *Census of India 1881, Bengal*, vol. 5, pt. 2, Table no. 29, Principal Occupations of Females, p. 908. All future references to 1881 occupational categories are on the basis of this table.

19. A.K. Bagchi, "Deindustrialisation in Gangetic Bengal" in Barun De, ed. *Essays in Honour of Susboban Sarkar* (Delhi: People's Publishing House, 1976), Table no. 5, p. 513.

20. *Census of India 1901: Bengal* (Delhi, 1903), vol. 5, pt. 2, Subsidiary Table 1. All future references to 1901 occupational distribution are on the basis of this table.

21. H.J. Colebrooke, *Remarks on the Husbandry and Internal Commerce of India 1794* in *Census of India 1951: West Bengal*, vol. 6, pt. 1C pp. 230-31.

22. Bankim Chandra Chattopadhyay's heroine Prafullakumari in the novel *Debi Chowdhurani* (1884) was in distress because her parents-in-law had refused to accept her in their house. She says to her widowed mother: "Why should we live by begging? ... Let us spin sacred threads for sale and get some money (a *kowri*) for that." *Debi Chowdhurani* in *Bankim Rachanawali* (Calcutta: Sahitya Sunsad, 1977), I, p. 789.

23. Lal Behari De, *Bengal Peasant Life* (1874; rpt. Mahadevprasad Saha, ed, Calcutta: Editions Indian, 1969), p. 50.

24. These songs are a part of an unpublished collection of folk songs, and have been collated by Smt. Bela Bandhopadhyay from diverse oral and vernacular sources, and from different communities of Bengal.

25. *Royal Commission of 1931*, p. 77. See also Mukul Mukherjee, "Impact of Modernization on Women's Occupations: A Case Study of Rice Husking Industry of Bengal," *Economic and Social History Review*, 20 (Jan.-March 1983), pp. 27-45.

26. *Census of India 1911: Bengal*, vol. 6, pt. 2, Table no. 15 and pt. 3, Table no. 15. Also, *Census of India 1931: Bengal*, vol. 5, pt. 2, Table

no. 10 and vol. 7, pt. 2, Table no. 10. Future references to 1911 and 1931 occupational distribution are based on these tables.

27. Cummins, *Review of Industrial Position*, p. 3.

28. Ibid., p. 6.

29. *1896 Labour Commission*, p. 16.

30. Dagmar Curjel, *Women's Medical Service of India: Report of an Enquiry into the Conditions of Employment of Women Before and After Child Birth in Bengal Industries* (Govt. of Bengal, Dept. of Commerce), File no. 2R-20/1923, April 1923 p. 12; henceforth referred to as *Curjel Report*.

31. P. Nolan, *Report on the Conditions of the Lower Classes of People in Bengal, 1888*, submitted to the Viceroy (Bengal, 1888). Henceforth referred to as *Dufferin Report*.

32. *Dufferin Report*, p. 4.

33. *Dufferin Report*, Subsidiary report for Presidency Division submitted by A. Smith. No-continuous pagination for subsidiary reports.

34. *Dufferin Report*, Subsidiary report for Chittagong Division submitted by Lyall, Commissioner.

35. *Dufferin Report*, Subsidiary report for Chotanagpur Division submitted by Stevens, Commissioner.

36. *Dufferin Report*, Subsidiary report for Patna Division submitted by J. Boxwell, Commissioner.

37. *Dufferin Report*, Subsidiary report for Bhagalpur Division submitted by Beerhan Deo Narayan, Asstt. Settlement Officer.

38. *Dufferin Report*, Subsidiary report for Puri Division submitted by C. Worseley, Commissioner.

39. *Dufferin Report*, Subidiary report for Howrah district submitted by Ritchie, Magistrate, Howrah district.

40. *Report of the Indian Factory Commission*, Proceedings of the 22nd meeting, (Calcutta, 22 Oct. 1890), testimony of the second witness, Taroni.

41. *1896 Labour Commission*, pp. 43-44.

42. Ibid., p. 3.

43. B. Foley, *Report on Labour in Bengal, 1906* (Calcutta: Govt. of Bengal, 1906), chap. 3, para 22, p. 19.

44. Ranajit Dasgupta's forthcoming work on the rural linkages of Bengal labour discusses this point.

45. See for example A.K. Sen, *Employment Technology and Development*

(Delhi: Oxford University Press, 1975), p. 37.

46. Ranajit Dasgupta, "Factory Labour in Eastern India," *Social and Economic History Review*, 13, no. 3 (1976), Table no. 10, p. 320; see also p. 326.
47. Several songs of Bihari women regarding the Calcutta jute mills and coal mines have been quoted by D.P. Saxena, *Rururban Migration in India* (Bombay: Popular Prakashan, 1977), pp. 175-78.
48. *Curjel Report.*
49. Ibid., p. 2.
50. *Royal Commission of 1931*, Evidence vol. 5, pt. 2, Oral Evidence-Bengal, 3 Feb. 1930, p. 5 E55.
51. *Curjel Report*, app., Ap iv.
52. Ibid., p. 5.
53. Ibid., p. 14.
54. Ibid., p. 13. See also evidence given by Manager, Soora Jute Mills.
55. Ibid., app., Ap iv.
56. Ibid., evidence given by Williamson of Kinnison Jute Mill.
57. Ibid., evidence given by Murray of Olive Jute Mill.
58. Ibid., p. 2.
59. Ibid., app., Ap x.
60. *Indian Factory Commission 1890*, Proceedings of meeting, Calcutta, 27 Oct. 1890.
61. Radhakamal Mukherjee, *The Indian Working Class* (Bombay: Hind Kitab, 1945), p. 246.
62. Ibid., p. 247.
63. *Curjel Report*, app., Ap iv. See also evidence given by Patterson of Union Jute Mill.
64. Samaresh Basu, *Jaggadal* (Calcutta: Bak, 1966) gives a vivid picture of the changing life in one jute mill area around the turn of the century.

Customs in a Peasant Economy:
*Women in Colonial Haryana**

PREM CHOWDHRY

IN HARYANA the control of women's behaviour through certain customs has been central to the affirmation of the solidarity of the dominant Jat peasant group. Such customs, emerging from the growth and demands of a patriarchy and interacting with specific geo-economic needs, have been largely constrictive for women. Further, when such customs came to be buttressed with the force of law by the colonial government, who became conscious agents in their perpetuation, the customs naturally became more binding upon Jat and other social groups in Haryana, making it either difficult or impossible for a woman to break out of their confines. The tenacious persistence of historically crystallized customs and attitudes made a mockery of attempts by women to contest these and often involved them in prolonged legal battles and open confrontations.

There is a peculiar contradiction in the dominant emergent customs and attitudes in rural Haryana in relation to women in the colonial period. On the one hand, the agrarian milieu shows the generally accepted indices of high status for women, i.e., bride-price, widow-remarriage, polyandry or its own sexual variants and full economic participation in agricultural activities resting on a relatively greater similarity of function with men. On the other

* This is a substantially revised version of my article, "Socio-Economic Dimensions of Certain Customs and Attitudes: Women of Haryana in the Colonial Period," *Economic and Political Weekly*.

I wish to thank Uma Chakravarti and the editors of the present anthology, Sudesh Vaid and Kumkum Sangari, for suggesting certain points for elaboration.

hand, it shows the region as also having indices of women's backwardness, i.e., female infanticide in different forms resulting in an extremely unequal female sex-ratio as compared to the male, *purdah* (seclusion) and the *ghunghat* (veil) custom, total neglect of and prejudice against female education, and the complete absence of women from any positions of power and decision making. This paper takes up the socio-economic aspects of such mutually contradictory indices, social customs and attitudes and analyses the dominant peasant cultural ethos which has accepted and sanctified them. In this connection, British administrative policy decisions as well as those of a reformist movement like the Arya Samaj, both of which sustained these customs, have also been examined. This paper also attempts to explore the social implications of these customs and the reasons behind the ostensibly 'liberal' attitudes towards women in the context of marriage, remarriage and sexuality etc. All these factors are seen in the historical context of overall colonial domination, the adoption of certain policies which, although not directly connected with women, nevertheless had profound effects on issues specifically relating to women. As such, this study also highlights the role of the colonial administration and its attitudes in retaining and reinforcing the emergent dominant social ethos of the Haryana peasantry.

I

The dominant caste and the peasant ethos

In the agrarian milieu of the Haryana region of Punjab, the socio-cultural ethos came to be coloured and determined generally by the agriculturist castes, and in particular by the land-owning classes. Among the agriculturist castes, the Jats emerge as the 'dominant caste'.[1] The model of the dominant caste in a given region as described by M.N. Srinivas is apposite for the Jats in Haryana.[2] Economically and numerically stronger than any other caste, the Jats satisfied yet another norm of the 'dominant caste', i.e., they did not occupy a low ritual status. Numerically they were found in very large numbers in the five districts of this region, viz., Ambala, Gurgaon, Hissar, Karnal and Rohtak, forming nearly one-third of the total population. They also held the bulk of agricultural land as proprietors. For instance, in Rohtak district in 1910, the Hindu Jats emerged as the owners of 60 per cent of the total cultivated land. In a very large number of 'Jat villages' of this region, they held a near monopoly of landownership ranging between 88 to 99 per cent. Besides, most other castes were in a relation of servitude to the landowning Jats who stood as the single largest receivers of services from the other castes. And, although the social status of Jats is somewhat difficult to define in terms of the ritualistic framework of caste hierarchies, the accepted social superiority of the Brahmin did not exist here or elsewhere in Punjab. The Brahmin could certainly be sacerdotally superior yet socially he was described as the "lowest of the low." Whatever superiority the Brahmin may have enjoyed declined severely by the early twenties with the propagation and acceptance of the Arya Samaj, especially among the landowning Jats of this region. On the other hand, regarding the Jats, who ritually ranked in Punjab after the Brahmin, Rajput and Khatri, the Punjab Census of 1901 laid down "there is no caste above the Jat." In this agrarian society, the norms as seen to be operating and also as encouraged by the British did not conform to ritualistic concepts and were necessarily related to the amount of land that was in the possession of a particular caste. Seen as such the Jats clearly emerge as the 'dominant caste' in social, economic and numerical terms, as well as in the emerging politics of this region.[3]

This ubiquitous domination by a single caste (despite internal economic disparities) set the tone and shaped the customs and attitudes that became common in rural Haryana. The emergent customs followed by most Jats came to be accepted and projected for the entire region, especially as many of these customs could be seen to be followed by nearly all lower castes as well as classes.

II

Socio-economic conditions: their significance for women

Haryana remained one of the most backward and underdeveloped regions of Punjab under the British. The needs of imperialism gave a very low priority to any improvement of agriculture in Haryana.[4] This region in any case had poorer resources as compared to most other parts of Punjab. Irrigation was extremely limited and British irrigational policies kept the region starved of this basic requirement which was the crucial determinant of agriculture. Apart from limited irrigation, precarious rainfall, recurrent floods due to periodic overflow of the river Jamuna, seasonal excesses and frequent *akal* (famines) spelt devastation for this region and its economy. Throughout, the official emphasis remained on low value food-cum-fodder crops and the region continued to be seen as primarily suited for the supply of draught animals to the rest of Punjab as also to certain other parts of India.

In this chronic famine ridden region, where large sections of the peasants tended to be subsistence or deficit producers, only a comparatively large holding could be economically viable. For example, in Rohtak district, a holding of at least twelve acres could be taken as an economic one.[5] This meant that only about 28 per cent of landholdings fell in this category.[6] The same was true, more or less, for the entire Haryana region. The *barani* (dependent on rainfall) nature of the region with its concomitant low yielding inferior crops and chronic crop failures made for a subsistence economy and hand to mouth living for an overwhelming majority of landowners. Deficient in any kind of resources, the small landowners relied mostly upon their family labour and some hired labour, if the need arose. Such an economy reinforced covetousness for male progeny. A male child came to be as essential as the life-giving rain. A popular local saying maintained:

meehṅ aur beṭṭyā te koon dhāppyā sai[7]

(Who can be satisfied without rain and sons;
for cultivation both are necessary.)

Moreover, given uncertain conditions, family labour requirements, and the high mortality rate, it was not considered either safe or sufficient to have only one male child:

ek āṅkh kā ke sulakshanā,
ek poot kā ke sapootā[8]

(Just as a one-eyed man can hardly be called lucky,
so also a man with only one son.)

Another proverb went on to maintain:

chohrā mure nirbhāg kā
chohri mure bhāgwān ki[9]

(The son of an unfortunate dies,
the daughter of a fortunate dies.)

This local proverb showing a marked preference for boys over girls, reflects the dominant social ethos. In very real terms this ethos manifested itself in the favourable male sex ratio. There was a great deal of difference in the male-female sex-ratio at any given age not only in Haryana but all over Punjab.[10] The British administration ascribed this imbalance to a distant past, before the annexation of Punjab, when female infanticide had been practised to a large extent.[11] However, by the time of the 1901 Census they were not willing to give it any significant contributory role and ascribed the uneven sex-ratio to other reasons like neglect of female children in earlier times (both pre-colonial and in the early years of British rule in Punjab), the high rate of mortality due to frequent child bearing starting at a very early age, and the neglect of women of advanced age. Additionally, in the all-too-frequent famines, droughts and epidemics, the first casualty were women.[12] All these factors undoubtedly combined to enable a different form of femicide to continue in order to keep the female ratio down, and resulted, in Punjab having the smallest proportion of females as compared to the major Indian provinces under the British.[13]

The socio-economy of this region has been emphasized because of its special significance for women and not merely to rationalize or explain the low female sex ratio. The hard subsistence level economy with total dependence on family labour for cultivation made women an economic asset. W.E. Purser and H.C. Fanshawe recognizing this, commented in their report on the revised land revenue settlement of the Rohtak district in 1880:

> Enquiry from people themselves, in almost every village of the district has shown that as long as a family has its proper complement of workers, male and female, it is well-to-do . . . where there is no woman in the family, the house is certain to fall into difficulties.[14]

Another graphic description of women's work showed:

> The women work as hard as the men if not harder. The heavy tasks of bringing in wood and fuel and water fall on them; they have to cook the food, and carry it daily to the fields; they have to watch the crops; to them the peeling of the sugarcane and picking of the cotton belongs; and when there is nothing else to do, they must always fill up the time

by tasks with the spinning wheel.[15]

A large number of local proverbs show that certain agricultural tasks such as weeding fell exclusively on women. Two proverbs from Karnal can be cited here as examples:

maiṅ koli nahiṅ duppaṭṭi
keyā chugegi kuppaṭṭi

(Cotton says you did not weed me when I had two leaves above the ground, what do you expect to pick now, bad woman.)

jo wahiṅ nalāye do paṭṭi
to kyā kamāe kuppaṭṭi[16]

(If weeding be not done when there are but two leaves, then what will you earn worthless woman.)

To this may be added the extensive animal husbandry work. Animal husbandry was a necessary supplement to this region's subsistence level economy. It meant tending, feeding, milking the cattle and making *lassi* (buttermilk) and *ghee* (refined butter). All this was the special preserve of women.

III

The colonial view of women: utility to agriculture

Hard work was a general feature all over rural Punjab. Yet, relatively speaking, due to the harsh unyielding geo-economic conditions of Haryana, the women worked harder than elsewhere in the Punjab province. The British officials' observations bear this out:

> It can be safely said that proportionately a large number of women are engaged in economic work in the Himalayan natural division than in the plains, and that in the latter the women of South-eastern districts such as Hissar, Rohtak and Gurgaon take a greater share of such work than the women of the Central districts with one or two exceptions. In the Himalayas, as well as in the South-east of the province, women take a large share in agricultural work and in some locations are believed to do it even better than their husbands. Women of North-western districts are also fairly active workers.[17]

Among these regional variations, women of certain caste groups were specially singled out for praise. For example, the Jatni (Jat woman) was hailed as an "economic treasure" by British officials, who wrote a great deal applauding the "help" she rendered to "an ideal cultivator and a revenue payer" i.e., the Jat.[18] The Jatni was universally praised thus:

bhali jaṭi jātni ki khurpi hāth
khet nivāre āpne khāvind ke sāth[19]

(Good kind Jatni, hoe in hand,
weeds the fields in company with her husband)

Another proverb maintained:

raṇ jaṭṭi, te hor sab chalti[20]

(A Jat wife for me, as all other women are a mere waste of money.)

The Rohtak Assessment Report of 1909 mentioned that a Jatni did not plough, dig or drive a cart, but there was no other form of agricultural labour which she did not perform. The women from other agricultural castes were also said to do as much work as the Jatni if not more.[21] Here one may include the women from lower castes as well. In fact these women showed a higher number of female workers than the other castes.[22] Those specially mentioned were from among the Chamars, Chuhras and Jhimars. They were described by the officials as "hard working,"[23] but because they did not belong to the landowning castes their being "economic assets" found no expression in official British accounts.

The caste groups who did not encourage their women to work outside home were the Bania, Khatri and Rajput among the Hindus, and the Pathan, Biloch, Sayyad, Shiekh and Ranghar or Rajput among the Muslims.[24] The colonial administrators' comments on these caste groups which were "conspicuous" for having "the smallest number of female workers" reveal their own attitude. For example, the Rajputs, both Hindu and Muslim, by the "common consent" of various British officials were considered to be "the worst cultivators in the Punjab" whose "land revenue dues remained frequently in arrears;" the Rajput's regard for his *izzat* (honour) forbade him to take any help from his wife who remained in purdah and was generally considered to be "an economic burden."[25] The Brahmins were also considered to be "inferior cultivators," because their women gave little or no assistance to the men in the fields beyond bringing them their meals.[26] For the same reason, the Pathans were considered "bad cultivators" and "very bad revenue payers;" the Biloch were described as "poor cultivators and heavily indebted."[27] The other castes being 'non-agriculturist castes', however, merited no mention.

Obviously, the British criterion for judging women was their usefulness to agriculture which was of supreme concern to them not only in terms of land revenue but also in terms of the general socio-economic stability and utility of this region. In fact, even the custom of purdah was seen from the point of view of women's non-availability for tasks other than the domestic as it led to women's seclusion and severely curtailed their availability for agricultural labour.[28] The British support to the social reformers' struggle against purdah therefore may well have emanated out of such concerns. Interestingly, this non-utilization of female labour was not only considered a handicap to the Indian peasant but was also considered to be one of the chief causes of Punjab poverty.[29] This fact made them take a very serious view of a social custom which prohibited women from sharing the work of their men. It was this custom which they felt could be substituted by the 'more progressive' western social norm. Comparing the two norms, British officials maintained in 1921:

> There is a vast waste of female labour, due primarily to custom and prejudice. In most other countries the proportion of female labour to the whole is high; while its efficiency is equal to the tasks performed; the contribution to the national dividend resulting from this forms an appreciable part of the whole. If there were in western countries a movement aiming at the exclusion of female labour for all except purely domestic tasks, that movement would endanger the whole economic fabric, and, if successful would involve those countries in ruin. The Punjab discards what in England and elsewhere is an absolutely necessary element in the maintenance of their civilization. The fact that there are tribes such as Brahmans and Rajputs which do not allow their womenfolk even to work in the fields is alone sufficient to explain their poverty. . . . In the course of generations the loss from the waste alone must have made material progress almost impossible. No European country could maintain its present standard of living without the assistance derived from female labour.[30]

The British officials' attempt to make "deeply ingrained Indian minds," see the need for involving women in agricultural work by projecting their own western example of "high present economic standards" was vastly frustrating. They confessed to experiencing "great difficulty" in making Indians accept their reasoning and getting the desired results.[31]

IV

Marriage and bride-price

The importance of women in the agrarian economy made marriage an acknowledged "economic necessity."[32] So much so that a man's inability to pay his revenue dues was put down to his unmarried status, since an "*akela aḍami*" (single man) was not expected to perform well agriculturally; and a widower was considered to be "half paralysed."[33]

Significantly, the so-called 'work qualities' of a prospective bride were looked for at the time of arranging marriages; the acknowledged requirement being, "*hāth-paer ki mazboot honi chāhiye, take khet-kivaṛ ka kaam thīk treh ho sake*"[34] (she should be physically strong, so that agricultural work can be performed well). The emphasis on these 'work qualities' also led them to disregard the girl's age and height etc., with the result that the girl was quite frequently older and sometimes taller than the boy. This fact was made a virtue of and a local proverb eulogizing it maintained:

baḍi bahu baḍe bhāg
chhotā banḍrā ghane suhāg[35]

(An older or taller wife brings luck,
as also a shorter or younger bridegroom).

The important role played by women in the economy led to a wide acceptance of the prevalent custom of sale and purchase of brides among the economically hard up peasantry. In the nineteenth century, except among a few better-off families, this custom was observed to have been universal among the agriculturist castes as well as the lower castes.[36] Among the lower castes bride-price was well signified in a local proverb:

nāi kis kā bhāi
chhori bech leyāva lugāi[37]

(The *nai* [barber] is no one's friend
he sells his daughter to buy himself a wife.)

Although looked upon as a "disgraceful custom" and admitted by Jats with a "certain amount of apology and obvious sense of shame," it was a practice that was gaining ground everywhere in the first decade of the twentieth century.[38]

Regarding the price of brides, Malcolm Lyall Darling, one of the most distinguished of Punjab officials who made a thorough and comparative study of varied aspects of social life in different regions of Punjab, maintained that it rose steadily with the rise in prices:

> In the fifties a bride could be had for Rs. 50, but nowadays in neither hill nor plain can anything worth having be got for less than three or four hundred rupees, and a serious epidemic may considerably raise the price. In Rohtak, for instance, where in 1918 influenza carried off 10 percent of the people, the price rose from Rs. 500 to Rs. 2000. In Hissar, on the other hand, the prolonged drought of 1919-21 reduced it from Rs. 2000 to Rs. 500.[39]

In individual cases "fancy prices" were paid, specially if the boy was handicapped in some way, or if he was considerably older or had an obvious defect of body or limb.[40]

It may be pointed out that payment of bride-price was one of the reasons why British officials denied that female infanticide existed in this region in any substantial way and offered other reasons for the low sex-ratio of females. The situation was indeed apparently contradictory, specially as the official perception of bride-price conceived it as "a compensation . . . for the family authority which was transferred to the husband."[41] Similarly a recent article interprets bride-price as a "compensatory payment to the family for the production loss they suffer on her departure."[42] Yet, even this apparent economic worth did nothing to raise her status. In practice, bride-price was most common among the lower economic strata of agriculturists. It was this factor which was responsible for not elevating the custom to respectability. The middle-level agriculturist with some standing had to pay bride-price to marry his son (the bride generally came from the poorer families who charged a price) and gave a dowry to marry his daughter, as a better alliance within the caste was always sought.[43] No girl was allowed to marry outside the caste, the norm being "*Jāṭ ki beṭi Jāṭ ko*" (A Jat girl must marry a Jat). Since there were no recognized 'socially superior' clans as such, status was determined by the amount of land held, and in the arid Haryana region the coveted wish was to get daughters or sisters married where canal irrigation existed.[44] This combination of bride-price and dowry made the existence of females a financial drain. Those accepting bride-price were looked down upon for this very practice and consequently could hardly affect a change in the dominant attitude of the others towards women. In turn, they blamed the female species for being there at all, as a woman's existence meant bride-price and bride-price spelt ultimate shame to the family; izzat among the agriculturists scored over economics, even in financially deprived households. Females therefore meant drain — financial for some and moral and ethical for the others. It is small wonder that bride-price even in its positive aspects could not represent high status for women in any real terms.

V

Widow remarriage or the custom of *karewa*

The agrarian needs which allowed bride-price also sanctified widow-remarriage. Like the former, this was also a feature which the agriculturist castes shared in common with the lower castes. However, the custom of widow-remarriage as followed here had special features of its own. Known as *karewa, karao*, or *chaddar andazi*, the custom was a throwback to the old Rig-Vedic *niyog* (levirate marriage) which was prevalent in the geographical region of Haryana Punjab and associated with the early Vedic Aryan settlements.[45] Karewa, a white sheet coloured at the corners, was thrown by the man over the widow's head, signifying his acceptance of her as his wife. This custom represented social consent for cohabitation. There could be certain variations.[46] For example, it could take the form of placing *churis* (glass bangles) on the widow's wrist in full assembly and sometimes even a gold *nath* (nose ring) in her nose and a red sheet over her head with a rupee tied in one of its corners. This could be followed by the distribution of *gur* (jaggery) or sweets. Significantly, this form of remarriage was not accompanied by any kind of religious ceremony, as no woman could be customarily married twice i.e., could go through the ceremony of *biah* (religious wedding). After karewa the widow merely resumed her jewels and coloured clothes which she had ceased to wear on her husband's death. So much so that sometimes mere cohabitation was considered sufficient to legitimize the relationship and it conferred all the rights of a valid marriage. However, for cohabitation to be accepted as remarriage it had to be cohabitation in the man's house. Mere visits to the woman were considered "adulterous."[47]

The Jats, as in other customs, led in the practice of Karewa and other agriculturist castes (except the Rajputs) followed suit. Interestingly, among the Brahmins, the reports indicate that karewa was being followed.[48] Even in a far-flung district like Muzaffargarh, the Brahmins had declared their adherence to the Jat custom. The settlement officer of this district pointed out that there was scarcely a Brahmin there who had even the slightest knowledge of the Hindu law books or was acquainted with their names.[49] The Brahmins of this province, who were not a priestly class but were mostly landowners, consequently followed the dominant social custom of this region in preference to the sanskritic model of the other Brahmins who brooked no remarriage at all and upheld *sati* (widow immolation) instead. Among other Hindu castes, the "low grade Khatris"[50] also followed this practice but others like the Bania and Kayastha did not do so, and among the Muslims nor did the Sayyads.[51] Castes that did not admit widow remarriage were contemptuous of this practice and looked down upon those who practised it.[52]

The widespread acceptability of karewa is reflected in local proverbs:

ājā beti lele phere
yo mergayā to aur bhotere[53]

(Come daughter get married, if this husband dies
there are many more.)

Another one maintained:

ek kanya sahānsar var[54]

(There are several bridegrooms available for one bride.)

Karewa, however, as a rule, was a levirate marriage in which the widow was accepted as wife by one of the younger brothers of the deceased husband; failing him the husband's older brother; failing him his agnatic first cousins etc. In 1934, in the Ambala district there was also the case of a Jat who claimed validity of custom regarding karewa marriage with his widowed daughter-in-law.[55] The case was lost by the father-in-law, who then appealed to the Lahore High Court. The High Court also rejected it and maintained that the custom of karewa marriage between a Jat and his widowed daughter-in-law was invalid, "being repugnant to the ideas of Jats." However, this judgement did not apparently lay down a general rule of custom applicable to the entire province. In another case decided shortly afterwards in 1936, the Hoshiarpur district judge took a totally opposite view and held, on the evidence, that such a remarriage was valid by custom.[56] Significantly, it may be noticed that the customs could and were sought to be extended specially as they had come to have legal sanction. The father-in-law's claim to the karewa custom has to be seen as an attempt to retain the widow within the family for a variety of reasons (given later) ranging from control of property and of her sexuality to control of her options regarding marriage partners. The reigning ideology behind this control, recorded by E. Joseph, significantly laid down:

> A female, minor or adult, is always under guardianship, while single she is under the guardianship of her father, if he be dead, of other relatives, in the order given [all male members]. So too when married until her *muklawa*, when she comes under the guardianship of her husband; on his death until remarriage she is under the guardianship of his family, whether she be minor or major.[57]

Therefore, the widow's right as to whom she could marry was not only severely restricted, it could be settled only by her late husband's family. And although the widow could not be compelled to remarry, she was not free to marry without their consent. So complete was the control over woman and on the question of her remarriage that it was freely admitted that the widow was often practically forced and made to yield to their wishes.[58] Any assertion to the contrary would be difficult to believe in a region which advocated:

zamin joi zor ki
zor ghāti hor ki[59]

(Land and wife can only be held through the use of force, when this fails they become another's.)

Karewa and the question of inheritance

The popularity of karewa among the overwhelming majority of landowning classes emanated out of the need for retaining landed property within the family. The main reason for making the marriage arrangements inside the family was to transfer control of her deceased husband's land from the widow (who succeeded to a life estate in the absence of male lineal descendants) to his brother or to a patrilineal family member, because a widow who remarried lost all her rights to property, even if she married her husband's brother.[60] Remarriage therefore deprived her of even the limited right to land which she came to possess after her husband's death, i.e., only a lifelong interest; ultimately the property passed to her husband's male line. In case she had children, her sons succeeded to the property and she had right only to suitable maintenance; her daughters and their issue had no right to inherit from the father. It was essential to deny the daughters any share in the inheritance, in order to retain land within the immediate kinship group. The daughters were only entitled to maintenance and to be "suitably betrothed and married."[61]

However, even this limited right of the widow was seen as a menace, because she could claim a partition of the property on certain grounds, i.e., when she could not secure the required maintenance.[62] But the onus of proving this was on her. This meant that the court either implicitly or explicitly took the position that the required maintenance was indeed being granted to her by her deceased husband's agnates. However, the fact that this view was contrary to reality was even acknowledged by the revenue officials. In their considered opinion the widow found it difficult to obtain her "fair share of produce" as long as the holding remained undivided.[63] A separate possession meant that the widow could get it cultivated through someone else as she was customarily not allowed to undertake full agricultural operations herself. A popular proverb from Karnal maintained:

Īkh ne bowen rānd
aur paden sānd[64]

(A widow may be able to sow sugar-cane, but it needs a strong man [literally a bull] to press out the cane.)

A separate possession also produced a fear, "often well founded," that it would lead to an "attempt to alienate" the property.[65] The widow could alienate the property, though not sell it, for her own maintenance, for her daughter's wedding or for payment of revenue, all the reasons dubbed as "strict necessity." That a lot of women had started to utilize this proviso can be seen from the constant appeals made to the Deputy Commissioner, protesting against widows who were accused of alienating their property "without necessity."[66]

This self assertion by widows in taking control of the economic resources after their husbands' death must have assumed such a proportion that, for a variety of reasons, government action against it became essential. J.M. Douie, compiler of ***The Punjab Land Administration Manual***, advised the revenue officials that the widow's attempts to partition the land "should be disallowed."[67] (The widow's right to control land had been legalized under the Land Revenue Act because after her husband's death she was held responsible for the payment of government revenue dues.) However, since legally such advice could not have held much weight, the only solution to the fast growing claims to partition was, according to official instruction, to be sought in "a firm anchoring of the widow in remarriage." This, the *Manual* instructed, could be the "only satisfactory arrangement against which she had no appeal."[68]

Strengthening karewa: colonial perception and policy

Such advice was an inevitable outcome of the colonial policy followed in Punjab, because of its economic, political and military importance, too well known to bear a recount here. The imperial government had, right from the beginning, adopted the "preservation of village community" as a settled policy for Punjab. To this end they advocated "cohering tribes" (rather than "their break up") through the operation of their customary laws as an essential prerequisite for controlling Punjab.[69] The general argument of British officials was that the mass of the agricultural population in this province did not follow either the Hindu or the Muslim law. Therefore, a general code of tribal custom was prepared by the settlement officers, who at each settlement had compiled the *rivaj-i-am* (record of customs and rights), in consultation with the village headmen of each principal landowning tribe in the district; these being acknowledgedly "men of most influential families in the village." Consequently the customs of the landowning class in regard to civil matters like succession, alienation, marriage, tenure of land, adoption and the like came to be settled primarily by the Punjab customary law, which then became the first rule of decisions.[70] However, the British perception of these customs, which they also made legally binding, is significant. For karewa they held:

> . . . most officers conversant with this tract of country have entertained, in the existence *sub rosa* of a system of polyandry. This institution is probably the first stage in development of a savage people after they have emerged from a mere animal condition of promiscuity. It is the concomitant of female infanticide. . . . The family is the first organisation, when all things, including the wife are owned in common. The eldest brother is the head of the house, but the younger brothers have their rights, and the universal survival of the *karewa* custom of widow remarriage among the Jats shows how the younger brother (though now it is not necessarily always the younger brother or any real brother) succeeds to the headship of the family on elder's death.[71]

In Punjab, the fundamental political interest of the British transcended their less well defined concern for 'social progress.' This 'low level' of civilization as signified by karewa had to be retained because the British concern lay in strengthening the hold of the existing peasant society over land; its break-up was inevitable if the widow was allowed to have her way.

The apprehension regarding the danger of social disequilibrium in Haryana was sharper because this region, with its insecure agricultural conditions, had provided the best recruiting ground for the British Indian Army. For example, in World War I, this region had contributed one fifth of the total recruitment from the whole of Punjab.[72] And although the karewa custom contributed significantly to the unceasing heavy recruitment (despite the insecurity of life and the equally heavy rate of mortality) the agricultural interests of the recruits' families could not be allowed to be jeopardized by the ever growing number of widows' claims. This could prove to be very costly to the imperial government and not only unsettle its military recruitment, but also the social equilibrium upon which its rule in the state was founded.

Moreover, even economically, such a demand, if conceded, would have only added to the fragmentation and sub-division of holdings and consequently to the fast growing smaller uneconomic holdings in this region, as elsewhere in Punjab,[73] which were posing a direct threat to the agricultural prosperity of the province and so to the collection of revenue. In fact, the fast spreading problem of the fragmentation of landholdings was serious enough for the Viceroy to order an inquiry in June 1936.[74] This fact had also led to government attempts at consolidation of holdings, the results of which were not noticeably fruitful.[75] The growing demands of the widows in this socio-economic milieu combined with an ever growing population dependent on agriculture, was certain to further compound the problem. It became necessary to issue instructions and give out administrative guidelines in this connection. The district officials were therefore instructed: "Often a young widow will present a petition to the Deputy Commissioner for sanction to marry a man of her choice, but with such application he is wise to have nothing to do."[76]

A woman's resistance to the peasant culture of remarriage which was designed to retain her within the family of her deceased husband was not allowed to surface. Petitions nevertheless continued to be made. Petitions were also made by widows, and even courts moved, to deny that karewa had taken place. This resistance shows that many peasant women perceived the karewa custom to be a repressive one. So common was this resistance that British officials noted in 1921 that criminal proceedings were most frequently resorted to by the deceased husband's brother by lodging a complaint under section 498 of the Indian Penal Code to counter the widows' attempts to escape by asserting that a marriage by karewa or chaddar andazi had taken place whereas it was firmly denied and challenged by the widows.[77] It was very difficult for a widow to prove the contrary for, as pointed out earlier, even cohabitation could be and was recognised as karewa. Once marriage or remarriage status was accepted, on no account could a Hindu woman claim release from it.[78] As against this, there was no limit to the number of wives a man could have either through *shadi* (a caste marriage) or by karewa. He could also expel his wife for unchastity through a practice called *tyag* (renunciation) which practically amounted to divorce, and also for change of religion which was said to automatically dissolve the marriage.[79] The customary law of the land, backed by the full force of the colonial administrators, safeguarded the landed property from a woman's possession. Interestingly, not allowing women to inherit property was a view which found a sympathetic and even an enthusiastic chord among many British officials. A curious parallel observation about the situation of women prevailing "backhome" as compared to that in Punjab discloses the ambivalent attitude of British officials towards women:

> . . . the proportion of females to males in England and Wales rises continuously from childhood to old age, indicative of the excessive care lavished on women in England qua women, and not merely qua child bearer. Social reformers may well stand aghast at the neglect of and the contempt for female life shown by all religious groups in the Punjab, but no less extensive, and, possibly fraught with serious consequences to the future of the race, is the excessive pampering of females in England. . . .[80]

An attempt on their part to understand this "great disproportion among females and males" resulted in the following conclusion:

> During the past half century there has been a steady tendency for females to acquire property and sums of money in their own right. Now, whereas, a man has through the force of tradition and social custom, a tendency to spend his money for the benefit of the woman, the woman has no traditional tendency to spend her money for the benefit of the man. The consequence is that, in enjoying the benefits of little comforts and luxuries, woman in England is steadily increasing her advantage over the man, and the effect of this process on the relative male and female mortality can hardly be negligible. In the Punjab the independent woman, i.e., the orphan daughter or widow, has under the customary law, only the right to maintenance, and she may never alienate the ancestral property except for necessity, the onus of proving which is put upon her.[81]

The 'dangers' of women inheriting and controlling property were evidently clear to those brought up in the British cultural milieu; they wanted no repetition of it in Punjab. The fact that the custom of karewa snatched away whatever little right of possession women in Haryana–Punjab had come to acquire as widows, was well known to them. They were fully aware of the nature and operation of this custom in relation to women. This can be seen from a perceptive observation of F. Cunningham, a British Barrister at Law, who compiled a draft gazetteer of Rohtak district between 1870 — 74. He wrote: "*Karewa* under these conditions may be called remarriage with reference to reasons affecting the women; but such unions often take place for causes which have regard to the men only."[82] Widow-remarriage — a seemingly progressive feature — continued to be applauded by the British administrators. The practice, however, as it was encouraged to exist, merely reinforced the social ethos which safeguarded the land in the family, clan and community. The British administrators' own attitudes regarding female inheritance were closely identified with the primary concern of the colonial government which did not want to disturb the existing rural society of Punjab.

Widow remarriage: The Arya Samaj and the brahminical code

The Arya Samaj made its own contribution to the practice of karewa in this region. It provided a justification drawn from the most ancient Hindu texts and offered protection to those who accepted it. In actual practice, the Arya Samaj Jat *updeshiks* and *bhajniks* (preachers and singers) emphasized the Vedic derived niyog i.e., the levirate aspect of it, whereas widow remarriage *per se* hardly formed a part of the programme they actually adopted. In fact, one of the major reasons for the popularity and acceptability of the Arya Samaj in this region was the legitimacy that it provided to this custom, which was looked down upon with great prejudice, and even horror, by the other upper caste Hindus, especially by commercial castes. In fact the widow-remarriage programme of the Arya Samaj remained extremely restricted elsewhere in Punjab.[83] Among the followers of the Arya Samaj in Punjab, predominantly the commercial castes, a distinction was drawn between virgin widows and those widows who had lived with their husbands or had children. The remarriage of the latter evoked very strong opposition, and remained socially unacceptable to many of the Arya Samajis themselves. In Haryana alone where the Arya Samaj merely legitimized its peculiar form (karewa), could widow remarriage be called a huge success.

The peasant ethos of Haryana–Punjab sanctified widow-remarriage for reasons of its own and even celebrated it by maintaining:

titar paṅkhi bādli
bidhwā kājal rekh
wuh barse yue ghar kare
ya maṅ nahiṅ bisekh[84]

(Just as a cloud shaped like a partridge feather means that it is going to rain, so a widow using *kajal* [kohl] or paying attention to her toilette means that she is going to remarry.)

This was in sharp contrast to the high caste Hindus who under the brahminical code prohibited widow remarriage completely and considered the children of such a marriage as illegitimate. Instead they had adopted an extremely repressive system for widows which condemned them to a living hell. Such a state, especially among the child-widows, had led to a wide scale social reform agitation in Bengal, Maharashtra and the south as a response to which the Widow Remarriage Act XV of 1856 was passed by the imperial government which legalized widow-remarriage. For rural Punjab this Act had no significance, as a form of widow remarriage was not only being observed but was also legally recognized under the customary law of the land operable in the courts. As such this Act made no difference. However, like the generally forced levirate marriage of the peasant culture which successfully kept landed property intact in the family and within the patrilineal clan, the Widow-Remarriage Act also successfully retained patrilineal hold over property by taking away from the widow her limited right over it in case of remarriage.[85] Interestingly, the social reformers, whether the Arya Samajis in the north, or the others in the east or south of India, were unanimous in emphasizing the remarriage of child-widows or virgins and were also unanimous in keeping a studied silence where inheritance and property matters were concerned.

VI

'Liberal' attitudes?

The agrarian milieu of Haryana which necessitated widow remarriage, with its own peculiar features, also imparted a somewhat flexible attitude and wide social acquiescence to certain emergent practices involving women. In the given geo-economic background (the adverse female sex-ratio, the prevalence of bride price with the wife as an agricultural-labour asset) emerged the concept of the woman being married to a family rather than to an individual. Translated in terms of hard reality this concept meant that two or three brothers would share a wife;[86] thus began a systematic and extensive sexual exploitation of women. In 1904, P.J. Fagan, a district level British official observed: "It is not uncommon among Jats and lower castes for a woman to be shared in common by several brothers, though she's recognised as the wife of only the eldest of them."[87] M.L. Darling, writing about the prevalence of this custom in the 1920s and identifying it as 'polyandry', similarly observed that the latter was not "unknown."[88] However, this kind of sexual exploitation did not always go unchallenged and at least one criminal case of adultery came up in the early twentieth century in which the accused cited in his plea the existence of this social custom which allowed him sexual access to his brother's wife.[89] Cases of worse sexual exploitation were also known. E. Joseph, recording the customary law of Rohtak district, observed:

> In point of fact the girl is often older than the boy. This is not an infrequent source of trouble that comes to the courts. . . . Certain villages which need not be named, have the evil reputation of deliberately getting girls older than their boy husbands in order that the father of the latter may have illicit enjoyment of them.[90]

From the sexual point of view, the two cases cited earlier, fathers-in-law wanting to marry their widowed daughters-in-law, may be taken as attempts to legitimize an already existing relationship.[91]

An oft repeated story of those days, popular even now,[92] not only reveals this sexual exploitation to be common knowledge but also its acceptance, albeit in a humorous and highly exaggerated manner. The story concerns a new bride who had four or five *jeths* and *devars* (older and younger brothers-in-law). All of them had free sexual access to her. After fifteen to twenty days of her marriage, the bride requested her mother-in-law to identify her husband from among them. Upon this the mother-in-law came out in the *gali* (narrow street) and started to howl loudly. When questioned, she replied: "It's difficult for me to live in this house any more. I have been married for forty years, yet even now I have never asked anyone to determine the identity of my husband. This bride of fifteen days is already asking about her's."

There were two other factors which seem to have provided grounds for the general acceptability of this custom. One was the emigration of men to seek work specially in the canal colonies (which offered better agricultural opportunities) as tenants or even as labourers and second, the wide scale recruitment into the British Indian Army from this arid and famine hit region. Both these factors meant that many married women had to live without their husbands for long stretches of time. On such occasions a man handed over his wife to his brother till he returned.[93] E. Joseph, the Deputy Commissioner and Settlement Officer of Rohtak district from 1905-10, writing about the 'liberal attitude' operating behind the acceptance of this practice, which also conveniently transferred the onus of desiring sexual favours on women, disclosed:

> A most respectable Jat of my acquaintance procured his son's resignation from the army because his wife could not be trusted alone, as he explained, all his younger sons were too small to assist in dealing with the difficulty.[94]

It was also considered a "common practice" to beget children from a devar or jeth while the husband was away serving in the army.[95] This fact, a logical corollary of the sexually exploitative custom, had to be accepted in the rural society of the time. A popular local story is illustrative of this acceptance. The dialogues proceed as follows:

First man : After how many years have you come home?
Second man : After three years.
First man : And how old is your child?
Second man : Two years.
First man : How come . . .?
Second man : (mildly) Well I had sent home my *dhoti*.[96]

Such is the reason why despite severe war casualties among the pick of the population and the absence of so large a proportion of the able bodied men from their homes, the birth rate was not affected.

The sexual exploitation of menial (low caste) women by the other agriculturists was a common feature which does not need much comment. However, interestingly, the difficulties experienced in obtaining a wife for the reasons explained above, led many agriculturists of this region to take wives from among the lower castes as well. Although it never became a norm as such or was practised on a wide scale, the economically hard up agriculturists were known to take recourse to it. For example, a Jat was stated to marry almost any woman he could.[97] Frequently these were women from the Chamar caste.[98] However, a faint pretence was kept that the girl was of his caste and an equally faint acceptance followed. A local belief maintains:

Jāṭ ek samunder hai aur jo bhi dariya es
saṁunder meiṅ paṭti hai woh samunder ki hi
bun jāti hai [99]

(The Jat is like an ocean and whichever river falls into this ocean loses its identity and becomes the ocean itself.)

The children of a Churhi or a Chamaran, whoever was accepted as a wife by a Jat, were called Jats though many times they were ridiculed as *churhi ke* or *chamaran ke.*[100] Such general social acceptance, despite derogatory references, is due to the fact that these social groups could not afford to, and indeed did not, attach undue importance to caste purity in case it was breached by the man; a woman, as pointed out earlier, was not allowed this freedom. This is aptly referred to in a local proverb:

beeraṅ ki kai jaat [101]

(Women have no caste.)

Moreover, within this subsistence economy the social practice was rationalized by maintaining the "*roṭi to bun jāgi, naam to chul jāgā, dono ka guzārā ho jāgā*"[102] (at least the food will be cooked; the family name will be carried on, both will somehow manage to live together). This practice of taking wives from lower castes was greatly frowned upon by British officials who declared it "a kind of disreputable matrimonial agency."[103] Given to applauding the "magnificient physique" of the so called superior agriculturist castes in agrarian and military professions, they actually bemoaned its biological 'deterioration' because of this practice.[104]

VII

Some further indices of the low status of women

Clearly, in Haryana a woman had come to be recognized and coveted as an economic necessity though only as a part of a man's property, and she was equated with food, a house and animals. A local proverb from Rohtak showed this:

saṅṭhi chaoul, bhaiṅs dūdh, ghar kulwanti nār,
chauthe tarang ki, bihist nishani char[105]

(Red rice, buffalo milk, a good woman in the house,
and a horse to ride, these four are heavenly things.)

Women provided labour for the peasant household, as well as for cultivation and for animal husbandry, all the while operating inside the male-dominated norms of the purdah culture — a culture of secluding women.[106] This culture represented a spatial boundary between man and woman, and was visible in Haryana in the normal six inches to a yard long ghunghat for the woman. However, the peasant economy, in which women provided an indispensable source of labour and thus could not be kept secluded, accommodated it by allowing her to work "shoulder to shoulder" with her man, but only in a ghunghat. Even the progressive Arya Samaj was not known (in this region) to preach against women observing ghunghat.[107]

The ghunghat culture, as perhaps somewhat distinct from the purdah culture, accepted and took for granted women's extreme labour without affording them any freedom. This attitude can be seen to be operating in other spheres as well. For example, in education, a region which had considered literacy to be useless ("*kālā akshar bhaiṅs barobar,*"[108] i.e., lack of literacy), was slowly realizing the importance of education, but only for boys. For the women it maintained:

beerbāṇni ghar ki bāṇni[109]

(A woman who remains at home adorns it.)

Generally used in reference to education, it emphasized that a woman should remain a housewife only and not jeopardize her position by stepping out of the house. Education therefore was looked upon with suspicion and was associated with an inevitable crumbling of the social structure.[110] Even the Arya Samaj which did a great deal for women's education in Punjab,[111] was quiet in its Haryana region. The Arya Samaj established Gurukuls but primarily for boys. The Kanya Pathshalas for girls were negligible in number and experienced a perennial shortage of both teachers and students.[112]

This social attitude also kept women away from any decision making process whether it was at home or in the wider sphere of *jaat-biradari* (caste-brotherhood), or in the village itself. At home they were never consulted even in matters of buying or selling of milch cattle, though cattle tending was generally an exclusive work domain of women.[113] And although women put in an equal if not larger share of work in the earning of money, its expenditure was the special and exclusive reserve of men, and was dictated to the minutest detail. An Ambala proverb maintained:

lekhā māwaṅ dhiāṅda
bakhshisha lakh laketi[114]

(Even if one gives away lakhs in charity,
a wife and a daughter must be held accountable.)

All that a woman had control over was merely a few rupees which her visiting relatives might have gifted to her.[115] Summing up this social milieu, the compiler of local customs in this region maintained:

> . . . in the present phase of customary law, especially among the Hindu Jat tribes, there is a strong disinclination to admit any independent power of the wife even over movables, however, acquired by her, apart from the wishes of her husband, who generally exercises an unfettered control over her estate.[116]

The customary law prevailing among the agriculturists regarded the wife and anything associated with her, whether her ornaments or her earnings, if they existed, as the property of her husband, about which she had no independent voice at all.

The attitude of keeping women secluded from all decision making, as reflected at home, was also projected outside. The women were never a part of the caste or the village *panchayat* (village council) although certain issues relating to them were frequently brought to it for decision making. These matters concerned women who had made runaway marriages with other caste men or had simply run away with someone belonging to their own village.[117] Such self assertion broke too many social norms and customs and was never accepted. The women were also not allowed to enter the village *chaupal*, that is the place where the panchayat customarily sat. The guarding of the chaupal as forbidden ground for women symbolized their complete seclusion, subordination and inferiority.

VIII

Conclusion

From the above account emerges a picture of Haryanavi peasant women perhaps best exemplified in their high visibility as the full working partners of men — but only in a ghunghat. The reality of ghunghat culture exposes the apparent contradiction in the co-existence of indices of high status and of low status for women in the region. The indices of high status like bride-price, widow remarriage, equal economic work partnership and a 'permissive' sexual climate, all emerge as customs evolved, dictated and enforced by the dominant peasantry of this region to suit its own peculiar socio-economic needs. They hardly had any relation to the needs of women. Therefore, in reality these indices were bereft of all validity as markers of high status and value. The customs encouraged by the British administrative policies, usually interpreted as indices of high status when combined with the discriminating practices also already operating, i.e., the low status indices, together became responsible for lowering the status of women in the colonial period. However, even within this tightly controlled peasant culture, as aided and abetted by the colonial government, occurred women's self assertion and protest against a system in which they shared the work but not its fruits. This can be seen in the widow's determination to hold on to her limited right over landed property and the challenge which the women posed to her marriage or to her remarriage in its levirate form. Women's perception of peasant customs as repressive also exposes the claims of high status indices. So outwardly the women of Haryana who have been projected as equal work companions of men and whose role has been celebrated by the British administrators, continued to remain men's inferior and subordinate counterparts — their status not above that of unpaid agricultural labourers.

It is perhaps needless to emphasize that once the socio-economic forces changed, the cultural ethos and the resultant customs and attitudes which these forces had moulded and determined also changed. This can be seen quite clearly in the wide scale changes which have occurred in Haryana in the post-colonial period which have catapulted this region from a backward subsistence level economy to the second richest state in India in the wake of the Green Revolution. These changes have had deep rooted socio-cultural effects specially in relation to women, in either completely or partially diluting many of the customs and social attitudes described above, in retaining or sharpening many others, or in introducing new ones. Apart from the wide scale changes in the socio-economic sphere the role of the independent Indian state may also be underlined. Just as the colonial state's policies had selectively reinforced social norms and customs, the post-independence state policies have had a revolutionizing effect on rural society. A single example, the introduction of the Hindu Code Bill of 1956, is illustrative.

Two of its provisions had direct bearing on Haryana's rural society. One was the Hindu Succession Act which gave equal right of succession to male and female heirs and second was the divorce clause which allowed Hindu women for the first time the right to seek divorce on a variety of grounds. The effects of these acts, which reversed the hitherto carefully maintained traditions and customs of society, need to be studied in the framework of wider socio-economic changes. Briefly speaking, their effects can be seen, on the one hand, in the violent reaction of a greatly strengthened patriarchal society forging newer weapons for the social control of women involving even physical violence and bloodshed, and on the other hand, in the greater intensification of women's resistance seen, apart from other evidence of self assertion, in the large influx of court cases involving inheritance, property and divorce. An understanding of the post-colonial period would require a separate study, which I propose to undertake later. Such a study alone would determine the extent and direction of change in various spheres involving women that is visible in the Haryana of today as compared to what existed in the colonial period.

NOTES

1. The agriculturist castes of Haryana, as notified under the Punjab Alienation of Land Act, 1901, were: Jat, Rajput, Pathan, Sayyed, Gujar, Ahir, Biloch, Ror, Moghal, Mali, Taga, Saini, Chauhan, Arain, Gaud Brahmin and Qoreshi.
2. For the concept and features of a 'dominant caste', see M.N. Srinivas, "The Dominant Caste in Rampura," *American Anthropologist*, 61 (Feb. 1959), pp. 1-16. M.N. Srinivas specifically mentions Jats as the 'dominant caste' in Punjab-Haryana in his *Caste and Modern India and Other Essays* (Bombay: Asia Publishing House, 1962), p. 90.
3. For a detailed discussion on 'Jat dominance' in Haryana and for the different sources consulted see Prem Chowdhry, "Jat Domination in South-East Punjab: Socio-Economic Basis of Jat Politics in a Punjab District," *The Indian Economic and Social History Review*, 19, nos. 3 & 4 (Oct.-Dec. 1983), pp. 325-46.
4. For details, see Prem Chowdhry, "The Advantages of Backwardness: Colonial Policy and Agriculture in Haryana," *Indian Economic and Social History Review*, 23, no. 3 (Oct.-Dec. 1986), pp. 236-88.
5. *Rohtak District Gazetteer, 1910*, vol. 3 A (Lahore, 1911), p. 68.
6. Calculated from the Board of Economic Inquiry, *The Size and Distribution of Agricultural Holdings in the Punjab* (Lahore, 1925), p. 16.
7. Jainarayan Verma, *Hariyanavi Lokoktiyan: Shastriye Vishaleshan* (Delhi: Adarsh Sahitya Prakashan, 1972), p. 123.
8. Ibid., p. 96.
9. Ibid., p. 30. The birth of a daughter was regarded as the equivalent of a decree of Rs. 2000 against her father. See M.L. Darling, *The Punjab Peasant in Prosperity and Debt.*, 2nd ed; (1925; rpt., New Delhi: Manohar Book Service, 1978), p. 5.

10. For details of female-male sex ratio see *Census of India: Punjab, 1931*, vol 17, pt. I, Report, p. 157.
11. The British officials agreed that among Jats, specially the Sikh Jats and Rajputs, female infanticide had been widely prevalent at the time of annexation of the province, but by 1901, it had dwindled to insignificant numbers. By 1931, it was confined to some individual families or groups of families which, according to them, did not influence the sex-ratio as such. See *Census of India: Punjab, 1931*, ibid., p. 154.
12. For details of these factors and other contributory reasons see *Census of India: Punjab, 1931*, ibid., p. 156.
13. Ratio of females per thousand males in different provinces of British India in 1931:
Punjab: 831; North West Frontier Provinces: 843; United Provinces: 906; Bihar and Orissa: 909; Bengal: 924; Madras: 1025; Bombay: 909; Central Provinces: 1000; Central India Agency: 948; Rajputana: 908. Although the proportion of the sexes was not uniform in different parts of Punjab or in the different castes (for example, the proportion of females among Jats had always been lower than among other castes), by and large the figures given for the whole of Punjab correspond to the detailed figures available for the different districts of Haryana. Source: *Census of India: Punjab, 1931*, ibid., p. 159. For the exact number of females per thousand males in different districts of Haryana see sub-table no. I, p. 163.
14. W.E. Purser and H.C. Fanshawe, *Report on the Revised Land Revenue Settlement: Rohtak District, 1873-79* (Lahore, 1880), p. 65; hereafter *Revised Land Revenue Settlement, Rohtak.*
15. *Rohtak District Gazetteer, 1910*, p. 96.
16. R. Maconachie, ed. *Selected Agricultural Proverbs of the Punjab* (Delhi: Imperial Medical Hall Press, 1870), p. 264.
17. *Census of India: Punjab, 1931*, p. 217.
18. Darling, *Punjab Peasant*, p. 35.
19. *Revised Land Revenue Settlement, Rohtak*, p. 53.
20. Darling, *Punjab Peasant*, p. 35.
21. Ibid., p. 33.
22. *Census of India: Punjab, 1931*, p. 217.
23. Ibid., p. 217.
24. Ibid. p. 217.
25. Darling, *Punjab Peasant*, p. 35. See also *The Settlement Report of the Ambala District*, 1893 (Lahore, 1893), p. 12.

26. *Rohtak District Gazetteer, 1910*, p. 77.
27. *Census of India: Punjab, 1931*, p. 217.
28. See Rushbrook William, Director, Central Bureau of Information, Govt. of India, *India in 1921-22* (Calcutta; Govt. Printing, 1922), p. 222.
29. *Census of India: Punjab and Delhi, 1921*, vol. 15 pt. I, Report, p. 363. Also see, *India in 1929-30* (Calcutta, 1931), p. 117.
30. *Census of India: Punjab and Delhi, 1921*, p. 363.
31. *India in 1929-30*, p. 119.
32. Darling, *Punjab Peasant*, p. 53.
33. Ibid., p. 53.
34. Personal interview with R.M. Hooda, Rohtak, 1 June 1986. Born in 1933, village Makrauli-Kalan, Rohtak Dist., a graduate from Jat College Rohtak (B.A., LLB) R.M. Hooda has been practising law since 1962 at the district level. He has ancestral land, 4-5 acres, in the village.
35. Verma, *Haryanavi Lokoktiyan*, p. 43. The fact of the wife being older than the husband also arose out of levirate marriages, described later on, in which a much older widow married her *devar* (husband's younger brother), who could be younger than her by four to ten years.
36. Darling, *Punjab Peasant*, p. 49.
37. Shanker Lal Yadav, *Haryana Pradesh Ka Loksahitya* (Allahabad: Central Book Agency, 1960), p. 423.
38. *Rohtak District Gazetteer, 1910*, p. 85.
39. Darling, *Punjab Peasant*, p. 50.
40. *Rohtak District Gazetteer, 1910*, p. 91.
41. W.M. Rattingan, *A Digest of Civil Law for the Punjab Chiefly Based on the CustomaryLaw as at Present Ascertained*, revised by Harbans Lal Sarin and Kundan Lal Pandit, 2nd ed. (1880; rpt. Allahabad: The University Book Agency, 1966), p. 737.
42. For an analytical study of bride-price and its socio-economic aspects see Indira Rajaraman, "Economics of Bride-Price and Dowry," *Economic and Political Weekly* 18, no. 8 (19 Feb. 1983), pp. 275-79.
43. For details of similar cases in Gujarat see Alice Clark, "Limitation on Female Life Chances in Rural Central Gujarat. *Indian Economic and Social History Review*, 20, no. 1 (March 1983), pp. 1-25.
44. *Revised Land Revenue Settlement, Rohtak*, p. 49.

45. Niyog was a practice of levirate marriage. Later, as during the Mahabharata times, niyog came to signify cohabitation by the wife with men other than her husband under certain specific conditions like impotency of the husband and the 'moral' and 'religious duty' to beget sons to continue the family line. See, for instance, the case of Kunti.
46. For details see C.L. Tupper, *The Punjab Customary Law* (Calcutta: Govt. Printing, 1881), vol.2, pp.93, 123; see also E. Joseph, *Customary Law of the Rohtak District, 1910* (Lahore: Govt. Printing, 1911), p. 45.
47. Joseph, *Customary Law Rohtak*, p. 46.
48. *Karnal District Gazetteer, 1976* (Chandigarh, 1976), p. 85.
49. Rattingan, *A Digest of Civil Law*, p. xvii.
50. *Census of India, Punjab and Delhi, 1911*, vol. 17, pt. 1, Report, p. 219.
51. *Karnal District Gazetteer, 1976*, p. 85.
52. *Rohtak District Gazetteer, 1910*, p. 85. All those who were interviewed for this article also confirmed this.
53. *Revised Land Revenue Settlement, Rohtak*, p. 53. Generally said in relation to the Jats, this proverb highlights the social ease about widow-remarriage.
54. Verma, *Haryanavi Lokoktiyan*, p. 43.
55. Rattingan, *A Digest of Civil Law*, p. 82.
56. Ibid. Nothing more is known about this case.
57. Joseph, *Customary Law Rohtak*, pp. 54-55 Until puberty a child bride stayed on with her natal family; *muklawa*, which customarily took place several years after the wedding ceremony, was the entry and establishment of the wife in her husband's home when the marriage was consummated.
58. Ibid., p. 45.
59. Maconachiė, *Agricultural Proverbs*, p. 280. This proverb is from Kangra, but according to R. Maconachie it revealed "a universal sentiment" of Punjab.
60. *Rohtak District Gazetteer, 1910*, p. 90. In certain areas and among specific agricultural castes of Haryana and Punjab different forfeiture customs applied. The customary norm which was to be operative in a particular case had to be decided by the court, on the basis of the custom applicable to the concerned parties. In any case the final result was the same, since the customary law prevailing amongst agricultural castes of Punjab regarded the wife's personal property as merged with that of the husband, he was also deemed entitled to all

the wife's earnings and even her ornaments. In other words, the woman both by marriage and by remarriage lost all control over moveable and immoveable property. See Rattingan, *A Digest of Civil Law*, pp. 204, 427, 747.

61. *Hissar Dist. Gazetteer, 1907*, vol. 2 A (Lahore, 1907), p. 229.
62. Joseph, *Customary Law Rohtak*, pp. 136-7.
63. Ibid., p. 40.
64. Maconachie, *Agricultural Proverbs*, p. 253.
65. J.M. Douie, *The Punjab Land Administration Manual*, 2nd ed. (1908; rpt. Chandigarh: Govt. of Punjab, 1971), pp. 270-71.
66. Joseph, *Customary Law Rohtak*, pp. 70-71.
67. Douie, *Punjab Land Administration*, pp. 270-71.
68. Ibid.
69. Tupper, *Punjab Customary Law*, vol. 1, pp. 17-19.
70. Ibid., vol. 2, pp. 86-88, 99-100.
71. *Rohtak District Gazetteer, 1910*, p. 88.
72. M.S. Leigh, *The Punjab and the War* (Lahore: Govt. Printing, 1922), pp. 61-62.
73. See Inquiry conducted by M.L. Darling, Financial Commissioner of Punjab, dated 3 June 1936, *Darling Papers* (South Asian Centre, Cambridge), Box 5, F.No. 1.
74. Ibid. See letter of Laithwait, Private Secretary to the Viceroy, 3 June 1936. The village surveys undertaken by the Punjab Board of Economic Inquiry 1920-40, also showed that in seven out of eight villages, in different districts of this region, the average area per owner had decreased noticeably in the last 30 years.
75. Darling, *Punjab Peasant*, pp. 240-41, 251-53.
76. *Rohtak District Gazetteer, 1910*, p. 90.
77. *Census of India: Punjab and Delhi, 1921*, p. 244.
78. Joseph, *Customary Law Rohtak*, pp. 40-41. See also *Gurgaon District Gazetteer, 1910* (Lahore 1911), p. 58.
79. Joseph, *Customary Law Rohtak*, pp. 35, 40.
80. *Census of India: Punjab and Delhi, 1921*, p. 234.
81. See views of Col. Forster, Director of Public Health, Punjab, in f.n., ibid., p. 234.
82. Cited in *Rohtak District Gazetteer, 1883-84* (Calcutta, n.d.), p. 51.

83. For details, see Kenneth W. Jones, *Arya Dharma: Hindu Consciousness in Nineteenth Century Punjab* (Delhi: Manohar Book Service, 1976), pp. 218-19.
84. Maconachie, *Agricultural Proverbs*, p. 46.
85. For the effects of customary law and Hindu law on widows and the remarriage question see Lucy Carrol, "Law, Custom and Statutory Social Reform: The Hindu Women's Remarriage Act of 1856," *Indian Economic and Social History Review*, 20, no. 4 (Oct.-Dec. 1983) pp. 363-89.
86. Darling, *Punjab Peasant*, p. 51. K.L. Rathi also confirmed the "sharing of women among brothers" to be a "common phenomenon" in the 1920s. He cited several cases in different villages in which there was only one married brother, but other brothers had free access to his wife. (Personal interview with K.L. Rathi, New Delhi, 24 May 1986. Born in 1912, village Rajlugarhi, Sonepat, K.L. Rathi is currently practising law in the Supreme Court. His large joint family had been in possession of 100 bighas of land.) R.M. Hooda was also of the same opinion. He saw the stark poverty of the region as responsible for this practice (personal interview with R.M. Hooda).
87. *Hissar District Gazetteer, 1904* (Lahore, 1908), p. 65.
88. Darling, *Punjab Peasant*, p. 51.
89. *Rohtak District Gazetteer, 1910*, p. 88. Verdict given not known.
90. Joseph, *Customary Law Rohtak*, p. 19.
91. R.M. Hooda also confirmed that this practice was widespread in the past. He, however, put the onus on the "inability of the young immature husband to satisfy his fully physically mature wife." According to him there were always some women who protested against the sexual demands of their fathers-in-law. Such women, he commented, were generally "packed-off" to the parents — an act which was considered to be a matter of "ultimate shame" for the natal family of the woman in question (personal interview with R.M. Hooda).
92. Personal interview with Smt. Chhotu Devi, village Dujjana, Rohtak district, 6 June 1986. Born in 1921, Chhotu Devi's late husband was a big landowner in Dujjana.
93. Darling, *Punjab Peasant*, p. 51.
94. *Rohtak District Gazetteer, 1910,* see f.n. p. 88.
95. Personal interview with R.M. Hooda.
96. Personal interview with Smt. Shanti Devi, Delhi, 9 June 1986. Born in 1921, Sonepat, Shanti Devi married a soldier who rose to the rank of a

colonel in the Indian Army. A *dhoti* is a length of cloth worn as a lower garment by men.

97. Darling, *Punjab Peasant*, p. 51.

98. Joseph, *Customary Law Rohtak*, p. 60. According to R.M. Hooda, low caste women, specially from among the Chamars worked shoulder to shoulder with the Jats in the fields. This led to "sexual promiscuity" due to the innumerable opportunities for close physical proximity. Because of this a large number of children among the Chamars came to be fathered by Jats and an equally large number among Jats by the Chamars. This fact also led many Jats to take wives from among the Chamars. According to Hooda, this practice continues to this day (personal interview with R.M. Hooda). E. Joseph, the British Settlement Officer of Rohtak district, also mentions a case brought to his notice in which a Jat woman was physically involved with a Chuhra (menial), and she was thrown out of the house for this reason. See Joseph, *Customary Law, Rohtak*, p. 42.

99. Personal interview with K.L. Rathi.

100. Personal interview with Shamsher Singh, Rohtak, 23 May 1986; a Jat agriculturist, Shamsher Singh is the owner of 12 1/2 bighas of good cultivable land in Haryana.

101. Verma, *Haryanavi Lokoktiyan*, p. 120.

102. Personal interview with Shamsher Singh.

103. *Census of India: Punjab and Delhi, 1911*, vol. 17, pt. 1, Report, p. 216.

104. Darling, *Punjab Peasant*, p. 51.

105. *Land Revenue Settlement, Rohtak*, p. 54.

106. For details of purdah culture, see Uma Chakravarti, "Pativrata" *Seminar*, no. 318 (Feb. 1986), pp. 17-20.

107. Personal interview with K.L. Rathi.

108. Verma, *Haryanavi Lokoktiyan*, p. 46.

109. Ibid., p. 46.

110. *Karnal District Gazetteer*, p. 87.

111. Kenneth W. Jones, *Arya Dharma*, pp. 107-8, 215-19. For the nature of education imparted to women by the Arya Samaj, see Madhu Kishwar, "Arya Samaj and Women's Education: Kanya Mahavidalya, Jallandar," Review of women studies in *The Economic and Political Weekly*, 21, no. 17 (26 April 1986), pp. 9-24.

112. Personal interview with K.L. Rathi.

113. Personal interview with R.M. Hooda.
114. Maconachie, *Agricultural Proverbs,* p. 209.
115. Personal interview with R.M. Hooda.
116. W.M. Rattingan, *A Digest of Civil Law,* p. 747.
117. Significantly, no marriage alliance was possible in the same vilage and consequently such cases were greatly frowned upon (Personal interview with R.M. Hooda).

Rural Women in Oudh 1917–47: *Baba Ramchandra and the Women's Question**

KAPIL KUMAR

OUDH (present day central Uttar Pradesh) witnessed a massive peasant uprising during the early 1920s — an outcome of the oppression and exploitation faced by the peasants at the hands of the British Raj and its allies — the *taluqdars* (landlord of a *taluqa,* a group of villages).[1] Amongst the peasants was a doubly exploited section — women. On the one hand, women faced all the miseries of the tenants and agricultural labourers and, on the other, they also suffered as women due to the rigid traditional structure of rural society. The peasant movement, organized under the leadership of Baba Ram Chandra,[2] not only brought to the fore the oppressed condition of the peasantry as a whole but also, more specifically, the question of the position of women. Official documents and private papers provide some evidence of the various issues that formed part of the movement in rural Oudh.[3]

In spite of the advances made in the field of historical investigation, the role of women from the oppressed social strata — particularly peasant women — in transforming economic, social and political life in the countryside stands neglected in historical analyses. This study attempts to highlight some of these aspects. However, in approaching the subject, an exclusively gender-based approach cannot explain social reality because rural women were (and are) not a homogenous social group. There were women taluqdars in the region who were as oppressive towards their tenants — male or

* I want to thank Tanika Sarkar, Sunita Tiwari Jassal, Gyanesh Kudaisiya, Sudesh Vaid, Kumkum Sangari and Deepti Mehrotra. Discussions with them helped to give final shape to the paper. An earlier version of this paper was presented at the Women's Studies Conference, Chandigarh, Oct. 1986 and History Department, Delhi University, Jan. 1988.

female — as any other taluqdar.[4] Similarly, there were women moneylenders whose profession firmly puts them in the category of an oppressive class. The women of these categories, due to their control over the means of production, had a dominant position in society with greater privileges and social security. The problems of these women and those of women from landlord families who had no direct control over the means of production, were largely related to social customs and patriarchy while those faced by women cultivators and agricultural labourers were economic as well as patriarchal. That is why a gender-class approach to the "history of feminism" is more useful than "feminist history".[5] This study is divided into sections dealing with the oppression of peasant women, Baba Ram Chandra's views on women and his personal experience, various issues related to women, political awakening amongst them and finally their participation in the freedom movement.

I

By the Taluqdari Settlement of 1858 the British government, in order to establish a social base in the Oudh countryside, recognized taluqdars as the "natural leaders" of the masses with absolute ownership rights in the land. Thus, the peasantry was converted into tenantry and agricultural labourers. The peasantry had made common cause with the princes and taluqdars in opposing the British. But the ultimate result of this struggle was that the princes and taluqdars not only compromised with the British but threw in their lot with the colonial power. The peasantry then onwards faced double oppression both by feudal lords and by the imperial government.

I have elsewhere discussed in detail the various forms of oppression faced by the tenantry.[6] Here I shall confine myself to the issue of exploitation of women. The number of women in the rural areas of Oudh in 1921 was 5,497,147 and that of men 5,851,754. Amongst ordinary cultivators, there were 1,635,036 female and 2,895,552 male actual workers, with 3,711,437 dependants.[7] There were only 2.1 per cent secure tenants, while 97.9 per cent cultivators were tenants-at-will, mostly with a seven year lease. Amongst these, 85.8 could be termed as poor peasants, 11.3 as middle peasants and only 2.9 as rich peasants.[8] Amongst agricultural labourers, 3,48,600 were women, 3,79,910 men along with 3,78,885 dependants. In the districts of Rai Bareily, Fyzabad, Gonda, Baharaich, Unnao, Sultanpur and Pratapgarh (i.e. in 7 of the 12 districts of Oudh), women outnumbered men as agricultural labourers. The agricultural labourers were a socially degraded class not only because of their occupation which kept them at the lowest economic stratum, but also because of the caste-structure. The bulk of the rural proletariat was drawn from 'low castes' who for generations had been prevented by the feudal aristocracy from owning land for cultivation in order to facilitate the supply of labour. They were not only paupers and serfs but 'untouchables' as well. The extreme economic and social pressure, to an extent, explains the large number of women amongst the labourers coming out to work. Moreover, the 'low castes' as compared to the 'high castes' were in greater number in these districts of Oudh. The number of actual workers whose income was from rent of agricultural land was 20,588 women and 57,279 men. There were 2,283 women moneylenders, as compared to 7,953 men in the trade.[9]

Foremost among the oppressive practices was the taking of *nazarana* (extra premium on rent) by landlords. This evil had penetrated to such an extent that some tenants were painfully forced to sell their daughters *(kanya vikray)* in order to raise nazarana:

> Bechai Misir sold his 12 year old daughter to a husband of 60 years for Rs 300. Ishri Dubey sold one daughter five year old to a husband 40 years and another daughter, aged 12 years, to a husband 30 years for Rs 300 each.
>
> The widow of Mahabadeo sold her daughter for Rs 200. Mahabir Brahman married his seven year old daughter to a husband aged 40 years and got Rs 200. The minor son of Thakur Din (deceased) sold his five year old sister to a husband 40 years old for Rs 300. Gayadin Dubey, as a last resort to save his family from ruin, sold his 10 year old daughter to a husband about 40 years old for Rs 400.[10]

We only have records of such cases reported from Pratapgarh and that too only for the years 1919-20. They came to light during the enquiry conducted by the Deputy Commissioner (D.C.) to investigate the causes of agrarian disturbances in the district. No such efforts were made in other parts of Oudh, but it appears that the results would not have been different. The vicious practice of kanya vikray was intensified by the fact that "there was enormous disparity in years between the ages of wife and husband" and the girl's marriage was often "consecrated before the funeral pyre of her husband." Kanya vikray "is considered the most heinous sin amongst orthodox Hindus and punishment is eternal hell for the father." The poor fathers were forced to take "recourse to sale as a last resort to preserve the family holding from slipping away."[11] Thus, in order to avoid a living hell in this world, they preferred incurring eternal damnation in the next world by selling their daughters. For the girls, it was a miserable existence. The parents who committed the sin, realized this, but felt helpless in the face of an oppressive economic and social structure. Many broke down in tears in the presene of the D.C. while narrating their pathetic accounts of such transactions.[12]

Murdafaroshi (selling of holdings after the death of the lease holder) was another weapon of the *taluqdari* (conferment of proprietorial rights in land) system and the worst victims were again women. Legally, the heirs of a lease-holder could not be evicted till the end of the seven year lease, but in practice immediately after the death of the lease-holder, the holding was let out to the highest bidder at enhanced rates by the landlord. The heir could save the holding only by paying nazarana. But many a time even after payment the holding was not restored. It is worth mentioning some cases related to women heirs:

a) A widow was evicted after her son's death, since the holding was in his name. Another tenant gave Rs 200 nazarana to get the holding, while she had to beg for her food.

b) A woman paid Rs 21 as nazarana to the landlord, yet she was forcibly evicted and rendered destitute.

c) A holding of four *bighas* (a measure of land) was taken away from a woman and thus a family of eleven was left destitute.

d) A woman with five children paid Rs 25 to the *zilledar* (landlord's manager) to get back her holding. Another Rs 25 was demanded and, on this pretext, she was refused possession.

e) A Gadaria woman's husband and his brother died of influenza. Twenty eight rupees stood as arrears in their name. The widow was forced to pay Rs 60 as nazarana but she could not get her 10 *biswas* (1/20th of a bigha) of land.

f) Six hundred rupees were demanded as nazarana from a woman and since she could not pay the sum she was evicted.

g) A peasant paid Rs 80 nazarana and obtained a holding in 1916. Next year, he died and his widow was evicted.

h) In 1915, a woman paid seven rupees per bigha as nazarana on the assurance that she would not be evicted. When her husband died she was asked to pay Rs 50 and, on her failure to pay, she was evicted.

i) Mussamat Sumera paid Rs 100 as nazarana. The money was sent by her sons working in Calcutta. Her land was not restored to her.

j) One hundred rupees were demanded from a woman for retaining her holding. She was told that another tenant was willing to pay the amount to acquire her holding. As she could not pay and as the landlord was insistent, she committed suicide.

k) A landlord got some *maufi* (free grant) land assessed to rent. Mussamat Rahmani, a very poor *faqiran,* (female religious mendicant; maufi land grants were sometimes given to religious mendicants) had to pay Rs 30 as nazarana to save her ancestral holding of three bighas. This caused "considerable resentment in the village," as it was considered a "sacrilege to lay hands on a faqiran's property."

l) A woman was evicted by the landlords's agent and left destitute. Her son had to migrate to Bombay to seek employment.[13]

During World War I, the taluqdars spared no effort to aid the British. In this process, they robbed their tenantry in the name of *larai chanda* (war donation) and *bharti chanda* (recruitment cess). False promises were made in order to lure peasants into recruitment. But the heirs of those who died at the front were evicted under the murdafaroshi proceedings. Numerous instances of such excesses can be cited.

a) Two members of a family died at the front. The widow of one of them was evicted under murdafaroshi. It was only at the intervention of the D.C. that the landlord returned 18 bighas to her. The D.C. commented: "It would have been a very hard case had the landholder not agreed."

b) A peasant died while his son was at the front. The landholder, a sub-inspector in the police, forcibly evicted the peasant's widow.

c) A soldier was killed at the front. His mother was evicted from their holding.

d) A pensioned soldier obtained a lease after paying nazarana. On his death, the widow was evicted from her holding of three bighas. With her two children, she wept bitterly before the D.C., as she had no means of livelihood whatsoever.[14]

Very often fights would break out among tenants due to the unscruplous practices of landlords. A man died leaving behind his heir, a minor daughter, under the guardianship of her uncle. Without formally evicting her, the landlord gave the lease to another peasant after taking Rs 250 nazarana. When the peasant went to take possession of the holding, the relatives of the minor girl opposed him and this resulted in a riot.[15] Here we find the relatives defending the rights of a minor girl because the encroacher was an outsider. However, in addition to harassment by the landlord, his zilledar and agents, women heirs—particularly widows—were very often harassed by male relatives who wanted to grab their holdings and property. Certain evidences show that women did hold leases in their own names but in most cases, they inherited them either as widows, mothers or daughters of the deceased male members of the family. This gave them a certain status as women controlling property/land. But due to the lack of permanent occupancy rights both women and men tenants were equally insecure.

The taluqdars and their agents imposed fines on the tenantry, both women and men, according to their whims. *Kumarg* (moral delinquency) was one such extortion realized from tenants accused of having: "illicit relations" with women from other families. These "illicit" relations included not only cases of adultery but also of intercaste sexual relations. Innocent peasants were often accused of having relations with this or that woman and, from fear of the landlords' power on the one hand and of social humiliation on the other, the peasants yielded to threats by landlords and paid fines as is borne out by the following instances:

a) Matabadal was fined Rs 51 because his name was associated with a Kurmi woman.

b) In a joint tenancy, after the death of one partner, his widow was made to complain, at the instance of the landlord, that her husband's partner was having relations with her. The partner was fined Rs 51.

c) A charge was brought against the daughter of one tenant that she was on terms of familiarity with one Nidhan Singh. The father of the girl was fined Rs 51 and one neem tree in addition.

d) In village Aspur Deosara, when an innocent tenant refused to pay kumarg, he was dragged and beaten up by the zilledar and his hut was burnt.[16]

At any given time we find a sizeable number of women taluqdars in the districts of Oudh.[17] In the estates managed by women taluqdars, as in those held by men, the peasants faced all kinds of hardships and exploitation. A *thakurain* taluqdar (Rajput woman landholder) in Pratapgarh had a boil on her leg which turned septic. She distributed Rs 15,000 to *sants* (religious men) who prayed for her recovery. The entire sum was realized from the peasants in the form of *pakawan* (a septic cess).[19] Thakurain Ajit Koer of Patti Saifabad had raised rents illegally by 150 per cent in her estate.[19] The thakurain of Amargarh estate was a known offender of the Rent Act and practised all kinds of oppression on her tenants. In 1936, she even had the houses of her tenants looted.[20] We have the petition of Mussamat Valli, widow of Brahma, whose five bighas of land were forcibly taken in 1938 by the thakurain and given to the zilledar for planting an orchard.[21] These instances indicate the class character of the women taluqdars. The control over land was the ultimate factor in determining relations between landlords and tenants and, at times, between tenants and agricultural labourers. Thus we find in the Baba Ram Chandra papers the case (July 1939) of a Brahmin peasant woman who would not pay wages to labourers. She was asked to appear before the Kisan Sabha (peasant organization). Her failure to do so was deemed an insult to the Sabha. The entire village socially boycotted her and this made her acknowledge the authority of the Sabha. She ultimately agreed to come under its protection.[22]

Another issue of concern, which indicates the status of women, was the marriage of infants and children common in the Oudh countryside. This is borne out from the following figures in Table I.

Table I

Marital status in Oudh (1921)

Age group	*Married males*	*Married females*	*Total*
0-1	118	133	251
1-5	4,261	4,674	8,935
5-10	57,087	85,542	142,629
10-15	163,052	256,548	419,600
15-20	235,006	343,666	578,672

SOURCE: Census of India 1921, United Provinces, Part 2.

Closely linked with the practice of child marriage was the problem of the large number of child widows in Oudh. Table 2 gives the figures of widows and widowers in Oudh.

Table 2

Marital status in Oudh (1921)

Age group	*Widows*	*Widowers*
0-1	23	2
1-5	271	174
5-10	3,611	2,562
10-15	8,736	7,261
15-20	14,052	13,047
Total	26,683	23,046

SOURCE: Census of India 1921, United Provinces, Part 2.

We shall discuss a little later how these inter-linked issues were taken up by the Kisan Sabha.

II

During 1917-18, Baba Ram Chandra came to the Oudh countryside and organized and led the most militant peasant movement of northern India in the course of the freedom struggle against the British. According to the D.C. (District Commissioner) of Pratapgarh, Ram Chandra became "a magnet of attraction" who supplied "some mental pabulum to a people intellectually starved in these out-of-the-way places."[23] His popularity knew no bounds. Not only men but women, with the permission of elders, would invite him inside the houses and discuss their problems.[24] This added to his knowledge on issues concerning women. It was a difficult task to raise issues related to women in a rigid, traditional feudal society like Oudh. Ram Chandra not only raised the issues but broke certain established norms in his personal life. His personal relations and experience with women shaped his attitude towards women in general and are worth recounting. Shridhar Balwant Jodhpurkar alias Baba Ram Chandra, a Maharashtrian Brahmin, left home at a young age. Though there was no *purdah* (seclusion of women) in his family, a lot of money had to be spent on a girl's marriage. He was critical of his father who brought in another wife: *Meré pitā né kalanka khaḍa kiyā,* (my father brought dishonour and trouble to our family) but, as a child, could not protest in front of him. The relations between the two women were far from cordial and both Ram Chandra and his mother faced a great deal of hardship. Eventually, due to his stepmother's attitude, he left home. His mother gave him 25 rupees as a parting gift and, of course, her blessings. Thereafter he met a *fakir* (religious mendicant) who was keen to take him on as his *chela* (disciple). Ram Chandra soon realized that the fakir was a fraud who "pretended to cure Hindu women through divine powers, cheated them and lured their young daughters and daughters-in-law into prostitution" (*Hindu striyon ko jhadtā phunktā va unhė thug kar jawān bahu betiyon ko bhagāne vālon ke akhadė me jā milātā thā.*[25]) Soon he parted company with him. For some time, he stayed with Ganga, a Marathi girl, but their different lifestyles made them part company. Wandering through different parts of the Central Provinces and Maharashtra, he reached Bombay. During this period, he had the varied experience of working as a coolie, a vendor and a labourer at a coal depot. He must have earned some money, for now he visited the Bombay Race Course. In his autobiographical writings, he mentions that he put money on a horse in the name of his mother and, by a stroke of good luck, won Rs 800. Out of this, he sent Rs 700 to his mother by money order. He also worked on a coal ship and, out of his earnings, remitted another Rs 400 to his mother.[26] We see here that Ram Chandra personally experienced the problems of polygamy in his parental house.

In 1905, Ram Chandra left for Fiji as an indentured labourer. The working conditions were extremely hard and punishments for workers were severe. His political activity began when the banana trees belonging to labourers were forcibly cut by an inspector. He had the trees loaded on carts and organized a procession to the Governor demanding redressal of the wrong committed. Under his leadership, the labourers were partially successful.[27] Ram Chandra was sentenced to three years imprisonment on charges of negligence of work. As a detenu, he was made to do domestic work at the Magistrate's house. As the memsahib was pleased with his work, his two-and-a half year term was pardoned on the condition that he would continue to work in the house.[28]

Ram Chandra has given an account of his stay in the house. The Magistrate (it is not known what nationality he was) had two daughters who tried various methods to attract him: *Ve apnė katāksh chakshuon se apnė vashibhoot karne ke liye kai prakār ke charitra kiya karti theen.*[29] (They used to look flirtatiously at me and try various means to seduce me).

Often he had to accompany them with soap, etc. to the pond for a bath. At times, he would join them and spend hours in the water. He complained that they ordered a tent and a phonogram machine from England without asking him and the cost was deducted from his salary. According to his own testimony, he accepted all this for two reasons. First, because if he refused he could be sent back to jail and, second, because he thought that since he had to stay in Fiji, he must get used to the lifestyle there. These two girls arranged his marriage to a "beautiful Chamarin" through Fiji rites. On the pretext of meeting this *chamarin* (women of the *chamar* low caste), the girls would visit Ram Chandra for sexual pleasure: *Is stri ke bahāne dono ladkiyān mere dhan, man haran ko mere paas aane lagin.*[30]

It was only when the two girls got married, that Ram Chandra shifted from their house along with his wife. Here two things need attention. First, that a marriage had taken place between a Maharashtrian Brahmin and a Chamarin; but Ram Chandra never reveals his wife's name, he only refers to her as a "beautiful Chamarin". Second, he blames the two girls for desiring sexual pleasure with him but is completely silent about his own feelings in the matter.

Ram Chandra acted in close cooperation with Manilal, an advocate, for the cause of indentured labourers.[31] In spite of this political relationship Ram Chandra was sad to see that Manilal had a memsahib as his mistress and that his wife had to face problems which she did bravely: "We and many Gujrati jewellers of Suva felt sorry for her and, at the same time, admired her courage and bravery."[32] Due to his political activities, Ram Chandra had to flee from Fiji. But before he did so, he transferred his property (two houses and some lands) to his wife, "the beautiful Chamarin." This was followed by a mutual divorce. Commenting on the condition of indentured women labourers in Fiji, he wrote:

> Regarding women it suffices to say that beautiful women are made to work at isolated places where both *gore* (white men) as well as *kale*

> (black men) seduce them. Pregnant women have to work right upto the time they deliver the child. Often this leads to miscarriage.[33]

During 1918-20, Ram Chandra was not only making efforts to mobilize the peasants against the British and the landlords but also attempting to articulate issues related to women. The very first programme he offered for the uplift of peasants in 1920 included the appointment of *updeshikas* (women teachers) to educate women in rural areas.[34] We shall discuss the role of women during the movement a little later.

Some time in the late 1920s Ram Chandra married Jaggi, a Kurmi by caste, and broke the caste norms once again. This marriage led to all kinds of vulgar propaganda against him by the landlords and by other opponents. Ram Chandra attributes this marriage to the advice of V.N. Mehta, a pro-peasant senior government official. A constant charge against Ram Chandra, levied by the landlords, was that he was an outsider, instigating peasants to "rebellion" in Pratapgarh. To counteract such attacks Mehta advised him to marry and settle down. Jaggi was the daughter of Kashi, his closest associate in the Kisan Sabha. He married her in the "English style". The marriage took place with Jaggi's consent.[35] But Ram Chandra's account makes it appear a political strategy. Jaggi accepts this and describes with pride the cordial relations between the two, and how under his influence she became an activist on the kisan front, on women's issues and in the freedom struggle.[36] It would be appropriate to mention here that though Ram Chandra died in 1950, Jaggi still continues to work as a Kisan Sabha activist in Pratapgarh. She led a movement against levy collection on wheat in 1976 —the emergency period — and went to jail. She also led a protest against a death in a family planning camp. As a consequence, she lost her pension as a freedom fighter which was only restored in 1983.[37] Though well over 90, she walks 10 to 15 kilometres a day for Kisan Sabha work.

III

In a frontal attack on patriarchal domination in the Oudh countryside Baba Ram Chandra wrote:

> Howsoever meritorious the women may be, their partners are not up to the mark because after marriage they imprison their wives in house-

> hold cages. They use them for sexual pleasure (*unkā bhog karten hain*). make them cook food and trap them in many other social hypocrisies (*dhakosala*).[38]

He felt perturbed because: "The women too regard their husbands as their *ishtdev* (gods) and dance to their tune." On the other hand, he felt: "Where the women get an upper hand, husbands become their slaves. They make all sorts of excuses in the name of their wives, when asked to participate in political activity or to fight for the redressal of their grievances."[39] Ram Chandra was against domination of either sex by the other. In fact what he had in mind was a monogamous, humane and moral form of family, based on greater rights for women. He preached: *Na joru se mard na mard se joru. Aisā koi ghar na rakhā jāye ki jodā na ho.* (No husband without wife, no wife without husband. There should be no home without a couple.)[40] He advocated that, "if men and women are to be kept happy, then both should have equal freedom" (*nar nāriyon ko sukhi rakhnā hai to dono ki swatantratā ek samān ho*).[41]

Ram Chandra's concern for the problems faced by women is also reflected in the way he tried to make the peasants aware of the changes which had been made in the Indian Penal Code. In a pamphlet under the title *Tāzerātė Hind ki Dafāin Badhā di gain,* (Penalties in the Indian Penal Code have been Enhanced) he familiarized the peasants with the punishments for major offences—murder, dacoity, instigation to communal rioting as well as offences against women:

Attacking a woman with bad intentions—ten years jail

Abducting a woman—*kalapani* (penal transportation)

Abducting a woman for prostitution—kalapani

Raping a woman—kalapani[42]

To this, he added a footnote *"baint bhi lagen ge"* (will be caned also). He cautioned that there will be a ten year jail term for those who kidnap a woman or use force to marry her and that such a forced marriage will have no legal status (*aisi zabardasti ki shādi kā koi kānuni asar na hogā*).[43] This establishes that Ram Chandra was opposed to the use of any form of violence or coercion on women. He regarded "reforms a must for women" and this, according to him, "would come when men reform themselves [in relation to women]".[44] It must be noted that Ram Chandra managed to get such a resolution passed in a totally male attended conference of the Kurmi Sangh sometime in the mid-1930s.[45]

Ram Chandra was very vocal against child marriage. In a leaflet titled *Ma Shatru Pita Bairi* (Mother Enemy, Father Illwisher) he warned parents against the ill effects of child marriage.[46] It appears from this leaflet that many a time parents would sell their minor daughters in marriage to more than one person. The young girl then virtually led a prostitute's life. This practice also often led to disputes. Such marriages, it appears, took place due to extreme economic hardship as in the cases of kanya vikray. Another factor which contributed to the rise of such marriages was the absence of occupancy rights in this region. The peasants of the neighbouring regions of Oudh were reluctant to marry their daughters to peasant-tenants "who may become beggars at the whim of their landlords."[47] Ram Chandra asked the peasants to show as much concern for their girls as they did for their animals.

> You make your animals mate only when they attain a particular age. You assert so much wisdom in the case of animals. If you do the same in relation to your child-daughters, the evil custom of child marriage will flee on its own from your houses.[48]

Ram Chandra accused old men and women (*budhe-budhiyan*) of committing the worst injustice against children by marrying young girls to aged men and young boys to aged women (*ye sabse badā annyāya hai*).[49] The sad part was that people were "infected with the disease of pardon" and these old people "were pardoned for their unjust acts only in consideration of their age." He preached that, had he been the king[50] he would have made these old persons stay in separate houses where they would be looked after. But he also saw it as a welfare problem and demanded state pension for all men and women above the age of 55 as well as for all widows.[51]

Ram Chandra advocated that if adultery was to be checked, then boys and girls should be married by taking into account their respective merits—that is arranged marriages should be based on considerations of compatibility, such as intelligence.[52] Here he was bringing in a new concept of conjugal relations based on the possibility of communication between partners.

Inter caste marriages were virtually absent due to rigid caste norms. The landlords upheld these norms and as part of their attempt to control social mobility, they would impose fines on peasants for breaking caste customs. One Kallu had to pay Rs 51 as fine to the landlord for bringing a wife from another sub-section of the Muslim community.[53] Thus, it was no surprise that Ram Chandra worked for reforms through caste *panchayats*.[54] Under his influence, the Kurmi Sangh resolved:

a) Marriage customs of the *biradari* (caste brotherhood) should be changed.

b) Marriage or *gauna* (post-puberty ceremonial bringing of girl bride to her husband's house) should take place with the signature/sanction of the head of the panchayat. If parents fail to do this, the marriage will have no legal sanction. It should be the duty of the *panch* (member of panchayat or village court) to ensure this practice or else he would be punished.

c) Reforms for women are necessary.

d) Women should not be sent to work in another person's house. Men should go upon payment of full wages only.

e) Reforms for women can be implemented only when men reform themselves in relation to women.

f) The fault of parents is that i) on the failure to produce children, they make the women run after *fakirs, sadhus, ojhas, pirs* and *mazars* (holy men and religious places) ii) if a child is born, they indulge in extravagance.[55]

This was an all male conference attended by 271 Kurmi representatives. Resolution (a) was to do away with the evils related to marriage, like child marriage and extravagant expenditure. Resolution (b) was for a kind of registration of marriage in village records. Here Resolution (d) should not be taken to mean a rejection of women's right to work but seen in the context of exploitative working conditions for women in the existing feudal structure. Women were the worst victims of *begar* (forced labour) as well as a target of sexual exploitation by the *karindas* (landlord's agents) and *sipahis* (soldiers) of landlords. At the same time the objective conditions were such that in order to be saved from sexual harassment women stood to lose their right to free movement and to certain forms of wage earning.

In another Kisan Council meeting at Rure—the headquarters of the Kisan Sabha—it was resolved that a) in household affairs all members of the family should have an equal say; b) there should be separate means of livelihood such as shops, etc. for women, so that after the death of their husbands they and their children would not starve or stay unclothed; c) old men and women should be looked after by everyone.[56]

But most important from the women's point of view were the resolutions brought forward by women themselves in this meeting. The initiative had been taken by Jaggi at the behest of Ram Chandra and Jhinguri Singh, another kisan activist.[57] These read:

> a) Only men are free to marry two to three women, instead of one. This should be stopped with immediate effect. Whoever has done so should be punished. A woman should also not have a second *mard* (man). If so she should be punished.
>
> b) One man and one woman can stay together. Their relations should not be treated as illegal.
>
> c) Such women (who stay with a man without formal marriage) should not be treated as belonging to any particular caste. They should not be dismissed as merely being there for producing children.
>
> d) If a woman stays with a man and bears a child, she should be respected as a *devi* (goddess). Those who do not bear sons should be respected as *kanyas* (daughters).[58]

Radical in nature, these resolutions were accepted in the meeting. They were aimed at obtaining social sanction for relationships otherwise regarded as *najayaz* (illegal). As women suffered in such relationships, these resolutions were also aimed at providing security for them. Here I would not treat Resolution (d) as merely an expression of patriarchal values in relation to the birth of a son. I shall look at it from the point of view of the status of such women. They are generally regarded as *kulta, patita,* or *kalankini* (immoral, fallen or bad women) but now the status being demanded was that of a goddess and of a daughter. This indicated a radical break with existing social relations, but the irony of it is that they could achieve this radical break only by accepting a traditional value — that is, by producing sons.

Rural women in Oudh in the 1930s had not only made such radical demands, they had also had them accepted in the Kisan Sabha. This was a significant step forward towards a higher status for women. And they had been considerably influenced and inspired by Ram Chandra in this regard.[59]

It is significant that Ram Chandra would not spare his closest associates in the Kisan Sabha if they maltreated women. When Bhagwandin left his wife after a quarrel, Ram Chandra's comment was: *Aaj ghar mein kaliyuga ki paithaari ho gai* (today the age of corruption has begun for the family).[60] In his words, Bhagwandin was in the wrong as he wanted to stay with a rich woman and desert his poor wife: *Is bechāri dhanheen ko adhuré mein chhoḍnā chāhatā hai* (he wants to abandon this poor helpless woman). Ram Chandra was concerned about what would happen to Bhagwandin's wife if the latter did abandon her. Moreover this could also bring a bad name to the Kisan Sabha. Ultimately Bhagwandin was persuaded to return to his wife.

I would also like to cite here some panchayat decisions found in Baba Ram Chandra's papers on petitions by women:

a) The case of Ramlal Satnami and Lilabai. Decision given by Devdas master and ten other members of the panchayat.[63]

The panchayat admitted that a just arbitration in this complicated case was difficult. It appears that Ramlal and Lilabai were disciples of a Satnami *guru* (preacher) Baba Santdasji. Lilabai was a widow and had a son. A relationship developed between Ramlal and Lilabai. It is also possible that the son was an offspring from this relationship. The exact situation is not clear, but it appears that Ramlal disowned responsibility and Lilabai wanted compensation in the form of money. The panchayat judges made it clear that they would rule out giving money as compensation and would first enquire into the exact nature of their relationship from Santdasji. The final decision was:

> The panchayat has handed over Lilabai to Ramlal. From today, Lilabai is the wife of Ramlal. But at the same time, they both are declared guilty—*gurudrohi* and *santdrohi* (of violating precepts of preacher and holy man). They should be socially boycotted for life. Now Ramlal has a right over Lilabai and will look after her son. But a social boycott will continue and whoever breaks it will be subjected to punishment.

This judgement treated Lilabai both as property and as a deprived woman. As property where Ramlal is given a right over her and as a deprived woman when she gets her right as a wife. Moreover, she alone is not treated as a degraded person as both of them are to be socially boycotted; the latter punishment was inflicted perhaps to check or discourage such relationships in future.

b) The case of Dhirajia Kurmin versus Sukhai Kurmi (April 1940).[64]

Dhirajia petitioned that her husband Sukhai was not looking after her welfare (***hamārā gujārā nahin kartā***) and asked that the panchayat should give her justice. The judges decreed that Sukhai should look after her, and if he failed to do so, a fine of Rs 51 would be realized from him and his wife would then be free to leave him. At the same time, she was warned not to do anything violating customary norms (***bekaayda***) without his permission. If she did, she would not be given a hearing and any other man who took her with him would also be fined Rs 51 and boycotted socially.

It appears from the judgement that the case was argued before the panchayat with both sides accusing the other of extra-marital relations. The judgement disproves the common belief that women could get no justice from the male-dominated panchayat. But at the same time the panchayat also tries to enforce a uniform but very strict code of sexual morality, perhaps as a means of gaining greater respectability for peasants.

c) *Petition of Lakhpati, village Maurahat (April 1947).*[65]

Lakhpati petitioned to get justice from the biradari. Jagan, her husband, had left her and for the last 18 years she had been looking after their daughter. She demanded: "I should get the money I spent on her during the last 18 years. I should be told the fault of my daughter. My daughter's case should be settled." Ram Chandra sent this petition to Guru Ramanugra of Kashi to explain. It appears that Jagan had become a *sadhu* (ascetic) and assumed the name Guru Ramanugra. His reply was that the girl should be sent to him: "I love my daughter...but you (Lakhpati) have no right to enjoy the happiness or sorrow of my house." In fact, Lakhpati had never made a claim for herself but the demand made by her indicates a growing awareness among women of their right to seek maintenance. Even if Lakhpati was in the wrong, which apparently was the reason for their separation, why should she alone bear the expense of bringing up the daughter?

In addition to these cases, we find petitions addressed to Ram Chandra by a number of exploited women:

a) Sona Harijan's daughter, Koeli, complained on 12.9.1940 that Thakur Jagol Singh had forcibly sown her lands. She had no faith in the *patwari* (village official), who was the *zamindar's* (landlord's) man. Her case, it was pleaded, should be taken up with the D.C. who must personally look into the matter.[66]

b) Kunau Kurmin, a widow residing in village Chandrahara, was forcibly evicted by the Taluqdar of Ramganj. She sought Ram Chandra's advice. "How should I live now?"[67]

c) Sumera Murain of village Fainha had 20 biswas land of a five rupee rental mortgaged to Jageshwar Pasi, a *mahajan* (moneylender). Jokhu Singh forcibly claimed the land. She had paid rent to the mahajan and now Jokhu also demanded it. On the other hand, the mahajan insisted that if she paid to Jokhu he would sue her. She asked Baba Ram Chandra, "What should I do now?"[68]

d) On 25.4.1942, Mussamat Maharaji of village Gharoli complained to the Congress office that, after the death of her husband Khedu, the zamindar did not let her enter her holding. Whenever she tried, her bullocks and plough were thrown out. If the Congress "does not take up her case she would starve, as she cannot resist the zamindar." The president of the Pratapgarh District Congress passed on the petition to Ram Chandra for action.[69]

e) Mussamat Hubrazi, a poor old Brahmin woman, complained that she had no one left in the house and, due to old age, she found it difficult to work. Two men—Devdutt and Suraj—would not let her enter her holding and beat her up whenever she tried to do so. She wanted the Congress to intervene and to make food and clothes available for her.[70]

All these problems were related not only to individual women but were a part of the wider problem—the exploitative character of the agrarian structure as a whole. They also indicated the faith reposed by women in Ram Chandra as the leader of the peasants.

Ram Chandra argued for upward mobility for lower caste women. When the Sarda Committee was seeking evidence he advised the village panchayat heads to demand a similar status for the women of "lower castes" as was enjoyed by "high caste" women.[71] Peasant women, however, must earn their right to a higher status by changing themselves into highly austere, pious and moral persons. What he had in mind was the image of a new kind of woman who would also enjoy a greater measure of equality with her husband. It was this model of the new peasant woman that made him propose certain measures which in fact restricted the free movement of women. In a write up on "*Oudh ki Nariyon per Merė Vichar*" (My Views on the Women of Oudh), he started by quoting Maithli Saran Gupta:

Nāri nindā nā karo nāri nar ki khān,
Nāri se nar hota hai Dhruv Prahalād saman.
(Do not talk ill of woman, she is the origin of man.
From her are born men like Dhruv and Prahalad).[72]

But then he wrote: "What should I do? I can't close my eyes to what's happening around." He was highly critical of women's love for jewellery and regarded this as the prime cause for adultery. This weakness, he believed, exposed them to exploitation by men. Something concrete was needed to check this 'weakness'. One measure which he recommended was to discontinue the custom of inviting dancing girls on auspicious occasions, as women of the house and neighbourhood tried to imitate their dress and jewellery.[73] Another measure was to impose restrictions on women for going to fairs and markets as this would not only check their meetings with lovers but also prevent them from getting involved with bangle-sellers and other men.[74] But along with this strict moral code he worked for the uplift of women. Wherever he came across a woman who had the slightest education, he would inspire her to educate other women in the village. Under his inspiration, Vidyavati wrote a booklet *Satnami Panch Kanya Daibati* and he published 2000 copies of this.[75] The book dealt with various problems faced by women. When he was in jail (1942-45), he kept reminding his wife Jaggi to look after the education of their daughters.[76]

IV

We find the first instance of active political participation by women in the peasant struggles in August-September 1920. When Ram Chandra was arrested for the first time, about 40,000 peasants surrounded Pratapgarh jail and the Government was forced to release him.[77] Women had taken an active part in this agitation and after this there was no going back. Incidentally, Ram Chandra and 32 other peasants had been arrested by the police on the complaint of a woman taluqdar —Chabiraj Kunwar—who was notorious for being very oppressive.[78]

Thakur Din Singh rose in revolt against the Raja of Parhat in October 1920. He directed the movement against landlords, moneylenders and traders. The police and taluqdari agents crushed the uprising with great difficulty and women were the worst sufferers. Villages were plundered and women molested in eight villages during the hunt for Thakur Din.[79]

The Ajodhaya Kisan Conference of December 1920 was a unique spectacle in the history of peasant struggles in India. About 50,000 to one lakh peasant men and women reached the town in spite of the cold weather. On his way to the meeting ground, Ram Chandra saw some very old women sitting exhausted by the long journey they had undertaken in order to attend the conference. He arranged an *ekka* (horse cart) to take them to the venue.[80] For the first time, women's presence was asserted separately from men in this historic meeting. Satya Devi spoke from the stage on behalf of women and assured their participation in the movement. This was greatly applauded from all sides.[81]

As if to test this assurance, the opportunity came that very day on the 20th of December. On the return journey there was trouble at the railway station. A clash took place over tickets and peasants offered *satyagraha* (passive resistance) by prostrating themselves on the railway tracks. Ram Chandra mentions that "women feeding their infants lay flat on the rail lines and would not budge. Hot water showers from rail engines and police lathi charge could not deter them." Ultimately they were allowed to board the trains.[82]

The peasant movement in Oudh assumed the dimensions of a class war as the desperate peasantry resorted to militant action on a large scale in Rai Bareily district. The year 1921 began with the *jacqueries* of Oudh peasants. The peasants, in their thousands, moved from one estate to another destroying the crops of the taluqdars.[83] Here, I shall confine myself to the role of women during the uprising.

On the 5th of January the peasants surrounded the *kothi* (palatial house) of taluqdar Tribhwan Bahadhur Singh at Chandania. The taluqdar was hated by his tenants because of his immoral and oppressive practices. The estate was virtually ruled by a prostitute, Achhijan, who was the taluqdar's mistress or "keep."[84] The peasants demanded the expulsion of Achhijan and the restoration of the real Rani (taluqdar's wife), exemption from nazarana and no more evictions.[85] The first demand indicates that the opposition to Achhijan was not only on account of her oppressive practices but also on grounds of morality as she had infringed on the rights of another woman—the wife. Of course, the person responsible for this infringement was the taluqdar himself. He refused to meet the demands of the peasants and many were arrested by the police.[86]

On the 24th of January there was a pitched battle between the police and taluqdar's men on the one side and peasants on the other in village Sehagaon Panchimgaon. One constable was killed with *lathi* (thick wooden staff) blows and two others were injured. In spite of firing by policemen, the women of the village did not remain passive in the struggle. They pelted brickbats from their housetops on the policemen.[87] The D.C. of Rai Bareily was perturbed by this development in the peasant movement.[88]

In Fyzabad district, on the 13th and 14th of January, large crowds consisting mainly of landlesss labourers moved about the Baskhari and Jehangirganj police circles, "looting" the zamindars, moneylenders, merchants and goldsmiths. The main targets of attack were the grain stores of the zamindars and mahajans. These crowds, numbering between 1,000 to 5,000 men, were followed by crowds of women who carried off the "booty" of their "pillage."[89] In many instances, women belonging to upper classes were subjected to humiliation, maltreated and abused by groups of oppressed women.[90] This demonstrates the awareness on the part of women of the class-contradictions of rural society. It would be interesting to mention here that two peasant leaders, Deo Narain and Kedarnath, were assaulted by Alopi, a Brahmin zamindar, on the 19th of January. Alopi regarded them as instigators and as such responsible for the "insult of his womenfolk during the riots."[91]

There was considerable interaction between the peasant movement in Oudh and the Non-Cooperation movement. Gandhi's name surfaced in different contexts during the peasant movement. Faruq Ahmed, a fakir, proclaimed that "Gandhi would ascend the throne of Delhi on 15th February" and "three lakhs of English ladies" would be "distributed at the Guhuana Sabha."[92] The talk of Gandhi ascending the throne is understandable but why English ladies are to be "distributed" is not at all clear. Is it to be seen as a sexually motivated statement to attract the men or was it a revengeful statement against the treatment meted out to peasant women by landlords? (There were a few British landlords in Oudh.) Or was there any case involving the honour of any local woman at the hands of an Englishman? There is no evidence to support any of these conjectures. However, Gandhi was projected in a totally different manner at the Guhuana Sabha on the 27th of January. Ram Devi compared Gandhi's agitation with the Mahabharata (Hindu epic) war: just as in the Mahabharata Draupadi's honour was at stake, Gandhi's agitation was seen to maintain the honour of Bharatmata (Mother India).[93] In fact, the peasants had their own perception of Gandhi and of his programme and were anxious about their economic emancipation.[94]

Active participation by women was a significant feature of the peasant movement in Oudh. The pelting of stones by women on the police party, their presence in hundreds during the Fyzabad uprising and the humiliation of upper class women at the hands of oppressed women, exhibited the revolutionary potential of the peasant women in the countryside.

On the 19th of February 1925, in Pratapgarh, an all women conference was held under the presidentship of Jai Kumari. It was described as a "Kisan devi ki sabha" and the following resolutions were passed:

a) A cow should be maintained by the panchayat in every village so that milk is available for small children.

b) After the death of the husband, and on confirmation of the proof of marriage, the wife should get her right. If the wife is not there then the son or daughter should have it.

c) For achieving these demands of *kisanin* (peasant women) we shall organize meetings in every village.

d) We will contribute one anna per woman and form women panchayats in every village.

e) We shall hold meetings in our own villages and for the redressal of our grievances we shall get our own laws constituted from the government.[95]

Whether future meetings were held or not we do not know, but this meeting itself was a turning point for women as it is, till today, the first known recorded charter of peasant women's demands.

Concrete efforts were made in the 1930s to form peasant women's organizations. Among the activists who took the initiative were the wives of the Kisan Sabha leaders. A Kisanin Panchayat was formed with Jaggi as its leader. This organization functioned as a branch of the Praja Sangh organized by Ram Chandra.[96] The aims of the Kisanin Panchayat were:

a) To fight the grievances faced by them as women.

b) To fight the grievances faced as peasants and agricultural labourers.

c) Political mobilization for the national movement.[97]

Quite important was the pledge — almost a kind of demand charter — which a kisanin had to sign and to promise to work for its attainment:

a) After the death of the husband, without paying anything [this seems an indirect reference to nazarana], we should have full right over the holding. And, there should be no eviction for five years.

b) The women from kisan families should not be forced to work under the threats of lathis, *dandas* (sticks) chains, etc.

c) Those who work as labourers should get full wages.[98]

Both the aims and the pledge of the Kisanin Panchayat were an overt expression of the oppression faced by women in the countryside. They demonstrate an awareness and a determination on the part of women to fight against such oppression.

Baba Ram Chandra used traditional customs and ceremonies to mobilize peasants against taluqdars and the British.[99] The Kisanin Panchayat also adopted such methods to create awareness amongst women. On the 14th of July 1933, a circular in Ram Chandra's handwriting read:

> Due to Jaggi's efforts, the benefits which kisanin have got will be celebrated by a *yagya* (religious rite) of Bala Devi (local goddess) *pujan* (worship). Jaggi will go with prominent members of her panchayat.[100]

What exactly the benefits were is not clear from this circular but in all probability the celebration was in connection with the acceptance of women's demands by the Kisan Council and Kurmi Sabha as mentioned earlier. The celebration of success through a yagya indicates that those very women who demanded a radical change in their economic and social status were not prepared to break away from rituals.

The Kisanin Panchayat organized exhibitions to educate the kisanin and these were financed by the Praja Sangh. In the account papers of the Sangh we find reference to one such exhibition held on 7 February 1934: "Bhagwandin and Jaggi's exhibition for kisanin was attended by kisanin from distant places. They stayed overnight. The expenditure was Rs 1 forinkpot, 8 annas..., wood 8 annas, food *(chabena)* Rs 3."[101] This indicates that women were undertaking journeys on their own to make themselves aware of various issues related to them and to strengthen their organization. We have on record two meetings (3 Sept 1933 and 25 April 1934) of the Praja Sangh which were largely attended by women from the three *tahsils* (district subdivisions) of Pratapgarh.[102] The Kisanin Panchayat would send separate invitation slips to women for such meetings: *Kisanino ki panchayat mein kisano ki mang ke sath milne ka utsav kiya jayega* (In their meeting the women will celebrate their joining the peasants in their demands).[103] These invitations, though signed by Jaggi, are in Ram Chandra's handwriting.

Some time in the mid or late 1930s a petition titled *"Anath Ablaon ki Pukar"* (The Helpless Women's Appeal) was sent to Prof. Braj Gopal Bhatnagar.[104] The petitioner signed herself as a "*dukhit praja ki abla*" (A helpless woman of the oppressed masses). The petition listed five grievances:

a) We are beaten with lathis.

b)Being forced to stand on a mudpot in the glaring sun we are watched with lustful eyes [obviously by landlords or their agents].

c)During *begar* they make us grind. If we refuse, we are beaten with lathis. They break our heads.

d)After the death of our husbands we are evicted from our holdings, houses, orchards, etc.

e) Thus, we cannot repay loans nor manage our family.

The petitioner further questioned *Kyā ham kisi ki byāhatā nahin hain.* (Are we not wives too?); *Is apmān ka dāvā kahān karen?* (Where should we appeal against such humiliation?); *ham dukhi ablā kyā karen?* (What should we, the aggrieved and oppressed women do?). A significant move to attract the attention of intellectuals towards the plight of oppressed rural women, this document too, like many others, was penned by Ram Chandra.

The late 1930s witnessed a sharp ideological struggle within the Indian National Congress.[105] The right wing leadership was particularly hostile towards the Kisan Sabha and at many places, peasant members of the Congress were not allowed to vote in the organizational elections. In the Pratapgarh countryside women had enrolled themselves in large numbers as four anna members of the Congress. These women were not just passive members. They played an important role not only during the direct action struggles but also in organizational matters. When a large number of women found their names missing in the voters list for organizational elections they flooded the D.C.C. (District Congress Committee) office with representations during 1938-39.[106]

Certain changes had been made in the tenancy laws during the Congress ministry in U.P. but they failed to meet peasant expectations. On the contrary it was the landlords who were able to extract some concessions from them. One among these was the enhanced power of the landlord to take over the lands which had been used for generations by the peasants for grazing their animals. In October 1940 Baba Ram Chandra organized a movement against this and more than 10,000 animals were taken in a procession to the D.C.'s office in Pratapgarh. It was a unique spectacle and in the words of Ram Chandra, "people were surprised to see that even animals had come to petition."[107] Women played a vital role in organizing this march. Maharani Devi, Gainda Devi and Paiga Devi had sent one ox each and many other women sent their animals which included cows, asses, goats, horses and even camels.[116] Laximin Kurmin has been mentioned as the most active participant in the movement.[108]

On 4 December 1940 during the individual satyagraha Jaggi made a request to the president of the Pratapgarh D.C.C. saying that since she was a Congress member from mandal 7, she should be issued a satyagrahi pass. She wanted to issue a statement before the D.C. and it was the responsibility of the D.C.C. to take her to his office. She asserted that her statement should be printed and distributed by the D.C.C. to all kisans and *mazurs* (labourers). She wanted to offer satyagraha because: a) peasants were oppressed; b) the government had insulted Mahatma Gandhi and all this had become unbearable.[109] It is important here to note that while offering satyagraha for the nationalist cause she stressed peasant oppression and this signifies the peasants' own perception of nationalism. A handwritten leaflet was issued under her signature appealing to the peasants to:

a) Never believe the alien Government or its servants and allies, nor help them in any way.

b) Not help or be with rajas and maharajas as they are the friends of the alien Government.

c)Look after your homes, family, lands and animals yourself.

d) Break all caste norms in crisis.

e) Not side with those who indulge in violence and looting.

f) Be with the poor and not with the rich as they are all one and at many places the taluqdars, small zamindars and capitalists, with the help of high classes and arms want to create disturbances.

She declared that she was marching fearlessly and that they should all do the same. "Don't get stuck at home" (*ghar na reha jana*).[110]

The Pratapgarh D.C.C. had made no call to women to participate but Jaggi insisted: "We women have come to offer satyagraha at Gandhiji's order."[111] Under her leadership ten other women offered satyagraha. Out of these eleven, nine went to jail but Jaggi and Sundra Devi were not allowed to do so by the D.C.C. The explanation given to them was that Mahatmaji had ordered that no women with small children could go to jail. Both of them had children in their laps and when I interviewed them, with great anguish they told me how they were deprived from going to jail and separated from their sisters due to Gandhiji's orders.[112]

All these women were from poor peasant families and belonged to different castes:

Mussamat Putta	— Harijan (Chamar)	
Sampati	— Kurmi	*(the first four are widows)*
Razi	— Kurmi	
Sukhi	— Teli	
Sukhmani	— Pasi	
Bubai	— Kurmi	
Putra	— Kurmi	
Abhilakhi	— Kurmi	
Basanti	— Brahmin	
Sundra Devi	— Ravidas[113]	

This caste composition was an important development as these women had joined hands cutting across rigid caste norms and demonstrated through this that satyagraha could be a combined effort of the oppressed.[114] But the high caste *vakil* (lawyer) leaders in the D.C.C. did not appreciate this as they were opposed to the peasants organizing as a class. Munishwar Dutt Upadyaya, an important Congress leader, commented: "Had the women from high families offered satyagraha it would have brought fame to the Congress. What could the women from Shudra (low caste) families bring?"[115] This was strongly resented by Sita Ram, Sundra Devi's husband. On 27 December he wrote to Baba Ram Chandra that Munishwar Dutt had insulted the Devis and as such he and many other men might not offer satyagraha.[116] But on Ram Chandra's advice they continued with the satyagraha.

I did get certain information in relation to the life and activities of the prominent women activists in the Kisan Sabha through interviews conducted during my field work. Mussamat Putta's husband was an agricultural labourer who never participated in the Kisan Sabha. He earned his wages and looked after the house whereas Putta was a Kisan Sahba whole timer, very vocal and very active. She was given the name Laali (red) by the peasants due to her militant and aggressive participation. Her husband did not oppose her participation.[117] Sampati was herself a peasant-tenant and was in the forefront of the kisan movement. The husbands of Abhilakhi and Putta were not active in the Kisan Sabha — the former's because of his occupation in agriculture and the latter's because of fear.[118] According to Jaggi, men never opposed the participation of their wives in political actions, rather they encouraged it and the wives of all Kisan Sabha leaders were active at the same level as the men. Even if they had objected the women would have defied them for " did not Ram tell Sita not to accompany him to the forest but Sita on her own decided to go."[119] Sita to Jaggi is a symbol not of a woman who followed her *patiparmeshwar* (husband-god) but of a woman who took her own decisions.

Sundra Devi had no political education in her parent's house. Hers was an arranged marriage with Sita Ram whose first wife had died after giving birth to a son. This was a political family. Sita Ram's father was a contractor and later on he bought a small zamindari in his wife's name. After his death his wife became a Kisan Sabha activist and in 1938 transferred her zamindari lands to the Congress.[120] Sundra Devi was encouraged by her mother-in-law and her husband to become active in the Kisan Sabha. During the 1942 movement Sita Ram was arrested and Sundra Devi went underground with her children. Soon Jaggi joined her and they faced tremendous hardships.[121]

It is important here to mention the kind of symbols Ram Chandra was using to mobilize peasants. Kaikeyi in the popular imagination, is regarded as an evil character who sent Rama to the forest. But Ram Chandra was all praise for her:

> In the *treta yuga*, when the freedom of India was abducted by Ravana of Lanka, there was a mother like Kaikeyi who created a way out to achieve independence. Had she not sent Rama to the forest who would have killed Ravana? Today in this *kaliyuga* if mothers act like Kaikeyi and offer their sons in the service of the country the *kalank* (shame) of mother India will go. But alas these days there are as many different feelings and opinions as there are mothers.[122]

Jaggi very proudly narrates how Ram Chandra used to advise her and other women to work for the uplift of women, of peasants and for the freedom struggle.[123]

V

This study is largely based on Ram Chandra's papers and there is ample scope for further investigation in the field. Yet, I have attempted to reconstruct the history of the rural women in Oudh. Three distinct voices are discernible in the study; 1) statements of women themselves cited in the Mehta Report and also found in the Ram Chandra papers; 2) issues raised by women under the tutelage of Ram Chandra; and 3) the concern shown by Ram Chandra and other kisan leaders for the plight of women in the countryside. These indicate that not only was there awareness of women's issues amongst both men and women but that both made a conscious effort to remedy specific grievances. This was not a one way process.

Ram Chandra's personal experience in relation to women did affect his views considerably — the stress on monogamy and sexual morality particularly was the direct result of what he had seen and experienced. Polygamy was described as a game of the rich (*baḍe logon kā khel hai*),[124] something which the poor peasant could not afford and should not think of. Moreover the justification for monogamy was sought by citing Rama who had only one wife — Sita.[125] He learnt a great deal from women about their problems either through direct dialogue or through intermediaries. He would urge the women to stand on their own feet, but being aware of the existing social reality he knew well that their amelioration would not come through their own efforts alone. The attitude of the men towards women had to be changed. Like all political and social reformers he was patronizing towards women but did not want them to be submissive. He struggled for transformation in the condition and status of women which he sought by using traditional and cultural idioms to mobilize them not only as peasants but also as a separate group — women. The organization of the Kisanin Sabha was an effort of this kind.

Once the women were organized and out in the movement did any tension emerge between them and Ram Chandra? There is no evidence yet to indicate this. Rather the evidence speaks otherwise. The entire women's movement collapsed after his death in 1950. What the situation is today is subject for another study.

NOTES

1. For details of the movement see Kapil Kumar, *Peasants in Revolt: Tenants, Landlords, Congress and the Raj in Oudh, 1886-1922* (Delhi: Manohar, 1984).
2. Ibid. Also see S.K. Mittal and Kapil Kumar, "Baba Ram Chandra and Peasant Upsurge in Oudh 1920-21," *Social Scientist*, 6, no. 11 (June 1978).
3. The most valuable source of information in this regard is the Baba Ram Chandra Papers (BRP) collected by the author during his field work. The papers are now preserved in the Nehru Memorial Museum and Library (NMML).
4. Various files of the Revenue Department and Settlement Reports give ample evidence in this regard.
5. See Elizabeth Fox-Genovese, "Culture and Consciousness in the Intelectual history of European Women," *Signs* 12, no. 3 (Spring 1987), p. 530.
6. See Kapil Kumar, *Peasants in Revolt*, pp. 14-70.
7. *Census of India 1921*, United Provinces, vol. 16, pt. 2.
8. Kapil Kumar, *Peasants in Revolt*, pp. 60-62, 218-20.
9. All figures are from *Census of India, 1921* vol. 16, pt. 2.
10. V.N. Mehta Report (MR) on *Agrarian disturbances in Pratapgarh*, F. No. 753/1920, Revenue, A, U.P. State Archives (UPSA), Lucknow.
11. Ibid.
12. Ibid.
13. All the cases cited are from MR.
14. Ibid.
15. Ibid.
16. Ibid.
17. A study of the District Gazetteers of Oudh shows that at any given time each district had women taluqdars.

18. F. Nos. 211-270/Oct. 1886, Leg. Dept., National Archves of India (NAI), Delhi.
19. *Oudh Revenue Administration Report, 1889-90,* p. 30.
20. BRP, Subject Files (SF)-II.
21. BRP, SF-9.
22. BRP, SF-10.
23. MR.
24. BRP, Speeches and Writings (SW), F. No. 2A.
25. Ibid.
26. Ibid.
27. Ibid.
28. Ibid.
29. Ibid.
30. Ibid.
31. For Manilal also see Suneet Chopra, "Bourgeois Historiography and the Peasant Question," *Social Scientist* 7, no. 11 (June 1977).
32. BRP, SW, F. No. 2A.
33. Ibid.
34. MR.
35. BRP, SW, F. No. 2A. Personal interview with Jaggi, village Daudpur, Tahsil Patti, Pratapgarh district, 14 June 1987. For a different view on this marriage see Deepti Mehrotra, "Women Participation in Peasant Movements in U.P." M. Phil. Thesis, Political Science Dept. Delhi University 1987.
36. Personal interview with Jaggi.
37. Ibid.
38. BRP, SF-3.
39. Ibid.
40. BRP, SW, F. No. 1A.
41. BRP, SF-11.
42. BRP, SW, F. No. 2A.
43. Ibid.
44. BRP, SW, F. No. 1A.
45. Ibid, No. 2A.
46. Ibid.
47. Commissioner Fyzabad to Chief Sect. to Govt. of U.P., 25 Nov. 1920. F. No. 753/1920, Rev., UPSA.
48. BRP, SW, No. 2A.
49. BRP, SW, No. 2B.
50. BRP, SF-16. According to Ram Chandra he used the word king because the people would understand *raja* (king) and *praja* (subjects) easily. BRP, SW, F. No. 2A.
51. BRP, SF-16. During the Congress ministry period Jaggi wrote to G.B.

Pant, the Premier of U.P., on 19 April 1938 demanding a pension for old men and women. She accused the Government and the landlords of grabbing the lands of old men and women and this made them dependent on family members. The family members, she asserted, had a meagre income and were unable to look after the old people. BRP, SF-15.

52. BRP, SF-16.
53. MR.
54. Among the various caste panchayats with which he was associated were the Kurmi Sangh, Harijan Sangh, Satnami Sabha and Tamoli Sabha, etc.
55. BRP, SW, F. No. 2A.
56. Ibid.
57. Personal interview with Jaggi.
58. BRP, SW, F. No. 2A.
59. Personal interview with Jaggi.
60. BRP, SF-6.
61. Ibid.
62. Personal interview with Jaggi.
63. BRP, SF-20. Saurabh Dube pointed out to me that the strict moral code which Ram Chandra was advocating for the Satnamis in fact took away much of the freedom which the Satnami women had in terms of man-woman relationships.
64. BRP, SF-II.
65. BRP, SF-10.
66. BRP, SF-20.
67. BRP, SF-9.
68. Ibid.
69. Ibid.
70. Ibid.
71. BRP, SW, F. No. 1A.
72. Ibid.
73. Ibid.
74. Ibid.
75. BRP, SF-4.
76. Ram Chandra to Jaggi, 14 April 1944, BRP, SF-26.
77. Kapil Kumar, *Peasants in Revolt*, pp. 96-102.
78. BRP, SW, F. No. 2C.
79. *Abhyudya*, 11 Dec. 1920.
80. BRP, SW, F. No. 2A.
81. C.I.D. Report on Ajodhaya meeting, F. No. 358/1920, Police, UPSA.
82. BRP, SW, F. No. 2A.
83. F. Nos. 195-216A/Feb. 1921-B, Home Pol., NAI.

84. Personal interviews with Kanhai Singh and Parag Singh, village Hamirmau, Rai Bareily district, 12 June 1977.
85. *Pratap*, 16 Jan. 1921.
86. *Independent*, 11 Jan.1921.
87. Shereff to Kaye, 24 Jan. 1921, F. No. 50/1921, Gen., UPSA.
88. D.C., Rai Bareily to Commissioner, 24 Jan. 1921, Ibid.
89. Nos. 195-216A 1921, Home Pol., NAI.
90. Porter to Hailey, 19 Jan. 1921, F. No. 50-3/1921, Gen., UPSA.
91. Nos. 195-216A 1921, Home Pol., NAI.
92. *Leader*, 24 June 1921.
93. C.I.D. Report on Guhuana Sabha, F. No. 50/1921, Gen. UPSA.
94. See Kapil Kumar, "Peasants' Perception of Gandhi and his Programme, Oudh 1920-22," *Social Scientist* 11, no.2 (Feb. 1983).
95. BRP, SF-4.
96. In an attempt to forge unity amongst various strata of peasants and small zamindars Ram Chandra had organized the Praja Sangh in the early 1930s.
97. BRP, SF-12.
98. BRP, SW, F. No. 2B.
99. Kapil Kumar, "Using the Ramcharitmanas as a Radical Text: Baba Ram Chandra in Oudh, 1920-50," in *Social Transformation and Creative Imagination*, ed. Sudhir Chandra (Delhi: Allied, 1984), pp. 311-34.
100. BRP, SF-11.
101. BRP, SF-12.
102. BRP, SF-6 & 25. In these meetings drug addiction and prostitution were denounced.
103. BRP, SF-10.
104. BRP, SF-4.
105. See Kapil Kumar, "Ideology, Congress and Peasants in 1930s: Class Adjustment or Submission?", *Social Scientist* 14, nos. 2-3 (Aug-Sept. 1986).
106. BRP, SF-20.
107. BRP, SF-18.
108. Ibid.
109. BRP, SF-9.
110. BRP, SF-9.
111. BRP, SF-9.
112. Personal interview with Jaggi: also with Sundra Devi, village Deosara, Tahsil Patti, Pratapgarh district, 16 June 1987.
113. BRP, SF-9.
114. For caste-class relationship in Oudh countryside see Kapil Kumar, *Peasants in Revolt*, pp. 223–24.
115. Sita Ram to Ram Chandra, 27 Dec. 1940, BRP, Correspondence.

116. Ibid.
117. Personal interview with Mathura s/o Putta Lali, village Atraura, Tahsil Patti, Pratapgarh district, 14 June 1987.
118. Personal interview with Mathura and Jaggi; also with Ram Bahadur Singh, village Rure, Tahsil Patti, Pratapgarh district, 14 June 1987.
119. Personal interview with Jaggi.
120. Personal interview with Sundra Devi. During my visit to Deosara I collected the papers of Sita Ram from Smt. Sundra Devi. The papers contain references to her mother-in-law and her small *zamindari*. The papers have been deposited in the NMML.
121. Personal interview with Sundra Devi.
122. BRP, SW, F. No. 2B. Within Hindu religious thought cosmic time is divided into four recurring *yugas* (periods) — *satyuga* is the golden period of virtue, *treta* wherein virtue and vice are in a proportion of three to one, *dvapara* where they are in equal proportion, and *kaliyuga,* the age of corruption.
123. Personal interview with Jaggi.
124. Ibid.
125. Ibid.

Notes on Contributors

NIRMALA BANERJEE is at present a Fellow at the Centre for Studies in Social Sciences, Calcutta. Her areas of work include issues of urban economics, ranging from urban planning to industrial economy and urban labour processes. She is the author of *Women Workers in the Unorganized Sector* (1985) and has also written articles for several journals. In recent years she has been increasingly involved, both as an academic and an activist, in women's issues.

SUMANTA BANERJEE is a freelance journalist who has written widely, both in India and elsewhere. He has published *India's Simmering Revolution: The Naxalite Movement in Bengal* (1984) and is currently completing work on another book, *The Parlour and the Streets: Elite and Popular Culture in Nineteenth Century Calcutta* (a project of the Indian Council of Social Science Research.

UMA CHAKRAVARTI teaches History at Miranda House College for Women, Delhi University. She is the author of *The Social Dimensions of Early Buddhism* (1987), and has co-authored *The Delhi Riots: Three Days in the Life of a Nation* (1987). She is currently engaged in research on caste, class and gender relations in early India and has also worked on the history of women and labouring groups. She has been active in both the women's and civil liberties movements in India.

PARTHA CHATTERJEE is currently Professor of Political Science at the Centre for Studies in Social Sciences, Calcutta. He is the author of *Arms, Alliances and Stability* (1975), *Bengal 1920-1947: The Land Question* (1984) and *Nationalist Thought and the Colonial World: A Derivative Discourse?* (1986), and co-author of *The State and Political Theory* (1978) and *Three Studies on Agrarian Structure of Bengal 1858-1947* (1982).

PREM CHOWDHRY teaches History at Miranda House College for Women, Delhi University. She is a regular contributor to several learned journals and is the author of *Punjab Politics: The Role of Sir Chhotu Ram* (1985). A keen painter, she is also currently engaged in revising for publication her research on 'The Socio-Economic, Cultural and Political Transformation of Haryana, 1937-1977,' (an Indian Council of Social Science Research project).

VASANTHA KANNABIRAN teaches literature at Reddy Women's College, Hyderabad, and is a founder member of Stree Shakti Sanghatana, an activist women's group. Along with other members of the group she has co-authored and co-edited an oral history of women in the Telangana movement entitled *Manaku Teliyani Mana Charitra* (Telugu, 1987) and its English translation *We were Making History: Life Stories of Women in the Telangana People's Struggle* (1989). She has co-edited *An Anthology of Women's Writings 1830-1987* (forthcoming). She is presently working on a project collecting texts for two documentary readers on the construction of gender in the late nineteenth and early twentieth centuries.

KAPIL KUMAR is Reader in history at the School of Humanities, Indira Gandhi National Open University in Delhi. He is the author of *Peasants in Revolt: Tenants, Landlords, Congress and the Raj in Oudh 1886-1922* (1984), and has edited *Congress and Classes: Nationalism, Workers and Peasants* (1984). He has also contributed articles to numerous books and journals.

K. LALITA is co-author and co-editor, along with other members of Stree Shakti Sanghatana, Hyderabad, of *Manaku Teliyani Mana Charitra* (Telugu, 1987), and its English translation *We Were Making History: Life Stories of Women in the Telangana People's Struggle* (1989). Actively involved in the women's movement and in research on women in the subsistence sector, she has also co-edited *An Anthology of Women's Writings 1830-1987* (forthcoming), and has written a book on women's bodies and health care. She is currently working on two documentary readers on the women's question.

LATA MANI is doing doctoral work for the History of Consciousness Programme at the University of California, Santa Cruz. She has published articles in several journals and is co-author, with Ruth Frankenberg, of a critical analysis of Edward Said's *Orientalism* entitled

Economy and Society (1985). Her research explores constructions of woman and tradition in colonial India. She has also been active in feminist politics.

KUMKUM SANGARI teaches Literature at Indraprastha College for Women, Delhi University. She has co-edited a collection of essays entitled *Women and Culture* (1985) and is currently engaged in extensive research on widow immolation in Rajasthan. She has written widely on American and Latin American literature, literary theory and women's studies and is at present working on a project on literature and colonialism. She is also Associate Editor of the *Journal of Arts and Ideas.*

VIR BHARAT TALWAR is a Hindi scholar who has been active in left movements and has worked extensively among tribals in India. He has edited *Philhal, Shalpatra* and *Jharkhand Varla*, socio-economic research journals in Hindi. His published work includes research papers on bonded labour, the national movement in the Hindi-speaking areas and a book, *Jharkhand ke Adivasi aur R.S.S.*

SUSIE THARU took her doctorate in literature from the Central Institute of English and Foreign Languages, Hyderabad and currently teaches there. She has written extensively on women, critical theory, modern European Drama, and her published works include *The Sense of Performance in Post Artaud Theatre* (1984), *Manaku Teliyani Mana Charita* (Telugu, 1987) and its English translation *We Were Making History: Life Stories of Women in the Telangana People's Struggle* (1989), both co-authored and co-edited with members of Stree Shakti Sanghatana, a women's group in Hyderabad of which she is a part. Her forthcoming publications include *An Anthology of Women's Writings 1830-1987* (co-edited with K. Lalita).

SUDESH VAID teaches literature at Indraprastha College for Women, Delhi University, and is active in both the women's and civil liberties movements. She has co-edited a collection of essays entitled *Women and Culture* (1985), and is currently engaged in extensive research on widow immolation in Rajasthan. She has published several articles in learned journals in India and elsewhere, as well as a book, *The Divided Mind: Studies in Select Novels of Defoe and Richardson* (1979).